Canon® EOS Rebel T4i/650D FOR DUMMIES®

Canon® EOS Rebel T4i/650D FOR DUMMIES®

by Julie Adair King

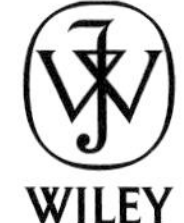

John Wiley & Sons, Inc.

Canon® EOS Rebel T4i/650D For Dummies®

Published by
John Wiley & Sons, Inc.
111 River Street
Hoboken, NJ 07030-5774

www.wiley.com

Published by John Wiley & Sons, Inc., Hoboken, New Jersey

Published simultaneously in Canada

Library of Congress Control Number: 2012948643

ISBN 978-1-118-33597-0 (pbk); ISBN 978-1-118-46190-7 (ebk); ISBN 978-1-118-46191-4 (ebk); ISBN 978-1-118-46192-1 (ebk)

Manufactured in the United States of America

10 9 8 7 6 5 4 3 2 1

About the Author

Julie Adair King is the author of many books about digital photography and imaging, including the best-selling *Digital Photography For Dummies.* Her most recent titles include a series of *For Dummies* guides to popular Nikon, Canon, and Olympus cameras. Other works include *Digital Photography Before & After Makeovers, Digital Photo Projects For Dummies, Julie King's Everyday Photoshop For Photographers, Julie King's Everyday Photoshop Elements,* and *Shoot Like a Pro!: Digital Photography Techniques.* When not writing, King teaches digital photography at such locations as the Palm Beach Photographic Centre.

An Ohio native and graduate of Purdue University, she now resides in West Palm Beach, Florida, and does not miss Midwestern winters even a little bit (although she very much misses friends who have not yet made the journey south).

Author's Acknowledgments

I am deeply grateful for the chance to work once again with the wonderful publishing team at John Wiley and Sons. Kim Darosett, Jennifer Webb, Steve Hayes, Barry Childs-Helton, and Patrick Redmond are just some of the talented editors and designers who helped make this book possible. And finally, I am also indebted to technical editor David Hall, without whose insights and expertise this book would not have been the same.

Publisher's Acknowledgments

We're proud of this book; please send us your comments at `http://dummies.custhelp.com`. For other comments, please contact our Customer Care Department within the U.S. at 877-762-2974, outside the U.S. at 317-572-3993, or fax 317-572-4002.

Some of the people who helped bring this book to market include the following:

Acquisitions and Editorial

Senior Project Editor: Kim Darosett

Executive Editor: Steven Hayes

Senior Copy Editor: Barry Childs-Helton

Technical Editor: David Hall

Editorial Manager: Leah Michael

Editorial Assistant: Leslie Saxman

Sr. Editorial Assistant: Cherie Case

Cover Photo: © Aldo Murillo / iStockphoto

Cartoons: Rich Tennant (`www.the5thwave.com`)

Composition Services

Project Coordinator: Patrick Redmond

Layout and Graphics: Carl Byers, Corrie Niehaus, Christin Swinford

Proofreaders: Jessica Kramer, Sossity R. Smith

Indexer: Christine Karpeles

Publishing and Editorial for Technology Dummies

Richard Swadley, Vice President and Executive Group Publisher

Andy Cummings, Vice President and Publisher

Mary Bednarek, Executive Acquisitions Director

Mary C. Corder, Editorial Director

Publishing for Consumer Dummies

Kathleen Nebenhaus, Vice President and Executive Publisher

Composition Services

Debbie Stailey, Director of Composition Services

Contents at a Glance

Table of Contents

Part III: Taking Creative Control 209

Introduction

In 2003, Canon revolutionized the photography world by introducing the first digital SLR camera to sell for less than $1,000, the EOS Digital Rebel/300D. And even at that then-unheard-of price, the camera delivered exceptional performance and picture quality, earning it rave reviews and multiple industry awards. No wonder it quickly became a best-seller.

That tradition of excellence and value lives on in the EOS Rebel T4i/650D. Like its ancestors, this baby offers the range of advanced controls that experienced photographers demand plus an assortment of tools designed to help beginners be successful as well. Adding to the fun, this Rebel also offers the option to record full high-definition video, plus an articulating, touchscreen monitor that's not only useful but also just plain cool.

The T4i/650D is so feature-packed, in fact, that sorting out everything can be a challenge, especially if you're new to digital photography or SLR photography, or both. For starters, you may not even be sure what SLR means, let alone have a clue about all the other techie terms you encounter in your camera manual — resolution, aperture, white balance, and ISO, for example. And if you're like many people, you may be so overwhelmed by all the controls on your camera that you haven't yet ventured beyond fully automatic picture-taking mode. That's a shame because it's sort of like buying a Porsche Turbo and never pushing it past 50 miles per hour.

Therein lies the point of *Canon EOS Rebel T4i/650D For Dummies*. In this book, you can discover not only what each bell and whistle on your camera does but also when, where, why, and how to put it to best use. Unlike many photography books, this one doesn't require any previous knowledge of photography or digital imaging to make sense of concepts, either. In classic *For Dummies* style, everything is explained in easy-to-understand language, with lots of illustrations to help clear up any confusion.

In short, what you have in your hands is the paperback version of an in-depth photography workshop tailored specifically to your Canon picture-taking powerhouse. Whether your interests lie in taking family photos, exploring nature and travel photography, or snapping product shots for your business, you'll get the information you need to capture the images you envision.

A Quick Look at What's Ahead

This book is organized into four parts, each devoted to a different aspect of using your camera. Although chapters flow in a sequence that's designed to take you from absolute beginner to experienced user, I also tried to make each chapter as self-standing as possible so you can explore the topics that interest you in any order you please.

Here's a quick look at what you can find in each part:

Part I: Fast Track to Super Snaps

This part contains four chapters that help you get up and running. Chapter 1 offers a brief overview of camera controls and walks you through initial setup and customization steps, including how to use the nifty touchscreen monitor. Chapter 2 explains basic picture-taking options, such as shutter-release mode and image quality settings, and Chapter 3 shows you how to use the camera's simplest exposure modes, including Scene Intelligent Auto and Creative Auto. Chapter 4 explains the ins and outs of using Live View, the feature that lets you compose pictures on the monitor, and also covers movie recording.

Part II: Working with Picture Files

As its title implies, this part discusses after-the-shot topics. Chapter 5 explains picture playback features, and Chapter 6 guides you through the process of transferring pictures from your camera to your computer and then getting pictures ready for print and online sharing. You can also get help with converting pictures shot in the Canon Raw file format (CR2) to a standard format in Chapter 6.

Part III: Taking Creative Control

Chapters in this part help you unleash the full creative power of your camera by moving into semi-automatic or manual photography modes. Chapter 7 covers the all-important topic of exposure; Chapter 8 offers tips for manipulating focus and color; and Chapter 9 provides a quick-reference guide to shooting strategies for specific types of pictures: portraits, action shots, landscape scenes, close-ups, and more.

Part IV: The Part of Tens

In famous *For Dummies* tradition, the book concludes with two top-ten lists containing additional bits of information and advice. Chapter 10 takes a look at ten more ways to customize your camera, and Chapter 11 offers a review of features that, though not found on most "Top Ten Reasons I Bought My Rebel T4i/650D" lists, are nonetheless interesting, useful on occasion, or a bit of both. Closing things out is a glossary that serves as a quick reference to the terminology you encounter as you explore digital photography and your camera.

Icons and Other Stuff to Note

If this isn't your first *For Dummies* book, you may be familiar with the large, round icons that decorate its margins. If not, here's your very own icon-decoder ring:

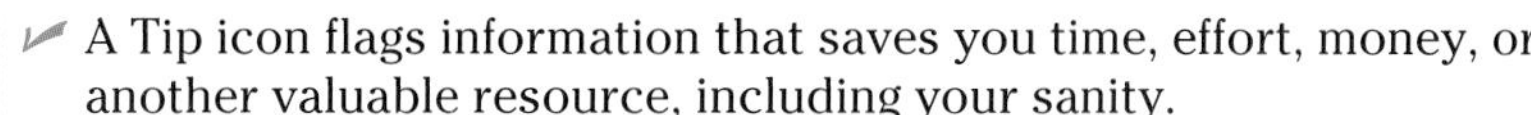

- A Tip icon flags information that saves you time, effort, money, or another valuable resource, including your sanity.

- When you see this icon, look alive. It indicates a potential danger zone that can result in much wailing and teeth-gnashing if it's ignored.

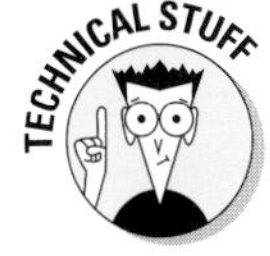

- Lots of information in this book is of a technical nature — digital photography is a technical animal, after all. But if I present a detail that's useful mainly for impressing your geeky friends, I mark it with this icon.

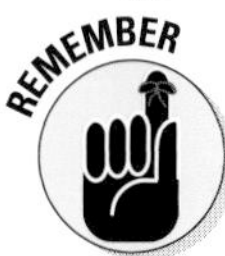

- This icon highlights information that's especially worth storing in your brain's long-term memory or to remind you of a fact that may have been displaced from that memory by another pressing fact.

Additionally, I need to point out a few other details that will help you use this book:

- **Other margin art:** Replicas of some of your camera's buttons and onscreen graphics also appear in the margins of some paragraphs and in some tables. I include these images to provide quick reminders of the appearance of the button or option being discussed.
- **Software menu commands:** In sections that cover software, a series of words connected by an arrow indicates commands you choose from the program menus. For example, if a step tells you, "Choose File⇨Export," click the File menu to unfurl it and then click the Export command on the menu.
- **Choosing camera menu and screen options:** In many cases, you can select a camera setting by tapping its name or symbol on the touchscreen or by using the *cross keys* — those four keys that surround the Set button — to highlight the name or icon and then pressing the Set button. To avoid having to spell all that out every time I describe a camera function that can be accessed either way, I use some verbal shorthand and simply tell you to choose the setting in question.
- **Book updates:** Occasionally, I need to make updates to technology books. If this book does have technical updates, they will be posted at `www.dummies.com/go/canoneosrebelt4i650dupdates`.

eCheat Sheet

As an added bonus, you can find an electronic version of the *For Dummies* Cheat Sheet at `www.dummies.com/cheatsheet/canoneosrebelt4i650d`. The Cheat Sheet contains a quick-reference guide to all the buttons, dials, switches, and exposure modes on your camera. Log on, print it out, and tuck it in your camera bag for times when you don't want to carry this book with you.

Practice, Be Patient, and Have Fun!

To wrap up this preamble, I want to stress that if you initially think that digital photography is too confusing or too technical for you, you're in very good company. *Everyone* finds this stuff a little mind-boggling at first. Take it slowly, experimenting with just one or two new camera settings or techniques at first. Then, every time you go on a photo outing, make it a point to add one or two more shooting skills to your repertoire. With some time, patience, and practice, you'll soon wield your camera like a pro, dialing in the necessary settings to capture your creative vision almost instinctively.

So without further ado, I invite you to grab your camera and a cup of whatever it is you prefer to sip while you read, and start exploring the rest of this book. Your Rebel T4i/650D is the perfect partner for your photographic journey, and I thank you for allowing me, in this book, to serve as your tour guide.

Part I
Fast Track to Super Snaps

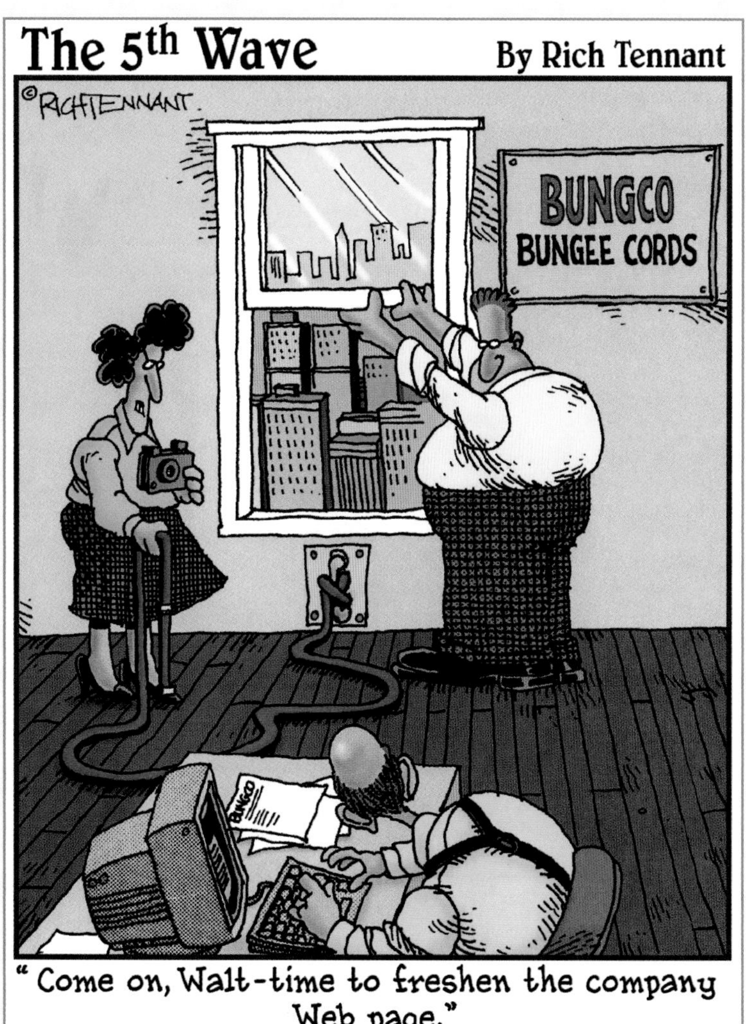

"Come on, Walt-time to freshen the company Web page."

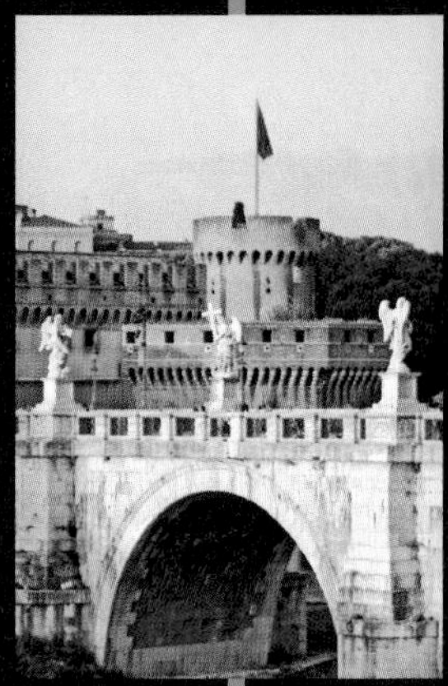

In this part . . .

Making sense of all the controls on your camera isn't a task you can complete in an afternoon — or, heck, in a week or maybe even a month. But there's no reason not to take great-looking pictures today. By using the point-and-shoot exposure modes, you can capture terrific images with very little effort. All you do is compose the scene, and the camera takes care of almost everything else.

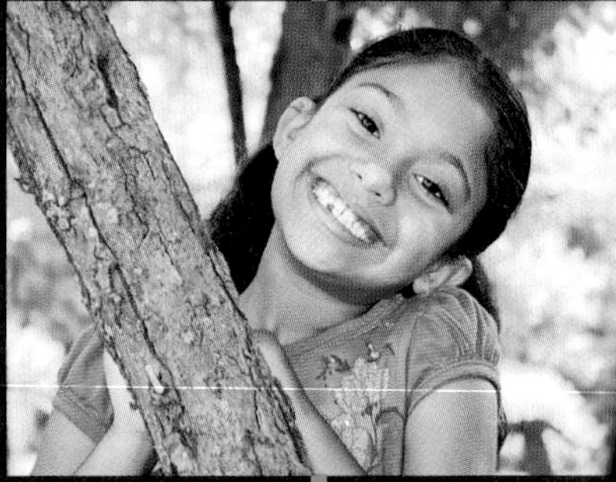

This part shows you how to take best advantage of your camera's most-automatic photography modes and also addresses some basic setup steps, such as adjusting the viewfinder to your eyesight and getting familiar with the camera menus, buttons, and dials. In addition, chapters in this part explain a few picture-taking settings that come into play in any exposure mode — and show you how to use your camera's Live View and movie-making features.

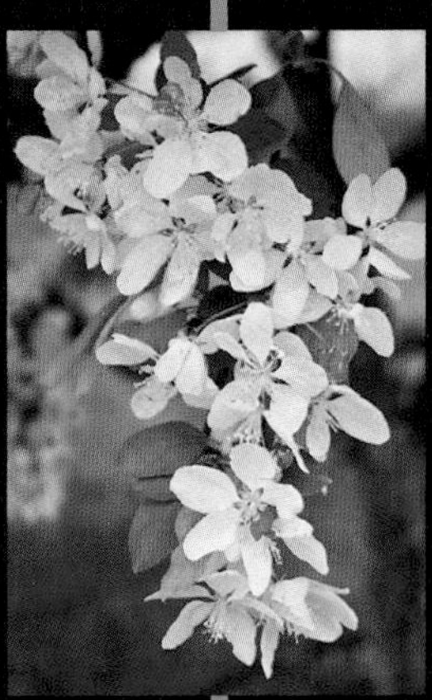

1

Getting the Lay of the Land

In This Chapter

- Using an SLR lens
- Adjusting the viewfinder and monitor
- Practicing touchscreen gestures
- Working with camera memory cards
- Getting acquainted with external camera controls
- Checking and changing camera settings
- Customizing basic camera operations

If you're like many people, shooting for the first time with an SLR (single-lens reflex) camera produces a blend of excitement and anxiety. On one hand, you can't wait to start using your new equipment, but on the other, you're a little intimidated by all its buttons, dials, and menu options.

Well, fear not: This chapter provides the information you need to get comfortable with your T4i/650D. Among other things, I show you how to attach and remove lenses, use the touchscreen monitor, and view and adjust camera settings. You'll also get an introduction to the camera's external controls as well as my advice about certain camera setup options.

Getting Comfortable with Your Lens

One of the biggest differences between a point-and-shoot camera and an SLR camera is the lens. With an SLR, you can swap lenses to suit different photographic needs, going from an extreme close-up lens to a super-long telephoto, for example. Additionally, an SLR lens has a movable focusing ring that lets you focus manually instead of relying on the camera's autofocus mechanism.

Of course, those added capabilities mean that you may need some help to take full advantage of your lens. To that end, the next several sections explain the process of attaching, removing, and using this critical part of your camera.

Attaching a lens

Your camera accepts two categories of Canon lenses: those with an EF-S design and those with a plain-old EF design.

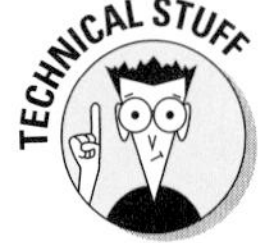

The EF stands for *electro focus;* the S, for *short back focus.* And *that* simply means the rear element of the lens is closer to the sensor than with an EF lens. And no, you don't need to remember what the abbreviation stands for — just make sure that if you buy a Canon lens other than one of the two sold as a bundle with the camera, it carries either the EF or EF-S specification. If you want to buy a non-Canon lens, check the lens manufacturer's website to find out which lenses work with your camera.

Two other lens acronyms to note: First, the 18–55mm and 18–135mm lenses that you can buy as part of a Rebel T4i/650D kit are *IS* lenses, which means that they offer *image stabilization,* a feature you can explore a few sections from here. Second, the 18–135mm kit lens also carries the designation *STM.* That abbreviation refers to the fact that the autofocusing system uses *stepping motor technology,* which is designed to provide smoother, quieter autofocusing.

Whatever lens you choose, follow these steps to attach it to the camera body:

1. **Remove the cap that covers the lens mount on the front of the camera.**
2. **Remove the cap that covers the back of the lens.**
3. **Locate the proper lens mounting index on the camera body.**

   A *mounting index* is simply a marker that tells you where to align the lens with the camera body when connecting the two. Your camera has two of these markers, one red and one white, as shown in Figure 1-1.

   Which marker you use to align your lens depends on the lens type:

   - *Canon EF-S lens:* The white square is the mounting index.
   - *Canon EF lens:* The red dot is the mounting index.

   If you buy a non-Canon lens, check the lens manual for help with this step.

4. **Align the mounting index on the lens with the correct one on the camera body.**

   The lens also has a mounting index. Figure 1-1 shows the one that appears on the 18–55mm kit lens. On the 18–135 STM kit lens, the index marker looks the same, but if you buy a different lens, check the lens instruction manual.

5. **Keeping the mounting indexes aligned, position the lens on the camera's lens mount.**
6. **Turn the lens in a clockwise direction until the lens clicks into place.**

   In other words, turn the lens toward the lens-release button, as indicated by the arrow in Figure 1-1.

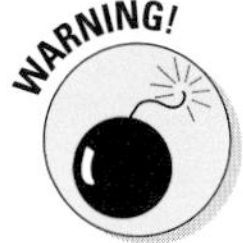

Always attach (or switch) lenses in a clean environment to reduce the risk of getting dust, dirt, and other contaminants inside the camera or lens. For added safety, point the camera slightly down when performing this maneuver; doing so helps prevent any flotsam in the air from being drawn into the camera by gravity.

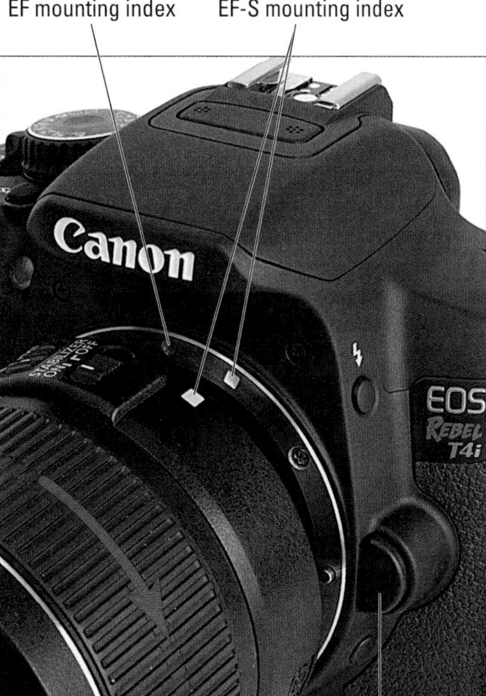

Figure 1-1: Place the lens in the lens mount with the mounting indexes aligned.

Removing a lens

To detach a lens from the camera body, take these steps:

1. **Locate the lens-release button on the front of the camera, labeled in Figure 1-1.**
2. **Grip the rear collar of the lens.**

   In other words, hold on to the stationary part of the lens that's closest to the camera body.
3. **Press the lens-release button while turning the lens toward the shutter-button side of the camera.**

   You can feel the lens release from the mount at this point. Lift the lens off the mount to remove it.
4. **Place the rear protective cap onto the back of the lens.**

   If you aren't putting another lens on the camera, cover the lens mount with the protective cap that came with your camera, too.

Zooming in and out

If you bought a zoom lens, it sports a *zoom ring*. Figure 1-2 shows you the location of the zoom ring on the two kit lenses; for other lenses, see your lens user guide. With the kit lenses, just rotate the zoom ring to zoom in and out. A few zoom lenses use a push-pull motion to zoom instead.

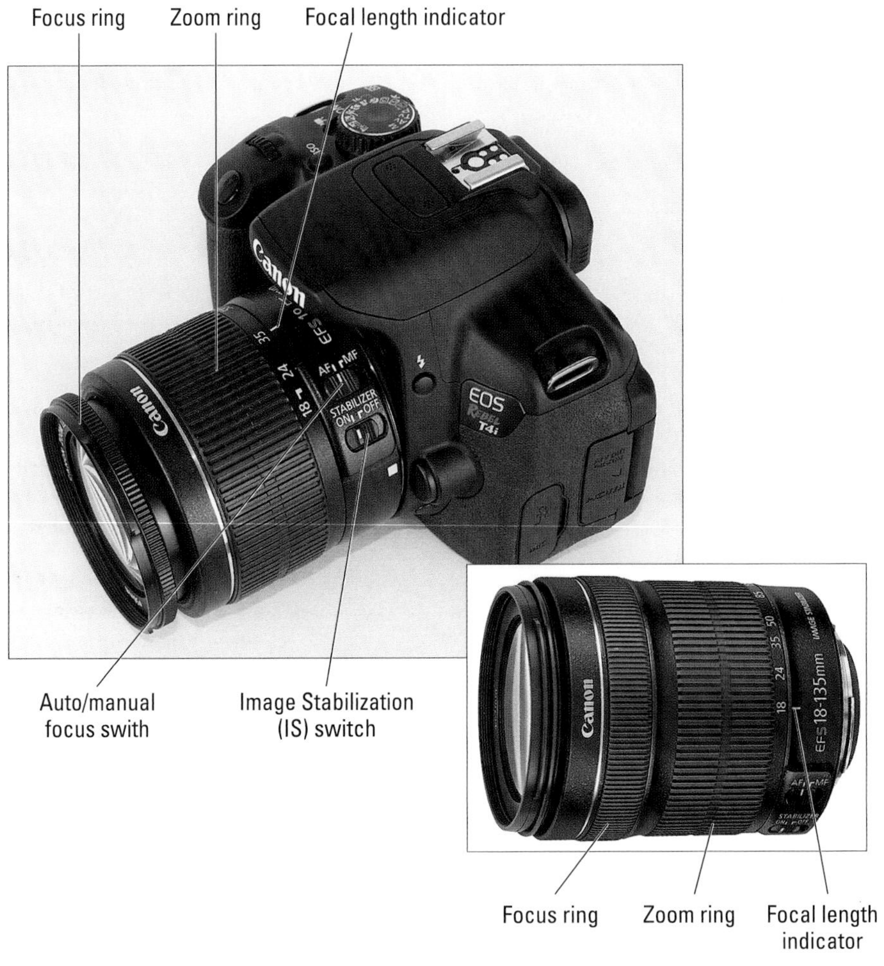

Figure 1-2: Here's a look at the two kit lenses.

The numbers around the edge of the zoom ring, by the way, represent *focal lengths*. Chapter 8 explains focal lengths in detail. In the meantime, just note that the number that's aligned with the white focal-length indicator, labeled in Figure 1-2, represents the current focal length.

Shifting from autofocus to manual focus (and back)

Your Rebel T4i/650D offers an excellent autofocusing system. With some subjects, however, autofocusing can be slow or impossible, which is why your camera also offers manual focusing. When using the viewfinder to compose photos, make the shift from auto to manual focus as follows:

1. **Set the AF/MF switch on the side of the lens to the MF position.**

   This switch sets the focus operation to either auto (AF) or manual (MF).

2. **Look through the viewfinder and twist the focusing ring until your subject comes into focus.**

   I labeled the focusing ring as it appears on the kit lenses in Figure 1-2. If you use another lens, the focusing ring may be located elsewhere, so check your lens manual.

   If you have trouble focusing, you may be too close to your subject; every lens has a minimum focusing distance. You also may need to adjust the viewfinder to accommodate your eyesight; the section "Adjusting the Viewfinder Focus" shows you how to take this step.

To return to autofocusing, just set the lens switch back to the AF position. In Movie mode (power switch set to the movie-camera icon) or Live View mode (when you use the monitor to compose images), turn the camera off before setting the lens switch to the MF position. This step is necessary to interrupt the continuous autofocusing system that's available for movie and Live View shooting. (Chapter 4 details Movie and Live View modes.)

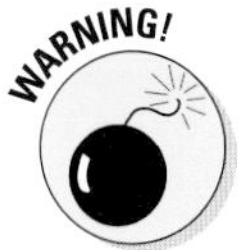

Chapter 8 provides more details about focusing. In the meantime, note this important bit of business about the 18–135mm STM kit lens: The focusing motor doesn't operate if the camera has gone to sleep because of the Auto Power Off feature, which I explain in the section "Setup Menu 2," later in this chapter. The lens itself goes to sleep if you don't perform any lens operations for a while. Either way, manual focus adjustments aren't possible when the lens is in this state, and automatic focusing during zooming may be delayed. You can wake the camera and lens up by pressing the shutter button halfway; give the lens a brief moment to wake up fully before you take a picture. (Please look in your camera manual for complete information about using this lens, which I don't have room to provide in this book.)

Using an IS (image stabilizer) lens

Both the kit lenses sold with the Rebel T4i/650D camera offer *image stabilization,* indicated by the initials *IS* in the lens name.

Image stabilization attempts to compensate for small amounts of camera shake that are common when photographers handhold their cameras and use a slow shutter speed, a lens with a long focal length, or both. Camera shake can result in blurry images, even when your focus is dead-on. Although image stabilization can't work miracles, it enables most people to capture sharp handheld shots in many situations that they otherwise couldn't. The feature works regardless of whether you use autofocusing or manual focusing, and it works for both still photography and movie shooting.

However, when you use a tripod, image stabilization can have detrimental effects because the system may try to adjust for movement that isn't actually occurring. Although this problem shouldn't be an issue with most Canon IS lenses, if you do see blurry images while using a tripod, try setting the Stabilizer switch (shown in Figure 1-2) to Off. You also can save battery power by turning off image stabilization when you use a tripod. If you use a monopod, leave image stabilization turned on so it can help compensate for any accidental movement of the monopod.

On non-Canon lenses, image stabilization may go by another name: *anti-shake, vibration compensation,* and so on. In some cases, the manufacturers recommend that you leave the system turned on or select a special setting when you use a tripod, so check the lens manual for information.

Whatever lens you use, image stabilization isn't meant to eliminate the blur that can occur when your subject moves during the exposure. That problem is related to shutter speed, a topic you can explore in Chapter 7. Chapter 8 offers more tips for blur-free shots and provides an explanation of focal length.

Getting Familiar with the Monitor

Perched on the top-right edge of the viewfinder is a tiny black knob, officially known as a *dioptric adjustment control*, that enables you to adjust the magnification of the viewfinder to your eyesight. I highlighted the knob on the left in Figure 1-3.

Adjusting the viewfinder to your eyesight is critical: If you don't, scenes that appear out-of-focus through the viewfinder may actually be sharply focused through the lens, and vice versa. Follow these steps to adjust your viewfinder:

1. **Remove the lens cap.**
2. **Look through the viewfinder and aim the lens at a plain surface.**

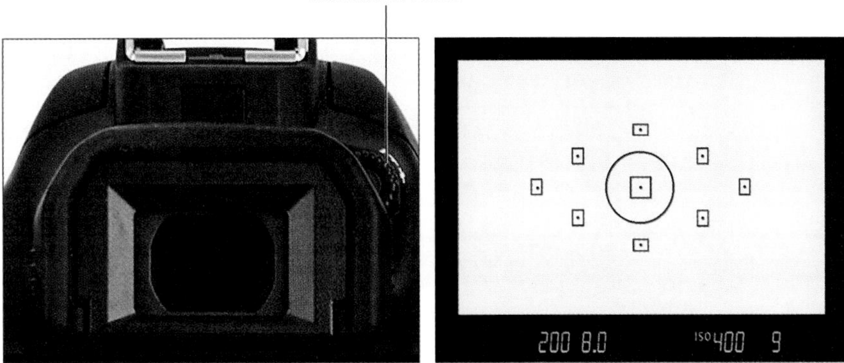

Figure 1-3: Roll the little knob to set the viewfinder focus for your eyesight.

3. **Concentrate on the markings in the center of the viewfinder or the exposure data at the bottom of the viewfinder.**

   In the viewfinder, the little squares with dots inside represent autofocus points, which you can find out about in Chapter 8; the circle that surrounds the center autofocus point is related to exposure metering, discussed in Chapter 7.

   If you don't see any exposure data at the bottom of the screen, press the shutter button halfway and release it to wake up the exposure meter.

4. **Rotate the dioptric adjustment knob until the viewfinder markings and exposure data appear sharp.**

If your eyesight is such that you can't get the display to appear sharp by using the dioptric adjustment knob, you can buy an additional eyepiece adapter. This accessory, which you pop onto the eyepiece, enables further adjustment of the viewfinder. Prices range from about $15–$30 depending on the magnification you need. Look for an E-series dioptric adjustment lens adapter.

Adjusting the Monitor Position

One of the many cool features of the T4i/650D is its articulating monitor. When you first take the camera out of its box, the monitor is positioned with the screen facing the back of the body, as shown on the left in Figure 1-4, protecting the screen from scratches and smudges. (It's a good idea to place the monitor in this position when you're not using the camera.) When you're ready to start shooting or reviewing your photos, you can place the monitor in the traditional position on the camera back, as shown on the right in Figure 1-4. Or for more flexibility, you can swing the monitor out and away from the camera body and then rotate it to find the best viewing angle, as shown in Figure 1-5.

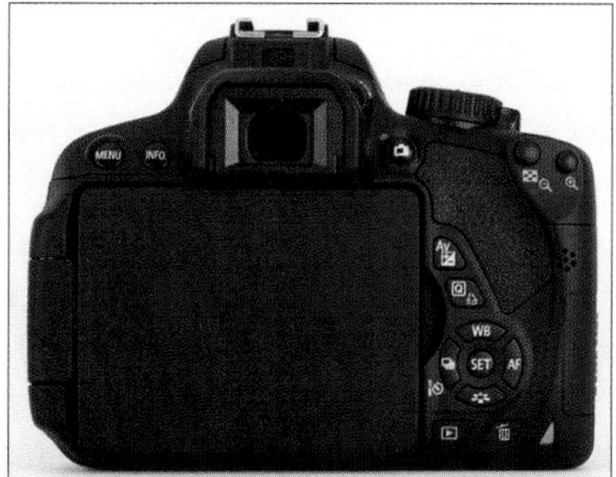

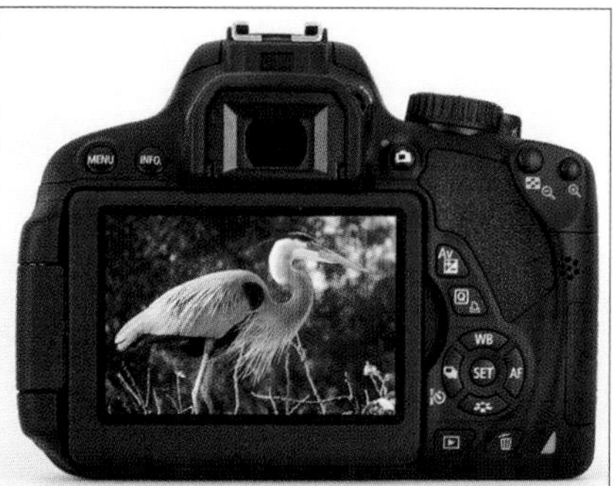

Figure 1-4: Here you see just two of the possible monitor positions.

Because playing with the monitor is no doubt one of the first things you did after unpacking your new camera, I won't waste space here walking you through the process of adjusting the screen. (If you need help, the camera manual shows you what to do.) But I want to offer a few monitor-related tips:

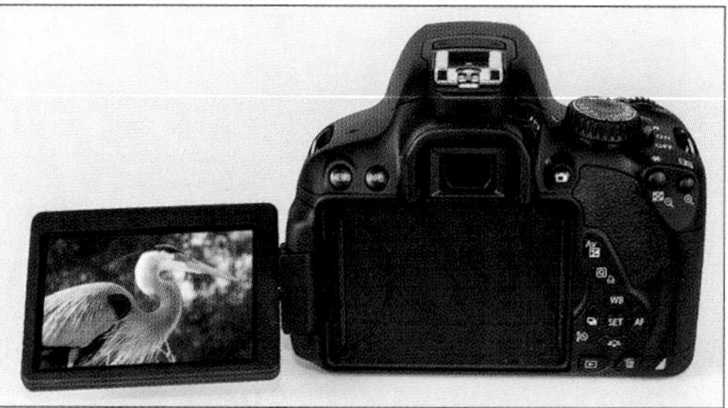

Figure 1-5: You also can unlock the monitor from the body and then rotate the screen to get the best view of things.

- **Don't force things.** Although the monitor assembly is sturdy, treat it with respect as you adjust the screen position. The monitor twists only in certain directions, and it's easy to forget which way it's supposed to move. So if you feel resistance, don't force things — you could break the monitor. Instead, rely on that feeling of resistance to remind you to turn the screen the other way.
- **Watch the crunch factor.** When positioning the monitor back into the camera (whether face in or face out), take care that nothing gets in the way. Use a lens brush or soft cloth to clean the monitor housing on the camera back so there's nothing in the way that could damage the monitor.

- **Clean smart.** To clean the screen, use only the special cloths and cleaning solutions made for this purpose. (You can find them in any camera store.) *Do not* use paper products such as paper towels because they can contain wood fibers that can scratch the monitor. And never use a can of compressed air to blow dust off the camera — the air is cold and can crack the monitor.

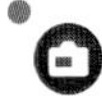

- **Live View photography has some drawbacks.** *Live View* is the feature that enables you to compose your photos using the monitor rather than the viewfinder. You switch the feature on and off by pressing the Live View button, which is found to the right of the viewfinder and looks like the icon shown in the margin here. The live display is also engaged when you set the camera to Movie mode (by moving the power switch to the movie-icon position).

  Live View may feel more comfortable than using the viewfinder if you're stepping up to the T4i/650D from a point-and-shoot camera that didn't have a viewfinder. But the monitor is one of the biggest drains on battery power, and autofocusing in Live View mode is slower than when you use the viewfinder. For these reasons and a few others you can explore in Chapter 4, I stick with the viewfinder for most photography and reserve the live display for movie recording. (You can't use the viewfinder in Movie mode.) Whatever you decide, note that if Live View or movie mode is enabled and you orient the monitor to face the same direction as the lens, the monitor may display a mirror image of your subject.

Using the Touchscreen

Just as cool as the monitor's flexibility is its touchscreen interface. You can choose menu commands, change picture settings, and scroll through your pictures by touching one or two fingers to the screen, just as you can with a tablet, smart phone, or other touchscreen device. During Live View shooting, you can even touch the screen to select a focus point and trigger the shutter release.

Throughout the book, I tell you exactly where and how to touch the screen to accomplish specific actions. For now, get acquainted with the terminology used to indicate these touchscreen moves, called *gestures* by those who feel the need to assign names to things such as this.

- **Tap:** Tap your finger gently on a screen item to select it. Give it a try: First, press the Menu button to display the menu screen on the monitor, as shown on the left in Figure 1-6. Along the top of the screen, you see one highlighted icon, representing the current menu, and a row of dimmed icons representing other menus. On the left side of Figure 1-6, Shooting Menu 1 is the current menu. To switch to another menu, tap its icon. For example, tap the icon for Setup Menu 2, labeled on the left in the figure, and that menu appears, as shown on the right.

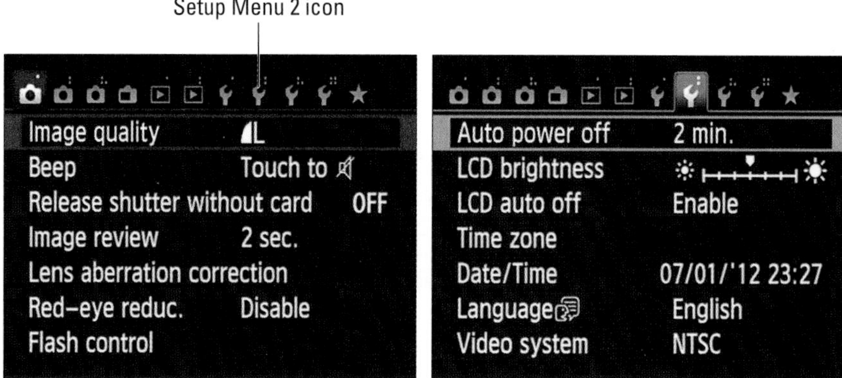

Figure 1-6: Tap the Setup Menu 2 icon to display that menu.

By "tap gently," I mean *gently* — you don't have to use force. To avoid damaging the screen, use the fleshy part of your fingertip, not the nail or any other sharp object, and be sure that your fingers are dry because the screen may not respond if it gets wet. Canon also advises against putting a protective cover over the monitor, such as the kind people adhere to their smart phones. Doing so can reduce the monitor's responsiveness to your touch.

- **Drag:** Drag your finger up, down, right, or left across the screen, according to my instruction. To try this gesture, first display Setup Menu 2 and tap the LCD Brightness item, shown on the left in Figure 1-7. Now you see the screen shown on the right. Now drag your finger across the scale at the bottom of the screen to adjust the screen brightness. Reset the marker to the middle of the bar after you're done playing around — the default brightness setting is best for giving you an accurate indication of picture brightness.

  On this particular screen, you also see triangles at either end of the scale. You can also tap those triangles to raise or lower the value represented on the scale. Either way, tap the Set icon to implement the setting and return to the menu.

- **Swipe:** Drag a finger quickly across the screen. You use this gesture, known in some circles as a *flick,* to scroll through your pictures in playback mode, a topic you can explore in Chapter 5.

- **Pinch in/pinch out:** To pinch in, place your thumb at one edge of the screen and your pointer finger at the other. Then drag both toward the center of the screen. To pinch out, start in the center of the screen and swipe both fingers outward. Pinching is how you zoom in and out on pictures during playback; again, Chapter 5 provides details.

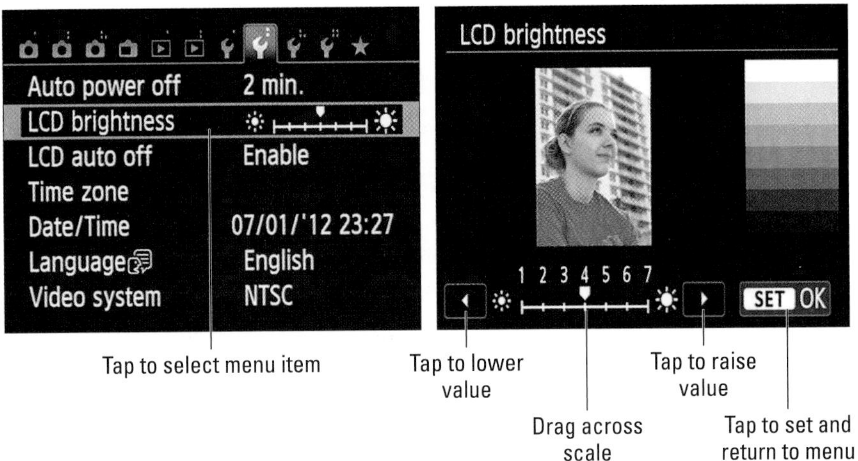

Figure 1-7: Tap the LCD Brightness item (left) and then drag left or right across a scale to adjust the setting (right).

You can control two aspects of touchscreen behavior:

- **Enable/disable the touchscreen:** By default, the touchscreen is enabled and ready to respond to your touch. But if you want to turn it off, you can do so via the Touch Control option on Shooting Menu 3. Tap the icon for Setup Menu 3, highlighted on the left in Figure 1-8, tap Touch Control to display the second screen in the figure, and then tap Disable.

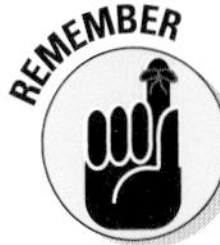

  To restore the touch function, press the Menu button to bring up the menu screens and then rotate the Main dial — that's the one just behind the shutter button — to select Setup Menu 3. Then use the up/down *cross keys* — the buttons above and below the Set button, respectively — to highlight Touch Control. Press the Set button, use the cross keys to highlight Enable, and press the Set button again.

- **Drive people crazy with touchscreen sounds:** Here's an option that you can use when you're in the mood to annoy people within earshot of your camera: You can tell the camera to emit a little "boop" sound every time you tap a touch-controlled setting. To do so, visit Shooting Menu 1, and look for the Beep setting, shown in Figure 1-9. The option that keeps the boop silent is Touch to Silence — silence indicated by a little speaker with a slash through it — as shown in the figure. Change the option to Enable to turn on the sound effect. The Disable setting turns off both the touchscreen sound and the normal beep tone that occurs when the camera finds its focus point.

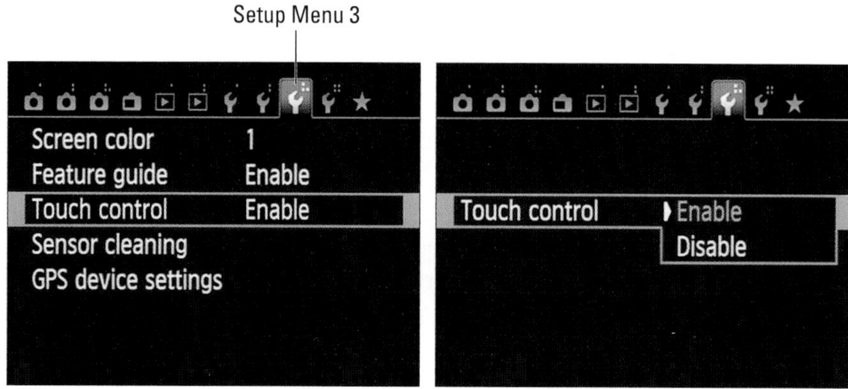

Figure 1-8: Enable or disable touchscreen control through this menu item.

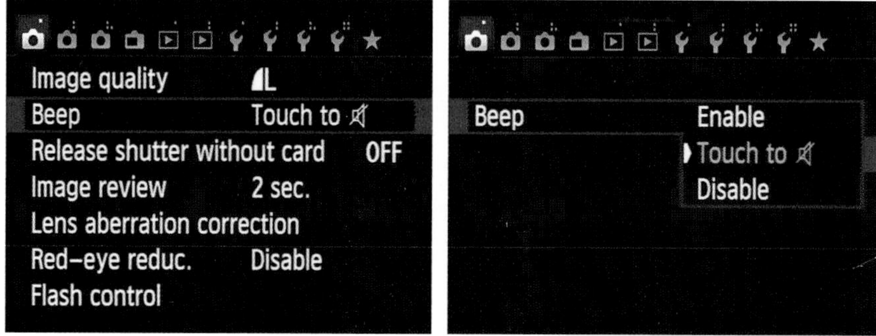

Figure 1-9: Set the Beep option to Touch to Silence to prevent the camera from making a sound when you tap a touch-controlled item.

Working with Memory Cards

Instead of recording images on film, digital cameras store pictures on *memory cards.* Your camera uses a specific type of memory card — an *SD card* (for *Secure Digital*), shown in Figures 1-10 and 1-11. You can also use *high-capacity* SD cards, which carry the label SDHC and come in capacities ranging from 4–32GB (gigabytes), and *extended-capacity* (SDXC) cards, which offer capacities higher than 32GB.

In addition to using regular SD cards, you camera accepts Eye-Fi memory cards, which are special cards that enable you to transmit images from the camera to the computer over a wireless network. It's a cool option, but the cards themselves are more expensive than regular cards and require some configuring that I don't have room to cover in this book. Additionally, Canon doesn't guarantee that everything will work smoothly with Eye-Fi cards, and directs you to the Eye-Fi support team if you have trouble. All that said, if an Eye-Fi card is installed in the camera, Setup Menu 1 offers an Eye-Fi Settings option that offers options related to the card. For more details, visit `www.eye.fi`.

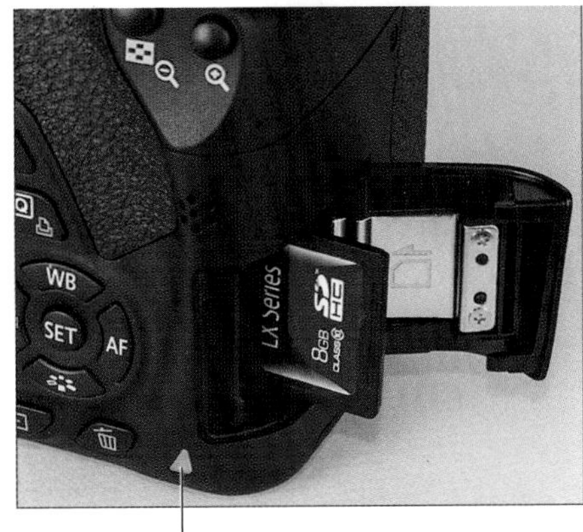

Figure 1-10: Insert the card with the label facing the camera back.

Whatever cards you choose, safeguarding them — and the images on them — requires a few precautions:

- **Inserting a card:** Turn the camera off and then put the card in the card slot with the label facing the back of the camera, as shown in Figure 1-10. Push the card into the slot until it clicks into place.

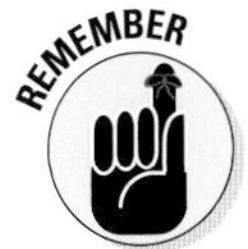

- **Formatting a card:** The first time you use a new memory card, *format* it by choosing the Format Card option on Setup Menu 1. This step ensures that the card is properly prepared to record your pictures. See the upcoming section "Setup Menu 1" for details.

- **Removing a card:** First, check the status of the memory card access light, labeled in Figure 1-10. After making sure that the light is off, indicating that the camera has finished recording your most recent photo, turn off the camera. Open the memory card door, as shown in Figure 1-10. Depress the memory card slightly until you hear a little click and then let go. The card pops halfway out of the slot, enabling you to grab it by the tail and remove it.

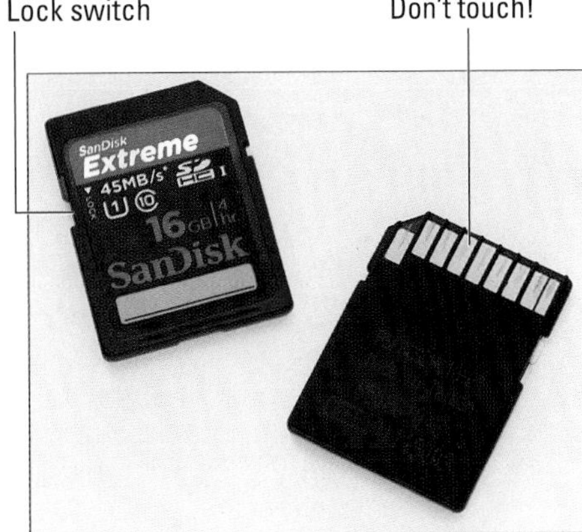

Figure 1-11: Avoid touching the gold contacts on the card.

Do you need high-speed memory cards?

Secure Digital (SD) memory cards are rated according to *speed classes:* Class 2, Class 4, Class 6, and Class 10, with the number indicating the minimum number of *megabytes* (units of computer data) that can be transferred per second. A Class 2 card, for example, has a minimum transfer speed of 2 megabytes, or MB, per second. In addition to these speed classes, The Powers That Be recently added a new category of speed rating, UHS, which stands for Ultra High Speed. UHS cards also carry a number designation; at present, there is only one class of UHS card, UHS 1. These cards currently offer the fastest performance. Your camera supports this new card speed.

Of course, with the increase in card speed comes a price increase, which leads to the question: How much speed do you really need? Well, for movie recording, Canon recommends a Class 6 card at minimum — the faster data-transfer rate helps ensure smooth movie-recording and playback performance. For still photography, users who shoot at the highest resolution or prefer the CR2 (Raw) file format may also gain from high-speed cards; both options increase file size and (thus) the time needed to store the picture on the card. (See Chapter 2 for details.)

As for picture downloading, how long it takes files to shuffle from card to computer depends not just on card speed, but also on the capabilities of your computer and, if you use a memory card reader to download files, on the speed of that device.

Long story short, if you want to push your camera to its performance limits, a high-speed card is worth the expense, especially for video recording. But if you're primarily interested in still photography or you already own slower-speed cards, try using them first — you may find that they're more than adequate for most shooting scenarios.

- **Handling cards:** Don't touch the gold contacts on the back of the card. (See the right card in Figure 1-11.) When cards aren't in use, store them in the protective cases they came in or in a memory card wallet. Keep cards away from extreme heat and cold as well.
- **Locking cards:** The tiny switch on the left side of the card, labeled *lock switch* in Figure 1-11, enables you to lock your card, which prevents any data from being erased or recorded to the card. Press the switch toward the bottom of the card to lock the card contents; press it toward the top of the card to unlock the data.

Exploring External Camera Controls

Scattered across your camera's exterior are a number of buttons, dials, and switches that you use to change picture-taking settings, review and edit your photos, and perform various other operations. Later chapters discuss all these camera functions in detail; the next few sections provide just a basic map to the external controls.

Topside controls

Your virtual tour begins on the top of the camera, shown in Figure 1-12.

The items of note here are

- **On/Off/Movie mode switch:** Okay, you probably already figured the first two points of this switch out, but what may not be clear is that setting the switch to the little movie-camera icon both turns on the camera and sets it to movie-recording mode. Set the switch to On for still photography.

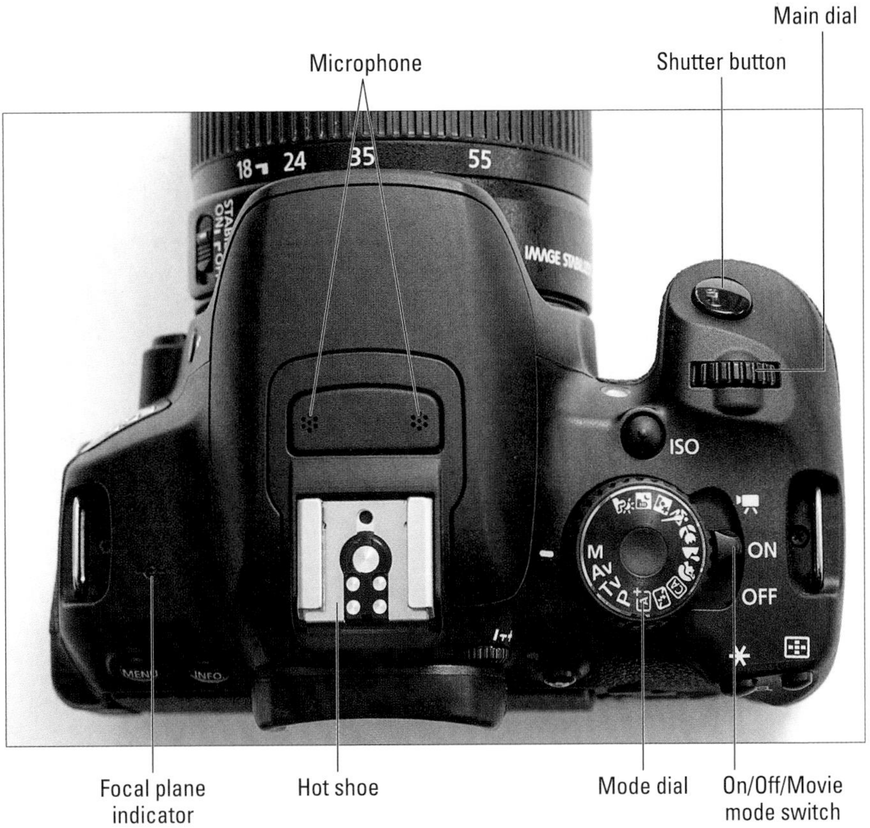

Figure 1-12: Here's a guide to controls found on top of the camera.

- **Mode dial:** Rotate this dial to select an *exposure mode,* which determines whether the camera operates in fully automatic, semi-automatic, or manual exposure mode when you take still pictures. Chapter 2 provides an overview of the exposure modes; the basic auto-everything mode is represented by the green A+ (for Scene Intelligent Auto) setting on the dial.
- **Main dial:** You use this dial when selecting many camera settings. (Specifics are provided throughout the book.) In fact, this dial plays such an important role that you'd think it might have a more auspicious name, but Main dial it is.
- **ISO button:** This button provides access to the ISO setting, which determines how sensitive the camera is to light. Chapter 7 details this critical exposure setting.

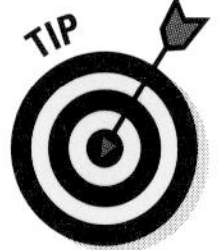

- **Shutter button:** You probably already understand the function of this button, too. But what you may not realize is that when you use autofocus and autoexposure, you can need to use a two-stage process when taking a picture: Press the shutter button halfway, pause to let the camera set focus and exposure, and then press the rest of the way to capture the image. You'd be surprised how many people mess up their pictures because they press that button with one quick jab, denying the camera the time it needs to set focus and exposure.
- **Flash hot shoe:** A *hot shoe* is a connection for attaching an external flash head. The contacts on the shoe are covered by a little black insert when you take the camera out of its shipping box; when you're ready to attach a flash head, remove the insert to reveal the contacts, as shown in Figure 1-12.

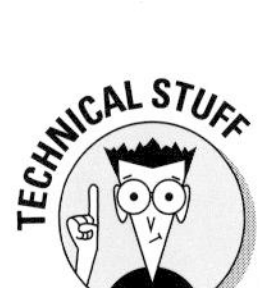

- **Focal plane indicator:** Should you need to know the exact distance between your subject and the camera, the *focal plane indicator* labeled in Figure 1-12 is key. This mark indicates the plane at which light coming through the lens is focused onto the negative in a film camera or the image sensor in a digital camera. Basing your measurement on this mark produces a more accurate camera-to-subject distance than using the end of the lens or some other external point on the camera body as your reference point.
- **Microphone:** The two clusters of holes just forward of the hot shoe lead to the camera's internal microphone. See Chapter 4 for details about choosing microphone settings for movie recording.

Back-of-the-body controls

Traveling over the top of the camera to its back, you encounter a smorgasbord of controls, including the knob you use to adjust the viewfinder to your eyesight, as discussed earlier in this chapter. Figure 1-13 gives you a look at the layout of the backside controls.

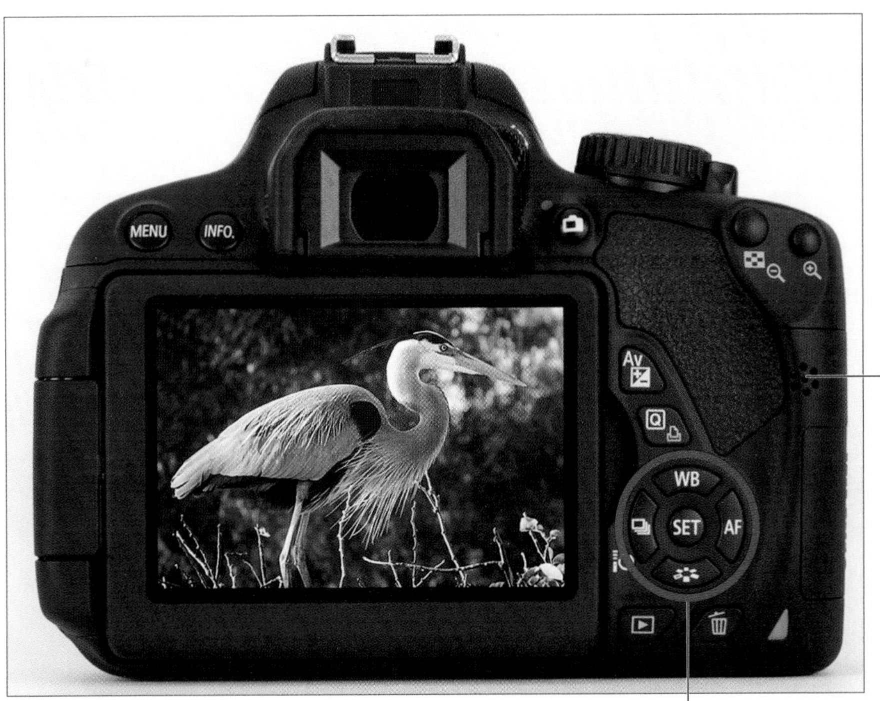

Figure 1-13: Having lots of external buttons makes accessing the camera's functions easier.

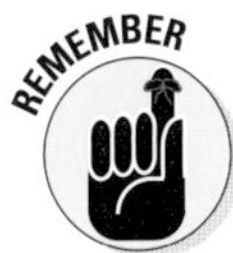

Throughout this book, pictures of some buttons appear in the margins to help you locate the button being discussed. So even though I provide the official names in the following list, don't worry about getting all those straight right now. Note, however, that some buttons have multiple names because they serve multiple purposes depending on whether you're taking pictures, reviewing images, recording a movie, or performing some other function. In this book, I refer to these buttons by the first label you see in the following list to simplify things. For example, I refer to the AF Point Selection/Magnify button as the AF Point Selection button. Again, though, the margin icons help you know exactly which button you're to press.

With that preamble out of the way, it's time to explore the camera back, starting at the top-right corner and working westward (well, assuming that your lens is pointing north, anyway):

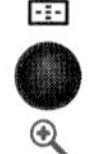

- **AF Point Selection/Magnify button:** When you use certain advanced shooting modes, you press this button to specify which of the nine autofocus points you want the camera to use when establishing focus. Chapter 8 tells you more. In Playback mode, covered in Chapter 5, you use this button to magnify the image display (thus the plus sign in the button's magnifying glass icon).

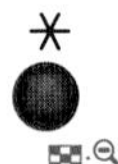

- **AE Lock/FE Lock/Index/Reduce button:** As you can guess from the official name of this button, it serves many purposes. The first two are related to still-image capture functions: You use the button to lock in the autoexposure (AE) settings and to lock flash exposure (FE). Chapter 7 details both issues.

  This button also serves two image-viewing functions: It switches the display to Index mode, enabling you to see multiple image thumbnails at once, and it reduces the magnification of images when displayed one at a time. Chapter 5 explains picture playback.

- **Speaker:** When you play a movie that contains an audio track, the sound comes wafting through these little holes, which lead to the camera's internal speaker.

- **Live View/Movie-record button:** You press this button to shift the camera into Live View mode and, when shooting movies, to start and stop recording. For the latter, you must first set the On/Off switch to the Movie position.

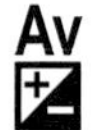

- **Exposure Compensation/Aperture button:** When you work in M (manual) exposure mode, you press this button and rotate the Main dial to choose the aperture setting, also known as the *f-stop.* In the other advanced exposure modes (P, Tv, and Av), you instead use the button and dial to apply *Exposure Compensation,* a feature that enables you to adjust the exposure selected by the camera's autoexposure mechanism. Chapter 7 discusses both issues.

- **Quick Control/Direct Print button:** You press this button to display the Quick Control screen, which gives you one way to adjust picture settings. (See "Taking advantage of the Quick Control screen," later in this chapter, for help.) As for the Direct Print button, it's used to print directly from the camera to a compatible printer. Chapter 11 covers this function.

- **Set button and cross keys:** Figure 1-13 points out the Set button and the four surrounding buttons, known as *cross keys.* These buttons team up to perform several functions, including choosing options from the camera menus. You use the cross keys to navigate through menus and then press the Set button to select a specific menu setting. You can find out more about ordering from menus later in this chapter.

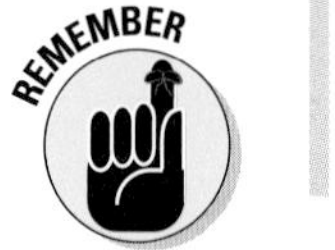

  In this book, the instruction "Press the left cross key" means to press the one to the left of the Set button, "press the right cross key" means to press the one to the right of the Set button, and so on.

The cross keys and the Set button also have nonmenu responsibilities, as follows:

- *When using the Quick Control screen, press the Set button to access options for the highlighted function.* Again, I provide full details on the Quick Control screen later in this chapter.
- *Press the right cross key to adjust the AF mode.* This option controls one aspect of the camera's autofocus behavior, as outlined in Chapter 8.
- *Press the left cross key to change the Drive mode.* The Drive mode settings enable you to switch the camera from single-frame shooting to continuous capture or self-timer/remote-control shooting. See Chapter 2 for details.
- *Press the down cross key to change the Picture Style.* Chapter 8 explains Picture Styles, which you can use to adjust color, contrast, and sharpness of your pictures.
- *Press the up cross key to change the White Balance setting.* The White Balance control, explained near the end of Chapter 8, enables you to ensure that your photo colors are accurate and not biased by the color of the light source.

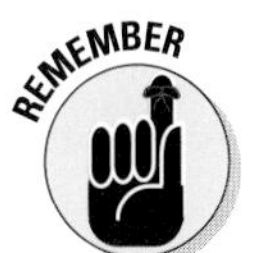

You can customize the function of the Set button; Chapter 10 explains how. But while you're working with this book, stick with the default setup, just described. Otherwise the instructions I give won't work. Also note that in Live View and Movie mode, the cross keys don't perform the aforementioned functions; you adjust the settings in other ways, as outlined in Chapter 4.

- **Playback button:** Press this button to switch the camera into picture-review mode. Chapter 5 details playback features.

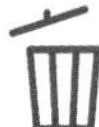

- **Erase button:** Sporting a trash can icon, the universal symbol for delete, this button lets you erase pictures from your memory card during playback. Chapter 5 has specifics.
- **Info button:** In Live View, Movie, and Playback modes, pressing this button changes the picture-display style, as outlined in Chapters 4 and 5, respectively.

  During shooting, you can press the Info button to turn off the monitor and to switch from the Shooting Settings display to the Camera Settings display. (Both displays are explained in detail later in this chapter.)
- **Menu button:** Press this button to access the camera menus, described in more detail later in this chapter.

Front odds and ends

On the front of the camera, you find the following features, labeled in Figure 1-14:

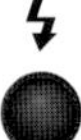

- **Flash button:** Press this button to use the built-in flash in the advanced exposure modes (P, Tv, Av, and M). See Chapter 2 for a flash primer; flip to Chapters 7 and 9 for more tips on flash photography.
- **Lens-release button:** Press this button to disengage the lens from the lens mount so that you can remove it from the camera. See the first part of this chapter for details on mounting and removing lenses.
- **Depth-of-Field Preview button:** When you press this button, the image in the viewfinder (or, in Live View mode, on the monitor) offers an approximation of the depth of field that will result from your selected aperture setting, or f-stop. *Depth of field* refers to how much of the scene will be in sharp focus. Chapter 8 provides details.

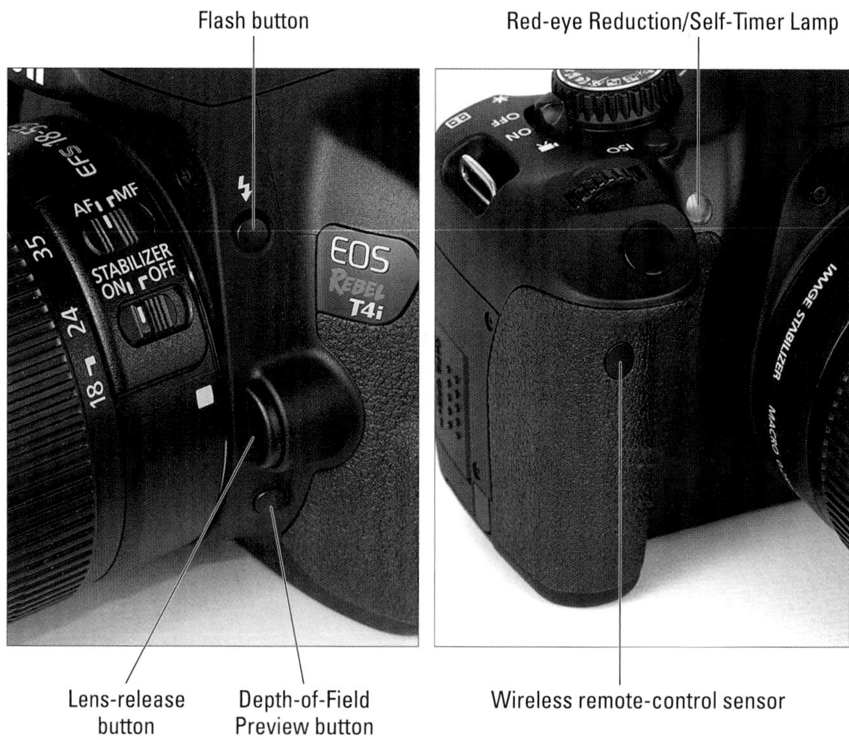

Figure 1-14: Press the Flash button to bring the built-in flash out of hiding when you shoot in the P, Tv, Av, or M exposure modes.

- **Red-Eye Reduction/Self-Timer Lamp:** When you set your flash to Red-Eye Reduction mode, this little lamp (see the right side of Figure 1-14) emits a brief burst of light prior to the real flash — the idea being that your subjects' pupils will constrict in response to the light, thus lessening the chances of red-eye. If you use the camera's self-timer feature, the lamp lights during the countdown period before the shutter is released. See Chapter 2 for more details about Red-Eye Reduction flash mode and the self-timer function.
- **Remote control sensor:** Labeled in the right image in Figure 1-14, the sensor can pick up the signal from the optional Canon wireless remote-control unit. The part number is Canon RC-6, and the remote sells for about $30.

Connection ports

Hidden under the two little covers on the left side of the camera, you find inputs for connecting the camera to various devices. The left side of Figure 1-15 shows you what lurks beneath the first cover; the right side of the figure shows the connections found under the second cover. Starting with the left side, the available connections are

- **Remote-control terminal:** As an alternative to using a wireless remote controller to trigger the shutter release, you can attach the Canon Remote Switch RS-60E3 wired controller here.

  The controller currently sells for about $30 and is a very worthwhile investment if you do a lot of long-exposure shooting (such as nighttime shots and fireworks). By using the remote control, you eliminate the chance that the action of your finger on the shutter button moves the camera enough to blur the shot, which is especially problematic during long exposures. And unlike a wireless remote, which must be positioned so that the signal reaches the sensor on the front of the camera, a wired remote can be operated from behind the camera (which is why it's my remote controller of choice).
- **Microphone jack:** If you're not happy with the audio quality provided by the internal microphone when you record movies, you can plug in an external microphone here. The jack accepts a 3.5mm stereo microphone miniplug. See Chapter 4 for all things movie-related.
- **A/V and USB connection terminal:** This connection point serves two purposes: You can connect your camera to a standard-definition television for picture playback via the optional AVC-DC400ST A/V (audio/video) cable, which sells for about $25. Chapter 5 explains this option. You use the same terminal to connect the camera to a computer via the supplied USB cable for picture downloading (although using a memory-card reader is usually a better alternative, for reasons you can explore in Chapter 6).

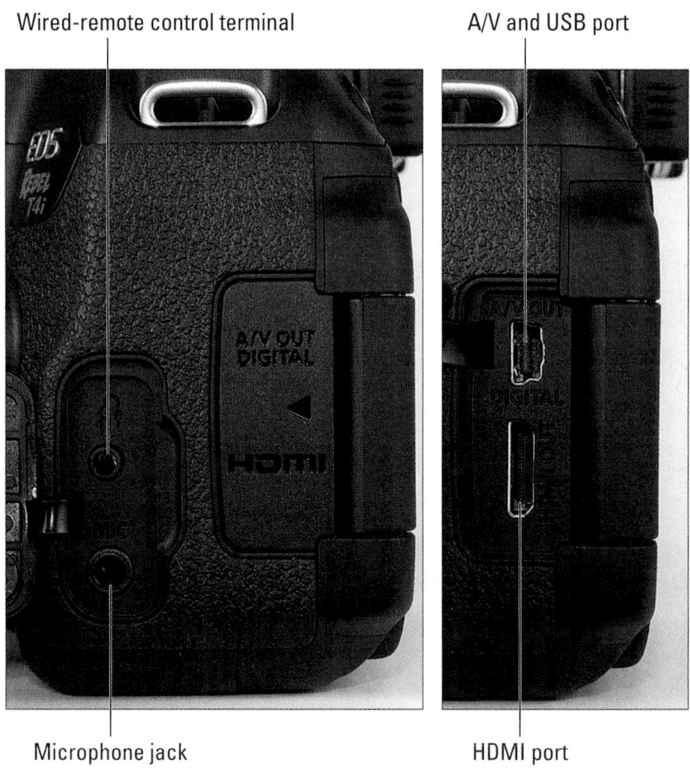

Figure 1-15: These two rubber covers conceal terminals for connecting the camera to other devices.

- **HDMI terminal:** For picture or movie playback on a high-definition television or screen, you can connect the camera via this terminal, using an optional HDMI male to mini-C cable. You'll pay about $50 if you buy Canon's version, the HTC-100 cable. (You can use other manufacturer's cables, but be sure they are of high quality.) Again, see Chapter 5 for details on connecting the camera to a TV.

If you turn the camera over, you find a tripod socket, which enables you to mount the camera on a tripod that uses a ¼-inch screw, plus the battery chamber. And finally, tucked just above the battery chamber, on the right side of the camera, is a little flap that covers a connection for attaching the optional AC power adapter kit ACK-E8; it sells for about $65. See the camera manual for specifics on running the camera on AC power.

Viewing and Adjusting Camera Settings

Your camera gives you several ways to monitor current settings and adjust them if needed. The next sections provide a quick introduction to viewing and changing settings; later chapters explain exactly how and where to access individual options.

Ordering from menus

You access many camera features via menus, which are described briefly in Table 1-1. As the table indicates, though, some menus appear only when you set the Mode dial to one of the advanced exposure modes (P, Tv, Av, and M). Similarly, when you switch to Movie mode (by setting the On/Off switch to the Movie position), the Live View menu disappears and the two Movie menus appear.

In case you didn't notice, the icons that represent the menus are color-coded. The Shooting, Live View, and Movie menus have red icons; the Setup menus sport yellow icons; the Playback menus have a blue symbol; and the My Menu icon is green. (Chapter 10 explains the My Menu feature, through which you can create your own, custom menu.)

Table 1-1 Rebel T4i/650D Menus

Symbol	*Open This Menu*	*To Access These Functions*
	Shooting Menu 1	Image Quality setting, Red-Eye Reduction flash mode, and a few other basic shooting settings
	Shooting Menu 2*	Advanced shooting options such as automatic exposure bracketing, metering mode, and color controls
	Shooting Menu 3*	Options for enabling the Dust Delete Data, Auto ISO limits, and noise reduction features
	Live View Menu***	Live View photography options
	Movie Menu 1**	Movie focusing, display, and exposure metering options

(continued)

Table 1-1 *(continued)*

Symbol	*Open This Menu*	*To Access These Functions*
	Movie Menu 2**	More movie settings, including recording size, sound recording, and video snap-shot (enable or disable)
	Playback Menu 1	Basic playback features, including protecting, rotating, and erasing images; also contains the Creative Filters and image-resizing features
	Playback Menu 2	Additional playback features, including picture rating, slide shows, histogram display, image jump, and HDMI control
	Setup Menu 1	Memory-card formatting plus basic customization options, such as the file-numbering system and automatic image rotation
	Setup Menu 2	More customization options, such as date/time and interface language
	Setup Menu 3	Touch-control option (enable/disable), additional customization options plus sensor cleaning and GPS device settings
	Setup Menu 4*	Custom Functions, copyright embedding, firmware information, and options for resetting camera functions to factory defaults
	My Menu*	User-customized menu setup

**Menu appears only when Mode dial is set to P, Tv, Av, or M*
***Menu appears only when On/Off switch is set to Movie position*
****Does not appear when camera is set to Movie mode*

I explain all menu options elsewhere in the book; for now, just familiarize yourself with the process of navigating menus and selecting menu options:

- **Display menus:** Press the Menu button. A screen similar to the one shown on the left in Figure 1-16 appears. Along the top of the screen, you see the icons shown in Table 1-1, each representing a menu. (Remember that the setting of the Mode dial determines which icons appear.)

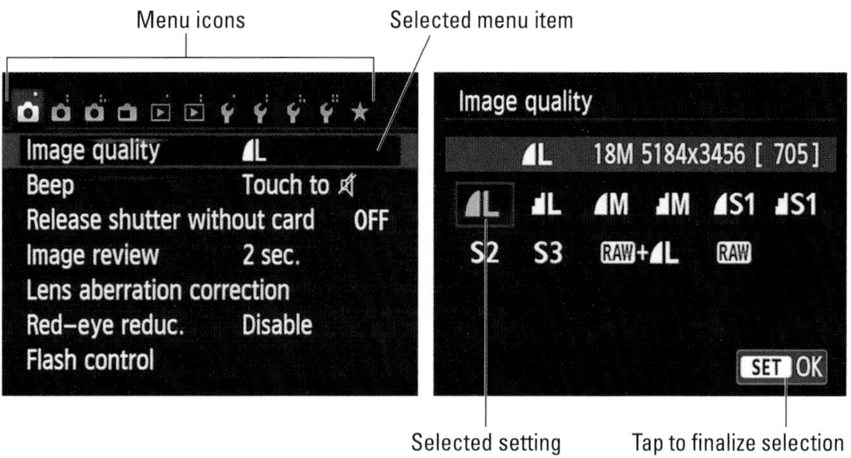

Figure 1-16: The icons at the top of the screen represent the different camera menus.

The highlighted icon marks the active menu; options on that menu appear automatically on the main part of the screen. In the left screen in Figure 1-16, Shooting Menu 1 is active, for example. The number of dots above the icon tells you the menu number — one dot for Shooting Menu 1, two dots for Shooting menu 2, and so on.

- **Select a different menu:** You have these options:
  - *Touchscreen:* Tap the menu icon.
  - *Cross keys or Main dial:* Press the right or left cross keys or rotate the Main dial to scroll through the menu icons.
- **Select and adjust a menu setting:** Again, you have a choice of techniques:
  - *Touchscreen:* Tap the menu item to display a screen of options related to that item. For example, to adjust the picture Image Quality, display Shooting Menu 1 and tap Image Quality to display the right screen in the figure. The current setting is highlighted and shown in blue; in the figure, Large Fine is the current setting, for example. Tap the setting you want to use and then tap Set to return to the menu. (See Chapter 2 for details on the Image Quality options.)

    In some cases, the available options appear right next to the menu item; just tap the setting you want to use to select it and return to the normal menu display. No need to tap a Set icon.
  - *Cross keys and Set button:* Press the up or down cross key to highlight the feature you want to adjust. Then press the Set button to display the available options. Use the cross keys to highlight your preferred setting and press the Set button again to lock in your choice.

Navigating Custom Functions

When you select Custom Functions from Setup Menu 4 — a menu available only when the Mode dial is set to P, Tv, Av, or M — you delve into submenus containing eight advanced camera settings. Navigating these screens involves a few special techniques.

Initially, you see a screen similar to the one shown on the left here. Some explanation may help you make sense of it:

- Custom Functions are grouped into four categories: Exposure, Image, Autofocus/Drive, and Operation/Others. The category number and name appear in the upper-left corner of the screen. In the figure, for example, Category 1, Exposure, is visible.
- The number of the selected function appears in the upper-right corner — Custom Function 1 is indicated in the figure here.
- Settings for the current function appear in the middle of the screen. The blue text indicates the current setting. The default setting is represented by the number 0.
- At the bottom of the screen, the top row of numbers represents the 8 Custom Functions, with the currently selected function indicated with a tiny horizontal bar over the number. The lower row shows the number of the current setting for each Custom Function; again, 0 represents the default. So in the figure, all the Custom Functions are currently using the default settings.

To scroll from one Custom Function to the next, tap left or right scroll arrows at the top of the screen or press the left or right cross keys. When you reach the setting you want to adjust, use either of these techniques:

- **Touchscreen:** Tap the setting you want to use. (In some cases, you may need to tap the up/down arrows on the right side of the screen — not shown in the figures — to scroll the list of settings.) The Set icon then appears, as shown on the right in the figure. Tap that icon to lock in your choice and exit the setting screen. Your selected setting appears in blue and the number at the bottom of the screen updates to show the number of the option you selected.
- **Buttons:** Press the Set button to activate the settings. Then use the cross keys to move the highlight box over the one you want to use and press the Set button.

To exit the Custom Function screens, press the Menu button or tap the Menu icon in the lower right corner of the screen (see the left screen in the figure).

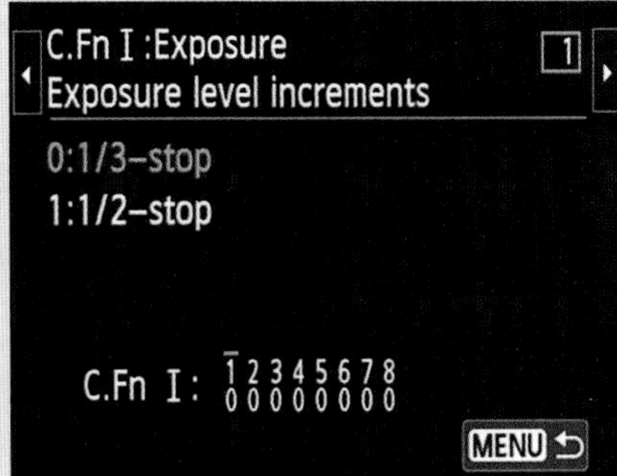

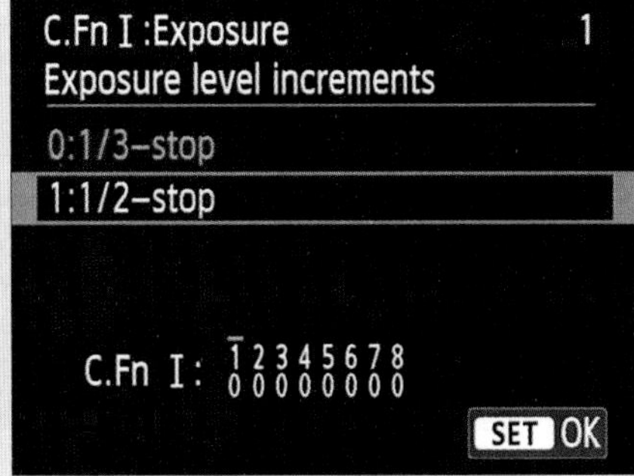

You can mix and match techniques, by the way: For example, even if you access a menu option via the control keys, you can use the touchscreen techniques to select a setting.

- **Exit menus and return to shooting:** Press the shutter button halfway and release it or press the Menu button again.

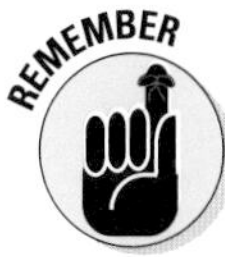

To save space in this book, I don't spell out both the button-push and touchscreen steps for selecting menu items. Instead, I just tell you to choose the item, using whichever method you prefer. Note that if you connect the camera to a TV or monitor, though, the touchscreen no longer is available, and you have to use the old-fashioned button-push method of selecting menu options.

Exploring the Shooting Settings display

Shown in Figure 1-17, the Shooting Settings screen displays the most critical photography settings — aperture, shutter speed, ISO, and the like. Note that the display shown here is relevant only to viewfinder photography, though. When you switch to Live View mode or Movie mode, you can choose to see some settings superimposed over your image in the monitor, but the process of adjusting settings and customizing the display is different. (See Chapter 4 for details.)

In addition, the data shown in the Shooting Settings display depends on the exposure mode you select. The figure shows data that's included when you work in one of the advanced modes, such as Tv (shutter-priority autoexposure). In the fully automatic modes and Creative Auto mode, you see far fewer settings because you can control fewer settings in those modes. Figure 1-17 labels two key points of data that are helpful in any mode, though: how many more pictures can fit on your memory card at the current settings and the status of the battery. A "full" battery icon like the one in the figure shows that the battery is charged. When the icon appears empty, you better have a spare battery handy if you want to keep shooting.

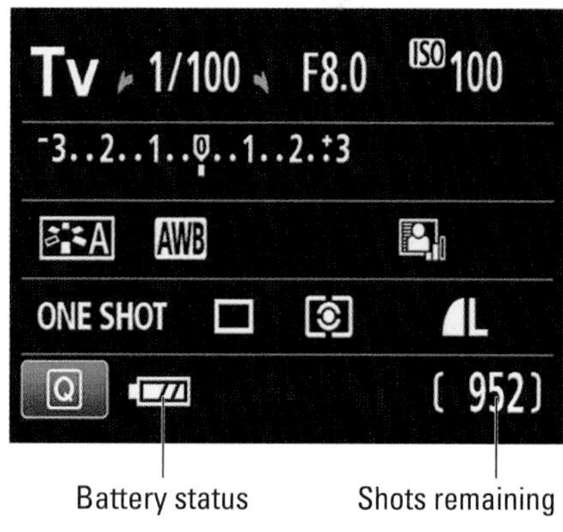

Figure 1-17: The Shooting Settings display gives you an easy way to monitor current picture settings.

Back to the Shooting Settings display: You use it to view settings and as a jumping off point for adjusting certain settings. Here's what you need to know:

- **Turning the display on and off:** By default, the display appears automatically when you turn on the camera and then turns off automatically if either of the following occurs:
  - *No camera operations are performed for about 30 seconds.* You can turn the display on again by pressing the shutter button halfway and then releasing it.
  - *You put your eye to the viewfinder.* See that little black box just above the viewfinder, shown in Figure 1-18? It's a sensor that detects the presence of your eye and tells the camera that because you're looking through the viewfinder, you no longer need the Shooting Settings screen on the monitor. The display comes back to life when you move your eye away from the sensor. ***Note:*** If you're wearing sunglasses, the sensor may not detect your eye. Also, the monitor does not turn off when menus are displayed.

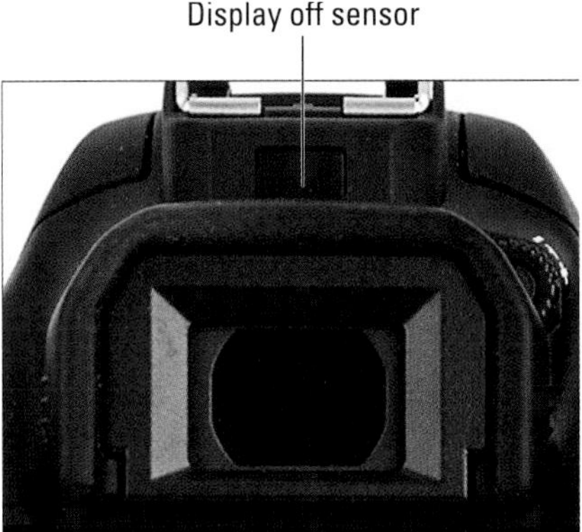

Figure 1-18: The Shooting Information display turns off automatically when the sensor detects your eye covering the viewfinder.

  To turn off the Shooting Settings display before the automatic shutoff occurs or if the sensor doesn't do its thing, press the Info button. Press again to display a second information screen, the Camera Settings display (explained a few sections from here); press once more to return to the Shooting Settings display.

- **Adjusting settings via the display:** You can adjust certain settings directly from the Shooting Settings display, as follows:
  - *Curved arrows bordering a setting mean that you can adjust the setting by rotating the Main dial.* For example, in the shutter-priority autoexposure mode (Tv, on the Mode dial), the shutter speed is bordered by the arrows, as shown in Figure 1-19, indicating that the setting is active and that rotating the Main dial changes the setting.

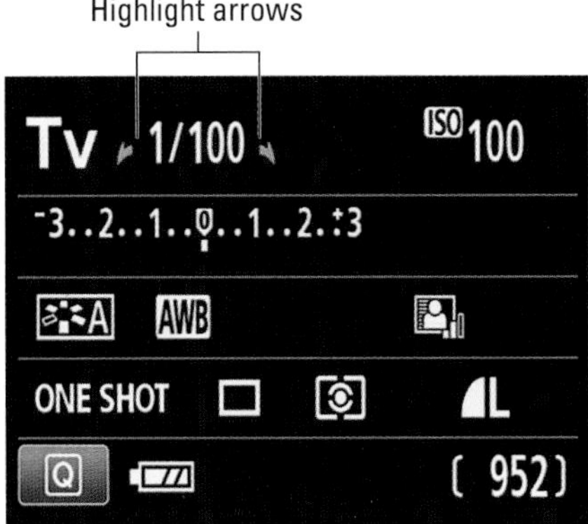

Figure 1-19: The arrows indicate that you can rotate the Main dial to adjust the setting.

Preserving battery power

If the battery indicator on the Shooting Settings display shows that you're running low on battery power, you can extend what power remains by using these tricks:

- Keep the monitor off as much as possible.
- Turn off Image Stabilization. On the kit lenses, set the Stabilizer switch to the Off position.
- Don't use flash. And keep the built-in flash head closed, too, because the camera keeps the flash charged while the head is raised, which drains power even when you're not shooting.
- Avoid keeping the shutter button pressed halfway for long periods; the exposure and autofocusing processes that are activated with a half-press also consume battery power.

- *You can access some settings by pressing the related function button.* For example, while the Shooting Settings screen is displayed and the Mode dial is set to P, Tv, Av, or M, pressing the ISO button takes you to the screen where you can adjust the ISO setting, as shown in Figure 1-20. These screens are officially known as Function Settings screens.

  After the Function Setting screen is displayed, you can select the setting via the touchscreen — just tap the option you want to use — or by using the cross keys to highlight the setting. To lock in your choice, tap return icon, labeled in the figure, or press the Set button.

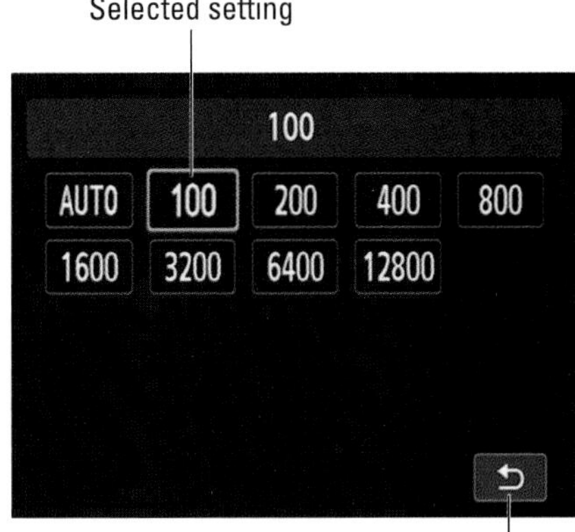

Figure 1-20: Some buttons take you directly to a settings screen; tap your choice and then tap the return arrow to return to the Shooting Settings screen.

Taking advantage of the Quick Control screen

The Quick Control screen enables you to change certain shooting settings without using the function buttons (ISO button, the Exposure Compensation button, and so on) or menus. You can use this screen to adjust settings in any exposure mode, but the settings that are accessible depend on the mode you select.

To try it out, set the Mode dial to Tv so that what you see on your screen looks like what you see in the upcoming figures. Then follow these steps:

1. **Display the Shooting Settings screen.**

   Either press the shutter button halfway and then release it, or press the Info button. (You may have to press the Info button a couple times to get to the Shooting Settings screen.)

2. **Use one of these methods to shift to Quick Control mode.**

   - *Tap the Q icon in the lower left corner of the screen.* I labeled it in Figure 1-21.

   - *Press the Quick Control button.* I also labeled the button in the figure.

   Either way, the screen shifts into Quick Control mode, and one of the options on the screen becomes highlighted. For example, the White Balance option is highlighted in Figure 1-22. (AWB stands for Auto White Balance.)

3. **Select the setting you want to adjust.**

   Either tap the setting on the touchscreen or use the cross keys to highlight it.

   TIP: When you first highlight a setting, a text tip appears to remind you of the purpose of the setting. If you find the text tips annoying, you can get rid of them by disabling the Feature Guide option on Setup Menu 3.

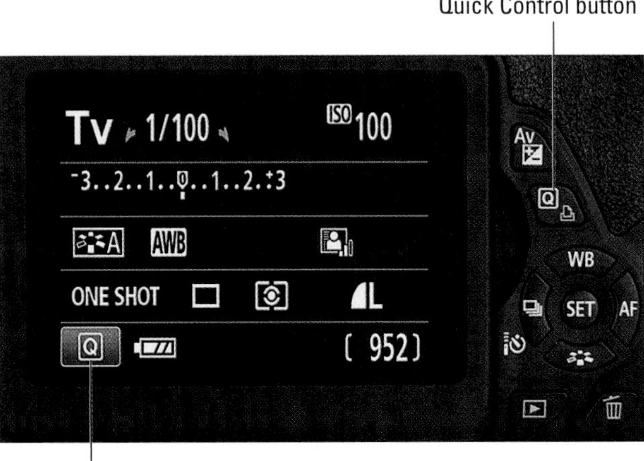

Figure 1-21: To shift to Quick Control mode, tap the Q icon or press the Quick Control button.

4. **Select the option you want to use.**

   You can use these techniques to take this step:

   - *To scroll through the available settings, rotate the Main dial.* The current setting appears at the bottom of the screen, as shown in the figure. Note the little wheel icon at the far right side of the text bar — it's your reminder to use the Main dial for this function.
   - *To display all the possible settings on a single screen, tap the option or press the Set button.* For example, if you're adjusting the White Balance setting and tap the icon or press Set, you see the screen shown in Figure 1-23. Then tap the option you want to use or highlight it by rotating the Main dial or using the cross keys. In some cases, the screen contains a brief explanation or note about the option, as shown in the figure, regardless of the setting of the Feature Guide option. After selecting your choice, tap the return icon, labeled in Figure 1-23 or press the Set button to return to the Quick Control screen.

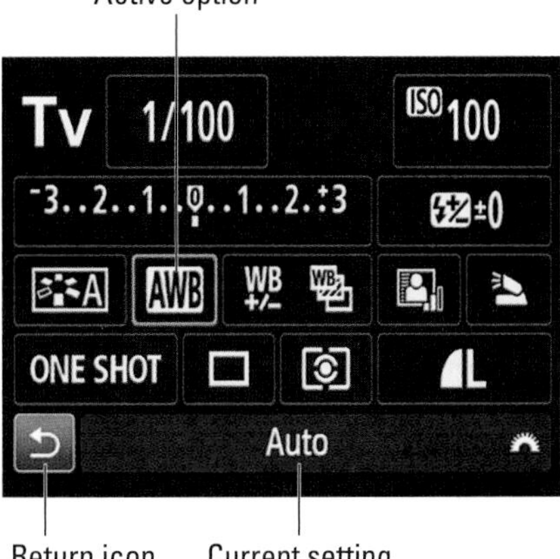

Figure 1-22: The active option appears highlighted.

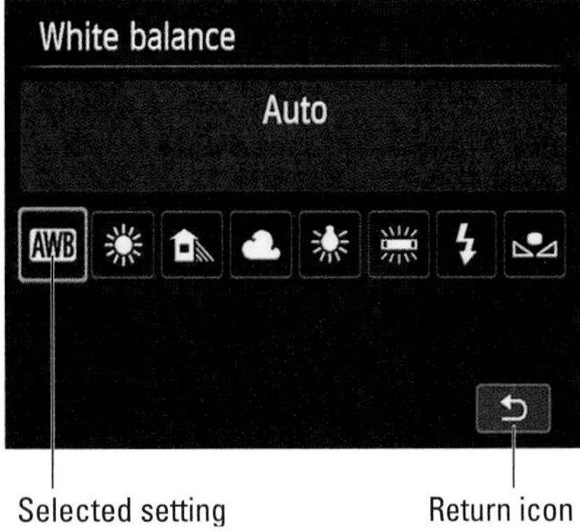

Figure 1-23: From the Quick Control screen, press Set to display all settings available for the currently selected option.

   A few controls require a slightly different approach, but don't worry — I spell out all the needed steps throughout the book.

5. **Exit Quick Control mode and return to shooting mode using any of these techniques.**

   - Tap the return symbol, labeled in Figure 1-22.
   - Press the Quick Control button.
   - Press the shutter button halfway and release it.

   You're returned to the Shooting Settings display.

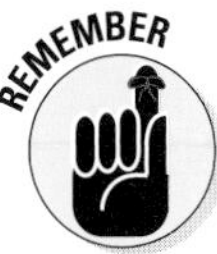

As with menu instructions, when I tell you to choose a certain option from the Quick Control screen, you can do so by using the touchscreen techniques or by using the "old-fashioned" methods involving the cross keys, Main dial, and Set button.

Decoding viewfinder data

When the camera is turned on, you can view critical exposure settings and a few other pieces of information in the data strip at the bottom of the viewfinder. Just put your eye to the viewfinder and press the shutter button halfway to activate the display. The data disappears after a few seconds; just press the shutter button halfway again to bring it back to life.

The data changes depending on what action you're undertaking and what exposure mode you're using. For example, if you set the Mode dial to Tv (for shutter-priority autoexposure), you see the data shown in Figure 1-24: shutter speed, f-stop (aperture setting), Exposure Compensation setting, and ISO setting. Additional data appears when you enable certain features, such as flash.

I detail each viewfinder readout as I discuss camera options throughout the book. But I want to explain now one often-confused value: The number at the far right end of the viewfinder (9, in Figure 1-24) shows you the number of *maximum burst frames.* This number relates to shooting in the Continuous capture mode, where the camera fires off multiple shots in rapid succession as long as you hold down the shutter button. (Chapter 2 has details.) Although the highest number that the viewfinder can display is 9, the actual number of maximum burst frames may be higher. At any rate, you don't really need to pay attention to the number until it starts dropping toward 0, which indicates that the camera's *memory buffer* (its temporary internal data-storage tank) is filling up. If that happens, just give the camera a moment to catch up with your shutter-button finger.

While you're looking through the viewfinder, you can adjust some shooting settings by using the Main dial alone or in conjunction with the function buttons, as you do with the Shooting Settings screen. For example, if you're working in one of the advanced exposure modes (P, Tv, Av, or M) and press the ISO button, all data but the current ISO setting dims, and you can then rotate the Main dial to change the setting. Press the shutter button halfway to return to the normal viewfinder display after changing the setting.

As for the markings in the center of the screen, the nine rectangles represent focusing points and the circle represents the frame area that's used if you set the Metering mode option to Spot metering. Chapter 8 talks about focusing; Chapter 7 explains how the Metering mode affects exposure.

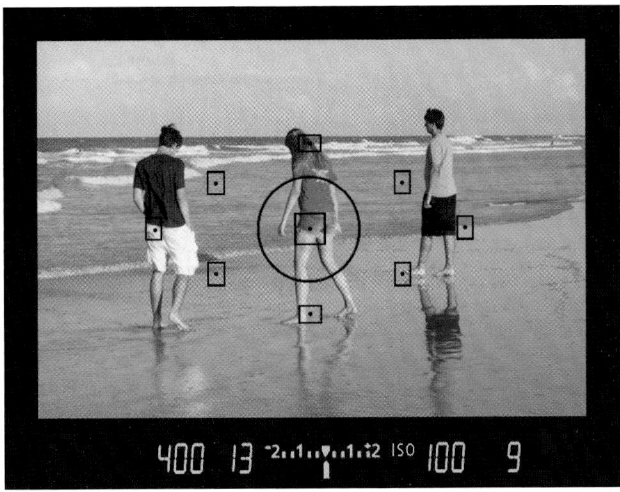

Figure 1-24: You also can view some camera information at the bottom of the viewfinder.

Checking the Camera Settings display

In addition to the Shooting Settings display, you can view a collection of additional settings data via the Camera Settings display, shown in Figure 1-25. This screen is purely an informational tool, however; you can't actually adjust any of the reported settings from this screen.

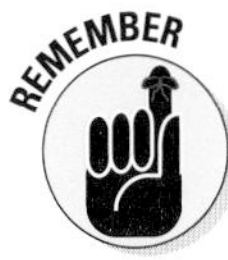

You get to the Camera Settings screen via the Info button. Pressing the button cycles you through three monitor states: displaying the Shooting Settings screen; turning the monitor off; and displaying the Camera Settings screen.

Freespace	6.23 GB
Color space	sRGB
WB Shift/Bkt.	0,0/±0
Enable	Enable
Enable	Disable
2 min.	On
Touch to	Enable
	07/03/2012 03:31:38

Figure 1-25: Press the Info button to cycle from the Shooting Settings screen to monitor off to this screen.

Figure 1-25 shows the settings that you can monitor via the screen when shooting in the advanced exposure modes. Again, that's P, Tv, Av, and M. Here are the details you can glean, with settings listed in the order they appear on the screen. After the first three lines, settings are presented two to a line — for example, the Live View Shooting and Touchscreen enable/disable settings share the fourth line of the screen.

- **Freespace:** This value indicates how much storage space is left on your camera memory card. How many pictures you can fit into that space depends on the Image Quality setting you select. Chapter 2 explains this issue.
- **Color Space:** This value tells you whether the camera is capturing images in the sRGB or Adobe RGB color space, an advanced option that you can investigate in Chapter 10.
- **White Balance Shift/Bracketing:** I cover these advanced color options in Chapter 8. All zeroes, as in the figure, indicate that White Balance shift and bracketing aren't in force.
- **Live View Shooting and Touchscreen:** The screen indicates whether these features are enabled. Chapter 4 details the first feature, which enables you to use your monitor instead of the viewfinder to compose your shots. See the earlier section "Using the Touchscreen" to find out about that aspect of your camera
- **Auto Sensor Cleaning and Red-Eye Reduction flash mode:** See the section "Setup Menu 3," later in this chapter, for more about automatic sensor cleaning; check out Chapter 2 for information about Red-Eye Reduction flash mode.
- **Auto Power Off and Auto Rotate:** For information on these two settings, see the upcoming sections, "Setup Menu 2" (for Auto Power Off) and "Setup Menu 1" (for Auto Rotate).
- **Beep and LCD Auto Off:** The first setting indicates the current setting of the Beep option on Shooting Menu 1, detailed in Chapter 10 as well as in the earlier section "Using the Touchscreen." For details about the second setting, LCD Auto Off, hop to the upcoming section "Setup Menu 2."
- **Date/Time:** The section "Setup Menu 2" also explains how to adjust the date and time. The little sun icon indicates that the camera is set to automatically spring forward or fall back according to the dictates of Daylight Savings Time.

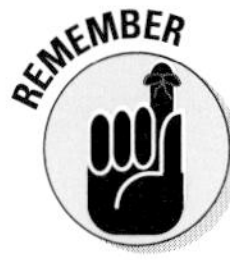

In exposure modes other than P, Tv, Av, and M, the Color Space and White Balance Shift/Bracketing information items don't appear because those other modes prevent you from adjusting those two features.

Of course, with the exception of the free card space value, you also can simply go to the menu that contains the option in question to check its status. The Camera Settings display just gives you a quick way to monitor some of the critical functions without hunting through menus.

Reviewing Basic Setup Options

One of the many advantages of investing in the Rebel T4i/650D is that you can customize it to suit the way *you* like to shoot. Later chapters explain options related to actual picture taking, such as those that affect flash behavior and autofocusing. The rest of this chapter details options related to initial camera setup, which are scattered throughout the four Setup menus. See Chapters 10 and 11 for a look at a few additional customization options.

Setup Menu 1

Start your camera customization by opening Setup Menu 1, shown in Figure 1-26, to access the following options:

- **Select Folder:** By default, your camera creates an initial file-storage folder named 100Canon and puts as many as 9999 images in that folder. When you reach image 9999, the camera creates a new folder, named 101Canon, for your next 9999 images. The camera also creates a new folder if you perform a manual file-numbering reset, a choice explained in the next bullet point.

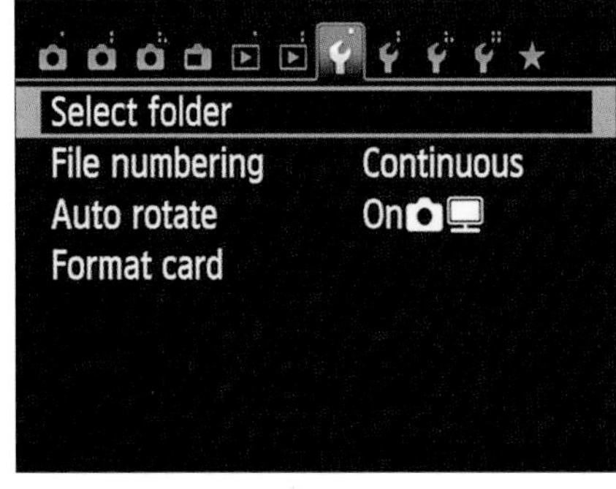

Figure 1-26: Press the Menu button and then choose Setup Menu 1 to display these options.

  If your memory card contains multiple folders, you must use the Select Folder option to choose the folder where you want to store the next photos you shoot. But selecting the menu option also leads to another neat feature: You can create your own storage folders at any time. You might create separate folders for each person who uses the camera, for example. Chapter 10 shows you how to create custom folders. Here's how to view which folder is active and choose a different one:

  - *See which folder is currently selected:* Choose Select Folder to display a list of all folders, with the current one highlighted and appearing in blue type. The number to the right of the folder name shows you how many pictures are in the folder. You also see a thumbnail view of the first and last pictures in the folder, along with the file numbers of those two photos.

  - *Choose a different folder:* Highlight it by using the cross keys or tapping it. Then tap Set or press the Set button to return to Setup Menu 1.

- **File Numbering:** This option controls how the camera names your picture files.

  - *Continuous:* This is the default; the camera numbers your files sequentially, from 0001 to 9999, and places all images in the same folder (100Canon, by default) unless you specify otherwise using the Select Folder option described in the preceding bullet point. This numbering sequence is retained even if you change memory cards.

    When you reach picture 9999, the camera automatically creates a new folder (101Canon, by default) and restarts the file numbering at 0001 — again, the folder issue being dependent on the status of the Select Folder option.

  - *Auto Reset:* If you switch to this option, the camera restarts file numbering at 0001 each time you put in a different memory card or create a new folder. I don't recommend this option because it's easy to wind up with multiple photos that have the same file number if you're not careful about storing them in separate folders.

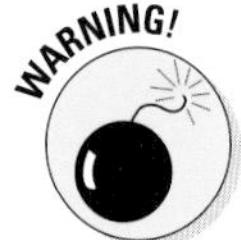

    Beware of one gotcha that applies both to the Continuous and Auto Reset options: If you swap memory cards and the new card already contains images, the camera may pick up numbering from the last image on the new card, which throws a monkey wrench into things. To avoid this problem, format the new card before putting it into the camera, as explained two bullet points from here.

  - *Manual Reset:* Select this setting if you want the camera to begin a new numbering sequence, starting at 0001, for your next shot. A new folder is automatically created to store your new files. The camera then returns to whichever mode you previously used (Continuous or Auto Reset) to number subsequent pictures.

- **Auto Rotate:** By default, your picture files include a piece of data that indicates whether the camera was oriented in the vertical or horizontal position when you shot the frame. Then, when you view the picture on the camera monitor or on the computer screen, the image is automatically rotated to the correct orientation. You also can choose to rotate the pictures only on the computer monitor or disable rotation altogether.

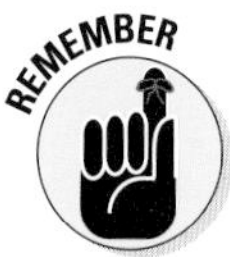

  When both computer and camera display rotation are enabled, you see a little camera icon and computer monitor icon next to the word On, as shown in Figure 1-26. If you see just the computer monitor icon, the pictures aren't rotated on the camera monitor. Choose Off to disable rotation on both displays.

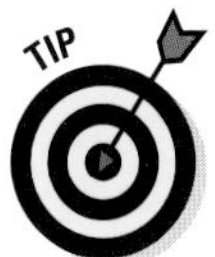

Even if automatic rotation is disabled, you can rotate a picture during playback using the Rotate Image option on Playback Menu 1. Chapter 5 explains how.

- **Format Card:** The first time you insert a new memory card, use this option to *format* the card, a maintenance function that wipes out any existing data on the card and prepares it for use by the camera.

If you previously used your card in another device, such as a digital music player, copy those files to your computer before you format the card. You lose *all* data on the card when you format it.

When you choose the Format option from the menu, you can perform a normal card formatting process or a *low-level* formatting by tapping the Low Level Format check box or by pressing the Erase button (the one marked with a trash-can symbol) to select the box. This option gives your memory card a deeper level of cleansing than ordinary formatting and thus takes longer to perform. Normally, a regular formatting will do, although performing a low-level formatting can be helpful if your card seems to be running more slowly than usual. However — and this is a however for anyone with a high-security clearance who's shooting pictures that should *never* fall into enemy hands — a regular-level formatting leaves enough bits of data intact that a determined computer whiz could recover your images. To prevent that possibility, do a low-level formatting or crush the card under your heel. Or run over it with your car. You can never be too safe, with all these spies running around looking just like your mild-mannered neighbor.

- **Eye-Fi Settings:** If an Eye-Fi memory card is installed, this menu option appears to enable you to control the wireless transmission between the camera and your computer. When no Eye-Fi card is installed, the menu option is hidden, as it is in Figure 1-26. I don't cover Eye-Fi cards in this book, but if you want more details about the product, visit `www.eye.fi`.

Setup Menu 2

Setup Menu 2, posing in Figure 1-27, contains these options:

- **Auto Power Off:** To help save battery power, your camera automatically powers down after a certain period of inactivity. By default, the shutdown happens after 30 seconds, but you can change the shutdown delay to 1, 2, 4, 8, or 15 minutes. Or you can disable auto shutdown altogether by selecting the Off setting, although even at that setting, the monitor still turns itself off if you ignore the camera for 30 minutes. Just give the shutter button a quick half-press and release or press the Menu, Info, Playback, or Live View button to bring the monitor out of hibernation.

- **LCD Brightness:** This option enables you to make the camera monitor brighter or darker. I show you how to take this step using the touchscreen in the section "Using the Touchscreen," earlier in this chapter, so I won't repeat all the details here. To use the buttons to control the setting, highlight the menu option, press Set, and then use the left and right cross keys to adjust the brightness value. Press the Set button to finish.

Auto power off	30 sec.
LCD brightness	
LCD auto off	Enable
Time zone	
Date/Time	07/03/'12 03:35
Language	English
Video system	NTSC

Figure 1-27: Setup Menu 2 offers more ways to customize basic operations.

If you take this step, what you see on the display may not be an accurate rendition of exposure. So keeping the brightness at its default center position is a good idea unless you're shooting in very bright or dark conditions. As an alternative, you can gauge exposure when reviewing images by displaying a Brightness histogram, a tool that I explain in Chapter 5.

- **LCD Auto Off:** This option controls whether the eye sensor above the monitor turns off the display when you put your eye to the viewfinder. It's enabled by default; set the option to Disable if you don't want the sensor to respond to your eye. (Refer to Figure 1-18 for a look at the sensor.)

- **Time Zone:** When you turn on your camera for the first time, it displays this option and asks you to set the time zone. I'm guessing that you already took this step, but here's the scoop on a screen value that may have caused you to scratch your head a little: The time displayed in the lower right corner of the screen is the difference between the Time Zone you select and Coordinated Universal Time, or UCT, which is the standard by which the world sets its clocks. For example, New York City is five hours behind UCT. This information is provided so that if your time zone isn't in the list of available options, you can select one that shares the same relationship to the UCT.

- **Date/Time:** You no doubt already set the date and time, too, but here's another fine point you may have missed: The setting directly to the right of the mm/dd/yy option — which enables you to specify the order of the month, day, and year values — tells the camera whether to automatically adjust the time of day for Daylight Savings Time. A sun symbol means the feature is enabled; a sun plus the word Off means that it's disabled. This setting is tied to the Time Zone option, so it should be set correctly automatically. But if not, tap the sun icon to display an arrow above and below the icon. Tap either one (or press the up/down cross keys) to turn the sun off and, with it, Daylight Savings Time adjustment.

Keeping the date/time accurate is important because that information is recorded as part of the image file. In your photo browser, you can then see when you shot an image and, equally handy, search for images by the date they were taken. Chapter 6 shows you where to locate the date/time data when browsing your picture files.

- **Language:** This option determines the language of any text displayed on the camera monitor.
- **Video System:** This option is related to viewing your images and movies on a television, a topic I cover in Chapter 5. Select NTSC if you live in North America or other countries that adhere to the NTSC video standard; select PAL for playback in areas that follow that code of video conduct.

Setup Menu 3

Setup Menu 3, shown in Figure 1-28, contains the following offerings:

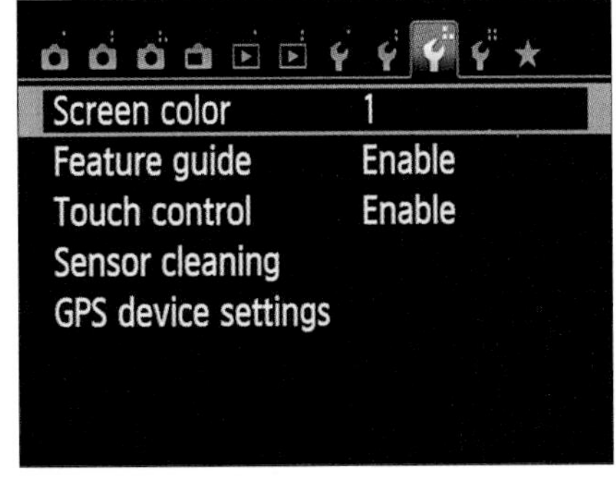

Figure 1-28: Still more customization features await on Setup Menu 3.

- **Screen Color:** If you don't like the default color scheme of the Shooting Settings display, you can choose from other schemes via the Screen Color option.
- **Feature Guide:** When this option is enabled and you switch exposure modes (via the Mode dial) or choose certain other camera options, notes appear on the monitor to explain the feature. For example, the left screen in Figure 1-29 shows the text that appears when you first set the Mode dial to Tv (shutter-priority autoexposure). The guide screens disappear as soon as you press a camera button or rotate the Main dial. You also can tap the explanation to make it go away.

  Although the Feature Guide screens are helpful at first, having them appear all the time is a pain after you get familiar with your camera. So I leave this option set to Disable — and for the sake of expediency in this book, I assume that you keep the option turned off as well. (If not, just don't be concerned when my instructions don't mention the screens in the course of showing you how to work the camera.)
- **Touch Control:** This setting enables or disables the touchscreen interface. For details on the touchscreen, flip back to the section "Using the Touchscreen."

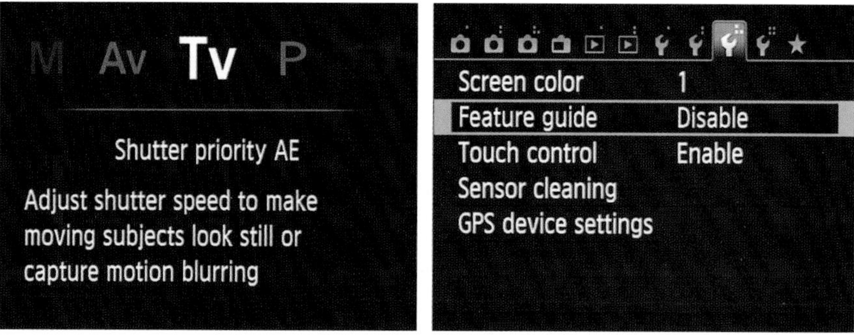

Figure 1-29: To stop the camera from displaying Help screens when you select certain camera options, disable the Feature Guide.

- **Sensor Cleaning:** Choose this option to access options related to the camera's internal sensor-cleaning mechanism. These work like so:
  - *Auto Cleaning:* By default, the camera's sensor-cleaning mechanism activates each time you turn the camera on and off. This process helps keep the image sensor — which is the part of the camera that captures the image — free of dust and other particles that can mar your photos. You can disable this option, but it's hard to imagine why you would choose to do so unless you turn your camera on and off a lot between shots, in which case the cleaning routine can get in the way of catching a fleeting moment.
  - *Clean Now:* Choose this option to initiate a cleaning cycle.
  - *Clean Manually:* In the advanced exposure modes (P, Tv, Av, and M), you can access this third option, which prepares the camera for manual cleaning of the sensor. I don't recommend this practice; sensors are delicate, and you're really better off taking the camera to a good service center for cleaning.

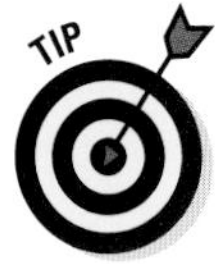

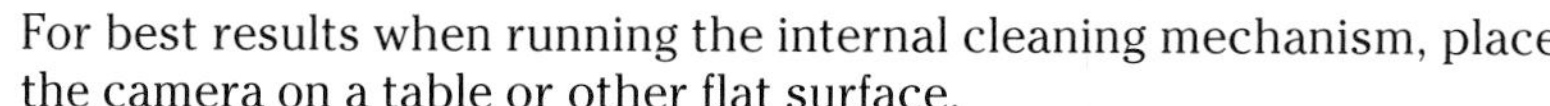

For best results when running the internal cleaning mechanism, place the camera on a table or other flat surface.

- **GPS Device Settings:** If you attach the optional GP-E2 GPS unit, settings related to its operation are available through this menu option.

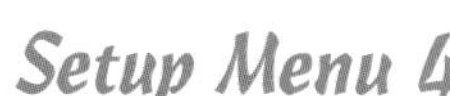

Setup Menu 4

Figure 1-30 shows Setup Menu 4, which you can access only in the advanced exposure modes. Again, those modes are P, Tv, Av, and M.

- **Certification Logo Display:** You have my permission to ignore this screen, which simply displays logos that indicate a couple electronics-industry certifications claimed by the camera. You can find additional logos on the bottom of the camera.

Why does this camera have two names?

You may notice that your camera manual, as well as this book, refers to your camera by two different names — EOS Rebel T4i and EOS 650D. What gives? The answer is that Canon assigns different names to a single camera model depending on the part of the world where it's sold. In fact, it even has a third name, the EOS KISS X6i, used in the Japanese market.

The *EOS* part, by the way, stands for Electro Optical System, the core technology used in Canon's autofocus SLR (single-lens reflex) cameras. According to Canon, the proper pronunciation is *EE-ohs,* which is also how you pronounce the name *Eos,* the goddess of dawn in Greek mythology.

With apologies to the goddess, I elected to save a little room in this book by shortening the camera name to simply T4i/650D.

By the way, shortly after the camera was released, Canon discovered a little glitch with respect to the camera names: On some models, when you look at the camera metadata in photo browsers that can display that data, the camera name shows up as KISS X6i even in countries that use the T4i name. The problem affects some units that have the number 3 as the second digit of the serial number. If this issue bothers you, check the Canon website for a service advisory related to the problem.

- **Custom Functions:** Selecting this option opens the door to *Custom Functions,* a set of features that are designed for people with some photography experience. Check out the sidebar "Navigating Custom Functions," earlier in this chapter, for some tips on making your way through these screens.

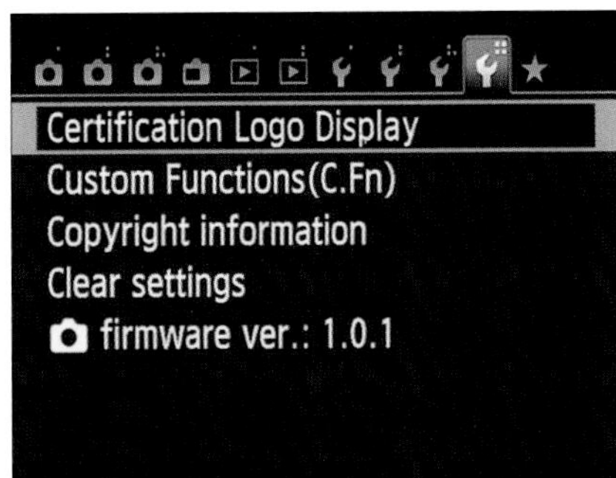

Figure 1-30: To display Setup Menu 4, you must set the Mode dial to P, TV, Av, or M.

- **Copyright Information:** Using this option, explained in Chapter 11, you can embed copyright information in the image metadata. *Metadata* is invisible text data that doesn't appear on the photo itself but can be read in many photo-viewer programs. Chapter 6 shows you how to view the metadata in the free Canon software that ships with your camera.

- **Clear Settings:** Via this option, you can restore the default shooting settings. You also can reset all the Custom Functions settings to their defaults.
- **Firmware Ver.:** This screen tells you the version number of the camera firmware (internal operating software). At the time of publication, the current firmware version was 1.0.1.

Keeping your camera firmware up-to-date is important, so visit the Canon website (`www.canon.com`) regularly to find out whether your camera sports the latest version. Follow the instructions given on the website to download and install updated firmware if needed.

2

Choosing Basic Picture Settings

In This Chapter

- Spinning the Mode dial
- Changing the shutter-release mode
- Adding flash
- Understanding the Image Quality setting (resolution and file type)

Every camera manufacturer strives to ensure that your first encounter with the camera is a happy one. To that end, the camera's default (initial) settings are selected to make it as easy as possible for you to take a good picture the first time you press the shutter button. At the default settings, your camera works about the same way as any point-and-shoot camera you may have used in the past: You compose the shot, press the shutter button halfway to focus, and then press the button the rest of the way to take the picture.

Although you can get a good photo using the default settings in many cases, they're not designed to give you optimal results in every situation. You may be able to take a decent portrait, for example, but probably need to tweak a few settings to capture action. Adjusting a few options can help turn that decent portrait into a stunning one, too.

So that you can start fine-tuning settings to your subject, this chapter explains the most basic picture-taking options, such as the exposure mode, shutter-release mode (officially called Drive mode), and the Image Quality option. They may not be the most exciting options (don't think I didn't notice you stifling a yawn), but they make a big difference in how easily you can capture the photo you have in mind.

Note: This chapter relates to still photography; for information about shooting movies, see Chapter 4. Also, I assume that you understand how to navigate menus and use the Quick Control screen. If not, head to Chapter 1 for help.

Choosing an Exposure Mode

The first picture-taking setting to consider is the exposure mode, which you select via the Mode dial, shown in Figure 2-1. Your choice determines how much control you have over two critical exposure settings — aperture and shutter speed — as well as many other options, including those related to color and flash photography.

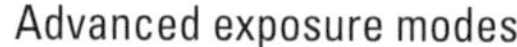

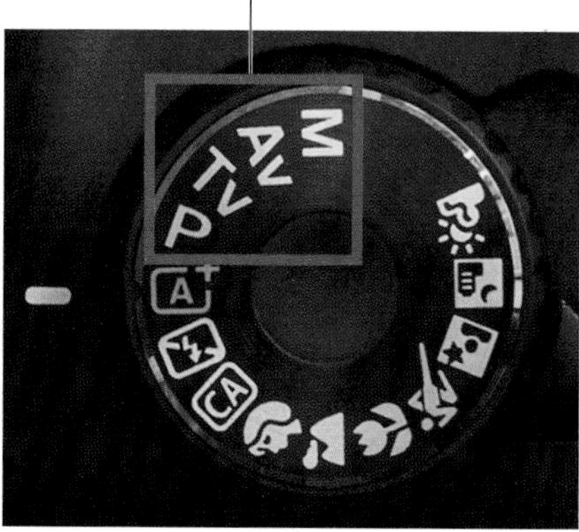

Figure 2-1: Settings on the Mode dial determine the exposure mode.

Canon categorizes the exposure modes as follows:

- **Basic Zone:** The Basic Zone category includes the following point-and-shoot modes, represented on the Mode dial with the icons shown in the margins:

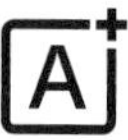

  - *Scene Intelligent Auto*: This is the most basic mode; the camera analyzes the scene in front of the lens, determines what settings would best capture that scene, and then handles everything but framing and focusing.

  - *Flash Off*: This one works just like Scene Intelligent Auto except that flash is disabled.

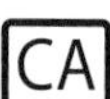

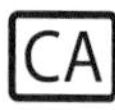

  - *Creative Auto*: This mode is like Scene Intelligent Auto on steroids, taking control of most settings but giving you an easy way to tweak some picture qualities, such as how much the background blurs.
  - *Image Zone modes:* This subgroup includes modes that are geared to capturing specific types of scenes:

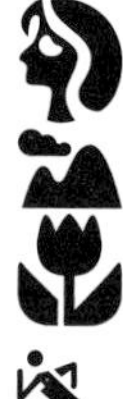

    Portrait, for taking traditional portraits

    Landscape, for capturing scenic vistas

    Close-up, for shooting flowers and other subjects at close range

    Sports, for capturing moving subjects (whether they happen to be playing a sport or not)

Night Portrait, for outdoor photographs of people at night. (Note the star over the person's head in the icon.)

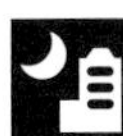

Handheld Night Scene, for taking pictures at night or in dim lighting without a tripod

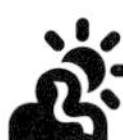

HDR Backlight Control, for getting better results with high contrast scenes, such as a dark subject set against a bright background. (The HDR stands for *high dynamic range; dynamic range* refers to the range of brightness values in an image.)

Chapter 3 tells you more about these modes, but be forewarned: To remain easy to use, all these modes prevent you from taking advantage of advanced exposure, color, and autofocusing features. You can adjust options discussed in this chapter, but the camera controls most everything else.

- **Creative Zone:** When you're ready to take more control over the camera, step up to one of the Creative Zone modes. This category includes the P (programmed autoexposure), Tv (shutter-priority autoexposure), Av (aperture-priority autoexposure), and M (manual exposure) modes, which I detail in Chapter 7.

Keeping track of all these *zones* is a little confusing, especially because the modes in the Image Zone category are often referred to generically in photography discussions as *creative scene modes* or *creative modes.* So to keep things a little simpler, I use the generic terms *fully automatic exposure modes* or *point-and-shoot modes* to refer to the Basic Zone modes — because, in a nutshell, that is the type of photography those zones provide — and *advanced exposure modes* to refer to the Creative Zone modes. For Creative Auto mode, which straddles the line between fully automatic and advanced, I use its full name to avoid inserting confusion into the mix. Okay, to avoid inserting any *additional* confusion.

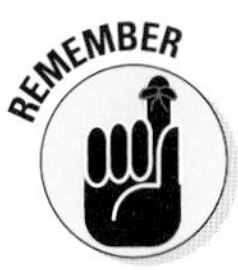

One very important — and often misunderstood — aspect about all the exposure modes: Although your access to exposure and color controls, as well as to some other advanced camera features, depends on the setting of the Mode dial, it has *no* bearing on your *focusing* choices. You can choose from manual focusing or autofocusing in any mode, assuming that your lens offers autofocusing. (Chapter 1 shows you how to set the lens to manual or autofocusing.) However, access to options that modify how the autofocus system works is limited to the advanced exposure modes (again, those are P, Tv, Av, and M).

Changing the Drive Mode

Setting the Drive mode tells the camera what to do when you press the shutter button: Record a single frame, record a series of frames, or record one or more shots after a short delay. Your camera offers the following Drive mode settings, which are represented in the camera displays by the symbols you see in the margin:

- **Single:** This setting records a single image each time you press the shutter button. In other words, this is normal photography mode. It's the default setting for all exposure modes except Portrait and Sports.

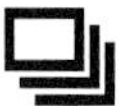

- **Continuous:** Sometimes known as *burst mode,* this mode records a continuous series of images as long as you hold down the shutter button. The camera can capture roughly 5 frames per second, but your mileage may vary, for the following reasons:
  - The number of frames per second depends in part on your shutter speed. At a slow shutter speed, the camera may not be able to reach the maximum frame rate. (See Chapter 7 for an explanation of shutter speed.)
  - Some other functions can slow down the continuous capture rate. For example, when you use flash, the frame rate slows because the flash needs time to recycle between shots. And if you use the AI Servo AF (autofocus) mode, detailed in Chapter 8, the rate may slow because the camera adjusts focus continually between frames in that mode. Finally, the speed of your memory card also plays a role in how fast the camera can transfer data to the card, which in turn affects the burst rate. In other words, consider 5 shots per second a best-case scenario.

  Continuous Drive mode is the default setting for Portrait and Sports modes. Having continuous capture available for portraits may seem odd, but it can actually help you capture the perfect expression on your subject's face — or, at least, a moment between blinks! (But if you use flash for your portrait, keep the previous tip in mind.)

- **Self-Timer: 10 second/remote control:** Want to put yourself in the picture? Select this mode, depress the shutter button, and run into the frame. You have 10 seconds to get yourself in place before the image is recorded.

  You can also use the self-timer function to avoid camera shake that can be caused by the mere motion of pressing the shutter button: Put the camera on a tripod and then activate the self-timer function to enable "hands-free" — and therefore motion-free — picture taking. As an alternative, you can trigger the shutter release with a wireless remote control or one that plugs into the camera's remote-control terminal. If you do, select this Drive mode. (For some remotes, you also may be able to use the following self-timer settings; check your remote's instruction manual to find out which options work with the unit.)

- **Self-Timer: 2 second:** This mode works just like the regular Self-Timer mode, but the capture happens just two seconds after you fully press the shutter button.

- **Self-Timer: Continuous:** With this option, the camera waits 10 seconds after you press the shutter button and then captures a continuous series of images. You can set the camera to record 2 to 10 images per each shutter release.

You can check the current Drive mode on the Shooting Settings screen. The icon representing the Drive mode appears in a different area depending on your exposure mode; the left screen in Figure 2-2 shows you where to look when shooting in Scene Intelligent Auto, for example, and the right screen shows where the icon hangs out when you use the advanced exposure modes. Both figures show the icon that represents the Single Drive mode.

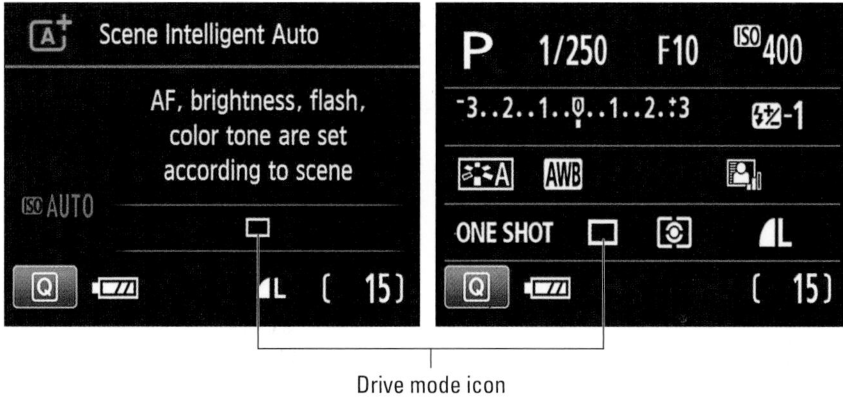

Figure 2-2: The Shooting Settings screen displays an icon indicating the current Drive mode.

To change the Drive mode, first display the Shooting Settings screen. (Give the shutter button a half press and release it or use the Info button to display the screen if necessary.) From there, you have two options:

- **Press the left cross key.** Notice that the key is marked by two of the Drive mode icons to help you remember its function, as shown on the left in Figure 2-3. After you press the cross key, you see the settings screen shown on the right in the figure. Select your choice by tapping it or by using the right/left cross keys. Then tap Set or press the Set button.

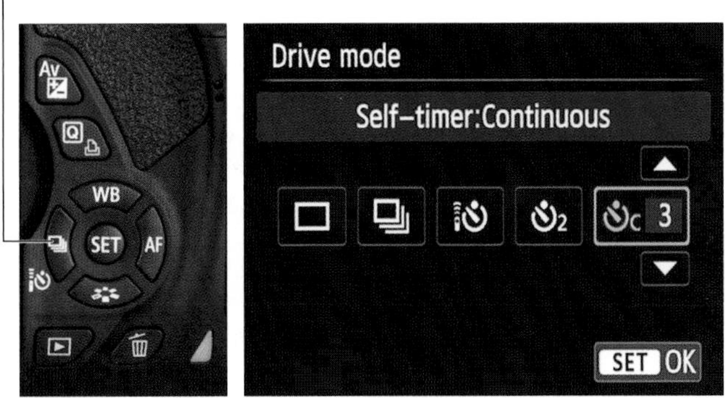

Figure 2-3: The fastest way to get to the Drive mode setting is to press the left cross key.

For the Self-Timer: Continuous mode, selected in the right screen of Figure 2-3, press the up or down cross key or tap the up or down arrows to set the number of continuous shots you want the camera to capture.

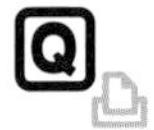

- **Use the Quick Control screen.** After you select the Drive mode icon, as shown on the left in Figure 2-4, the name of the current setting appears at the bottom of the screen. Rotate the Main dial to cycle through the available settings. Note that the figure shows you how things look in the advanced exposure modes; in the full auto modes, all the Drive mode icons appear in the area reserved for that setting.

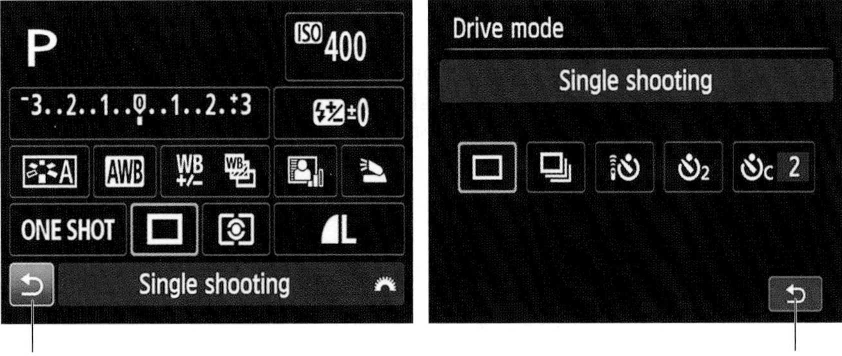

Figure 2-4: But you also can change the setting via the Quick Control screen.

To see all available options in the P, Tv, Av, or M exposure modes, press the Set button or tap the Drive mode icon to access the screen shown on the right in Figure 2-4. Highlight your choice and then press Set or tap the return arrow, labeled on the right in the figure, to return to the Quick Control screen. Again, if you choose the Self-Timer: Continuous mode, press the up/down cross keys or tap the up/down arrows (not shown in the figure) to set the number of continuous shots. To finalize things and return to the Quick Control screen, tap the arrow highlighted on the right in the figure or press the Set button. Give the shutter button a quick half-press and release to return to shooting mode.

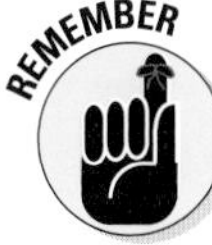

Whichever route you go to change the Drive mode, remember these key points:

- **Check the Drive mode before each shoot.** For the P, Tv, Av, and M exposure modes, your selected Drive mode remains in force until you change it. For the other exposure modes, the camera reverts to the default Drive mode if you rotate the Mode dial to a different exposure mode. So put this setting on the list of options to review every time you set out with your camera.
- **Cover the viewfinder for self-timer or remote shooting.** Any time you take a picture without your eye to the viewfinder, light can seep in through the viewfinder and mess with exposure metering. For that reason, Canon includes a little viewfinder cover on the camera strap. Chapter 4 shows you how to install the cover, which is also recommended for Live View shooting and movie recording.
- **To cancel self-timer shooting after the countdown starts, press the Drive mode button (left cross key).** If you're like me, though, the camera will take the shot long before you remember this trick. Well, no worries — that's why the camera has an Erase button.
- **Consider using Mirror Lock-Up for long exposures.** Although using the self-timer or remote-control Drive modes to shoot hands-free ensures that the action of pressing the shutter button doesn't shake the camera enough to blur the photo, you can add another layer of security by enabling Mirror Lock-Up.

  Here's the deal: The camera's optical assembly includes a little mirror whose job it is to reflect the scene coming through the lens onto the viewfinder. When you press the shutter button, the mirror moves out of the optical path so that the scene can be recorded by the image sensor. With a long exposure time, the mirror action can be enough to create a slight blur, so the camera enables you to delay the shutter release until after the mirror movement is complete. This feature, called Mirror Lock-Up, is available via a Custom Function and requires a special shooting technique; Chapter 11 provides details.

Using the Flash

The built-in flash on your camera offers an easy, convenient way to add light to a too-dark scene. But whether you can use flash or prevent it from firing depends on your exposure mode, as outlined in the next few sections.

TIP

Before you digest that information, note these universal tips:

- **The viewfinder and monitor offer cues regarding flash status.** A little lightning bolt like the one in the lower-left corner of Figure 2-5 tells you that the flash is enabled. The word "Busy" along with the lightning bolt means that the flash needs a few moments to recharge. Flash recycling status also appears on the Shooting Settings screen.
- **The effective range of the built-in flash depends on the ISO setting.** The ISO setting affects the camera's sensitivity to light; Chapter 7 has details. At the lowest ISO setting, ISO 100, the maximum reach of the flash ranges from about 7.5 to 12 feet, depending on whether you're using a telephoto or wide angle lens, respectively. To illuminate a subject that's farther away, use a higher ISO speed or an auxiliary flash that offers greater power than the built-in flash.
- **Don't get too close.** Position the lens at a minimum distance of about 3.5 feet from the subject, or the flash may not illuminate the entire subject.
- **Watch for shadows cast by the lens or a lens hood.** When you shoot with a long lens, you can wind up with unwanted shadows caused by the flash light hitting the lens. Ditto for a lens hood.

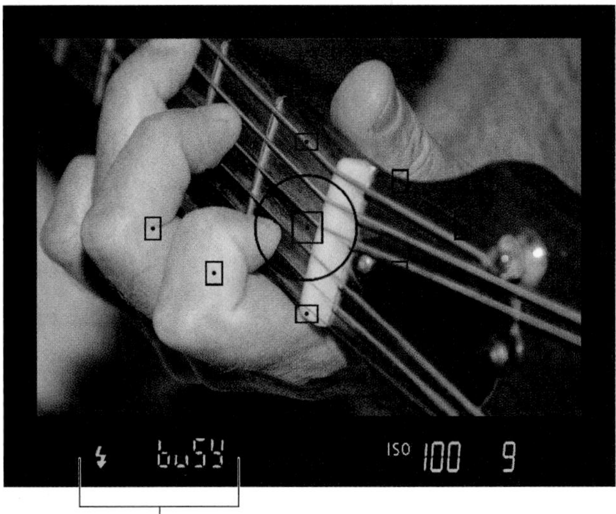

Figure 2-5: A Busy signal means that the flash is recharging.

Using flash in the fully automatic modes

In the fully automatic exposure modes, whether flash is available depends on the exposure mode. Here's how things shake out:

- **Scene Intelligent Auto, Portrait, Close-up, and Night Portrait:** If the camera thinks extra light is needed, it automatically raises and fires the built-in flash. Otherwise the flash remains closed.
- **Landscape, Sports, HDR Backlight Control, and Flash Off modes:** Flash is disabled.

  Disabling flash in the Flash Off mode makes sense, of course. But why no flash in Sports and Landscape mode, you ask? Well, Sports mode is designed to enable you to capture moving subjects, and the flash makes that more difficult because it needs time to recycle between shots. On top of that, the maximum shutter speed possible with the built-in flash is 1/200 second, which often isn't fast enough to ensure a blur-free subject. Finally, action photos usually aren't taken at a range close enough for the flash to reach the subject, which is also the reason why flash is disabled for Landscape mode.

  Lack of flash in HDR Backlight Control mode is a little more difficult to explain. In this mode, which is designed for shooting high-contrast scenes (scenes with both very light and very dark areas), the camera records three images at three different exposures and then blends the result to retain more detail in both the highlights and shadows. Light from the flash would mess up the exposure calculations the camera uses to produce this result. In addition, the recycling time that the flash needs between shots would slow down the rate at which the camera captures the three shots. And if you're handholding the camera, that slower frame rate increases the chances that you may move the camera slightly between frames, preventing the images from properly aligning when they're merged. Suffice it to say, no flash in HDR Backlight Control mode is a Good Thing.
- **Handheld Night Scene mode:** In this mode, the camera takes four frames in rapid succession and merges them to get a sharper result than you might otherwise obtain when handholding the camera in dim lighting. By default, flash is turned off, and this is the best choice if you're shooting landscapes. But if you're photographing people or a close-up subject at night, using the flash helps illuminate the subject. Either way, hold the camera as still as possible while the shots are being recorded to get the best results.

  You can see the current flash setting in Handheld Night Scene mode in the Shooting Settings display, as shown on the left in Figure 2-6; enable and disable the flash via the Quick Control screen, as shown on the right. After highlighting the icon as in the second screen, rotate the Main dial to change the setting. Or tap the icon or press Set to display the settings screen and then choose the setting you want to use. (Again, see Chapter 1 for complete details on using the Quick Control screen.)

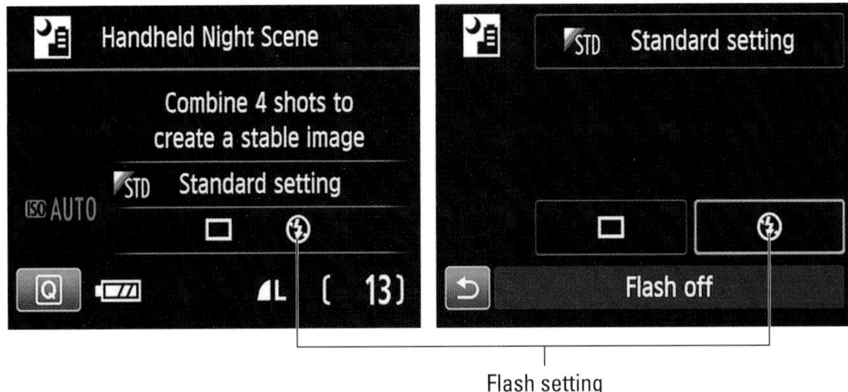

Figure 2-6: In Handheld Night Scene mode, enable flash via the Quick Control screen.

If flash is available, you can enable Red-Eye Reduction flash, which is designed to help eliminate those "devil eyes" that often plague flash portraits. You can find details on that option, enabled via Shooting Menu 1, later in this chapter.

Using flash in Creative Auto mode

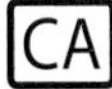

Although Creative Auto mode is like Scene Intelligent Auto in many respects, it gives you some input over various picture characteristics, including whether flash is used. In fact, you can choose from three flash modes:

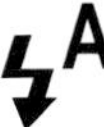

- **Auto flash:** The camera decides when to fire the flash, basing its decision on the lighting conditions.

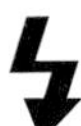

- **On:** The flash fires regardless of the lighting conditions. You may hear this flash mode referred to as *force flash* because the camera is forced to trigger the flash even if its exposure-brain says there's plenty of ambient light. This flash mode is sometimes also called *fill flash* because it's designed to fill in shadows that can occur even in bright light. Whatever you call it, this option causes the flash to pop up as soon as you press the shutter button halfway. The flash will fire for subsequent shots until you change the flash mode to Auto or Off.

- **Off:** The flash does not fire, no way, no how. Even if the built-in flash is raised because you used it on the previous shot, it still won't fire until you shift the flash mode to Auto or On.

You can view the current flash setting in the Shooting Settings screen, which appears in Creative Auto mode as shown on the left in Figure 2-7. Chapter 3 explains the other stuff you see on the screen and provides more details about using Creative Auto mode.

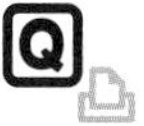

Set the flash mode via the Quick Control screen, as illustrated on the right in Figure 2-7. The fastest option is to highlight the icon and then rotate the Main dial to cycle through the three flash settings. If you use flash, also see the upcoming section related to Red-Eye Reduction flash, which may improve flash portraits.

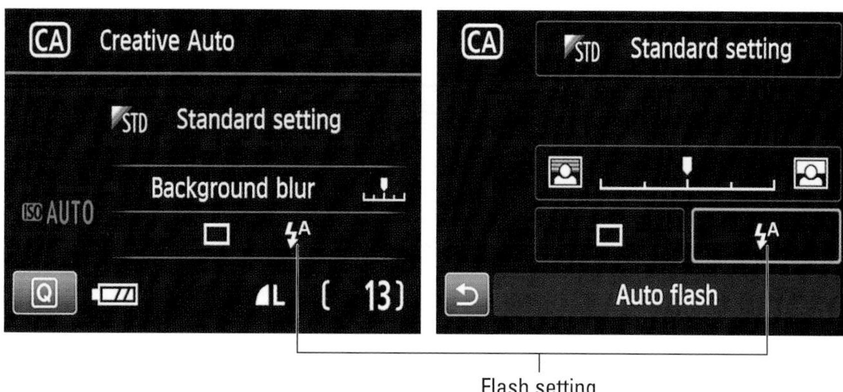

Figure 2-7: Use the Quick Control screen to change the flash setting in Creative Auto mode, too.

Enabling flash in the advanced exposure modes

In the P, Tv, Av, and M exposure modes, you don't choose from the Auto, On, and Off flash modes available in Creative Auto mode. Instead, if you want to use the built-in flash, you press the Flash button on the side of the camera. (Refer to Figure 2-8.) The flash pops up and fires on your next shot. Don't want flash? Just close the flash unit. There is no such thing as auto flash in these exposure modes — but don't worry, because using flash (or not) is one picture-taking setting you definitely want to control, for reasons you can explore in Chapter 7.

You do, however, have access to flash options that aren't available in the fully automatic exposure modes or Creative

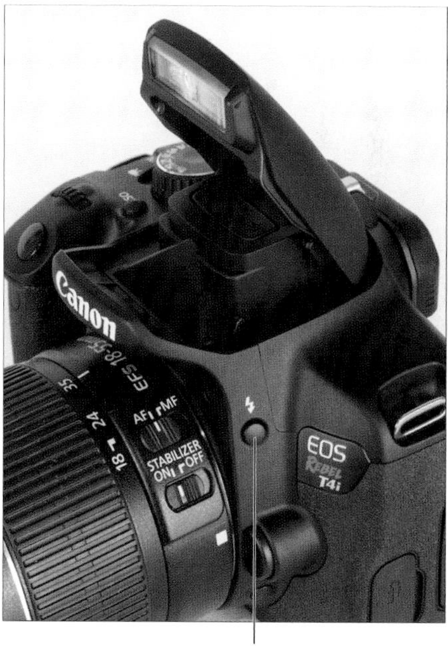

Figure 2-8: In the advanced exposure modes, press the Flash button to raise the built-in flash.

Auto mode. Until you're ready to dig into those features — again, head to Chapter 7 to explore them — just make sure that when you enable flash, the Quick Control screen displays a Built-in Flash Function symbol that looks like the one shown in Figure 2-9. That symbol — note that it doesn't appear until you raise the flash or shift to the Quick Control screen — represents the Normal flash firing setting. If another symbol appears, use the Quick Control screen to select the Normal setting; the other two options set the flash to trigger off-camera flash units.

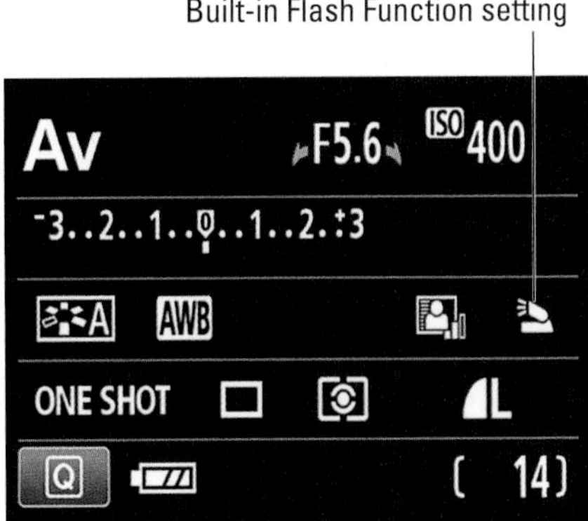

Figure 2-9: Select this option unless you want to use the built-in flash as a wireless trigger for other flash units.

Using Red-Eye Reduction flash

Red-eye is caused when flash light bounces off a subject's retinas and is reflected back to the camera lens. Red-eye is a human phenomenon, though; with animals, the reflected light usually glows yellow, white, or green.

Man or beast, this issue isn't nearly the problem with the type of pop-up flash found on your T4i/650D as it is on non-SLR cameras. Your camera's flash is positioned above the lens, a position that lessens the chances of red-eye. However, red-eye may still be an issue when you use a lens with a long focal length (a telephoto lens), you shoot subjects from a distance, or the ambient lighting is very dim.

If you notice red-eye, try enabling Red-Eye Reduction flash. When you turn on this feature, the Red-Eye Reduction Lamp on the front of the camera lights up when you press the shutter button halfway and focus is achieved. The purpose of this light is to shrink the subject's pupils, which helps reduce the amount of light that enters the eye and, thus, the chances of that light reflecting and causing red-eye. The flash itself fires when you press the shutter button the rest of the way. (Warn your subjects to wait for the flash, or they may stop posing after they see the light from the Red-Eye Reduction Lamp.)

You can enable this feature in any exposure mode that permits flash. The control lives on Shooting Menu 1, as shown in Figure 2-10.

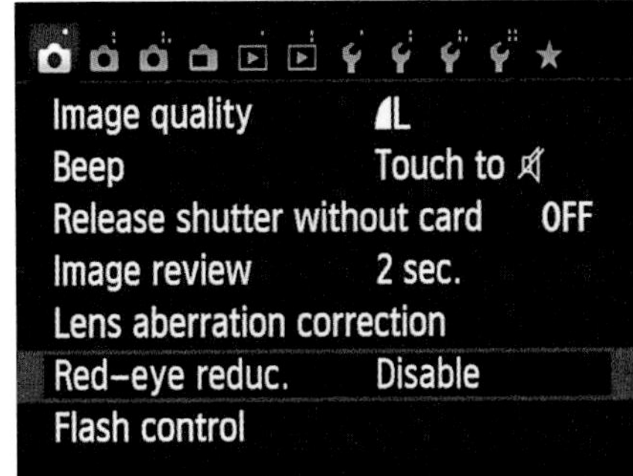

Figure 2-10: Turn Red-Eye Reduction flash mode on and off via Shooting Menu 1.

The viewfinder and Shooting Settings display don't offer any indication that Red-Eye Reduction is enabled. The Camera Settings screen shows the current status, however; look for the little eyeball icon and the word *Enable* or *Disable,* shown in Figure 2-11. You can get to this screen by displaying the Shooting Settings screen and then pressing the Info button twice — your first press turns off the monitor, the second takes you to the Camera Settings display. But I find it just as easy to check the feature status on Shooting Menu 1.

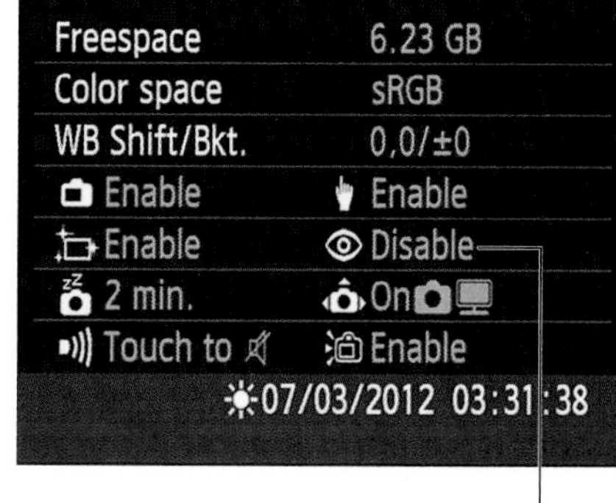

Figure 2-11: You can view the Red-Eye Reduction status in the Camera Settings screen as well as on Shooting Menu 1.

After you press the shutter button halfway in Red-Eye Reduction flash mode, a row of vertical bars appears in the center of the viewfinder display, just to the left of the ISO value. A few moments later, the bars turn off one by one. For best results, wait until all the bars are off to take the picture. (The delay gives the subject's pupils time to constrict in response to the Red-Eye Reduction Lamp.)

Controlling Picture Quality

Almost every review of the T4i/650D contains glowing reports about the camera's top-notch picture quality. Getting the maximum output from your camera, however, depends on choosing the right capture settings. Chief among them is the appropriately named Image Quality setting. This control determines two important aspects of your pictures: *resolution,* or pixel count; and *file format,* which refers to the type of computer file the camera uses to store your picture data.

Resolution and file format both play a large role in the quality of your photos, so selecting the Image Quality setting is an important decision. Why not just dial in the setting that produces the maximum quality level and be done with it? Well, that's the right choice for some photographers. But because that maximum setting has some disadvantages, you may find that stepping down a notch or two on the quality scale is a better option, at least for some pictures.

To help you figure out which setting meets your needs, the rest of this chapter explains exactly how resolution and file format affect your pictures. Just in case you're having quality problems related to other issues, though, the following section provides a handy defect-diagnosis guide.

Diagnosing quality problems

When I use the term *picture quality,* I'm not talking about the composition, exposure, or other traditional characteristics of a photograph. Instead, I'm referring to how finely the image is rendered in the digital sense.

Figure 2-12 illustrates the concept: The first example is a high-quality image, with clear details and smooth color transitions. The other examples show five common digital-image defects. Each defect is related to a different issue, and only two are affected by the Image Quality setting. So if you aren't happy with your picture quality, first compare your photos with those in the figure to properly diagnose the problem. Then try these remedies:

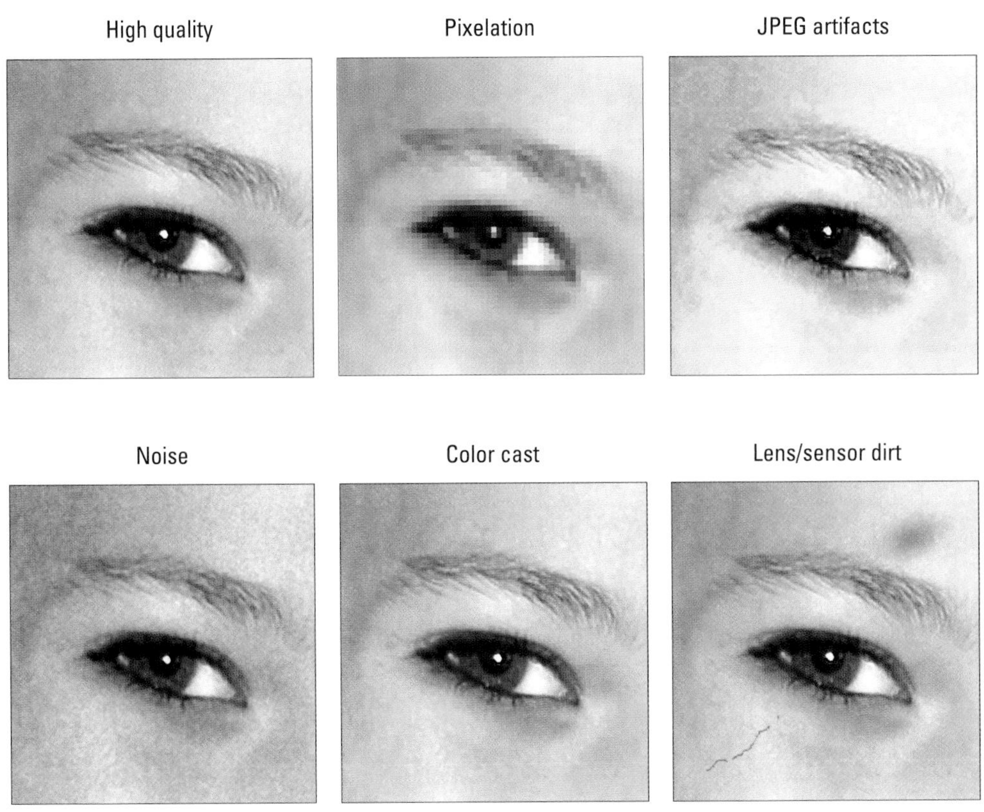

Figure 2-12: Refer to this symptom guide to determine the cause of poor image quality.

- **Pixelation:** When an image doesn't have enough *pixels* (the colored tiles used to create digital images), details aren't clear, and curved and diagonal lines appear jagged. The fix is to increase image resolution, which you do via the Image Quality setting. See the upcoming section, "Considering Resolution: Large, Medium, or Small?" for details.
- **JPEG artifacts:** The "parquet tile" texture and random color defects that mar the third image in Figure 2-12 can occur in photos captured in the JPEG *(JAY-peg)* file format, which is why these flaws are referred to as *JPEG artifacts.* This defect is also related to the Image Quality setting; see the "Understanding File Type (JPEG or Raw)" section, later in this chapter, to find out more.
- **Noise:** This defect gives your image a speckled look, as shown in the lower-left example in Figure 2-12. Noise is most often caused by a high ISO setting (an exposure control) or by long exposure times (shutter speeds longer than one second). Chapter 7 explores these topics in detail.
- **Color cast:** If your colors are seriously out of whack, as shown in the lower-middle example in Figure 2-12, try adjusting the camera's White Balance setting. Chapter 8 covers this control.
- **Lens/sensor dirt:** A dirty lens is the first possible cause of the kind of defects you see in the last example in Figure 2-12. If cleaning your lens doesn't solve the problem, dust or dirt may have made its way onto the camera's image sensor. Try using the camera's internal cleaning mechanism, accessed via Setup Menu 3 and detailed in Chapter 1. If that doesn't do the trick, professional sensor cleaning is in order; many camera stores offer this service.

One important point regarding Figure 2-12: I took some mild image-processing liberties to exaggerate the flaws in the examples to make the symptoms easier to see. With the exception of an unwanted color cast or a big blob of lens or sensor dirt, these defects may not even be noticeable unless you print or view your image at a very large size. And the subject matter of your image may camouflage some flaws; most people probably wouldn't detect a little JPEG artifacting in a photograph of a densely wooded forest, for example. In other words, don't consider Figure 2-12 as an indication that your camera is suspect in the image quality department. First, *any* digital camera can produce these defects under the right circumstances. Second, by following the guidelines in this chapter (and the others mentioned in the preceding list), you can resolve any quality issues that you may encounter.

Decoding the Image Quality options

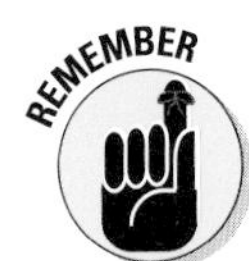

Your camera's Image Quality setting determines both the image resolution and file format of the pictures you shoot. Your options for changing the setting depend on your exposure mode, as follows:

- **Quick Control screen (P, Tv, Av, and M modes only):** After highlighting the setting, as shown on the left in Figure 2-13, rotate the Main dial to cycle through the available settings. Or if you prefer, press the Set button or tap the setting icon to display the screen shown on the right in Figure 2-13, which displays all the options at once. Choose the setting you want to use and then tap the return arrow or press the Set button to return to the Quick Control screen. To return to shooting mode, give the shutter button a quick half-press and release it.
- **Shooting Menu 1 (any exposure mode):** You also can adjust the Image Quality setting through this menu, as illustrated in Figure 2-14.

If you're new to digital photography, the Image Quality settings won't make much sense to you until you read the rest of this chapter, which explains format and resolution in detail. But even if you're schooled in those topics, you may need some help deciphering the way that the settings are represented on your camera. As you can see from Figures 2-13 and 2-14, the options are presented in rather cryptic fashion, so here's your decoder ring:

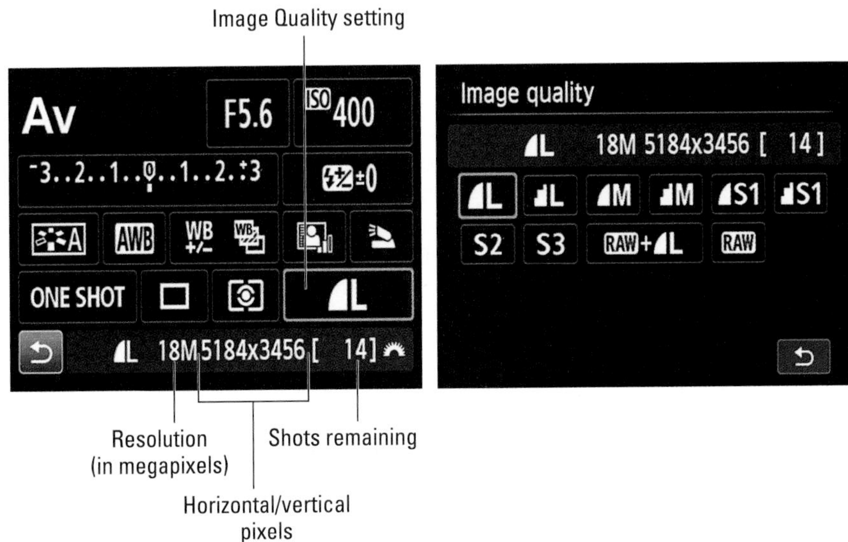

Figure 2-13: In the advanced exposure modes, you can change the Quality setting via the Quick Control screen.

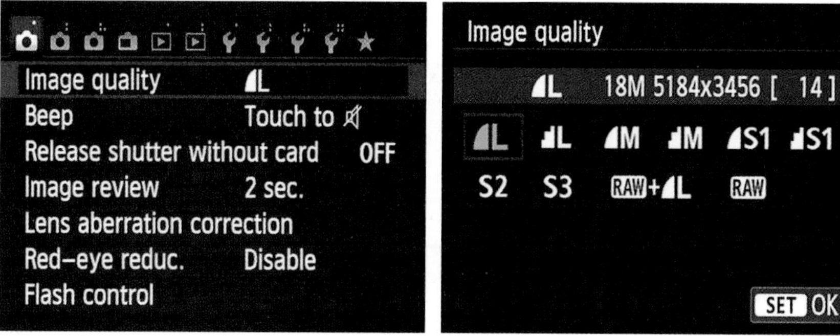

Figure 2-14: You also can select the Image Quality option via Shooting Menu 1.

- At the bottom of the Quick Control screen, you see three bits of information about the current Image Quality setting, as labeled in Figure 2-13: the *resolution,* or total pixel count (measured in megapixels), the horizontal and vertical pixel count, and the number of subsequent shots you can fit on your current memory card if you select that Image Quality setting. (The Main dial icon to the right of the Image Quality settings is a reminder to use that dial to change settings.) The next section explains pixels and megapixels.
- This same informational bar (less the Main dial icon) appears at the top of the screen when you change the setting via Shooting Menu 1 or the settings screen (see the right screens in Figures 2-13 and 2-14). The next two rows of both screens show icons representing the Image Quality settings.
- The settings marked with the little arc symbols capture images in the JPEG file format, as do the S2 and S3 settings. The arc icons represent the level of JPEG *compression,* which affects picture quality and file size. You get two JPEG options: Fine and Normal. The smooth arcs represent the Fine setting; the jagged arcs represent the Normal setting. Both S2 and S3 use the JPEG Fine recording option. And no, I don't know why they don't sport the arc icons — maybe the arc-supplier guy was sick the day that S2 and S3 got added to the mix. At any rate, check out the upcoming section "JPEG: The imaging (and web) standard" for details about all things JPEG.
- Within the JPEG category, you can choose from five resolution settings, represented by L, M, and S1, S2, and S3 *(large, medium,* and *small, smaller, smallest).* See the next section for information that helps you select the right resolution.

- You also can capture images in the Raw file format. All Raw files are created at the Large resolution setting, giving you the maximum pixel count. One of the two Raw settings also records a JPEG Fine version of the image, also at the maximum (Large) resolution. The upcoming section "Raw (CR2): The purist's choice" explains the benefits and downsides to using the Raw format.

Which Image Quality option is best depends on several factors, including how you plan to use your pictures and how much time you care to spend processing your images on your computer. The rest of this chapter explains these and other issues related to the settings.

Considering Resolution: Large, Medium, or Small?

To choose an Image Quality setting, the first decision you need to make is how many pixels you want your image to contain. *Pixels* are the little square tiles from which all digital images are made; *pixel* is short for *pic*ture *el*ement. You can see some pixels close up in the right image in Figure 2-15, which shows a greatly magnified view of the eye area in the left image. (If your photo viewer has a zoom tool that enables you to greatly magnify an image, you can inspect the pixels in your own photos.)

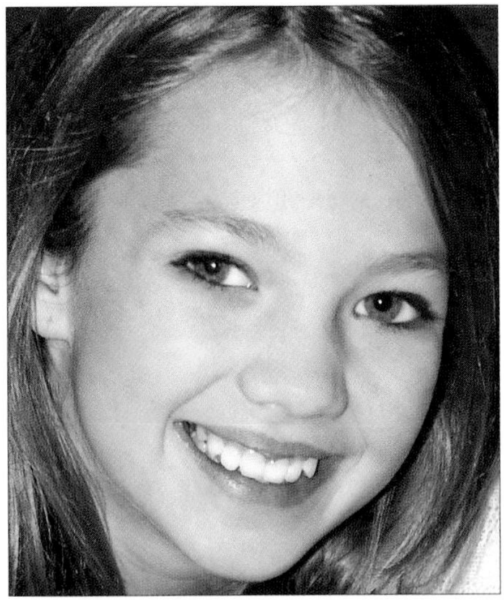

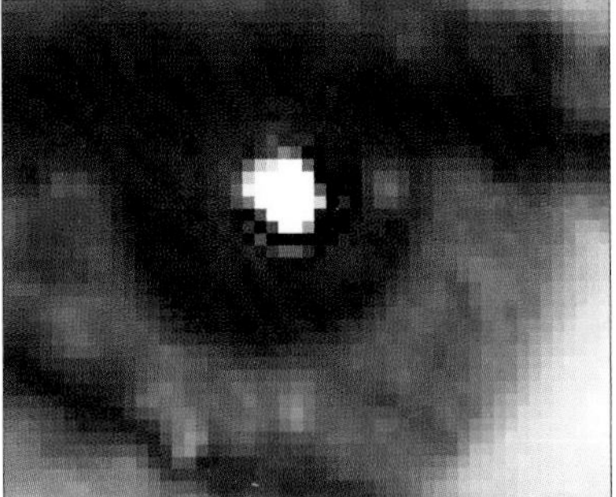

Figure 2-15: Pixels are the building blocks of digital photos.

The number of pixels in an image is referred to as its *resolution.* Your camera offers five resolution levels: Large, Medium, and Small (1–3), represented on the list of Image Quality settings by the initials L, M, and S (1–3). Table 2-1 shows you the pixel count that results from each option. If you select Raw as your Quality setting, images are always captured at the Large resolution value.

Table 2-1 The Resolution Side of the Image Quality Settings

Symbol	*Setting*	*Pixel Count*
L	Large	5184 x 3456 (18 MP)
M	Medium	3456 x 2304 (8 MP)
S1	Small 1	2592 x 1728 (4.5 MP)
S2	Small 2	1920 x 1280 (2.5 MP)
S3	Small 3	720 x 480 (0.35 MP)

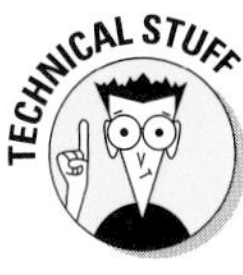

In the table, the first pair of numbers in the Pixel Count column represents the *pixel dimensions* — the number of horizontal pixels and the number of vertical pixels. The values in parentheses indicate the total resolution, which you get by multiplying the horizontal and vertical pixel values. This number is usually stated in *megapixels,* or MP for short. The camera displays the resolution value using only one letter M, however. (Refer to Figures 2-13 and 2-14.) Either way, 1 MP equals 1 million pixels.

Resolution affects your pictures in three ways:

- **Print size:** Resolution determines the size at which you can produce a high-quality print. If you don't have enough pixels, your prints may exhibit the defects you see in the pixelation example in Figure 2-12, or worse, you may be able to see the individual pixels, as in the right example in Figure 2-15.

  How many pixels you need depends on your photo printer, but a good minimum threshold is 200 pixels per linear inch, or *ppi,* of the print. To produce an 8 x 10 print at 200 ppi, for example, you need a pixel count of 1600 x 2000, or just less than 2 MP. For professional publication, you may be required to submit photos at a higher ppi — the publishers of this book, for example, require 300-ppi images. If you're printing your own photos, experiment to see whether you get better results at a higher ppi; in some cases, you won't see any difference at all.

Even though many photo-editing programs enable you to add pixels to an existing image, doing so isn't a good idea. For reasons I won't bore you with, adding pixels — known as *upsampling* — doesn't enable you to successfully enlarge your photo. In fact, resampling typically makes matters worse. The printing discussion in Chapter 6 includes some example images that illustrate this issue.

- **Screen display size:** Resolution doesn't affect the quality of images viewed on a monitor, television, or other screen device the way it does for printed photos. Instead, resolution determines the *size* at which the image appears. This issue is one of the most misunderstood aspects of digital photography, so I explain it thoroughly in Chapter 6. For now, just know that you need *way* fewer pixels for onscreen photos than you do for printed photos. In fact, the smallest resolution setting available on your camera, 720 x 480 pixels (S3), is plenty for e-mail sharing.
- **File size:** Every additional pixel increases the amount of data required to create a digital picture file. So a higher-resolution image has a larger file size than a low-resolution image.

Large files present several problems:

  - You can store fewer images on your memory card, your computer's hard drive, and removable storage media such as a DVD.
  - The camera needs more time to process and store the image data, which can hamper fast-action shooting.
  - When you share photos online, larger files take longer to upload and download.
  - When you edit your photos in your photo software, your computer needs more resources and time to process large files.

As you can see, resolution is a bit of a sticky wicket. What if you aren't sure how large you want to print your images? What if you want to print your photos *and* share them online? I take the better-safe-than-sorry route, which leads to the following recommendations:

- **Shoot at a resolution suitable for print.** You then can create a low-resolution copy of the image for use online. In fact, Playback Menu 1 has a built-in Resize tool that can do the job. Chapter 6 shows you how to use that feature.
- **For everyday images, Medium is a good choice.** Even at the Medium setting, your pixel count (3456 x 2304) is far more than you need for an

8 x 10" print at 200 ppi, and almost exactly what you need for an 8 x 10" print at 300 ppi.

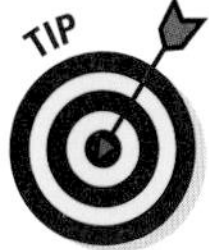

- **Choose Large for an image that you plan to crop, print very large, or both.** The benefit of maxing out resolution is that you have the flexibility to crop your photo and still generate a decent-sized print of the remaining image. Figure 2-16 offers an example. I wanted to fill the frame with the butterfly, but couldn't do so without getting so close that I risked scaring it away. So I kept my distance and took the picture at the Large setting, resulting in the composition shown on the left in the figure. Because I had oodles of pixels in that photo, I could crop it and still have enough pixels left to produce a great print, as you see in the right image. In fact, I could have printed it at a much larger size than you see here, but then I would have had to cut some of my fascinating prose, which is too painful to consider. For me, anyway.

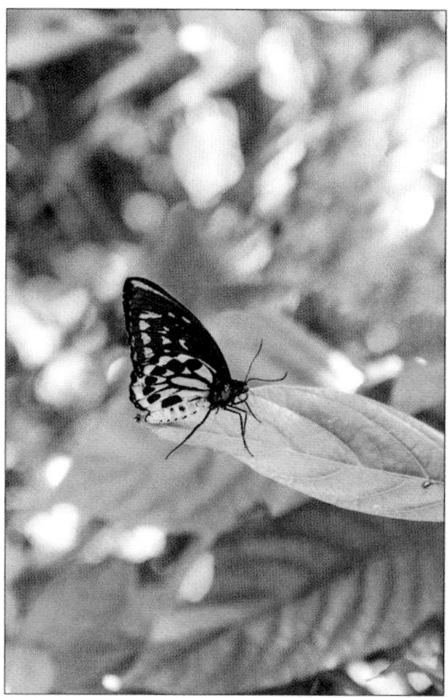

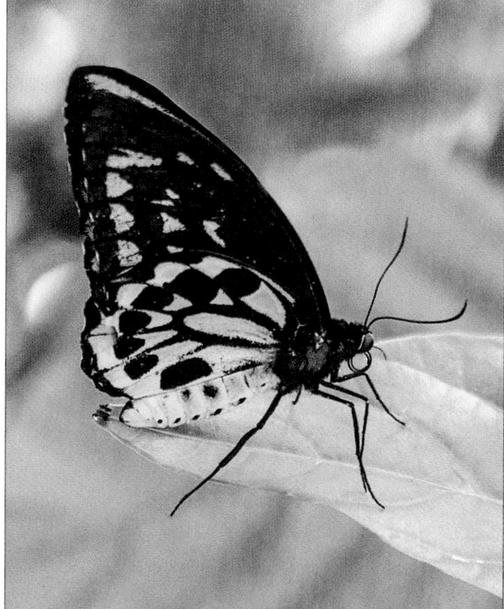

Figure 2-16: When you can't get close enough to fill the frame with the subject, capture the image at the Large resolution setting (left) and crop later (right).

How many pictures fit on my memory card?

Image resolution (pixel count) and file format (JPEG or Raw) together contribute to the size of the picture file which, in turn, determines how many photos fit in a given amount of camera memory. The following table shows you the approximate size of the files, in megabytes (MB), that are generated at each of the resolution/format combinations on your T4i/650D. (The actual file size of any image also depends on other factors, such as the subject, ISO setting, and Picture Style setting.) In the Image Capacity column, you see approximately how many pictures you can store at the setting on an 8GB (gigabyte) memory card.

Picture Capacity of an 8GB Memory Card

Symbol	*Quality Setting*	*File Size*	*Image Capacity*
L	Large/Fine	6.4MB	1140
L	Large/Normal	3.2MB	2240
M	Medium/Fine	3.4MB	2150
M	Medium/Normal	1.7MB	4200
S1	Small 1/Fine	2.2MB	3350
S1	Small 1/Normal	1.1MB	6360
S2	Small 2/Fine	1.3MB	5570
S3	Small 3/Fine	0.3MB	21560
RAW	Raw	30.9MB	290
RAW L	Raw+Large/Fine	40MB*	230

**Combined size of the two files produced at this setting.*

Understanding File Type (JPEG or Raw)

In addition to establishing the resolution of your photos, the Image Quality setting determines the *file type,* which refers to the kind of data file that the camera produces. Your camera offers two file types — JPEG and Raw (sometimes seen as *raw* or *RAW*), with a couple variations of each. The next sections explain the pros and cons of each setting.

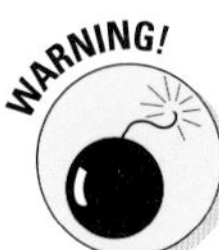

File type is also sometimes referred to as file *format.* Don't confuse that use of the word with the Format Card option on Setup Menu 1, which erases all data on your memory card.

JPEG: The imaging (and web) standard

This format is the default setting on your camera, as it is for most digital cameras. JPEG is popular for two main reasons:

- **Immediate usability:** JPEG is a longtime standard format for digital photos. All web browsers and e-mail programs can display JPEG files, so you can share them online immediately after you shoot them. You also can get JPEG photos printed at any retail outlet, whether it's an online or a local printer. Additionally, any program that has photo capabilities, from photo-editing programs to word-processing programs, can handle your files.
- **Small files:** JPEG files are smaller than Raw files. And smaller files mean that your pictures consume less room on your camera memory card and on your computer's hard drive.

The downside — you knew there had to be one — is that JPEG creates smaller files by applying *lossy compression.* This process actually throws away some image data. Too much compression leads to the defects you see in the JPEG artifacts example in Figure 2-12, earlier in this chapter.

On your camera, the amount of compression that's applied depends on whether you choose an Image Quality setting that carries the label Fine or Normal. The difference between the two breaks down as follows:

- **Fine:** At this setting, very little compression is applied, so you shouldn't see many compression artifacts, if any. Canon uses the symbol that appears in the margin here to indicate the Fine compression level; however, the S2 and S3 settings both use the Fine level even though they don't sport the symbol.

- **Normal:** Switch to Normal, and the compression amount rises, as does the chance of seeing some artifacting. Notice the jaggedy-ness of the Normal icon, as shown in the margin? That's your reminder that all may not be "smooth" sailing when you choose a Normal setting.

Note, though, that the Normal setting doesn't result in anywhere near the level of artifacting that you see in the example in Figure 2-12. Again, that example is exaggerated to help you recognize artifacting defects and understand how they differ from other image-quality issues. In fact, if you keep your image print or display size small, you aren't likely to notice a great deal of quality difference between the Fine and Normal compression levels. The differences become apparent only when you greatly enlarge a photo.

Given that the differences between Fine and Normal aren't all that easy to spot until you really enlarge the photo, is it okay to shift to Normal and enjoy the benefits of smaller files? Well, only you can decide what level of quality your pictures demand. For most photographers, the added file sizes produced by the Fine setting aren't a huge concern, given that the prices of memory cards fall all the time. Long-term storage is more of an issue; the larger your files, the faster you fill your computer's hard drive and the more DVDs or CDs you need for archiving purposes. But in the end, I prefer to take the storage hit in exchange for the lower compression level of the Fine setting. You never know when a casual snapshot is going to be so great that you want to print or display it large enough that even minor quality loss becomes a concern. And of all the defects that you can correct in a photo editor, artifacting is one of the hardest to remove. So I stick with Fine when shooting in the JPEG format.

To make the best decision, do your own test shots, carefully inspect the results in your photo editor, and make your own judgment about what level of artifacting you can accept. Artifacting is often much easier to spot when you view images onscreen. It's difficult to reproduce artifacting here in print because the printing press obscures some of the tiny defects caused by compression. Your inkjet prints are more likely to reveal these defects.

If you don't want *any* risk of artifacting, bypass JPEG and change the file type to Raw (CR2). The next section offers details.

Raw (CR2): The purist's choice

The other picture-file type that you can create is *Camera Raw,* or just *Raw* (as in, uncooked) for short.

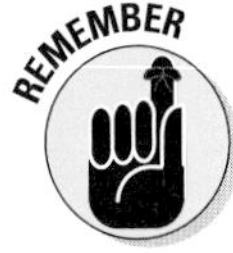

Each manufacturer has its own flavor of Raw files; Canon's are CR2 files (or, on some older cameras, CRW). You'll see that three-letter designation at the end of your picture filenames on your computer.

Raw is popular with many advanced photographers for two reasons:

- **Greater creative control:** With JPEG, internal camera software tweaks your images, adjusting color, exposure, and sharpness as needed to produce the results that Canon believes its customers prefer (or according to certain camera settings you chose, such as the Picture Style). With Raw, the camera simply records the original, unprocessed image data. The photographer then copies the image file to the computer and uses software known as a *raw converter* to produce the actual image, making decisions about color, exposure, and so on, at that point. The upshot is that "shooting Raw" enables you, not the camera, to have the final say on the visual characteristics of your image.
- **Higher bit depth:** *Bit depth* is a measure of how many color values an image file can contain. JPEG files restrict you to 8 bits each for the red, blue, and green color components, or *channels,* that make up a digital image, for a total of 24 bits. That translates to roughly 16.7 million possible colors. On your camera, a Raw file delivers a higher bit count, collecting 14 bits per channel.

Although jumping from 8 to 14 bits sounds like a huge difference, you may not ever notice any difference in your photos — that 8-bit palette of 16.7 million values is more than enough for superb images. Where having the extra bits can come in handy is if you really need to adjust exposure, contrast, or color after the shot in your photo-editing program. In cases where you apply extreme adjustments, having the extra original bits sometimes helps avoid a problem known as *banding* or *posterization,* which creates abrupt color breaks where you should see smooth, seamless transitions. (A higher bit depth doesn't always prevent the problem, however, so don't expect miracles.)

- **Best picture quality:** Because Raw doesn't apply the destructive compression associated with JPEG, you don't run the risk of the artifacting that can occur with JPEG.

But just like JPEG, Raw isn't without its disadvantages:

- **You can't do much with your pictures until you process them in a Raw converter.** You can't share them online, for example, or put them into a text document or multimedia presentation. You can print them immediately if you use the Canon-provided software, but most other photo programs require you to convert the Raw files to a standard format first. Ditto for retail photo printing. So when you shoot Raw, you add to the time you spend in front of the computer instead of behind the camera lens. Chapter 6 gets you started processing your Raw files using your Canon software.
- **Raw files are larger than JPEG files.** Unlike JPEG, Raw doesn't apply lossy compression to shrink files. This means that Raw files are significantly larger than JPEG files, so they take up more room on your memory card and on your computer's hard drive or other file-storage devices.

Whether the upside of Raw outweighs the down is a decision that you need to ponder based on your photographic needs, schedule, and computer-comfort level. If you decide to try Raw shooting, you can select from the following Image Quality options:

- **RAW:** This setting produces a single Raw file at the maximum resolution (18 MP).
- **RAW+Large/Fine:** This setting produces two files: the Raw file plus a JPEG file captured at the Large/Fine setting. The advantage is that you can share the JPEG online or get prints made immediately and then process your Raw files when you have time. The downside, of course, is that creating two files for every image eats up substantially more space on your memory card and your computer's hard drive.

My take: Choose Fine or Raw

At this point, you may be finding all this technical goop a bit much, so allow me to simplify things until you have time or energy to completely digest all the ramifications of JPEG versus Raw:

- If you require the absolute best image quality and have the time and interest to do the Raw conversion process, shoot Raw.
- If great photo quality is good enough for you, you don't have wads of spare time, or you aren't that comfortable with the computer, stick with one of the Fine JPEG settings.
- If you want to enjoy the best of both worlds, consider Raw+Large/Fine — assuming, of course, that you have an abundance of space on your memory card and your hard drive. Otherwise creating two files for every photo on a regular basis isn't really practical.
- Select JPEG Normal if you aren't shooting pictures that demand the highest quality level and you aren't printing or displaying the photos at large sizes. The smaller file size also makes JPEG Normal the way to go if you're running low on memory-card space during a shoot.

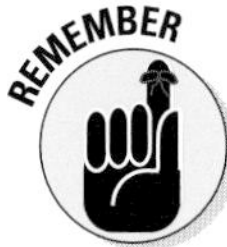

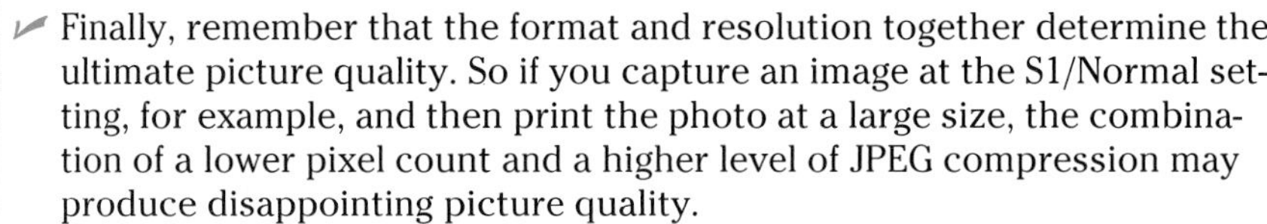

- Finally, remember that the format and resolution together determine the ultimate picture quality. So if you capture an image at the S1/Normal setting, for example, and then print the photo at a large size, the combination of a lower pixel count and a higher level of JPEG compression may produce disappointing picture quality.

3

Taking Great Pictures, Automatically

In This Chapter

- Shooting your first pictures
- Setting focus and exposure automatically
- Getting better results by using the automatic scene modes
- Understanding the Ambience and Lighting/Scene Type features
- Gaining more control with Creative Auto mode

Are you old enough to remember the Certs television commercials from the 1960s and '70s? "It's a candy mint!" declared one actor. "It's a breath mint!" argued another. Then a narrator declared the debate a tie and spoke the famous catchphrase: "It's two, two, two mints in one!"

Well, that pretty much describes the Rebel T4i/650D. On one hand, it provides a range of powerful controls, offering just about every feature a serious photographer could want. On the other, it also offers fully automated exposure modes that enable people with no experience to capture beautiful images. "It's a sophisticated photographic tool!" "It's as simple as 'point and shoot'!" "It's two, two, two cameras in one!"

Of course, you probably bought this book for help with your camera's advanced side, so that's what other chapters cover. This chapter, however, is devoted to your camera's point-and-shoot side, explaining how to get the best results from the fully automatic exposure modes.

Although the fully automated modes work in Live View mode, where you use the monitor to compose your shots, some picture-taking steps (including autofocusing) are different than when you use the viewfinder. This chapter assumes that you're using the viewfinder; see Chapter 4 for help with Live View photography.

As Easy As It Gets: Auto and Flash Off

For the most automatic of automatic photography, set your camera's Mode dial to one of the following two settings:

- **Scene Intelligent Auto:** The name of this mode, labeled in Figure 3-1, refers to the fact that the camera analyzes the scene and selects the picture-taking options that it thinks will best capture the subject.
- **Flash Off:** Also labeled in the figure, this mode does the same thing as Scene Intelligent Auto, except flash is disabled. This mode provides an easy way to ensure that you don't break the rules when shooting in locations that don't permit flash.

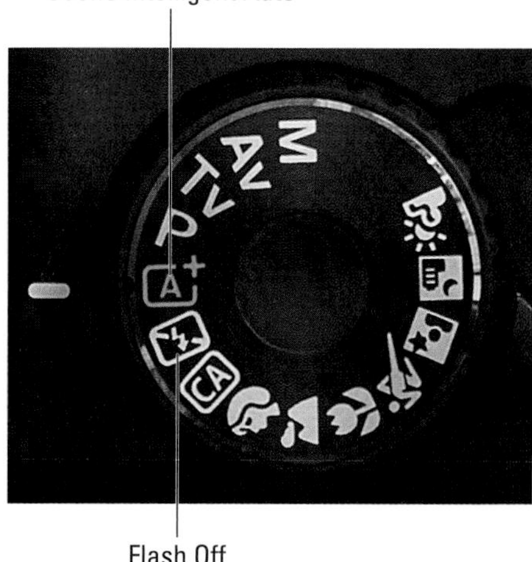

Figure 3-1: These two modes are identical except one disables flash.

In either mode, follow these steps to take a picture:

1. **Set the focusing switch on the lens to the AF (autofocus) position, as shown in Figure 3-2.**

   The figure features the 18–55mm kit lens; the switch looks the same on the 18–135mm kit lens. If you own a different lens, the switch may look and operate differently; check your lens manual for details. (Note that these steps assume that your lens offers autofocusing; if not, ignore autofocusing instructions and focus manually.)

2. **Unless you're using a tripod, set the Stabilizer switch to the On setting, as shown in Figure 3-2.**

   Image stabilization helps produce sharper images by compensating for camera movement that can occur when you handhold the camera. If you're using a tripod, you can save battery power by turning stabilization off. Again, if you use a lens other than one of the two kit lenses, check your lens manual for details about its stabilization feature, if provided.

3. **Check the Drive mode on the Shooting Settings display.**

   By default, the camera sets the Drive mode to Single, which means that you capture one picture with each press of the shutter button. But you can switch to one of the other Drive modes if you prefer.

   You can view the current Drive mode in the Shooting Settings display, as shown in Figure 3-3. The fastest way to access the Drive mode settings is to press the left cross key after displaying the Shooting Settings screen; see Chapter 2 if you need help understanding your options. You can also use the Quick Control screen, covered in Chapter 1, to adjust the setting.

4. **Select the Image Quality setting via Shooting Menu 1.**

   Chapter 2 spells out the intricacies of this setting. If you're not up for digesting the topic, keep the setting at the default (Large/Fine). The icon representing that setting looks like the one shown in Figure 3-3.

5. **Looking through the viewfinder, frame the image so that your subject appears under an autofocus point.**

   The *autofocus points* are those nine tiny rectangles clustered in the center of the viewfinder, as shown in Figure 3-4. (Ignore the circle; it's related to a special exposure metering mode that Chapter 7 explains.)

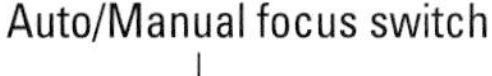

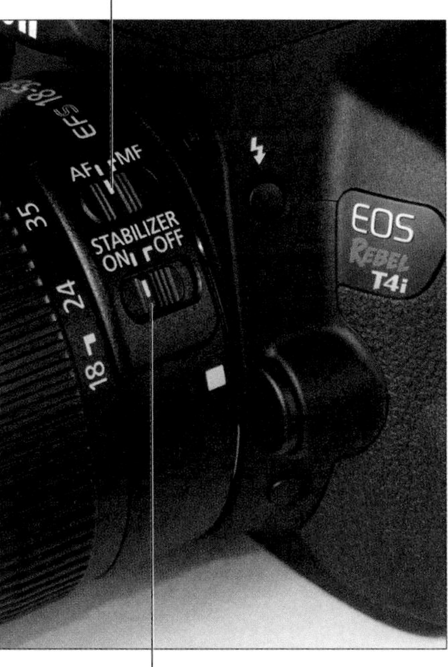

Figure 3-2: Set the lens switch to AF to use autofocusing.

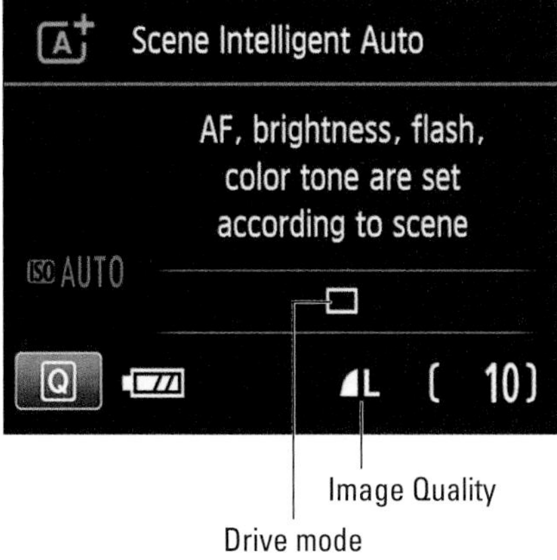

Figure 3-3: In Scene Intelligent Auto and Flash Off modes, you still have control over the Drive mode and Image Quality settings.

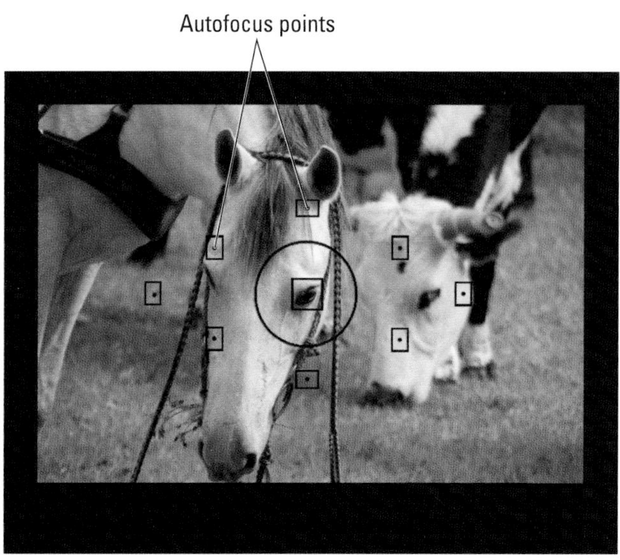

Figure 3-4: The tiny rectangles in the viewfinder indicate autofocus points.

Framing your subject so that it falls under the center autofocus point typically produces the fastest and most accurate autofocusing.

6. **Press and hold the shutter button halfway down.**

   The camera's autofocus and autoexposure systems begin to do their thing. In dim light, the flash pops up if the camera thinks light is needed when you use the Scene Intelligent Auto exposure mode. Additionally, the flash may emit an *AF-assist beam,* a few rapid pulses of light designed to help the autofocusing mechanism find its target. (The *AF* stands for autofocus.)

   After the camera meters exposure, it displays its chosen aperture (f-stop) and shutter speed settings at the bottom of the viewfinder. In Figure 3-5, for example, the shutter speed is 1/500 second, and the f-stop is f/6.3. You also see the current ISO setting and the maximum burst rate (in this case, 100 and 9, respectively). (Chapter 7 details shutter speed, f-stops, and ISO; see Chapter 1 for information about the maximum burst rate.)

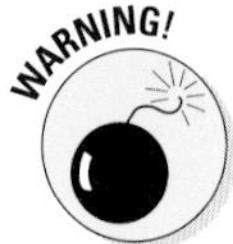

If the shutter speed value blinks, the camera needs to use a slow shutter speed to expose the picture. Because any movement of the camera or subject can blur the picture at a slow shutter speed, use a tripod and tell your subject to remain as still as possible.

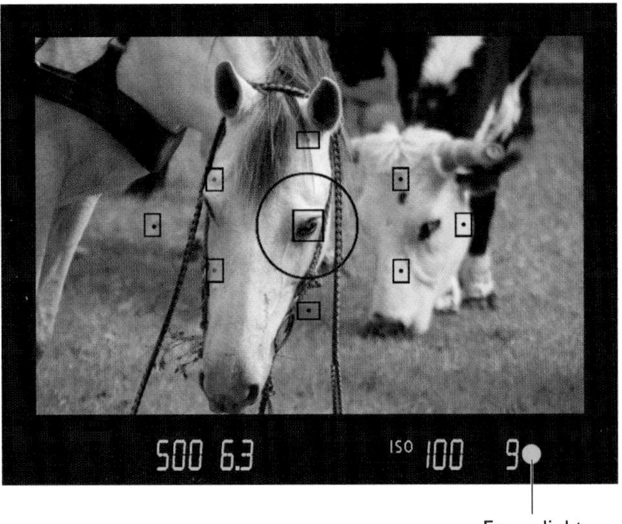

Figure 3-5: When you photograph stationary subjects, the green focus indicator lights when the camera locks focus.

7. **Pause to give the camera time to set focus.**

   This step is critical! If you simply press the shutter button down in one continuous motion, the camera may not be able to set focus correctly.

   When focus is established, one or more of the autofocus points blink red to indicate which areas of the frame are in focus. For example, in Figure 3-5, the points on the horse's face are lit, showing that everything under those points is in focus.

   In most cases, you also hear a tiny beep, and the focus indicator in the viewfinder lights, as shown in Figure 3-5. Focus is now locked as long as you keep the shutter button halfway down. Typically the camera focuses on the closest object; if you want to set focus elsewhere, your easiest option is to use manual focusing.

   These focus signals vary if the camera senses motion in front of the lens, however. You may hear a series of small beeps, and the focus lamp may not light. Both signals mean that the camera switched to an autofocusing option that enables it to adjust focus as necessary up to the time you take the picture. As long as you keep the subject within the area covered by the autofocus points, focus should be correct.

8. **Press the shutter button the rest of the way down to record the image.**

While the camera sends the image data to the camera memory card, the memory card access lamp on the lower-right corner of the camera back lights. Don't turn off the camera or remove the memory card while the lamp is lit, or you may damage both camera and card.

When the recording process is finished, the picture appears briefly on the camera monitor. By default, the review period is two seconds; you can adjust the timing via Shooting Menu 1. See Chapter 5 to find out more about picture playback.

I need to add just a few more pointers about the Scene Intelligent Auto and Flash Off modes:

- **Exposure:** In dim lighting, the camera may need to use a very high ISO setting, which increases the camera's sensitivity to light, or very slow shutter speed (longer exposure time), especially if you use the Flash Off mode. Unfortunately, both can create *noise,* a defect that makes your picture look grainy. See Chapter 7 for tips on dealing with this and other exposure problems.
- **Flash:** In Scene Intelligent Auto mode, you can set the flash to the Red-Eye Reduction mode (the control lives on Shooting Menu 1). Chapter 2 provides the full story and offers some basic tips for flash photography.
- **Autofocusing:** If the camera can't establish focus, you may be too close to your subject. Additionally, some scenes simply confuse autofocusing systems — water, highly reflective objects, and subjects behind fences are some problematic subjects. Just switch to manual focusing and set focus yourself as outlined in Chapter 1.
- **Color:** Color decisions are also handled for you automatically. Normally, the camera's color brain does a good job of rendering the scene, but if you want to tweak color, you're out of luck.

Taking Advantage of Scene (Image Zone) Modes

In Scene Intelligent Auto and Flash Off modes, the camera tries to figure out what type of picture you want to take. If you don't want to rely on the camera to make that judgment, you can choose from one of seven Image Zone modes, more commonly known as *scene modes* because they're designed to capture specific scenes using traditional recipes. For example, most people prefer portraits that have softly focused backgrounds. So Portrait mode selects settings that can blur the background. And action shots typically show the subject frozen in time, so that's the route the camera takes in Sports mode.

Scene modes also apply color, exposure, contrast, and sharpness adjustments to the picture according to the traditional characteristics of the scene type. Landscape mode produces more vibrant colors (especially in the blue-green range, for example).

The next section provides an overview of using scene modes; following that, you can find details about the individual modes.

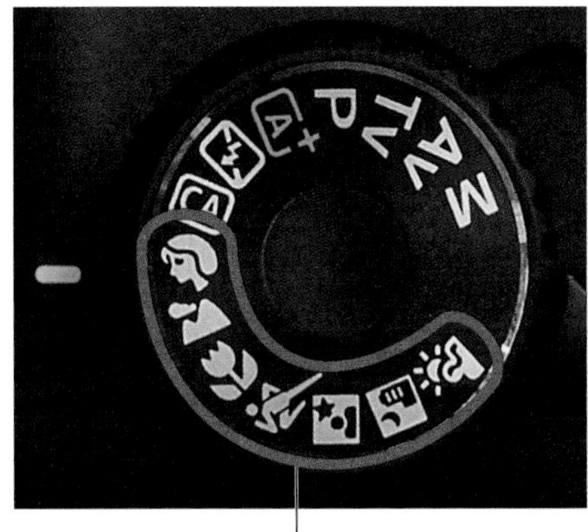

Figure 3-6: These icons represent automatic exposure modes geared to specific types of scenes.

Trying out the scene modes

To select a scene mode, turn the Mode dial to the icon that represents the type of picture you want to take. Figure 3-6 highlights all the scene modes; Table 3-1 shows the symbol that represents each mode and explains what type of picture the mode is designed to shoot.

Table 3-1 Scene (Image Zone) Modes

Use This Mode . . .	*For This Type of Picture*	
	Portrait	Portraits featuring soft backgrounds and soft, flattering skin tones
	Landscape	Landscapes featuring vivid blues and greens; both foreground and background appear in sharp focus. Flash is disabled.
	Close-up	Still-life photos taken at close range; produces sharp subject with softly focused background
	Sports	Action shots that freeze subject motion; flash is disabled.
	Night Portrait	Portraits at night or in very dim lighting; combines flash with slow shutter speed for brighter backgrounds.

(continued)

Table 3-1 *(continued)*

Use This Mode . . .	***For This Type of Picture***	
	Handheld Night Scene	Low-light pictures without a tripod; camera records four images and combines them to create sharper image
	HDR Backlight Control	Scenes with both very dark and very bright areas; camera records three shots at different exposures and merges them for more detail in shadows and highlights. Flash is disabled.

After you select a scene mode, the Shooting Settings screen displays information similar to what you see on the left in Figure 3-7. The exact information varies according to the scene mode; the figure shows the screen for Portrait mode. Depending on the scene mode, you may be able to adjust the following settings:

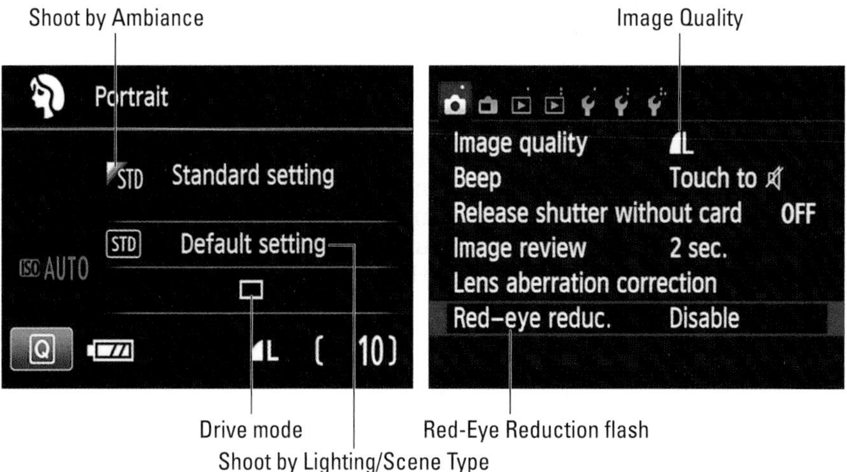

Figure 3-7: Some scene modes enable you to adjust a few settings via the Quick Control screen or Shooting Menu 1.

- **Shoot by Ambience:** This option, available in all the scene modes except HDR Backlight Control, enables you to play with image colors and request a darker or brighter exposure on your next shot. The section "Shoot by Ambience," later in this chapter, explains your choices. Look for the setting marked by the little triangle symbol, as labeled on the left in Figure 3-7; adjust the option via the Quick Control screen.
- **Shoot by Lighting or Scene Type:** This option, also labeled in the figure, is available only in Portrait, Landscape, Close-up, and Sports modes. It manipulates color and is primarily designed to eliminate color casts that can occur in some types of lighting. Check out "Shooting by Lighting or Scene Type," also later in this chapter, for details. Again, this setting is accessed by the Quick Control screen.
- **Drive mode:** The icon representing this setting appears in the area labeled on the left in Figure 3-7. Close-up, Landscape, Night Portrait, Handheld Night Scene, and HDR Backlight Control modes set the Drive mode to Single (one shot per each shutter-button press) by default; Portrait and Sports modes use the Continuous Drive mode. You can switch to any other Drive mode, however; see Chapter 2 for details.
- **Flash:** For Handheld Night Scene mode, you can enable or disable flash via the Quick Control screen. For other modes that permit flash, you don't have control over whether the flash fires but you can enable or disable Red-Eye Reduction flash via Shooting Menu 1 (refer to the right screen in Figure 3-7).
- **Image Quality:** You can change this setting, which controls resolution and file type, only via Shooting Menu 1. Chapter 2 explains the impact of that setting; if you're unsure of which option to choose, stick with the default (Large/Normal). The symbol next to the menu item should look like the one shown in Figure 3-7 — the L with the smooth arc beside it. Note that you can't use the Raw Image Quality setting for the HDR Backlight Control and Handheld Night Scene modes.

As for the actual picture-taking process, everything works pretty much as outlined in the steps provided earlier in the first section of this chapter. You do need to be aware of a few variations on the theme, which I spell out in the upcoming sections detailing each scene mode.

Portrait mode

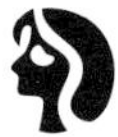

Portrait mode is designed to produce the classic portraiture look featured in Figure 3-8: a sharply focused subject against a blurred background. In photography lingo, this picture has a *short depth of field.*

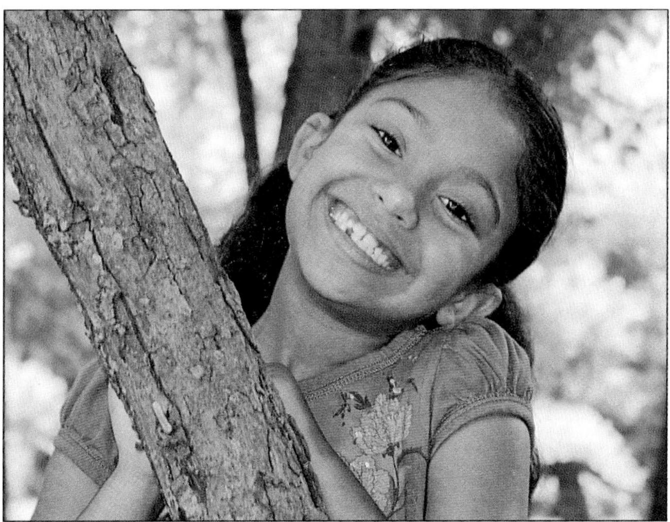

Figure 3-8: Portrait setting produces a softly focused background.

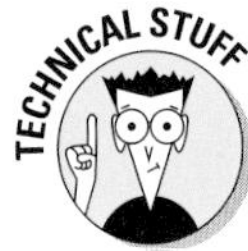

One way to control depth of field is to adjust an exposure control called *aperture,* or *f-stop setting,* so Portrait mode attempts to use an f-stop setting that produces a short depth of field. But the range of f-stops available to the camera depends on the lens and the lighting conditions, so one picture taken in Portrait mode may look very different from another. Additionally, the amount of background blurring depends on a couple other factors, all covered in Chapter 8. In other words, your mileage may vary.

Along with favoring an f-stop that produces a shorter depth of field, Portrait mode results in a slightly less sharp image, the idea being to keep skin texture soft. Colors are also adjusted to enhance skin tones. A few other facts to note:

- **Drive mode:** The Drive mode is set to Continuous by default, which means that the camera records a series of images in rapid succession as long as you hold down the shutter button. This technique comes in handy if your subject can't be counted on to remain still for very long — a toddler or pet, for example. But you have the option of changing to any of the other Drive modes. See Chapter 2 for Drive mode details.
- **Flash:** The flash fires if the camera deems extra lighting is needed. For outdoor portraits, this can pose a problem: Flash generally improves outdoor portraits, and if the ambient light is very bright, the camera may not think you need flash. You can switch to Creative Auto mode or one of the advanced exposure modes to take control of flash firing.

If the camera does pop up the flash, you can enable or disable Red-Eye Reduction flash via Shooting Menu 1.

- **Autofocusing:** Portrait mode employs the One-Shot AF (autofocus) mode. This is one of three AF modes, all detailed in Chapter 8. In One-Shot mode, the camera locks focus when you press the shutter button halfway. Typically the camera locks focus on the closest object that falls under one of the nine autofocus points.

If your subject moves out of the selected autofocus point, the camera doesn't adjust focus to compensate, as it does if it senses a moving object when you shoot in Scene Intelligent Auto or Flash Off mode.

Landscape mode

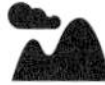

Landscape mode, designed for capturing scenic vistas, city skylines, and other large-scale subjects, produces a large depth of field. As a result, objects both close to the camera and at a distance appear sharply focused, as in Figure 3-9.

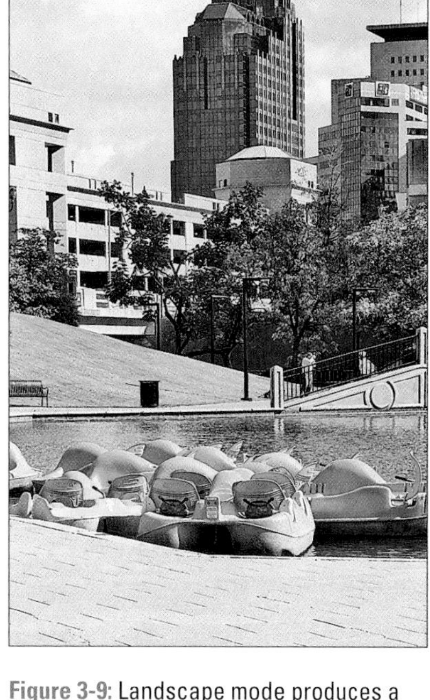

Figure 3-9: Landscape mode produces a large zone of sharp focus.

Like Portrait mode, Landscape mode achieves its depth-of-field goal by manipulating the aperture (f-stop) setting. Consequently, the extent to which the camera can succeed in keeping everything in sharp focus depends on your lens and on the available light. To fully understand this issue and other factors that affect depth of field, see Chapters 7 and 8.

Whereas Portrait mode tweaks the image to produce soft, flattering skin tones, Landscape mode results in sharper, more contrasty, photos. Color saturation is increased as well, and blues and greens appear especially bold. Other critical settings work as follows:

- **Drive mode:** The default setting is Single, which records one image for each press of the shutter button. As with the other scene modes, you can switch to any of the other Drive modes if you prefer. See Chapter 2 for an explanation of all your options; adjust the setting by pressing the left control key while the Shooting Settings screen is displayed.

- **Flash:** The built-in flash is disabled, which is typically no big deal. Because of its limited range, the flash is of little use when shooting most landscapes, anyway. But for some still-life shots, such as of a statue at close range, a flash may prove helpful. Try switching to Creative Auto mode, detailed later in this chapter, if you want to use flash.
- **Autofocusing:** Landscape mode uses One-Shot autofocusing; focus locks when you press the shutter button halfway. Focus usually is set on the nearest object that falls under one of the nine autofocus points.

Close-up mode

Switching to Close-up mode doesn't enable you to focus at a closer distance to your subject than normal as it does on some non-SLR cameras. The close-focusing capabilities of your camera depend entirely on the lens you use. (Your lens manual should specify the minimum focusing distance.)

Choosing Close-up mode does tell the camera to try to select an aperture (f-stop) setting that results in a short depth of field, which blurs background objects so that they don't compete for attention with your main subject. I took this creative approach to capture the orchid in Figure 3-10, for example. As with Portrait mode, though, how much the background blurs varies depending on a number of factors, all detailed in Chapter 8. For greater background blurring, move the subject farther from the background, use a telephoto lens (or zoom to the longest focal length your lens offers), and get closer to the subject.

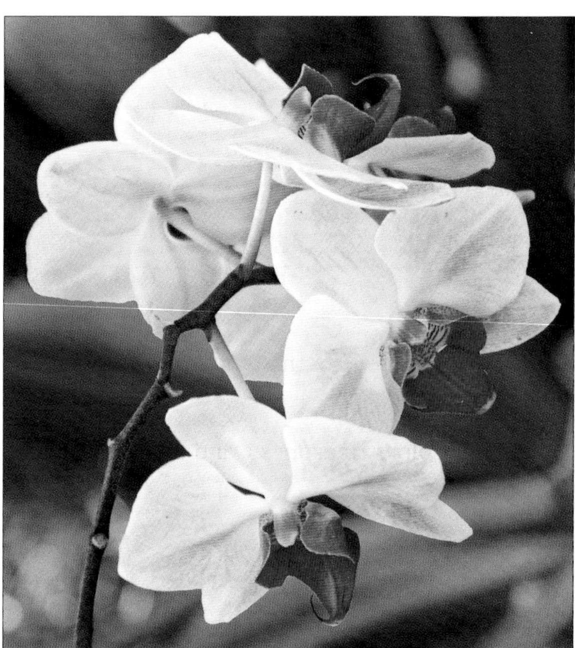

Figure 3-10: Close-up mode also produces short depth of field.

As far as color, sharpness, and contrast, the camera doesn't play with those characteristics as it does in Portrait and Landscape modes. So in that regard, Close-up mode is the same as Scene Intelligent Auto and Flash Off modes.

Other settings that apply to Close-up mode:

- **Drive mode:** The Drive mode is set to Single by default, so you record one photo each time you fully press the shutter button. However, you can use any of the other options you prefer. Don't know how those work? Chapter 2 explains.
- **Flash:** Flash is set to Auto, so the camera decides whether the picture needs the extra light from the flash. If the camera enables the flash, you can turn Red-Eye Reduction flash on or off via Shooting Menu 1.
- **Autofocusing:** The AF mode is set to One-Shot mode; again, that means that when you press the shutter button halfway, the camera locks focus, usually on the nearest object. If you have trouble focusing, first make sure that you're not *too* close up: Remember, every lens has a minimum close-focusing distance. Then just use manual focusing if the camera has trouble locking on your subject in autofocus mode.

See Chapter 8 for more details about AF modes and other focusing issues. Chapter 9 offers additional tips on close-up photography.

Sports mode

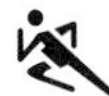

Sports mode results in a number of settings that can help you photograph moving subjects, such as the soccer player in Figure 3-11. First, the camera selects a fast shutter speed, which is needed to "stop motion." *Shutter speed* is an exposure control that you can explore in Chapter 7.

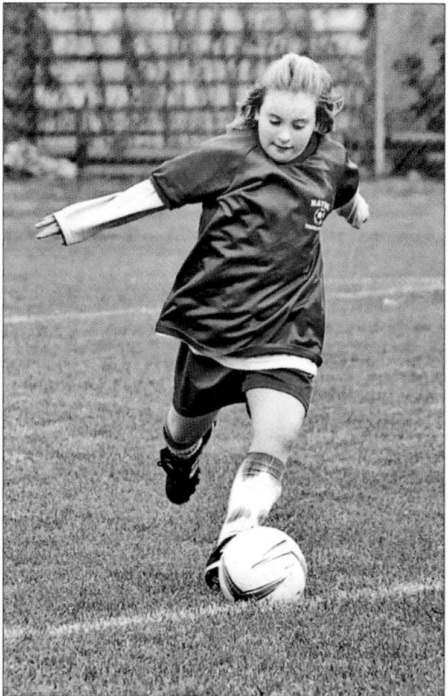

Figure 3-11: To capture moving subjects and minimize blur, try Sports mode.

Colors, sharpness, and contrast are all standard in Sports mode, with none of the adjustments that occur in Portrait and Landscape mode. Other settings to note include the following:

- **Drive mode:** To enable rapid-fire image capture, the Drive mode is set to Continuous by default. This mode enables you to record multiple frames with a single press of the shutter button. To find out about other Drive mode options, see Chapter 2.
- **Flash:** Flash is disabled, which can be a problem in low-light situations but also enables you to shoot more

quickly because the flash needs time to recycle between shots. In addition, disabling the flash permits a faster shutter speed; when the flash is on, the maximum shutter speed is 1/200 second, which may not be fast enough to freeze quickly moving subjects. (See Chapter 7 for details about flash and shutter speeds.)

- **Autofocusing:** The AF mode is set to AI Servo, which is designed for focusing on moving subjects. When you press the shutter button halfway, the camera establishes focus on whatever is under the center focus point. But if the subject moves, the camera attempts to refocus up to the moment you take the picture.

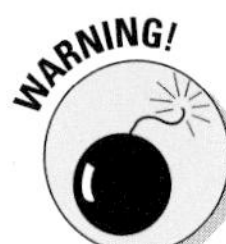

For this feature to work correctly, you must adjust framing so that your subject remains within one of the autofocus points.

The other critical thing to understand about Sports mode is that whether the camera can select a shutter speed fast enough to stop motion depends on the available light and the speed of the subject itself. In dim lighting, a subject that's moving at a rapid pace may appear blurry even when photographed in Sports mode. And the camera may need to increase light sensitivity by boosting the ISO setting, which has the unhappy side effect of creating *noise,* a defect that looks like grains of sand.

To fully understand shutter speed and ISO, visit Chapter 7. See Chapter 8 for focusing help, and for more tips on action photography, check out Chapter 9.

Night Portrait mode

As its name implies, Night Portrait mode is designed to deliver a better-looking portrait at night (or in any dimly lit environment). Night Portrait does so by combining flash with a slow shutter speed. That slow shutter speed produces a longer exposure time, which enables the camera to rely more on ambient light and less on the flash to expose the picture. The result is a brighter background and softer, more even lighting.

Shutter speed is covered in detail in Chapter 7. For now, the important thing to know is that the slower shutter speed used by Night Portrait mode means that you probably need a tripod. If you try to handhold the camera, you run the risk of moving the camera during the long exposure, resulting in a blurry image. Your subjects also must stay still during the exposure.

Night Portrait mode also differs from regular Portrait mode in that it renders the scene in the same way as Scene Intelligent Auto in terms of colors, contrast, and sharpness. So shots taken in Night Portrait mode typically display sharper, bolder colors than those taken in Portrait mode.

Other Night Portrait settings to note:

- **Drive mode:** The default setting is Single, but you also can switch to any of the other Drive mode options. Check out Chapter 2 for details.
- **Flash:** Flash is enabled when the camera thinks more light is needed — which, assuming that you're actually shooting at night, should be most of the time. You can set the flash to Red-Eye Reduction mode (Shooting Menu 1) if you prefer. See the section "Using Red-Eye Reduction flash," in Chapter 2, for help.
- **Autofocusing:** The AF mode is set to One-Shot, which locks focus when you press and hold the shutter button halfway down.

Handheld Night Scene mode

Any camera movement during an exposure can blur your photo. And when you take a picture in dim lighting, the risk is increased because the camera needs a longer exposure time, meaning you have to hold the camera still longer. That's the scenario that led to the Handheld Night Scene mode: As its name implies, it's designed to produce a sharper picture when you handhold the camera in dim lighting.

When you press the shutter button, the camera records four shots in quick succession. Then it analyzes the images and blends them together in a way that reduces blurring while still producing a good exposure. Don't worry about the details — just know that this magic formula, whatever it is, works pretty well, although pictures may not be as sharp as when you use a tripod.

You don't have to reserve this setting for just nighttime shots, despite the mode name, by the way. For example, I used it to capture the shot in Figure 3-12, taken from the top flight of stairs inside a lighthouse. I knew it would be enough of a struggle to climb up the 200-some steps to get to that vantage point, and I wasn't about to add a tripod to my load. So I just leaned over the railing, pointed the camera downward, held my breath, and pressed the shutter button. At a shutter speed of 1/40 second — slow by photographic standards — that would normally be a recipe for a blurry image, but with the help of the Handheld Night Scene mode, the shot is acceptably sharp.

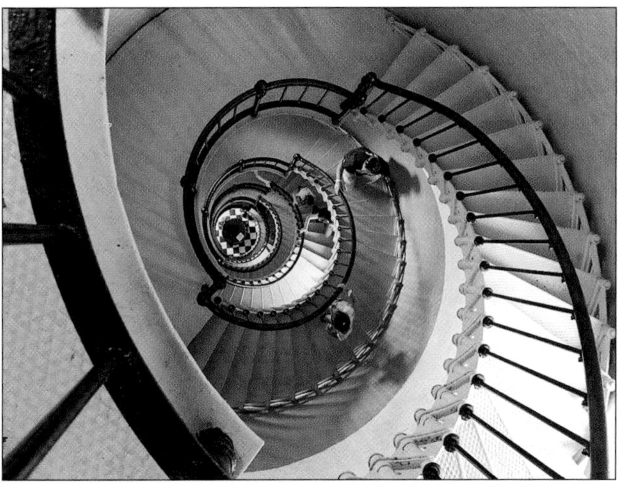

Figure 3-12: I used Handheld Night Scene to capture this handheld shot from a vantage point at the top of a lighthouse.

A couple of points about this mode:

- **Drive mode:** The Single Drive mode is set by default, but the camera records the four successive images with one press of the shutter button anyway, as if you were using the Continuous Drive mode. Setting the Drive mode to Continuous has no effect — you still get just four shots per shutter press. You can, however, use the Self-Timer modes to delay the capture of those four shots. And if you use the Self-Timer Continuous mode, you can capture up to 10 bursts of four frames, resulting in 10 final images. There is a short delay between each burst because the camera needs time to process and merge the frames. Again, see Chapter 2 for the complete scoop on Drive mode.
- **Flash:** You can set the Flash mode to on or off, as indicated by the icon on the Shooting Settings screen, labeled in Figure 3-13. Make the adjustment via the Quick Control screen. For landscapes, disable flash, as shown in the figure, but for portraits, flash is a good idea. The flash fires on the first frame to guarantee that your subject will be well lit, and then the other three frames are taken without flash. Warn your

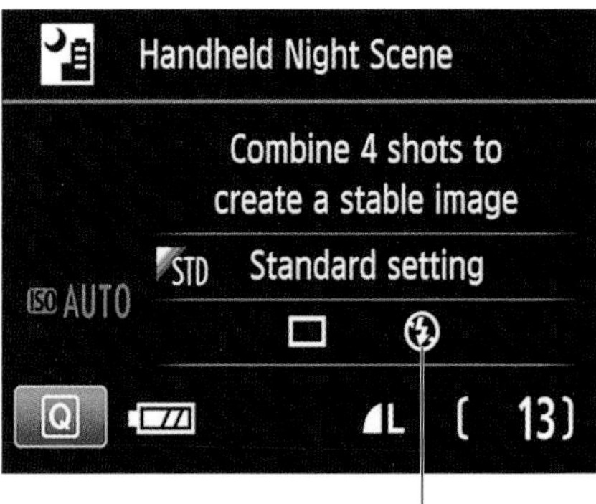

Figure 3-13: Disable flash when photographing landscapes in Handheld Night Scene mode.

subjects to remain still even after the flash fires, or they may appear blurry in the photo.

Using flash can result in a couple other problems, too: If you're really close to your subject, the image may appear too bright. Back away a little to see if that solves the problem. Additionally, if both subject and background are within the reach of the flash, the camera may have trouble aligning the four frames, resulting in a blurry photo.

- **Autofocusing:** The One-Shot AF mode is in force, so focus is locked when you press and hold the shutter button halfway down.

- **Frame area:** The angle of view of the final image is a little smaller than what you see through the viewfinder. This occurs because the camera usually needs to crop the image a little in order to get the four frames to align properly. The actual size of the image remains the same — it just contains a slightly smaller frame area than normal. So compose your image with a little extra margin around the edges to compensate.
- **Moving subjects:** Moving subjects may create blur in your picture because they'll be captured at slightly different areas in each frame. For example, if you look closely at my lighthouse shot, you may be able to notice some blurring of the people climbing the stairs.

- **Image Quality:** This mode works only with images recorded in the JPEG format. In fact, you can't select Raw or Raw+JPEG as the file format when this mode is active. If you select Raw or Raw+JPEG prior to selecting the Handheld Night Scene mode, the camera automatically changes the format to Large/Fine.

Finally, give the camera all the help you can by holding it as still as possible while the four frames are being captured. If possible, find a ledge or other surface on which you can brace the camera, and try tucking your elbows into your sides for additional stability.

HDR Backlight Control mode

When a scene contains both very dark and very bright areas, the camera has a difficult time recording the entire range of brightness values — its "eyes" aren't nearly as adept as ours at seeing the whole picture, as it were. That's where the HDR Backlight Control feature comes in.

A bit of background about the terminology: *HDR* stands for *High Dynamic Range. Dynamic range* refers to the range of brightness values that a device can record. HDR refers to an image that contains a greater spectrum of brightness values than can normally be captured by a camera. In order to produce this result, the photographer records a series of images at different exposures and then uses HDR software to merge the images in a way that results in more detail in both the darkest and brightest parts of a photo.

About the Backlight Control part of the mode name? Well, a backlit image is one in which the light source is behind the subject, which often produces a photograph background that's well exposed but a subject that's too dark. If you tweak exposure settings, you can get your subject to be bright, but not without also brightening the background and, usually, *blowing out the highlights,* or making the lightest areas of the scene *too* bright. HDR Backlight Control to the rescue: It helps brighten up the darkest parts of the image while holding onto more highlight detail than is otherwise possible.

Here's how the HDR Backlight Control setting works: When you press the shutter button, the camera records three images, adjusting exposure between each frame. One frame is exposed to capture the highlights, another for the *midtones* (areas of medium brightness), and another for the shadows. Then the three are merged into one final HDR image. You can see an example in Figure 3-14. I took the left picture using the Scene Intelligent Auto mode; for the right image, I used HDR Backlight Control. Both the highlight and the shadow areas in the HDR version contain more detail. Note, too, that the frame area for the two images is slightly different: As with the Handheld Night Scene, the camera needs to crop the image a little in order to properly align the multiple frames into one.

Scene Intelligent Auto

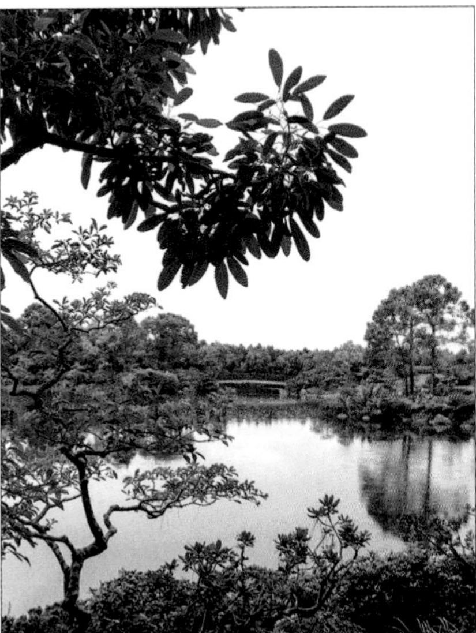

HDR Backlight Control

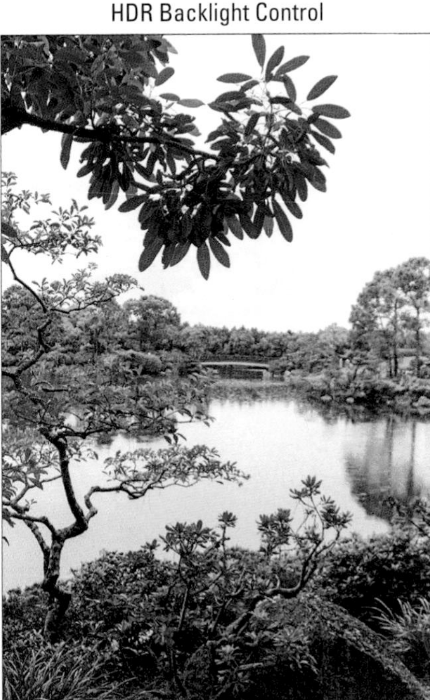

Figure 3-14: Try shooting high-contrast scenes with HDR Backlight Control to retain more detail in both shadows and highlights.

Although this exposure mode sounds like a magical answer to a common problem, you shouldn't expect miracles. HDR Backlight Control mode doesn't always completely correct backlight problems — the results are best when the subject and background aren't extremely different in brightness. Also, if you're interested in doing the type of HDR work that's popular in today's photography circles, you should know that the type of HDR images featured in most photography magazines and websites require more than three exposures. Often, HDR enthusiasts combine more than five frames for a single HDR image. And with the HDR Backlight Control option, you don't have any input on the shift in exposure between frames or the way that the images are merged, as you do when you combine the exposures on the computer. But for a small — and easy to accomplish — improvement in dynamic range, give the HDR Backlight Control a try, remembering these pointers:

- **Shooting tips:** You'll get the best images by following a couple rules:
  - *Use a tripod:* This ensures that each of the three captured frames records the exact same image area, helping the camera to properly align them when merging them into the final HDR image.
  - *Avoid scenes with moving objects.* Anything moving in the scene will probably appear at partial opacity in different parts of the frame in the merged image. On the other hand, you may be able to claim that you captured a ghost in your picture . . . .
  - *Frame a little loosely.* Then, when the images are merged, you won't lose important parts of the scene due to the cropping that occurs in the merge process.
- **Image Quality:** Like the Handheld Night Scene mode, HDR Backlight Control is a JPEG-only creature. You can't shoot in the Raw format in this mode.
- **Drive mode:** The camera fires off three shots in succession with each press of the shutter button, regardless of whether the Drive mode is set to Single or Continuous mode. You can use one of the Self-Timer modes to delay the shutter release if desired.
- **Flash:** Flash is disabled.
- **Autofocus:** One-Shot AF is used, so focus is locked when you press and hold the shutter button halfway.

Modifying scene mode results

With the Scene Intelligent Auto and Flash Off modes, what you see on the playback monitor is what you get — you can't modify the camera settings to get different results on the next shot. But with certain scene modes, you can play around a little with color, sharpness, contrast, and exposure through the Shoot by Ambience and Shoot by Lighting/Scene Type features.

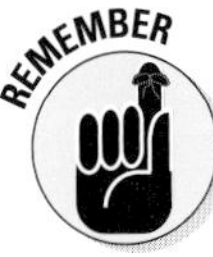

Key words here: play around *a little.* These features don't give you anywhere near the level of control as the advanced exposure modes (P, Tv, Av, and M) or even as much as Creative Auto mode, explained at the end of this chapter. But they do offer an easy way to start exploring your creative possibilities and begin thinking about how *you* want to record a scene.

My only beef with these two features is that they aren't presented in the most user-friendly fashion, especially for the novice photographer — heck, even for the advanced photographer. For starters, the feature names don't give you a lot of information about what you can accomplish by using them. And the displayed names of the default settings — shown on the Shooting Settings screen in Figure 3-15 — are Standard and Default. Well, that's helpful, huh? Then again, if it weren't for confusing stuff like this, you might not need my input, so I probably shouldn't complain.

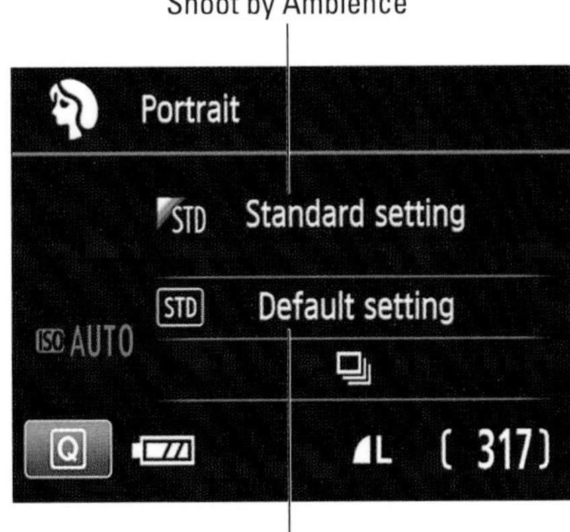

Figure 3-15: These settings enable you to adjust picture color, contrast, sharpness, and exposure when shooting in the scene modes.

At any rate, here's a quick explanation of each feature:

- **Shoot by Ambience:** With this option, you can affect the color, exposure, contrast, and sharpness of your pictures. This option is available in all the scene modes except HDR Backlight Control. You also can use it in Creative Auto mode, explained later in this chapter.
- **Shoot by Lighting or Scene Type:** This option, available in Portrait, Landscape, Close-up, and Sports modes, is designed to remove unwanted color casts that can occur if the camera can't properly compensate for the color of the light source (for example, the warm red glow of candlelight may cause skin colors to look too red).

The next two sections give you a better idea of what you can accomplish with these options; following that, you can find step-by-step instructions for using them on your next shot.

Taking a look at the Shoot by Ambience options

In Chapter 8, I introduce the Picture Style feature, which enables you to choose how the camera "processes" your original picture data when you use one of the JPEG Quality settings. (Chapter 2 explains JPEG.) You can choose the Landscape Picture Style for bold, sharp colors, for example, or select

Portrait to give skin a warm, soft look. (Yes, the camera offers Landscape and Portrait exposure modes and Landscape and Portrait Picture Styles. Don't get me started.)

You can control Picture Styles only in the advanced exposure modes, however — that option is off limits in the other modes. But as compensation, the scene modes (except HDR Backlight Control) and Creative Auto mode give you Shoot by Ambience, which lets you accomplish results similar to those that you could achieve by using Picture Styles. You also get two Shoot by Ambience settings that enable you to achieve exposure adjustments similar to what you can produce with Exposure Compensation, another feature that's available only in the advanced exposure modes.

Don't waste time wondering why Canon doesn't just let you access those features in the first place — it'll only drive you as crazy as me. Just have fun playing with the Shoot by Ambience settings, which work as follows:

- **Standard:** Consider this the "off" setting. When you select this option, the camera makes no adjustment to the characteristics normally produced by your selected scene mode.
- **Vivid:** Increases contrast, color saturation, and sharpness.
- **Soft:** Creates the appearance of slightly softer focus.
- **Warm:** Warms (adds a reddish-orange color cast) and softens.
- **Intense:** Boosts contrast and saturation (color intensity) even more than the Vivid setting.
- **Cool:** Adds a cool (blue) color cast.
- **Brighter:** Lightens the photo.
- **Darker:** Darkens the photo.
- **Monochrome:** Creates a black-and-white photo, with an optional color tint.

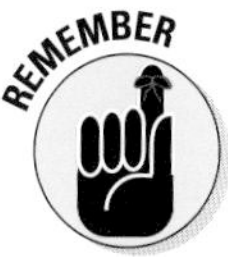

All adjustments are applied *in addition* to whatever adjustments occur by virtue of your selected scene mode. For example, Landscape mode already produces slightly sharper, more vivid colors than normal. If you add the Vivid Shoot by Ambience option, you amp things up another notch.

In addition, you can control the amount of the adjustment through a related setting, Effect (another less-than-clear feature name, if you ask me). You can choose from three Effect levels — Low, Standard, and Strong or Low, Medium, and High, depending on the adjustment you choose. In the case of the Monochrome setting, the Effect setting enables you to switch from a black-and-white image to a monochrome image with a warm (sepia) or cool (blue) tint.

As a quick example of the color effects you can create, Figure 3-16 shows the same subject taken at four different Shoot by Ambience settings. I took all pictures in the Landscape scene mode. For the three variations — Vivid, Warm, and Intense — I applied the maximum level of adjustment, setting the Effect option to Strong.

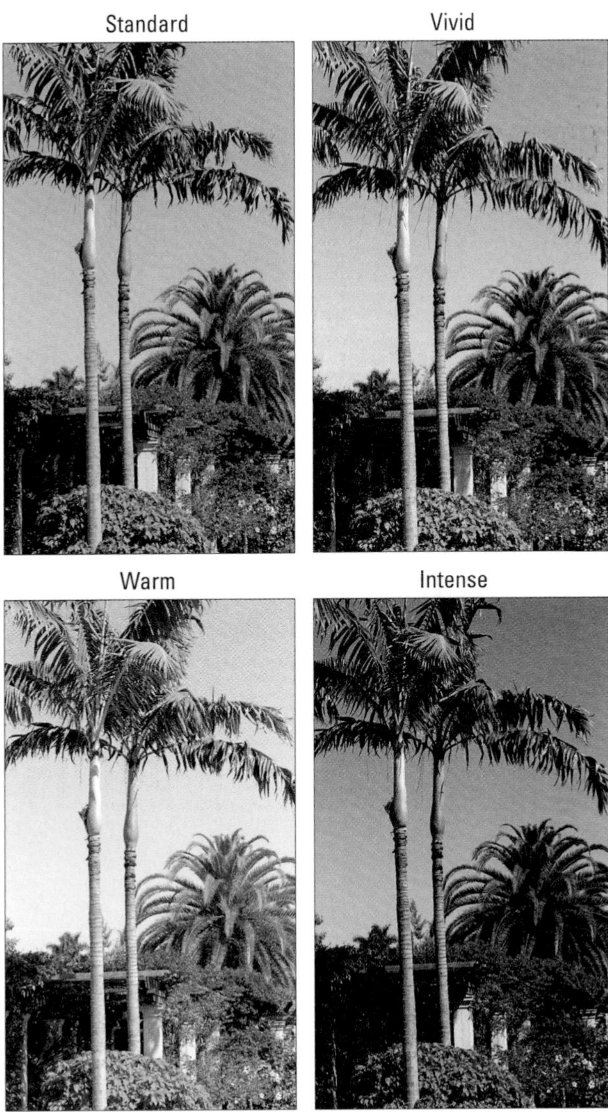

Figure 3-16: To create these Shoot by Ambience variations, I used the maximum amount of adjustment for the Vivid, Warm, and Intense settings.

Although the color effects are entertaining, I think you'll get more use out of the Brighter and Darker settings, as they give you a way to overrule the camera's exposure decisions. For example, in the left image in Figure 3-17, the exposure of the background was fine, but the flower was overexposed. So I set the Shoot by Ambience option to Darker, set the Effect option to Medium, and shot the flower again.

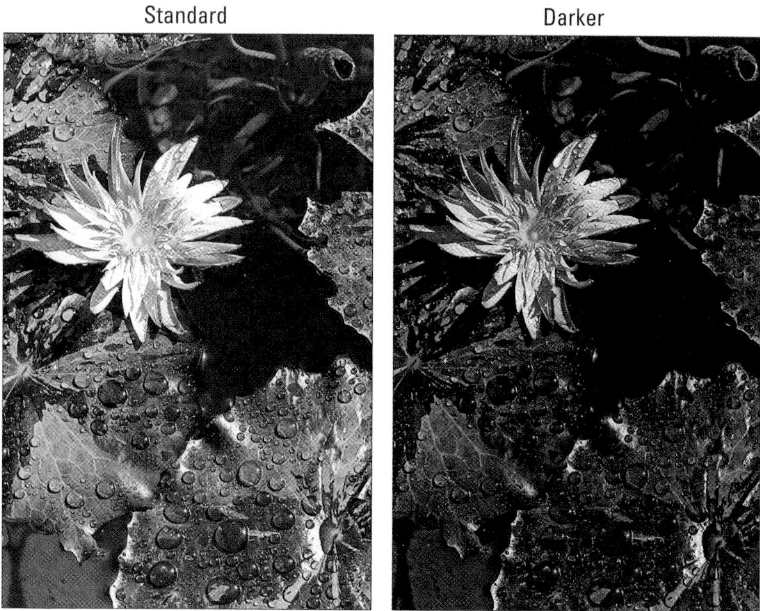

Figure 3-17: If the initial exposure leaves your subject too bright, choose the Darker setting and reshoot.

Because the Shoot by Lighting or Scene Type feature also affects image colors, it's a good idea to consider both options together. So the next section explains this second "Shoot by" feature; following that, I provide step-by-step instructions for enabling both options.

Eliminating color casts with Shoot by Lighting or Scene Type

This option might be better named "Eliminate Color Cast" because that's what it's designed to do: remove unwanted color casts that can occur when the camera makes a *white balance* misstep.

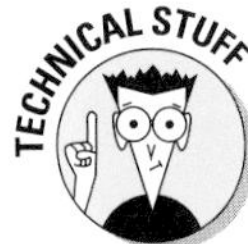

Chapter 8 explains white balancing fully, but in short, it has to do with the fact that every light source emits its own color cast — candlelight, a warm hue; flash, a slightly cool hue, and so on. The camera's White Balance setting is the mechanism that compensates for the color of the light so that colors in the scene are rendered accurately.

Normally, the camera uses automatic white balancing and things turn out just fine. But if a scene is lit by different types of light, each throwing its own color bias into the mix, the camera sometimes gets confused, and colors may be out of whack. The left image in Figure 3-18 has an example — a white-balance error caused the scene to be too yellow. The image on the right shows the correct image colors.

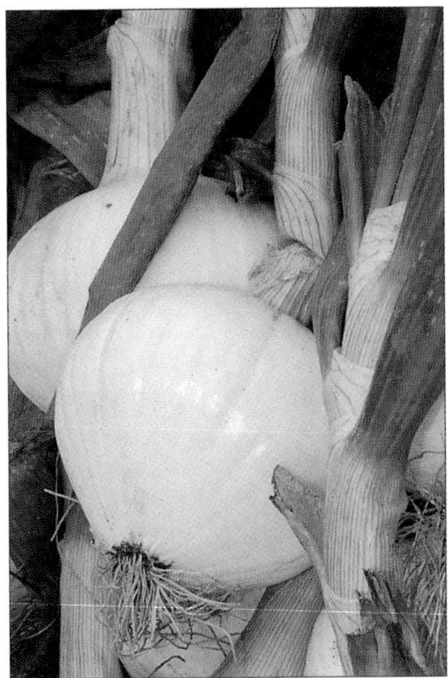
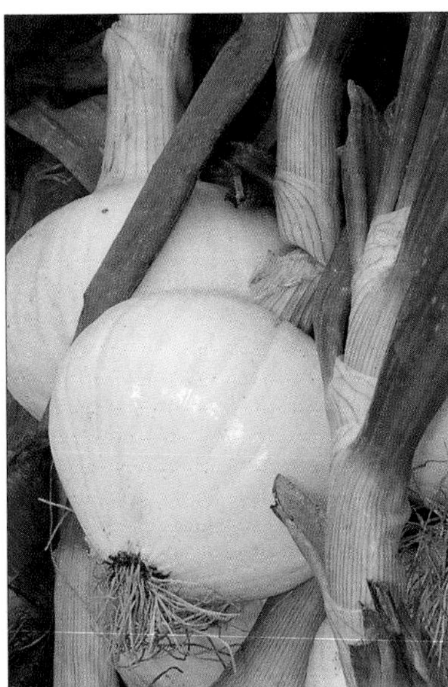

Figure 3-18: If your photo has a color cast (left), you may be able to use the Shoot by Lighting/Scene Type option to eliminate it (right).

In the advanced exposure modes, you deal with color casts by changing the White Balance setting; again, Chapter 8 shows you how. You can't access the White Balance setting in the scene modes, but in Portrait, Landscape, Close-Up, and Sports modes, you can use the Shoot by Lighting or Scene Type option to tell the camera to balance colors for a specific light source.

You can choose from the following settings:

- **Default:** Colors are balanced for the light source automatically.
- **Daylight:** For bright sunlight.
- **Shade:** For subjects in shade.
- **Cloudy:** For shooting under overcast skies.

- **Tungsten Light:** For incandescent and tungsten bulbs; not available for Landscape scene mode.
- **Fluorescent Light:** For subjects lit by fluorescents (although this may not be suitable for some compact-fluorescent lights — try tungsten if you get bad results). Also not available for Landscape scene mode.
- **Sunset:** Helps capture brilliant sunset colors, especially when you're shooting into the sun. (P.S.: Don't aim the lens directly at the sun or look through the viewfinder directly into the sun. You can damage the camera and hurt your eyes.)

Don't worry if you don't know which setting will produce the correct colors — as explained in the next section, you can use the Live View feature on your camera to preview the effect of each setting.

Adjusting (and previewing) the "Shoot by" settings

As the examples in Figures 3-16 through 3-18 illustrate, the two "Shoot by" options together determine your final photo colors and exposure. So being able to preview the possible combinations of settings without having to take a bunch of shots to experiment would be great, yes?

Well, luckily, you can enjoy that advantage in Live View mode — the feature that enables you to compose pictures using the monitor instead of the viewfinder. As you vary the Shoot by Ambience and Shoot by Lighting or Scene Type settings, the Live View display updates to show you how the subject will be rendered. (Note that the Live View preview isn't always 100% accurate, especially in terms of image brightness, but it's fairly close.)

For reasons that I spell out in Chapter 4, I recommend that you use the viewfinder for still photography. So in the following steps, which explain how to select the "Shoot by" settings, I show you how to choose and preview the effects using Live View and then switch back to the viewfinder before actually taking the picture. Canon recommends that you set the Shoot by Lighting or Scene Type option first, so that's how the steps flow.

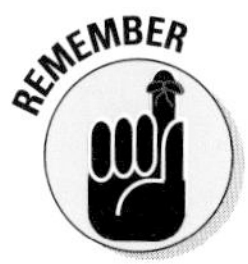

The Shoot by Lighting or Scene Type options are available in the Portrait, Landscape, Close-up, and Sports modes only, and Shoot by Ambience is off limits in HDR Backlight Control mode. So to try out the following steps, set the camera to Portrait, Landscape, Close-up, or Sports mode.

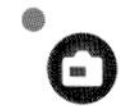

1. **Press the Live View button to shift to Live View mode.**

   The viewfinder goes dark, and the scene in front of the lens appears on the monitor. You also see various icons and markings superimposed atop the scene; exactly what appears depends on the shooting mode and certain other camera settings.

2. **Compose the shot.**

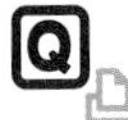

3. **Shift to Quick Control mode.**

   You can get there by tapping the Q icon in the upper-right corner of the screen or by pressing the Quick Control button, shown in the margin here. The two icons labeled on the left in Figure 3-19 represent the Shoot by Ambience and Shoot by Lighting/Scene Type options.

4. **Select the Shoot by Lighting or Scene Type option, as shown on the left in Figure 3-19.**

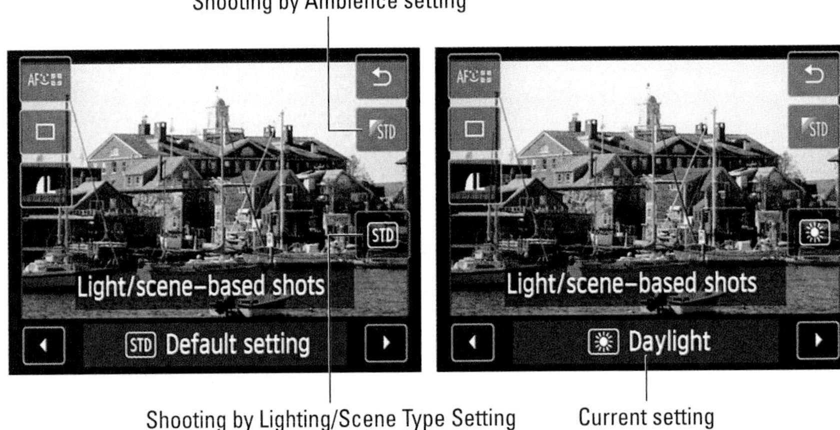

Figure 3-19: You can see the effects of changing the setting on the Live View display.

   You can tap the setting or use the cross keys to select it. The name of the current setting then appears at the bottom of the screen. For example on the left side of Figure 3-19, the Default (no adjustment) setting is selected.

5. **Rotate the Main dial to cycle through the settings.**

   You also can tap the arrows on either side of the setting, displayed at the bottom of the screen, to scroll through the options.

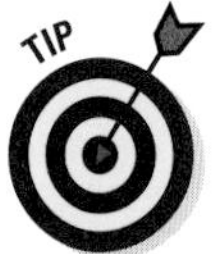

This setting, as I explain in the preceding section, is designed to remove unwanted color casts from a scene. But there's nothing preventing you from using the option to *add* a slight cast to the scene if your heart so desires. You may like the effect of making your subject look a little warmer or cooler, and again, you can see the results of each setting on the camera monitor. What impact any setting has on your subject depends on the actual lighting conditions. In the right example in Figure 3-19, choosing the Daylight option made colors warmer, for example.

6. **Select the Shoot by Ambience option, labeled on the left in Figure 3-20.**

   You can either tap the icon to select it or use the cross keys to highlight it. By default, the Standard setting is used.

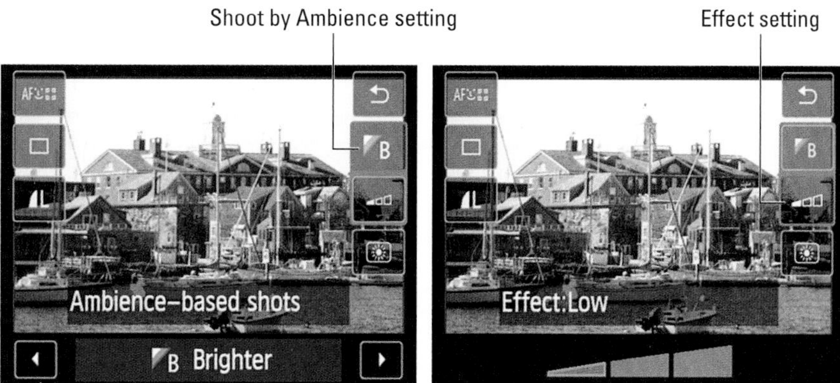

Figure 3-20: After highlighting the Shoot by Ambience option (left), rotate the Main dial to change the setting and display the Effect setting.

7. **Rotate the Main dial to change the Shoot by Ambience setting.**

   Or, again, you can tap the arrows on either side of the setting name at the bottom of the screen. On the left side of Figure 3-20, I selected the Brighter setting.

   As soon as you rotate the dial, you see the impact of the newly selected ambience setting on the scene. In addition, the Effect setting, which determines the level at which the adjustment is applied, becomes available. I labeled this option on the right side of Figure 3-20.

8. **Select the Effect setting and rotate the Main dial to set the level of the adjustment.**

   Again, either use the cross keys to highlight the setting or just tap the icon. You then can rotate the Main dial to choose from Low (one notch on the little gauge), Standard or Medium (medium impact, represented by two notches), or Strong (three notches). Or just tap the bars on the Effect scale to change the setting.

9. **When you're happy with the results of the two options, press the Live View button to exit Live View mode.**

The monitor goes dark, and you can once again see your subject through the viewfinder. The Shoot by Ambience and Shoot by Lighting or Scene Type settings you dialed in remain in force until you change the Mode dial or turn the camera off.

10. **Take the picture.**

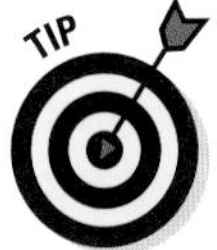

If you already know what settings you want to use, you can get the job done more quickly by staying out of Live View mode and just using the Quick Control screen to dial in both options. Again, keep in mind that the Lighting or Scene Type feature works only in the Portrait, Landscape, Close-up, and Sports mode, and you can't access the Ambience option in HDR Backlight Control mode. Refer to Figure 3-15 to see the location of the two settings on the Shooting Settings screen; see Chapter 1 for help using the Quick Control screen.

Gaining More Control with Creative Auto

When you use the scene modes, described in the preceding few sections, the camera selects settings that render your subject using the traditional "look" for the scene — blurry backgrounds for Portrait mode, greater depth of field and bold colors for Landscapes, and so on. Depending on the scene mode, you may be able to modify colors and exposure somewhat by using the Shoot by Ambience and Shoot by Lighting or Scene Type options, but all in all, you're fairly limited as to the look of your pictures.

Creative Auto mode enables you to take a bit more control. As its name implies, this mode is still mostly automatic, but if you check the monitor after taking a shot and don't like the results, you can make the following adjustments for your next shot:

- Enable or disable the flash.
- Adjust color, sharpness, contrast, and exposure through the Shoot by Ambience option, as explained in the preceding few sections.
- Soften or sharpen the apparent focus of the picture background.

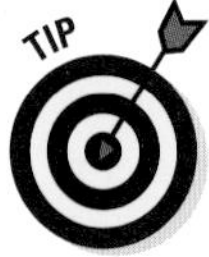

What about the Shoot by Lighting or Scene Type option that's available in the scene modes? Sorry, that dog won't hunt in Creative Auto mode. But remember that using that option typically isn't necessary: It's designed to fix white-balancing issues, and in Creative Auto mode, the camera uses automatic white balancing, which works well for the majority of shooting situations.

Here's how to use Creative Auto mode:

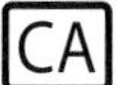

1. **Set the Mode dial on top of the camera to the CA setting.**

   The Creative Auto version of the Shooting Settings screen appears on the monitor, as shown in Figure 3-21. (If you don't see the screen, press the Info button or press the shutter button halfway and then release it.)

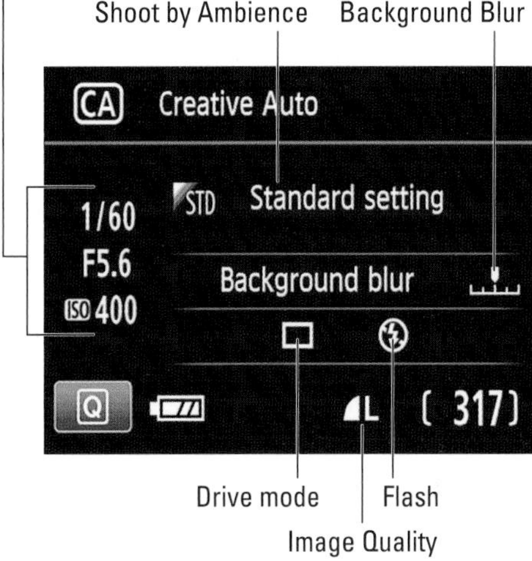

Figure 3-21: In Creative Auto mode, the Shooting Settings screen displays this information.

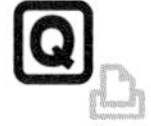

2. **To adjust the Drive Mode, Flash, and Shoot by Ambience settings, use the Quick Control screen.**

   As usual, you can either tap the Q icon on the screen or press the Quick Control button (shown in the margin here). Either way, one of the settings becomes highlighted, and a text label appears at the bottom of the screen to remind you what the highlighted setting does. In Figure 3-22, for example, the Background Blur setting is highlighted.

3. **Select the setting you want to adjust.**

   Either tap the setting or use the cross keys to highlight it.

4. **Adjust the selected setting.**

   See the upcoming list for details about each setting. After selecting an option, the easiest way to change the setting is to rotate the Main dial. For all but the Background blur option, you can also tap the setting icon to display a screen containing all the available options; select your choice and tap the return arrow to go back to the Quick Control screen.

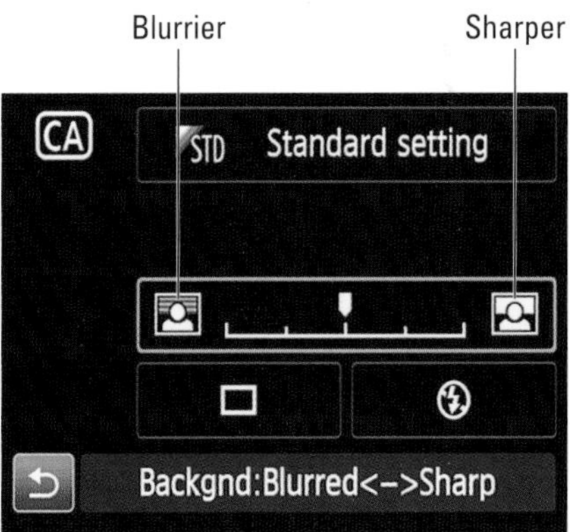

Figure 3-22: Use the Quick Control screen to adjust the Drive mode, Flash, and Shoot by Ambience settings.

5. **After selecting all the options you want to use, exit the Quick Control screen by pressing the shutter button halfway and releasing it.**

   You also can tap the return arrow or press the Quick Control button again. Either way, the monitor returns to the Shooting Settings display.

6. **To adjust the Image Quality setting, use Shooting Menu 1.**

   As with the other exposure modes discussed in this chapter, you can't change that setting via the Quick Control screen in Creative Auto mode.

7. **Frame, focus, and shoot.**

   From this point on, everything works as outlined for the Scene Intelligent Auto mode, explained in the first section of this chapter.

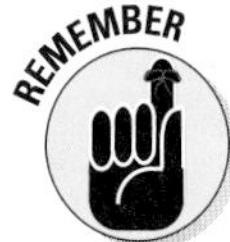

The settings you choose remain in effect from shot to shot. If you turn the camera off or switch to a different exposure mode, though, the settings return to their defaults.

Now for the promised explanations of how the Creative Auto options work:

- **Shoot by Ambience:** This setting enables you to alter how the camera processes the photo, enabling you to tweak color, contrast, and exposure slightly. The earlier section "Taking a look at the Shoot by Ambience options" explains this feature.
- **Background Blur:** This feature gives you some control over depth of field, or the distance over which focus appears acceptably sharp. Consider the images in Figure 3-23, for example. In both shots, I set focus on the flag. But the left image features a long depth of field, so both the flag and the tractor in the background are sharp. The right image has a very shallow, or short, depth of field, so the tractor is blurry.

  Unfortunately, this feature doesn't play nice with the flash. If you set the flash mode to On, the Background Blur bar becomes dimmed and out of your reach when the flash pops up. Ditto if you set the flash mode to Auto and the camera sees a need for flash.

  Assuming that the flash doesn't get in your way, press the Quick Control button or tap the Q icon to shift to the Quick Control screen, highlight the setting, and then use the Main dial to move the little indicator on the bar to the left to shorten depth of field, which makes distant objects appear blurrier. You can also drag your fingertip along the blurring scale or tap the icons at either end of the scale to adjust the setting. Either way, shift the indicator to the right to make distant objects appear sharper.

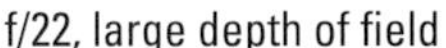

f/22, large depth of field

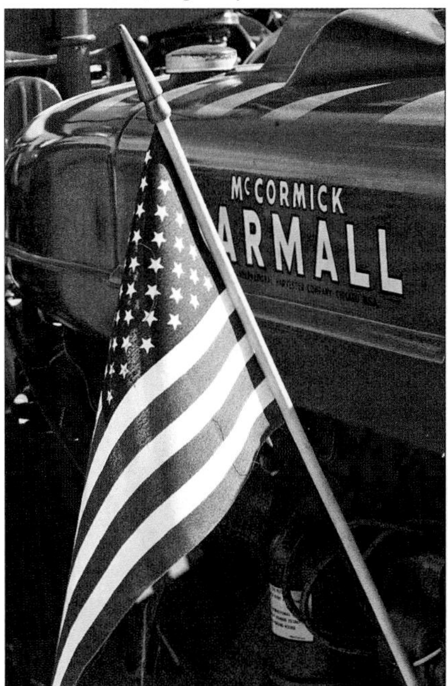

f/2.8, short depth of field

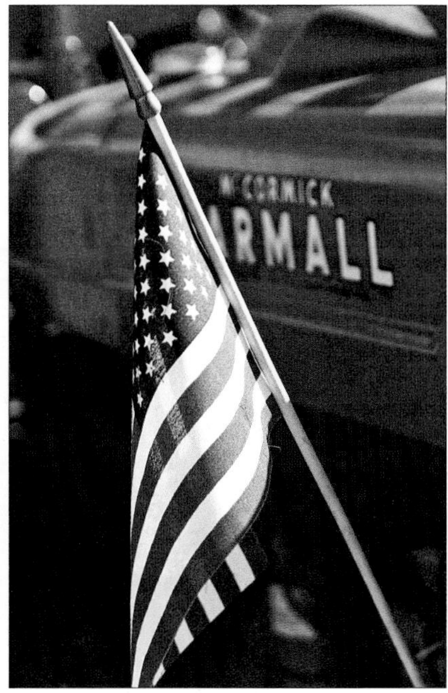

Figure 3-23: You can choose to make background objects appear sharp (left) or blurry (right).

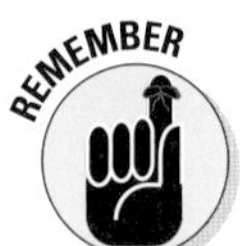

The camera creates this shift in depth of field by adjusting the aperture setting (f-stop), which is an exposure control you can explore in Chapter 7. A lower f-stop number produces a more shallow depth of field, for a blurrier background, as shown on the right in Figure 3-23; a higher f-stop setting produces a greater depth of field, for a sharper background, as shown on the left.

The range of f-stops available to the camera depends on your lens. Additionally, because aperture also plays a critical role in exposure, the range of f-stops the camera can choose — and, therefore, the extent of focus shift you can achieve with this setting — depends on the available light. The camera gives priority to getting a good exposure, assuming that you'd prefer a well-exposed photo to one that has the background blur you want but is too dark or too light. Understand, too, that when the aperture changes, the camera also must change the shutter speed, ISO (light sensitivity setting), or both to maintain a good exposure.

At slow shutter speeds, moving objects appear blurry, regardless of your depth of field. But even for still subjects, a slow shutter speed creates the risk that camera shake during the exposure will blur the image. A blinking shutter speed value in the viewfinder or Shooting Settings display alerts you to a potentially risky shutter speed; put your camera on a tripod to avoid the risk of camera shake. Figure 3-21 shows you where to find the shutter speed and f-stop settings in the Shooting Settings display. (You may need to press the shutter button halfway and release it to wake up the exposure meter and force the exposure settings to appear.)

To find out more about depth of field, aperture, shutter speed, ISO, and exposure, see Chapters 7 and 8. In the meantime, note these easy ways to tweak depth of field beyond using the Background Blur slider:

- *For blurrier backgrounds,* move the subject farther from the background, get closer to the subject, and zoom in to a tighter angle of view, if you use a zoom lens.
- *For sharper backgrounds,* do the opposite of the above.

- **Drive mode:** You can choose from any Drive mode option, all explained in Chapter 2. Remember that you can access the settings by pressing the left cross key as well as by using the Quick Control screen.
- **Flash:** You can choose from three flash settings, which are represented on the Shooting Settings screen by the icons in the margin:
  - *Auto:* The camera fires the flash automatically if it thinks extra light is needed to expose the picture.
  - *On:* The flash fires regardless of the ambient light.
  - *Off:* The flash doesn't fire.

  For the Auto and On settings, you can use the Red-Eye Reduction flash feature, found on Shooting Menu 1. See Chapter 2 for more information about flash photography.

4

Exploring Live View Shooting and Movie Making

In This Chapter

- Getting acquainted with Live View and Movie modes
- Customizing the monitor display
- Exploring autofocusing options
- Selecting camera settings and taking pictures in Live View mode
- Recording and playing movies

Like many dSLR cameras, yours offers *Live View,* a feature that enables you to use the monitor instead of the viewfinder to compose photos. You must rely on the monitor to compose shots during moving recording; using the viewfinder isn't possible.

In many respects, shooting in Live View mode is no different from using the viewfinder. But a few aspects, such as autofocusing, are quite different. So the first part of this chapter provides an overview of the Live View and Movie mode features and clues you in on some precautions to take to avoid damaging the camera when using either feature. Following that, you can find details on taking still photos in Live View mode and shooting and viewing movies.

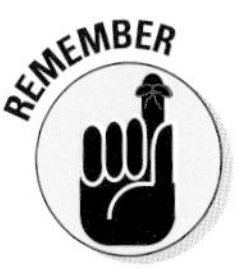

Note: When looking at figures in this chapter, you'll notice that data at the bottom of the screen appears differently on your monitor than it does in the figures. In the figures, data displays against a plain black bar, but on your screen, it's superimposed over the image. In some cases, this also applies to data at the top of the screen. The difference is due to the technology I use to capture the image that the monitor displays; for reasons that I won't bore you with, it's not possible to capture the superimposed data properly. I trust the discrepancy won't throw you off too much.

Getting Started

The basics of taking advantage of Live View and Movie modes are pretty simple:

- **Enabling Live View:** The first step to taking advantage of Live View is to visit the Live View menu and ensure that the Live View Shoot option is enabled, as shown in Figure 4-1. Otherwise pressing the Live View button, which toggles Live View on and off, has no effect unless you set the On/Off switch to Movie mode, in which case the button starts and stops recording.

  As with certain other menus, the options on the Live View menu vary depending on your exposure mode. The right menu in Figure 4-1 reveals options available when you shoot in the fully automated exposure modes; the left menu shows the two additional options available in the P, Tv, Av, and M exposure modes.

Live View shoot.	Enable
AF method	☺+Tracking
Continuous AF	Enable
Touch Shutter	Disable
Grid display	Off
Aspect ratio	3:2
Metering timer	16 sec.

Live View shoot.	Enable
AF method	☺+Tracking
Continuous AF	Enable
Touch Shutter	Disable
Grid display	Off

Figure 4-1: The Live View Shoot option determines whether Live View photography is possible.

  Why would you want to disable Live View, you ask? Because it's easy to hit the Live View button accidentally and switch to Live View when you don't really want to go there.

- **Toggling between viewfinder photography and Live View photography:** To switch from viewfinder shooting to Live View mode, press the Live View button, labeled on the left in Figure 4-2 and shown in the margin. As soon as you press the button, you hear a clicking sound as the internal mirror that normally sends the image from the lens to the viewfinder flips up. Then the scene in front of the lens appears on the monitor, and you can no longer see anything in the viewfinder. Instead of the normal Shooting Settings screen, you see the Live View version, with symbols representing certain camera settings displayed over the live image, as shown in Figure 4-3. Don't panic if your screen doesn't show the same data — you can customize this display, as outlined two sections from here.

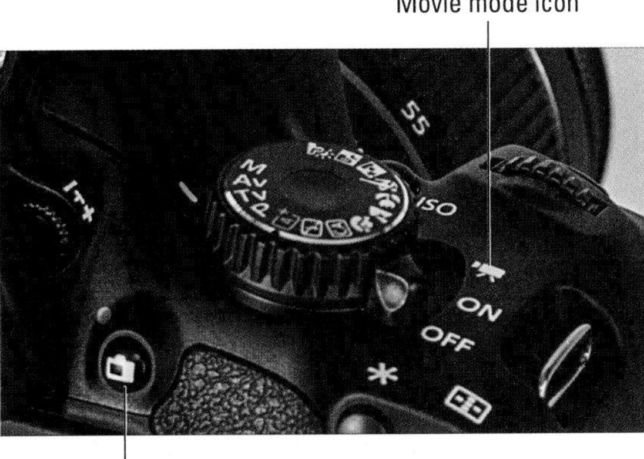

Figure 4-2: For still photography, press the Live View button to engage Live View; for movies, set the On/Off switch to the Movie position and then press the Live View button to start and stop recording.

Press the Live View button a second time to return to viewfinder photography. The camera also automatically shifts out of Live View mode if you move the Mode dial from a fully automatic mode to P, Tv, Av, or M mode (and vice versa) or if you select the HDR Backlight Control or Handheld Night Scene mode. Just press the Live View button to return to Live View mode.

- **Turning Movie mode on and off:** To set the camera to Movie mode, move the On/Off switch to the little movie-camera icon, labeled in Figure 4-2. Just as when you switch to Live View mode, the viewfinder blanks out, and the monitor displays the live scene along with some shooting data. See the later sections "Customizing the display" and "Customizing Movie Recording Settings" to sort out what you see on the screen. To exit Movie mode and return to viewfinder photography, rotate the On/Off switch to the On position.

  Note that when you change the Mode dial setting, the monitor may go dark and ask you to press the Live View button to redisplay the live scene even though the On/Off switch is still in the Movie position.

- **Shooting photos:** Most steps are the same as for viewfinder photography — frame, focus, and press the shutter button. Autofocusing methods, however, are quite different, as I explain in the upcoming treatise "Focusing in Live View and Movie Modes." You also have two options not available for viewfinder photography:

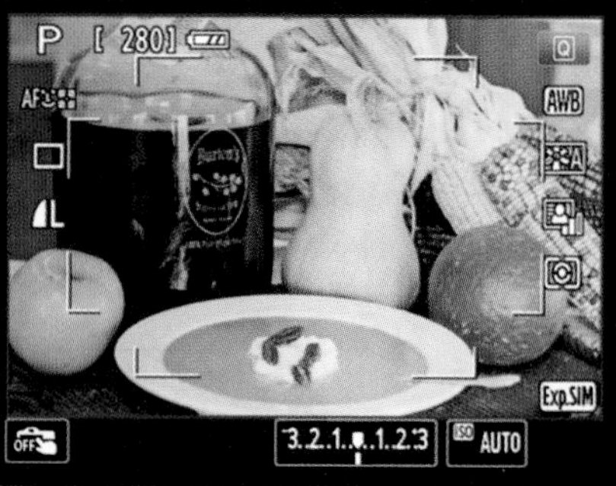

Figure 4-3: Picture data is superimposed over the live preview.

  - *Touch shutter and focusing:* You can focus and snap a picture simply by tapping the focus spot on the monitor. Or you can tell the camera to focus only and await your press of the shutter button to actually take the picture. See the previously mentioned focusing section along with "Using the touch shutter," also later in this chapter, for details.
  - *Aspect ratio options:* Through the Aspect Ratio option on the Live View menu, you can change the picture proportions from the normal 3:2 aspect ratio to 4:3, 16:9, or 1:1. "Setting the photo aspect ratio," later in this chapter, tells you more.

- **Recording movies:** After setting the On/Off switch to Movie, press the Live View button to start and stop recording. (The little red circle near the button — the universal movie-record symbol — reminds you of the button's function for movie capture.) Press again to stop recording.
- **Adjusting camera settings:** For the most part, you use the same techniques as for viewfinder photography, selecting options on the menus, using the Quick Control screen, and so on. I provide details throughout the chapter. But note these critical differences up front:
  - *The touchscreen Quick Control icon resides in the upper-right corner of the screen.* (Refer to Figure 4-3.) During viewfinder shooting, it's in the opposite corner. But during Live View photography, that corner is occupied by the Touch Shutter control, and during movie recording, it hosts a control related to continuous autofocusing. I have no idea why they didn't just put those symbols in the top-right corner and leave the Q icon in its normal position. They never ask me about these things.
  - *Certain buttons don't perform the same functions as during viewfinder photography.* For example, the cross keys don't access their normal options: AF mode, White Balance, and so on. Nor does the AF Point Selection button play a role in focusing as it does during viewfinder photography.

- *Non-Canon flash units don't fire in Live View mode.* You'll have to do business with Canon if you want to use flash for Live View photography.
- *Movie-recording options don't become available until you switch to Movie mode.* After you do, the Live View menu disappears, and Movie Menu 1 and Movie Menu 2 take its place. Those menus contain the major recording settings. You also can access several movie-recording settings via the Quick Control screen.
- *Exposure modes work differently in Movie mode.* The camera operates as it does in Scene Intelligent Auto mode for all Mode dial settings except P, Tv, Av, and M. Furthermore, you can control aperture and shutter speed only in M (manual exposure) mode. In P, Tv, and Av modes, the camera controls exposure, although you gain control over other settings, such as White Balance, that you don't have in Scene Intelligent Auto mode.

For specifics on adjusting settings for photography, see "Shooting Pictures in Live View Mode;" for help with adjusting movie settings, see "Customizing Movie Recording Settings," both later in this chapter.

- **Viewing photos and movies:** Press the Playback button to look at your images and movies. To switch back to shooting, give the Playback button another press or give the shutter button a half-press and then release it. Check out the end of this chapter to discover some special options available for movie playback; see Chapter 5 for details on playback features available for still photos and a couple that work for both photos and movies as well as for video snapshots, a specialty movie function that I cover in Chapter 11.

As you may have guessed from the fact that I devote a whole chapter to the topic of Live View photography and movie recording, these points comprise just the start of the story, however. The rest of the chapter goes into detail about all your photographic and movie-recording options. First, though, the next section provides some general safety tips to keep your camera happy when you use either feature.

Live View and Movie mode cautions

Be aware of the following safety rules when you use Live View and Movie modes:

- **Cover the viewfinder to prevent light from seeping into the camera and affecting exposure.** The camera ships with a little cover designed just for this purpose. In fact, it's conveniently attached to the camera strap. To install it, first remove the rubber eyecup that surrounds the viewfinder by sliding it up and out of the groove that holds it in place. Then slide the cover down into the groove and over the viewfinder, as shown in Figure 4-4. (Orient the cover so that the *Canon* label faces the viewfinder.)

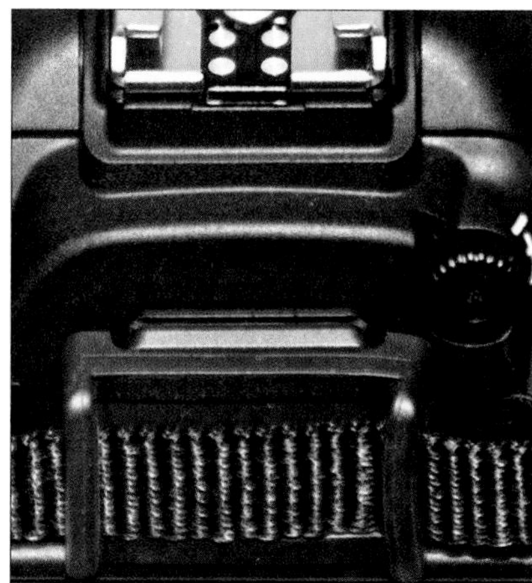

Figure 4-4: Use the rubber cover on the camera strap to prevent light from seeping through the viewfinder and messing up exposure metering.

- **Using Live View or Movie mode for an extended period can harm your pictures and the camera.** This damage can occur because using the monitor full-time causes the camera's innards to heat up more than usual, and that extra heat can create the right electronic conditions for *noise,* a defect that looks like speckles of sand.

  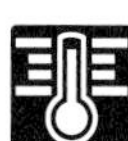

  Perhaps more critically, the increased temperatures can damage the camera. The symbol

  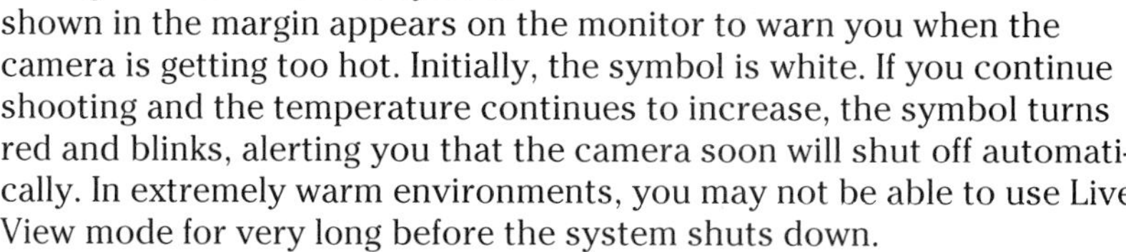

  shown in the margin appears on the monitor to warn you when the camera is getting too hot. Initially, the symbol is white. If you continue shooting and the temperature continues to increase, the symbol turns red and blinks, alerting you that the camera soon will shut off automatically. In extremely warm environments, you may not be able to use Live View mode for very long before the system shuts down.

- **Aiming the lens at the sun or other bright lights also can damage the camera.** Of course, you can cause problems doing this even during normal shooting, but the possibilities increase when you use Live View and Movie mode. You not only can harm the camera's internal components but also the monitor.

- **Live View and Movie modes put additional strain on the camera battery.** The monitor is a big consumer of battery juice, so keep an eye on the battery-level icon to avoid running out of power at a critical moment.

  By default, the camera powers down automatically after 30 seconds of inactivity. You can adjust this automatic shutdown timing via the Auto Power Off option on Setup Menu 2. If you set that menu option to disable, the camera turns the monitor off anyway after 30 minutes of inactivity (the camera remains on, however).

- **The risk of camera shake during handheld shots is increased.** When you use the viewfinder, you can help steady the camera by bracing it against your face. But when you compose shots using the monitor, you have to hold the camera away from your body to view the screen, making it harder to keep the camera absolutely still. As Chapter 7 explains, any camera movement during the exposure can blur the shot, so using a tripod is the best course of action for Live View photography. The same is true for movie recording — unless you like that "jiggling frame" effect that seems to be all the rage with some Hollywood directors.

If you do handhold the camera, enabling Image Stabilization can compensate for a bit of camera shake; Chapter 1 discusses this feature. For still photos, also experiment with the Handheld Night Scene mode, covered in Chapter 3.

Because of these complications, I don't use Live View for still photography very often. Rather, I think of it as a special-purpose tool geared to situations where framing with the viewfinder is cumbersome. I find Live View most helpful for still-life, tabletop photography, especially in cases that require a lot of careful arrangement of the scene.

For example, I have a shooting table that's about waist-high. Normally, I put my camera on a tripod, come up with an initial layout of the objects I want to photograph, set up my lights, and then check the scene through the viewfinder. Then there's a period of refining the object placement, the lighting, and so on. If I'm shooting from a high angle, requiring the camera to be positioned above the table and pointing downward, I have to stand on my tiptoes or get a stepladder to check things out through the viewfinder between each compositional or lighting change. At lower angles, where the camera is tabletop height or below, I have to either bend over or kneel to look through the viewfinder, causing no end of later aches and pains to back and knees. With Live View, I can alleviate much of that bothersome routine (and pain) because I can adjust the articulating monitor so that I can see how things look no matter what the camera position.

Customizing the display

You can choose from a few different Live View and Movie mode display options, each of which adds different types of information to the screen. Here's a look at your decorating possibilities:

- **Press Info to change the amount and type of data displayed.** Figure 4-5 shows the screen as it appears in each of the four styles available for Live View photography when you use the P exposure mode. (Data varies according to your exposure mode, focusing mode, and other settings.) In Movie mode, some data changes to show movie-recording options instead of still-photography settings, and the upper-right display shown in Figure 4-5 is not available.

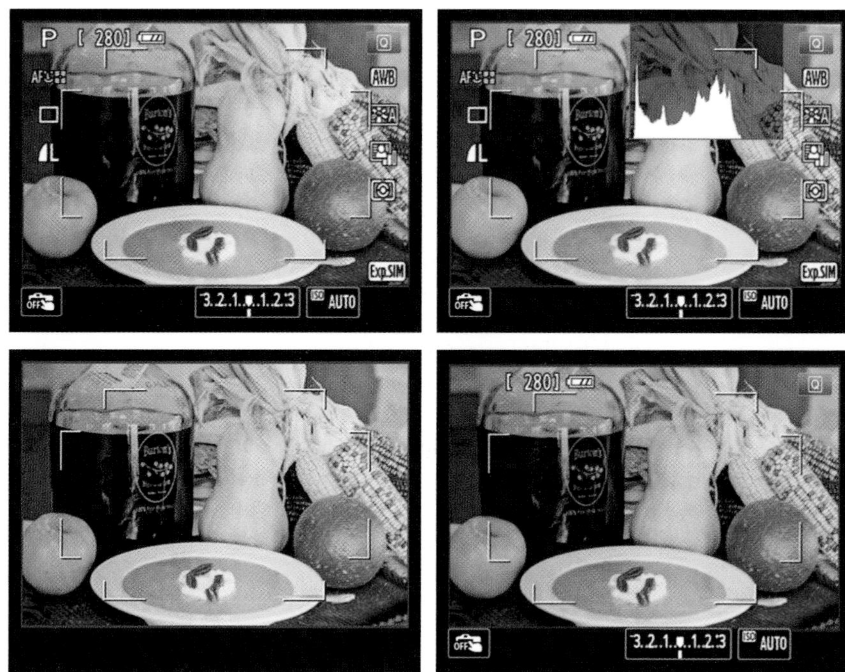

Figure 4-5: Press the Info button to cycle through the four Live View display styles.

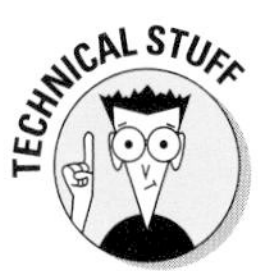

The chart in the upper-right corner of the top-right screen in Figure 4-5 is a *Brightness histogram,* which is a tool you can use to gauge whether your current settings will produce a good exposure — again, though, only for Live View photography. See the discussion on interpreting a Brightness histogram in Chapter 5 to find out how to make sense of what you see. But note that when you use flash, the histogram is dimmed; the histogram can't display accurate information because the final exposure will include light from the flash and not just the ambient lighting. The histogram also is dimmed if you use the Handheld Night Scene or HDR Backlight Control exposure modes or set the shutter speed to Bulb, an option available only in the M (manual) exposure mode. Chapter 7 has details on bulb shooting.

As for the other onscreen data, you can get an overview of the Live View symbols in the later section "Adjusting other Live View picture settings" and find out about the movie symbols in the section "Customizing Movie Recording Settings." The rectangular markings you see in each of the four examples in Figure 4-5 relate to autofocusing; see the next section for a primer in Live View and Movie mode autofocusing.

- **Display a grid:** To assist you with composition, the camera can display a grid on the monitor, as illustrated in Figure 4-6.

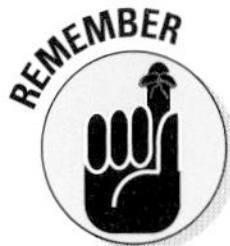

Where you turn the grid on depends on whether you're in Live View mode or Movie mode:

- *Live View mode:* Live View menu (left screen in Figure 4-7).
- *Movie mode:* Movie Menu 1 (right screen in Figure 4-7).

You can choose from two grid styles: Grid 1 gives you loosely spaced gridlines, as shown in Figure 4-6; Grid 2 offers a more tightly spaced grid.

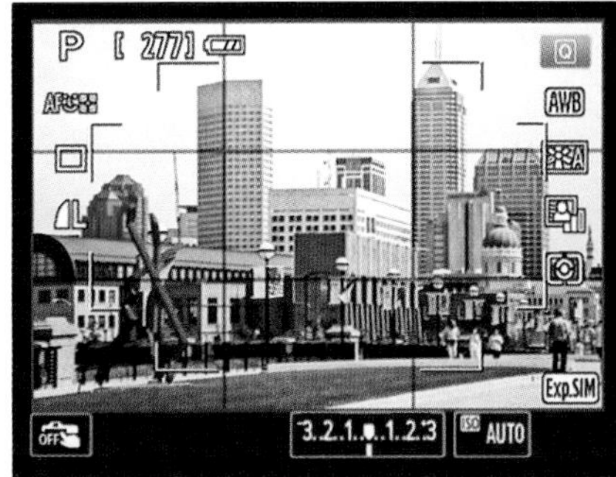

Figure 4-6: The grid is helpful for checking the alignment of objects in the scene.

- **Metering Timer:** By default, exposure information such as f-stop and shutter speed disappears from the display after 16 seconds if you don't press any camera buttons. If you want the exposure data to remain visible for a longer period, you can adjust the shutdown time, but only if the Mode dial is set to P, Tv, Av, or M. Again, the option lives on the Live View menu for still photography; in Movie mode, on Movie Menu 1. The metering mechanism uses battery power, so the shorter the cutoff time, the better.

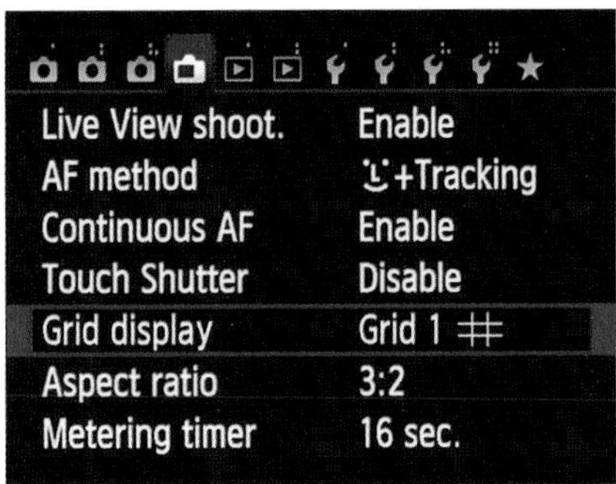

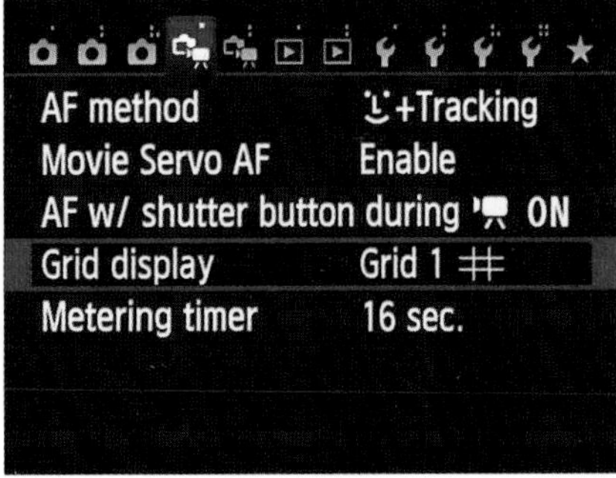

Figure 4-7: For still photography, adjust the grid display via the Live View menu (left); for Movie mode, via Movie Menu 1 (right).

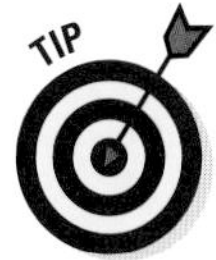

- **Viewing the display on a TV:** You can send the monitor signal to a television via a standard A/V cable or an HDMI cable (both must be purchased separately) for shooting as well as for playback. Chapter 5 provides help with connecting the camera to a TV. Keep in mind, though, that you lose all touch screen operations when the camera is tethered to a TV or monitor; you must use camera buttons to control things.

  In addition, you can connect the camera to your computer with the supplied USB cable and then use the Canon EOS Utility software (provided in your camera box) to operate the camera remotely. You can even see the Live View preview on your computer monitor. See the software manual, provided on one of the two CDs in the camera box, for more information. You might want to take advantage of this feature when your presence near the camera might be disruptive, as when shooting wildlife, or dangerous, as when your kid asks you to record a movie of the class science experiment.

Focusing in Live View and Movie Modes

Assuming that your lens supports autofocusing, you can choose from auto or manual focusing, just as you can with viewfinder photography. But both focusing methods involve some different options and techniques than viewfinder focusing, which I cover in Chapter 8.

For autofocusing, you can control a couple aspects of how the system works:

- **Continuous autofocusing:** By default, the camera initiates autofocusing as soon as you enable Live View or Movie mode. The next section explains the whys and wherefores of this feature.
- **Autofocus (AF) mode:** This option determines which part of the frame the camera uses to set focus and whether you choose that spot or let the camera make the call. Later sections in this chapter walk you through the steps of using each autofocus mode.

Having these options gives you lots of autofocus flexibility, but getting a handle on all of them takes a little time. The next sections detail each option; as you read through the text, have your camera handy so you can experiment with the settings to see which ones you like best. Following that, you can find details on manual focusing and a special option that enables you to magnify the live view display to ensure that focus is set correctly.

Disabling continuous autofocusing

Your camera is set by default to start autofocusing as soon as you engage Live View or Movie mode. You may be able to see the picture going in and out of focus and hear the autofocus motor as the camera searches for a focusing target. For still photography, the idea is to have the camera find a preliminary focusing target so that when you press the shutter button halfway to set the final focusing distance, the camera can lock focus more quickly. For movies, continuous autofocusing is designed to track your subject as it moves through the frame during the recording.

This feature, called Continuous AF (autofocus) for Live View mode and Movie Servo AF for Movie mode, presents some downsides:

- **When recording movies with sound, the internal microphone may pick up the noise of the autofocus motor.** The solution is to use an external microphone and place it far enough from the camera that it doesn't pick up the focusing sounds or to disable continuous autofocusing. Focusing with some lenses is quieter than with others — for example, the 18–135mm STM kit lens, created especially for smooth zooming and quieter operation when shooting movies, is better in this regard than the 18–55mm kit lens.
- **Continuous autofocusing may falter in some scenarios.** The focusing system can have trouble locking in on subjects moving very quickly toward or away from the lens as well as on subjects that are very close to the lens.

  In addition, during movie recording, zooming the lens may cause continuous autofocusing to be temporarily interrupted. And if your subject moves toward or away from you or you pan the camera (move it up, down, right or left to follow the subject), the subject may momentarily appear larger or smaller in the frame. Using slower camera movements can result in smoother, less obvious focus transitions.
- **This feature is a power hog.** The other disadvantage of continuous autofocusing is that all that activity by the autofocusing motor is a big drain on the camera battery. So if you plan to use continuous autofocus a lot, you may want to invest in a spare battery so you don't run out of battery juice during a shoot.
- **For Live View photography, you can't use Quick mode autofocusing with continuous autofocusing.** As its name implies, Quick mode is the fastest of the camera's Live View autofocusing options. Unfortunately, if you set the AF mode to Quick, the camera disables continuous autofocusing automatically. It's re-enabled when you switch to one of the other AF modes. (Quick mode AF isn't available for movie recording.)
- **To switch to manual focusing, you must first turn the camera off if continuous autofocusing is in progress.** Don't simply move the lens switch to the MF position — turn the camera off, set the lens switch, and then the camera on again. If you make this change when continuous autofocusing is in progress, you may damage the camera or the lens.

For these reasons, I typically disable continuous autofocusing for still photography. For shots in which my subject may be moving — making continuous focus tracking a plus — I prefer to go back to viewfinder photography because it offers faster focus tracking with less battery drain. (Chapter 8 has details on viewfinder autofocusing.)

How you enable or disable continuous autofocusing depends on whether you're shooting still photos or shooting movies:

- **Live View photography:** Turn the feature on and off via the Continuous AF option on the Live View menu, as shown in Figure 4-8. Remember, when Quick mode autofocus is in force, this option is unavailable and so is dimmed in the menu.

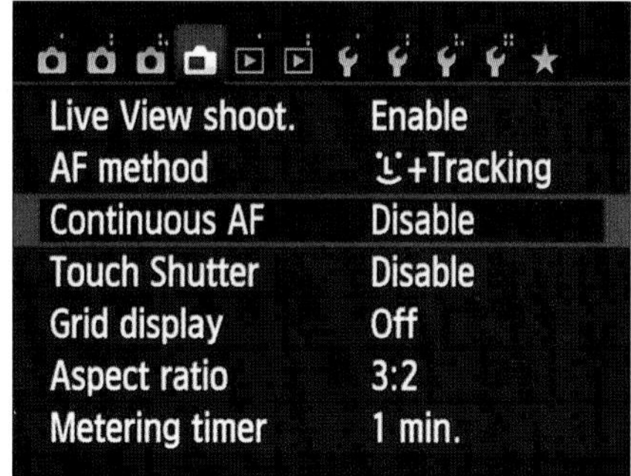

Figure 4-8: You can save battery power by turning off continuous autofocusing.

TIP

When continuous autofocusing is enabled, you lock focus by pressing and holding the shutter button halfway down. When you release the button, continuous autofocusing begins anew. You also can modify the AE Lock button so that it temporarily stops continuous autofocusing when pressed. To use this option, set Custom Function 6 to AF/AF Lock no AE Lock. I suggest that you bypass this option until you're fully familiar with your camera, though, because my instructions elsewhere assume that you haven't made this change to the button's function.

- **Movie mode:** In Movie mode, you can turn off Movie Servo AF via Movie Menu 1, as shown on the left in Figure 4-9. You also can turn the feature off by tapping the touch-screen icon labeled on the right in the figure. A green dot on the icon means the feature is enabled; tap the icon to hide the dot and turn off continuous autofocusing. Note that if you disable the feature via the menu, the screen icon no longer appears.

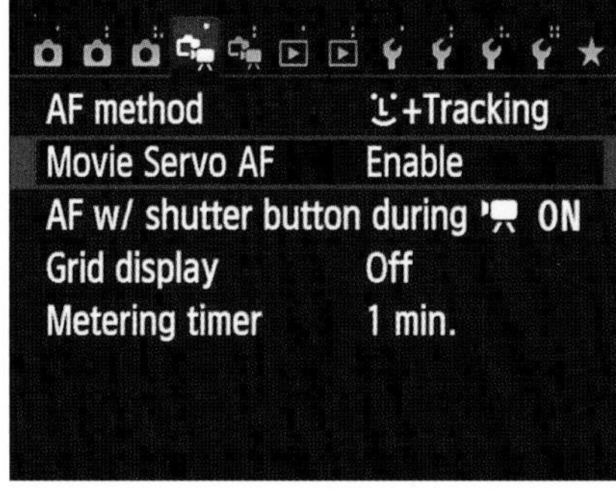

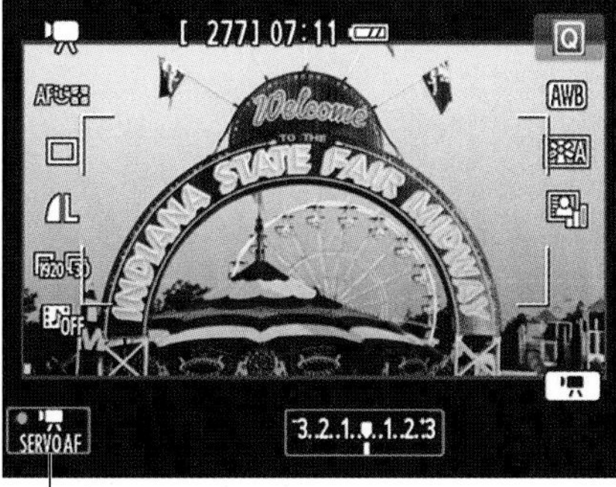

Movie Servo AF on/off icon

Figure 4-9: In Movie mode, the feature is called Movie Servo AF and can be disabled via Movie Menu 1 (left) or the touch screen (right).

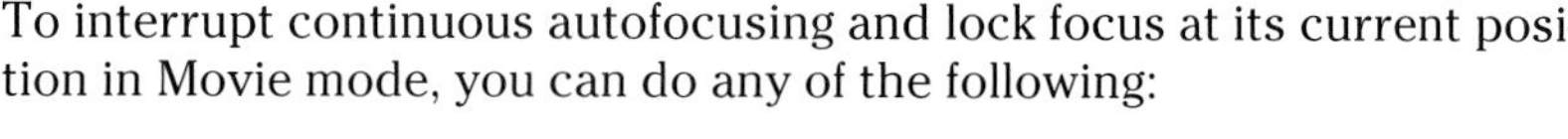

To interrupt continuous autofocusing and lock focus at its current position in Movie mode, you can do any of the following:

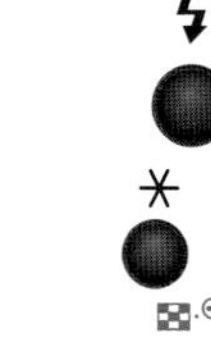

- *Tap the Movie Servo AF screen icon.* Tap again to restart continous autofocusing.
- *Press the Flash button.* Press again to go back to continuous autofocusing.
- *Press and hold the AE Lock button.* This option, again, requires setting Custom Function 6 to the AF/AF Lock no AE Lock setting.

Your second icon tap or button press resumes continuous autofocusing.

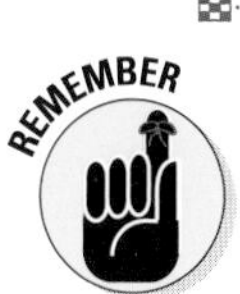

You also can set focus by pressing the shutter button halfway. If you turn off Movie Servo AF, you then can release the shutter button, and focus will remain locked at the current focus distance. Otherwise, continuous autofocusing begins again when you release the shutter button.

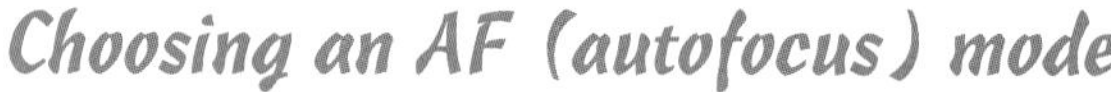

Choosing an AF (autofocus) mode

For autofocusing, the AF (autofocus) mode setting determines the focusing method, as it does for viewfinder shooting. But the AF mode options for Live View and Movie autofocusing work differently from the normal ones, which I cover in Chapter 8. For Live View photography, you get all four of the following options, represented on the display by the icons you see in the margins. For Movie mode, you lose the Quick mode option.

Upcoming sections detail the AF modes; here's a quick introduction to each one:

- **Face+Tracking:** This setting is the default. If the camera detects a face, it automatically focuses on that face. When no faces are detected, the camera instead uses the FlexiZone-Multi autofocusing option.
- **FlexiZone-Multi:** The camera automatically selects the focusing point, usually locking onto the closest object. In the P, Tv, Av, and M modes, you can limit the camera's choice of focusing areas by selecting one of several focus zones spread throughout the frame.
- **FlexiZone-Single:** You specify which of the available focusing points the camera should use to establish focus.
- **Quick mode:** In this mode, the camera uses the same nine-point autofocusing system as it does for viewfinder photography. As its name implies, Quick mode offers the fastest autofocusing of the Live View AF options. The downside to Quick mode is that it blanks out the Live View display temporarily as it sets focus, which can be a little disconcerting if you're not expecting it to happen. And, as mentioned a few paragraphs ago, it's not available for movie recording.

Even with Quick mode, autofocusing is slower than when you use the viewfinder to compose your pictures. The difference has to do with how the camera performs the focusing operation, a technical detail not worth exploring here. Just know that for fastest autofocusing, shift out of Live View mode and go with the viewfinder.

When you do you choose Live View mode or set the camera to Movie mode, an icon representing the current AF mode appears in the upper-left corner of the display, as shown on the left in Figure 4-10.

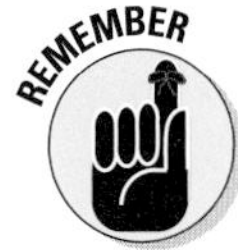

Don't see the AF icon? Press Info to cycle through the various Live View display modes until one appears. What other data shows up depends both on the display mode and your exposure mode; the screens in Figure 4-10 show the monitor as it appears in the P (programmed autoexposure) mode with all data but the histogram displayed — that is, the default display mode.

To change the AF mode setting, you can't press the AF button (right cross key) as you can during viewfinder shooting. Instead, use either of these methods:

- **Quick Control screen:** This option is fastest. Press the Quick Control button or tap the Q icon, also highlighted in Figure 4-10. Then highlight the icon that represents the focusing method, as shown on the right in the figure. You can either tap the icon or use the up/down arrow keys to highlight it. Then rotate the Main dial to cycle through the settings or just tap the icon representing the mode you want to use (the icons are at the bottom of the screen).

  Note that the figure on the right shows the screen as it appears during Live View photography; you don't see the fourth option (Quick mode AF) in Movie mode. To exit the Quick Control screen, tap the Return arrow or press the Quick Control button. To change another setting, tap its icon instead.

- **Menus:** For still photography, chose the AF mode via the Live View menu, as shown on the left in Figure 4-11. For Movie recording, look for the option on Movie Menu 1, as shown on the right.

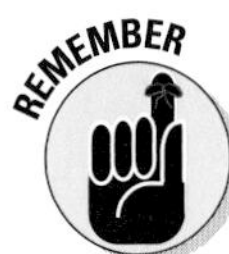

Your chosen AF mode remains in force until you change it, even if you turn the camera off, change exposure modes, or do some viewfinder shooting before your next Live View or movie-recording session.

Face+Tracking autofocusing

AF

In this mode, which is the default for both still photography and movie recording, the camera searches for faces in the frame. If it finds one, it displays a white focus frame over the face, as shown in Figure 4-12.

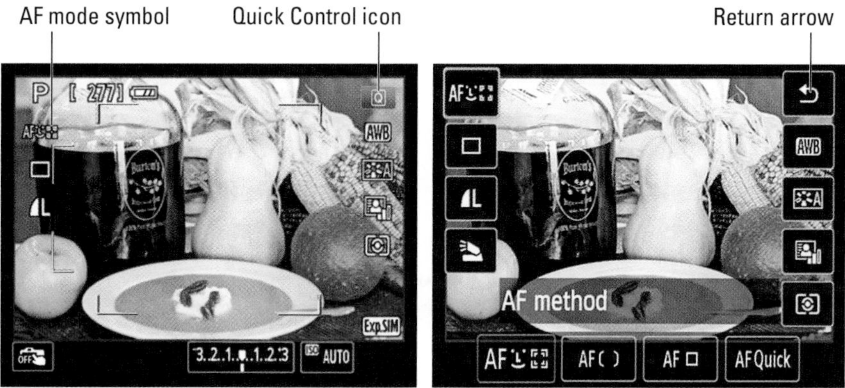

Figure 4-10: In Quick Control mode, highlight the AF icon and then rotate the Main dial to change the setting.

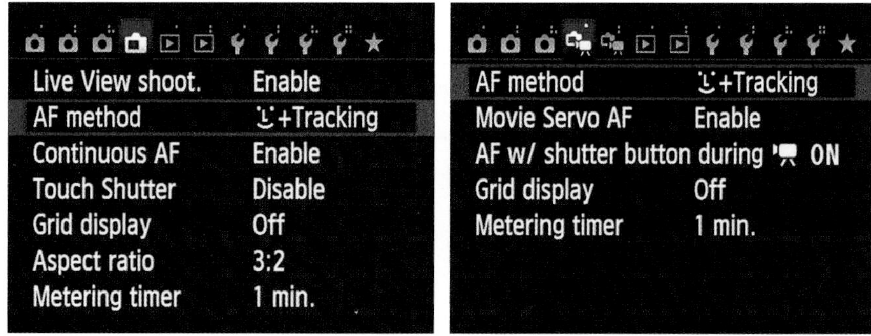

Figure 4-11: You also can adjust the autofocusing method via the Live View menu for still photos (left) or via Movie Menu 1 for movie recording (right).

In a group shot where more than once face is recognized by the camera, you see arrows on either side of the focus frame. To choose a different face as the focusing target, either press the left/right cross keys or just tap the face.

If continuous autofocusing is enabled, the camera automatically focuses on the selected frame. To lock focus on the face, press and hold the shutter button halfway down. When focus is locked, the focus frame turns green and the camera emits a tiny beep. (You can disable the sound effect via the Beep option on Shooting Menu 1.) If focus isn't successful, the focus frame turns orange.

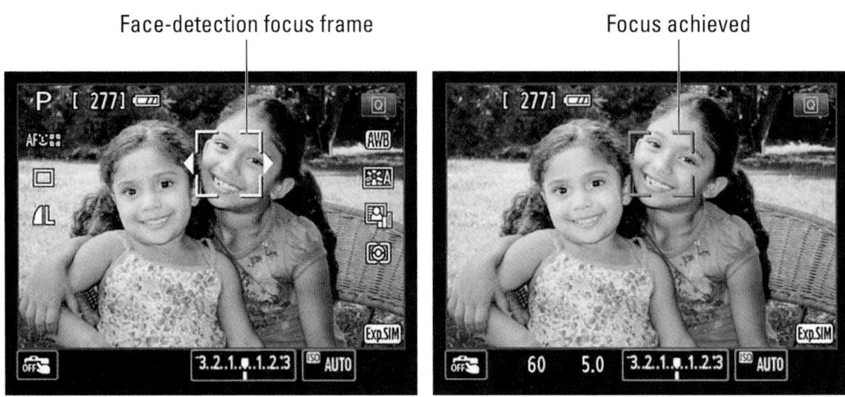

Figure 4-12: The white frame represents the face chosen for focusing; the frame turns green when focus is achieved.

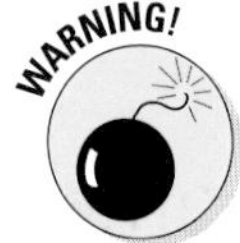

When the conditions are *just right* in terms of lighting, composition, and phase of the moon, this setup works fairly well. However, it has a number of "issues":

- People must be facing the camera to be detected — the feature is based on the camera recognizing the pattern created by the eyes, nose, and mouth. So if you're shooting the subject in profile, don't expect face detection to work.
- The camera may mistakenly focus on an object that has a similar shape, color, and contrast to a face.
- Face detection sometimes gets tripped up if the face isn't just the right size with respect to the background, is tilted at an angle, is too bright or dark, or partly obscured.
- Autofocusing isn't possible when a subject is very close to the edge of the frame. The camera alerts you to this issue by displaying a gray frame instead of a white one over your subject. You can always temporarily reframe to put the subject within the acceptable autofocus area, press and hold the shutter button halfway to lock focus, and then reframe to your desired composition.

If the camera can't detect a face, it automatically shifts the AF mode to FlexiZone-Multi autofocusing, in which the focus point is automatically selected by default. See the next section for details on that AF mode.

FlexiZone-Multi autofocusing

By default, this focusing mode is based on invisible focus points spread throughout the area indicated by the framing marks you see in Figure 4-13.

Framing marks

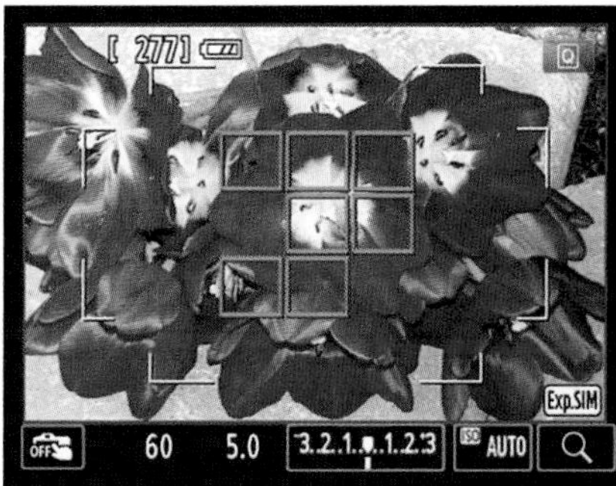

Figure 4-13: In fully automatic exposure modes, compose your shot so your subject is within these framing marks.

In the fully automated exposure modes, you don't have any control over which of the points the camera uses to establish focus. Typically, focus is set on the object closest to the camera. When you press the shutter button halfway, one or more focus points turns green, as shown on the right in the figure, to indicate the areas of the frame that were used to establish focus. You also hear a tiny beep indicating that focus is set.

When you set the mode dial to P, Tv, Av, or M, you can break the focusing area into several smaller zones — thus, *FlexiZone* focusing — and limit the camera to finding its focusing point within one of those zones.

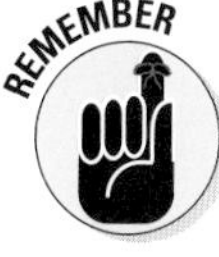

Exactly how many focusing points and zones are available depends on the following factors:

- **Live View photography:** The key here is the Aspect Ratio setting on the Live View menu. By default, the picture aspect ratio is 3:2 and you get 31 focusing points and nine focus zones. But if you change the aspect ratio, things change:
  - *3:4 and 1:1 aspect ratios:* 25 focus points and 9 zones
  - *16:9 aspect ratio:* 21 focus points and 3 zones
- **Movie mode:** You get 21 focus points and 3 zones *unless* the Movie Recording Size option (Movie Menu 2) is set to 640 x 480, in which case you get 25 points and 9 zones.

Yeah, I hear you — this stuff gets a little deep in the weeds. But don't worry too much about how many points and zones are available — it's not like you can control them, anyway — and just remember the techniques you use to select a zone, which are pretty easy:

- **Switch from automatic focus point selection to zone selection:** First, remember to set the Mode dial to P, Tv, Av, or M. Then press the Set button or the Erase button (the blue trash-can button). As soon as you press either button, you see a large rectangle indicating the current focus zone, as shown in Figure 4-14. An icon telling you that you're in zone mode also appears on the screen, as labeled in the figure.

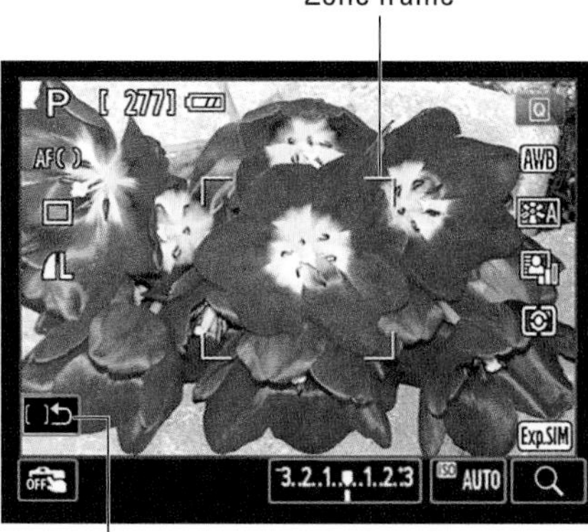

Figure 4-14: Press the Set button to toggle to zone focusing and then tap an area of the frame to locate the zone frame.

- **Select the focus zone:** Tap the subject to display a frame that represents the closest zone frame. Or use the cross keys to move the zone frame.

- **Quickly select the center zone:** Press the Set button or the Erase button again.
- **Switch back to automatic focus selection:** Tap the icon labeled Exit Zone Mode in Figure 4-14 or press the Set or Erase button one more time.

The focusing technique for zone focusing is the same as for automatic selection: If continuous autofocusing is enabled, the camera hunts for its focus point in the zone frame. If you press and hold the shutter button halfway, the frame turns green and you hear the focus beep, indicating that focus is locked as long as you keep the shutter button pressed halfway.

FlexiZone-Single autofocusing

Even more flexible than FlexiZone-Multi's zone mode, this AF mode lets you select a specific autofocus point. Not only is this autofocusing method available in any exposure mode, it's easy to use.

You see a single, small focus frame at the center of the screen, as shown on the left in Figure 4-15. The figure shows how the frame looks in Live View mode; in Movie mode, it's a little larger. Either way, the next step is to move the frame over your subject. For example, I moved the frame over the soup garnish in the right screen in the figure. You can either use the cross keys to adjust the frame position or, if the touch screen is enabled, just tap the screen to place the frame. (Enable the touch capability via Setup Menu 3.)

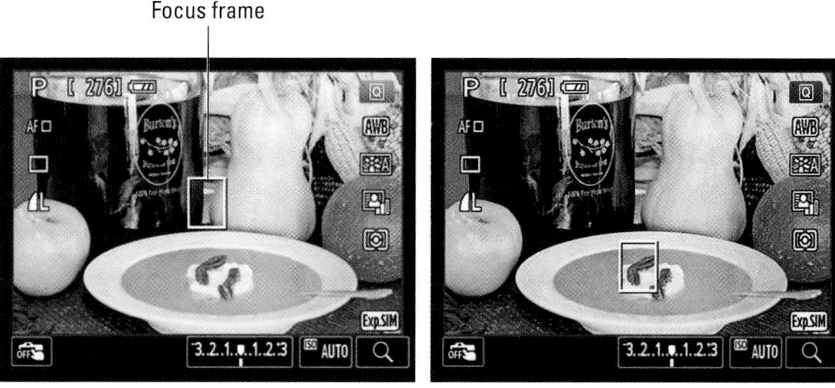

Figure 4-15: In FlexiZone-Single mode, use the cross keys or tap the screen to move the focus frame over your subject.

As in FlexiZone-Multi mode, you can press the Set button or Erase (trash can) button to immediately move the focus frame back to the center of the frame.

Focusing works the same as in the AF methods already discussed: Press the shutter button halfway to set and lock focus. The focus frame turns green when focus is achieved. The camera also emits a beep, unless you turned off that function (through the Beep option on Shooting Menu 1). If the camera can't focus on the spot you selected, the frame turns orange.

If continuous autofocusing is enabled, the camera bases focus on the focus frame and adjusts focus as needed up to the time you press the shutter button halfway to lock focus.

Quick mode autofocusing

As its name implies, Quick mode offers the fastest autofocusing during Live View or movie shooting. It's based on the same nine-point focusing grid used for viewfinder photography, so may feel more familiar to you than the other AF methods. Also, Canon recommends that you use this mode when shooting with certain EF lenses; as I write this, the list of affected lenses appears on page 159 of the English version of the camera manual. With those lenses, the other autofocus modes can be problematic.

So why isn't Quick mode the default setting? Well, it's a little more complex to use. In addition, the monitor display goes dark during the time the camera is focusing, which can throw off the unsuspecting photographer. Finally, you can't use Quick mode for movie shooting — it's only for still photography. Nor is continuous autofocusing, explained earlier in this chapter, available for Quick mode.

If those limitations don't affect you, here's what you need to know about using Quick mode. After you select this AF mode, rectangles representing the nine autofocus points appear in the center of the screen, as shown on the left in Figure 4-16.

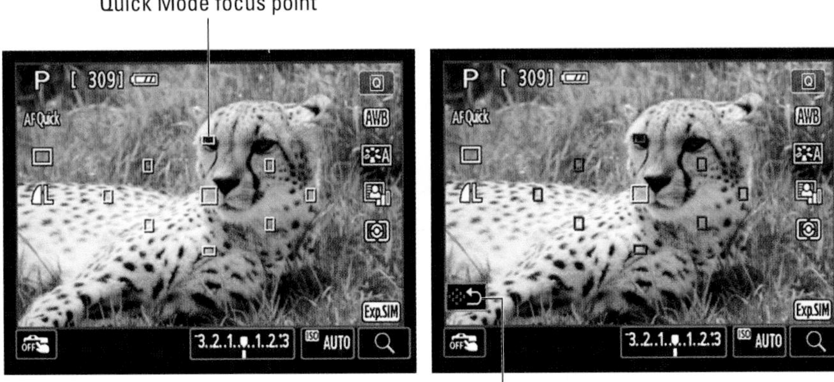

Figure 4-16: In Quick AF mode, the small rectangles represent autofocus points.

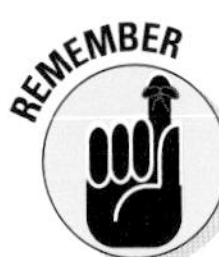
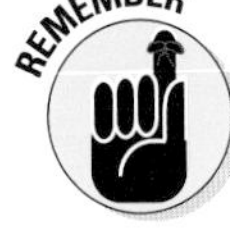

In Scene Intelligent Auto, Flash Off, Creative Auto, and the scene modes (Portrait, Landscape, and so on), the camera automatically selects which of the nine points to use when focusing. Typically, focus is established on the closest object. In P, Tv, Av, or M exposure mode, you can stick with automatic focus point selection or choose one of the nine points. Use these techniques to take advantage of these options:

- **Switch from auto to manual point selection:** Do any of the following:
  - *Press the Set button.*
  - *Press the Erase button.*
  - *Tap the point you want to use for focusing.*

  The selected point appears white; the other points are dimmed. For example, on the right screen in Figure 4-16, the center point is selected.
- **Selecting a focus point:** After switching to manual point selection, use the cross keys to highlight the focus point you want to use. You also can simply tap the point, assuming that touch screen operation is enabled (Setup Menu 3).

You can press the Set or Erase button to quickly select the center focus point (although just tapping it is just as fast).

- **Return to automatic point selection:** Tap the little return icon labeled on the right in Figure 4-16. Or press the Set or Erase button. (You need to press twice if any point but the center point is selected because your first button press selects that center point.)

Regardless of whether you use automatic or single point selection, set focus by pressing and holding the shutter button halfway down. The monitor turns off and the autofocusing mechanism kicks into gear. (It may sound as though the camera took the picture, but don't worry — that isn't actually happening.) When focus is achieved, the camera beeps, the Live View display reappears, and, in auto selection mode one or more of the focus points appears green to tell you which areas of the frame are in focus. For single point selection, just your chosen point turns green. Focus remains locked as long as you keep the shutter button pressed halfway; press the button the rest of the way to take the picture.

If the camera can't find a focusing target, the focus point (or points) turn orange and blink. Try using manual focusing, explained next, or getting a little farther away from your subject — you may be so close that you're exceeding the minimum focusing distance of the lens.

Manual focusing

Manual focusing is the easiest of the Live View focusing options — and in most cases, it's faster, too. First, ensure that the continuous autofocusing system isn't engaged. You can turn the option off via the Continuous AF option on the Live View menu or, for Movie mode, via the Movie Servo AF option on Movie Menu 1.

Then simply set the lens switch to the MF position if you're using one of the kit lenses or a similarly featured lens and twist the lens focusing ring to bring the scene into focus. On the monitor display, the letters MF take the place of the usual AF mode icon.

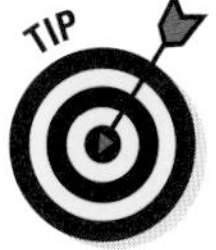

I find that most people who shy away from manual focusing do so because they don't trust their eyes to judge focus. But thanks to a feature that enables you to magnify the Live View preview, you can feel more confident in your manual focusing skills. See the next section for details.

Zooming in for a focus check

Here's a cool focusing feature not available during viewfinder photography: Whether you're focusing manually or using autofocus, you can magnify the Live View display to ensure that focus is accurate.

This trick works during manual focusing or in any AF mode except Face+Tracking mode (that's the default AF mode, by the way). After setting focus, follow these steps to magnify the display:

1. **Press the AF Point Selection button or tap the Zoom icon in the lower right corner of the screen (refer to Figure 4-17).**

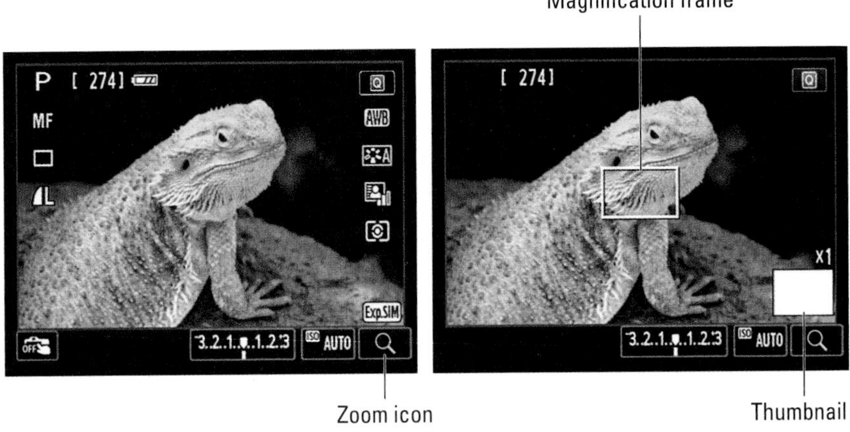

Figure 4-17: Tap the Zoom symbol (left) to switch to magnified view (right).

Note that the button has a blue label that shows a magnifying glass with a plus sign — the universal symbol for zoom in. (During playback, you press the same button to magnify the playback display.)

After you press the button or tap the icon, most of the shooting data disappears and you see a magnification frame somewhere on the screen plus a white box in the lower right corner, as shown on the right in Figure 4-17. The white rectangle is a thumbnail representing the entire image area.

Where the magnifying rectangle appears depends on your focusing mode. For manual focus and FlexiZone Multi, it's at the center of the frame, as shown in the figure, or the center of the selected zone, if you used zone selection. But for FlexiZone-Single or Quick mode when you use manual-point selection, the frame appears over the selected focus point.

The value x1 appears above the thumbnail to show you that you're viewing the image at its regular size (no magnification).

2. **Move the focusing frame over your subject if needed.**

   You can either tap the screen or use the cross keys to position the frame. For example, on the left side of Figure 4-18, I moved the frame over the eye.

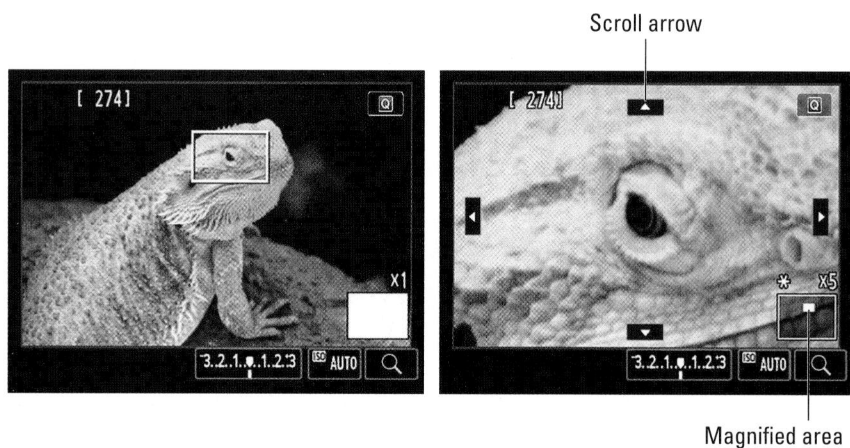

Figure 4-18: Tap the screen to position the frame (left); tap the scroll arrows to shift the magnified display (right).

3. **Press the AF Point Selection button or tap the Zoom icon again to magnify the display.**

   Your first press of the button displays a view that's magnified five times, as shown on the right in Figure 4-18. Now the thumbnail icon changes, and the tiny white rectangle indicates the area of the frame you're viewing. Additionally, little arrows appear on each side of the frame; I labeled these as scroll arrows in the figure.

   If needed, tap the scroll arrows (I labeled one in the figure) or press the cross keys to reposition the magnification frame.

   Press the AF Selection Point button or tap the Zoom icon again for a ten-times magnification.

4. **To exit magnified view, press the AF Point Selection button or tap the Magnify icon again.**

Pretty cool, yes? Just a couple of tips on using this feature:

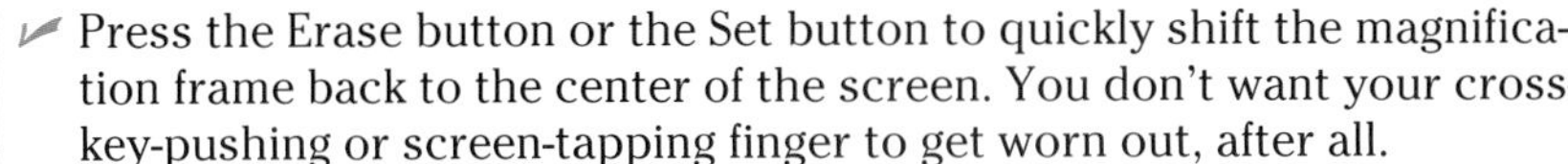

- Press the Erase button or the Set button to quickly shift the magnification frame back to the center of the screen. You don't want your cross-key-pushing or screen-tapping finger to get worn out, after all.

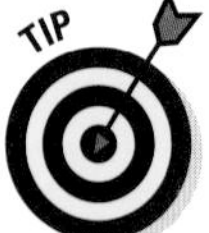

- Magnification is available only in Live View and Movie mode. But there's no reason you can't set initial focus in viewfinder mode, switch to Live View to check focus, and then shift back out of Live View mode to take the picture. Just make sure you don't change the camera position along the way, or the focusing distance may vary.
- If you use the FlexiZone-Single AF mode or Quick Mode, you can press the shutter button halfway to set focus while in magnified view.
- Be sure to exit magnified view before you actually take the picture. Otherwise exposure may be off. However, if you *do* take the picture in magnified view, the entire frame is captured — not just the area currently displayed on the monitor.

Shooting Pictures in Live View Mode

After sorting out the focusing rigmarole, understanding the rest of the options involved in Live View photography are a piece of cake. The next two sections explain one Live-View only picture setting — Aspect Ratio — and show you how to adjust other picture settings in Live View mode. Then I walk you through the process of actually taking a picture in Live View mode. (Finally, you say!)

Setting the photo aspect ratio

When you shoot with the viewfinder, the camera takes photos with a traditional 3:2 *aspect ratio* (the relationship of a photo's width to its height). But in Live View mode, you can choose a different aspect ratio if you shoot in the P, Tv, Av, or M exposure modes. Select one of the following aspect ratios from the Live View menu, as shown in Figure 4-19:

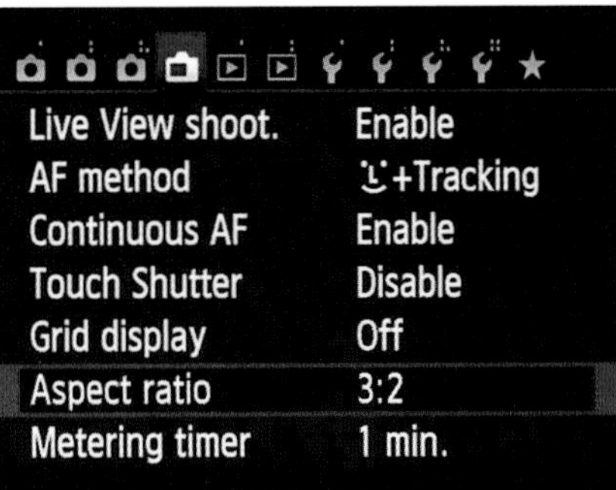

Figure 4-19: When you use Live View in the advanced exposure modes, you can change the picture aspect ratio.

- **3:2:** The standard aspect ratio and the same as 35mm film (as well as a 4 x 6-inch print)
- **4:3:** The same aspect ratio as older televisions and computer monitors

- **16:9:** Uses the same aspect ratio as most new TVs and monitors
- **1:1:** Produces square photos

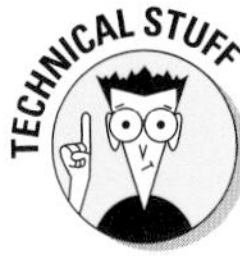

How many pixels your image contains depends on the aspect ratio; at the 3:2 setting, you get the full complement of pixels delivered by your chosen Image Quality setting. (Chapter 2 explains that setting.) Note, too, that if you set the Image Quality option to record JPEG pictures, the camera creates the different aspect ratios by cropping a 3:2 original — and the cropped data can't be recovered. Raw photos, although they appear cropped on the camera monitor, actually retain all the original data, which means you can change your mind about the aspect ratio later, when you process your Raw files. (Read about that subject in Chapter 6.)

At any setting except 3:2, the Live View display shows crop lines to indicate the area of the frame that will be captured at the chosen aspect ratio. For example, the crop lines in Figure 4-20 represent the 1:1 aspect ratio. (As I mentioned at the beginning of the chapter, your screen may look slightly different than mine because of the video-capture process used to record the monitor screens for this book.)

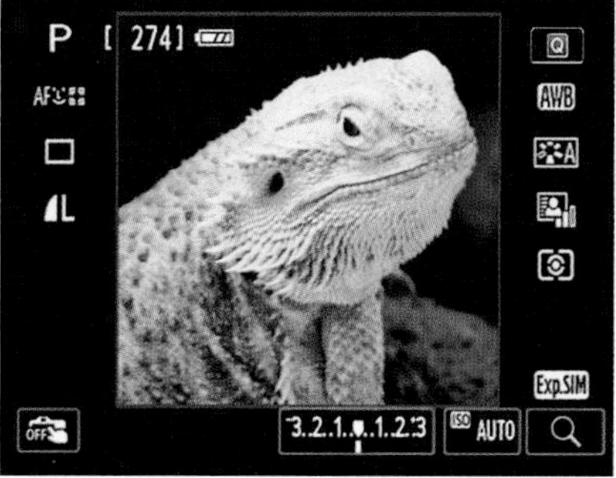

Figure 4-20: At aspect ratios other than 3:2, crop lines indicate the area of the frame that will be included in the photo.

Adjusting other Live View picture settings

Before I get into the details of adjusting picture settings, I want to point out the following limitations so you don't waste your time trying to figure out how to use the related features in Live View mode:

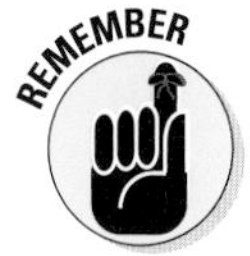

- **The cross keys don't access their normal picture-setting functions.** When Live View is active, you use the cross keys to perform certain focusing functions, as explained earlier in this chapter. Because they're used for this purpose, the cross keys no longer provide quick access to the White Balance, AF mode, Picture Style, and Drive mode settings. Instead, you change those settings via the Quick Control screen. You also can select the AF mode via the Live View menu and the Picture Style from Shooting Menu 2.
- **The AF Point Selection button also doesn't function as it does for viewfinder photography.** During viewfinder shooting, you use this button to toggle between automatic focus-point selection and single-point selection, as outlined in Chapter 8. But in Live View mode, the button magnifies the display so that you can check focus, as explained in the earlier section "Zooming in for a focus check."

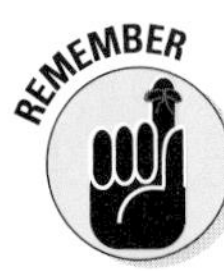

- **Certain Custom Functions are disabled or limited.** See the sidebar "Custom Functions and Live View/Movie modes," later in this chapter for details.
- **Some flash options are affected.** To wit:
  - *Flash Exposure Lock is disabled.* I cover this handy feature in Chapter 7.
  - *The modeling flash feature found on some Canon Speedlite flash units doesn't work.*
  - *Non-Canon flash units don't work in Live View mode.*
  - *The sound of the shutter release is different.* When you take a flash shot in Live View mode, the camera's shutter sound leads you to believe that two shots have been recorded; in reality, though, only one photo is captured.
- **Exposure is calculated differently in Continuous Drive mode.** You can use Continuous Drive mode (introduced in Chapter 2), but the camera uses the exposure settings chosen for the first frame for all images. And as with flash shots, you hear two shutter sounds for the first frame in the continuous sequence.

Now that you know what you can't do, here's what you *can* do. First, when Live View is enabled, you can set the display to reveal many of the same picture settings that normally appear on the Shooting Settings screen — and then some. Figure 4-21 shows screen as it appears when you shoot in the P, Tv, Av, or M modes and display the maximum shooting data. (This mode is the default; press the Info button to switch from that display to one of the three other display styles, all illustrated in Figure 4-5.)

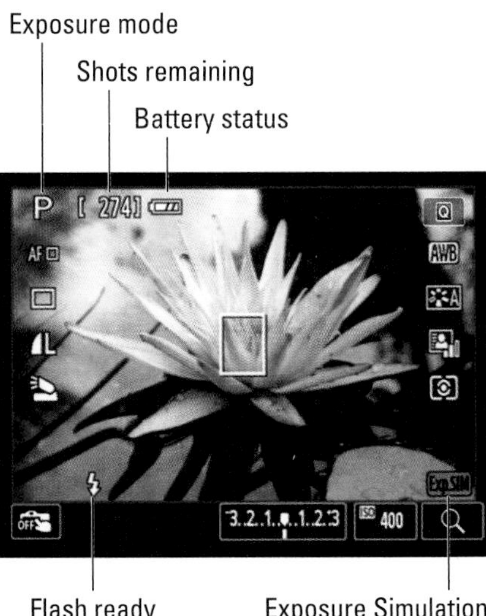

Figure 4-21: Symbols representing the current picture settings appear on the Live View display.

The onscreen symbols break down into three categories: Information only symbols; settings that you can adjust via the Quick Control screen; and options you can access by tapping the touch screen. Here's how things shake out when you use the display mode shown in Figure 4-20. Again, the screen shows settings available for the advanced exposure modes; when you shoot in the fully automatic or Creative Auto modes, less data appears onscreen because you can control fewer picture settings.

- **Information only data:** Labeled in Figure 4-21, this data includes
  - *Exposure mode:* For the figure, the P (programmed autoexposure) mode was in force. When you shoot in the Scene Intelligent Auto mode (the green A on your camera dial), an icon representing the type of scene the camera detected appears along with the exposure mode symbol. Your camera manual has a long list of icons that indicate what type of photo the camera detected — but if I were you, I wouldn't waste time memorizing them. If you have a certain scene type in mind, you're better off choosing a scene mode or, better yet, stepping up to the P, Tv, Av, or M exposure modes so that you can control all the picture characteristics.
  - *Battery status:* A full battery icon means the battery is good to go. Remember that Live View shooting depletes the battery faster than normal shooting, so keep an eye on that status icon.
  - *Flash ready symbol:* If the flash is raised, you see the little lightning bolt symbol, as in the figure, when the flash is charged and ready to fire.
  - *Exp. Sim:* In the lower-right corner, you also see an Exp Sim symbol, which stands for Exposure Simulation. If the symbol blinks or is dimmed, the camera can't provide an accurate exposure preview, which can occur if the ambient light is either very bright or very dim. Exposure Simulation is also disabled when you use flash in Live View mode because the camera can't simulate how the flash light will affect the exposure. A white Exp Sim symbol means that what you see on screen will be close to the final exposure.
  - *AEB:* This symbol appears to the left of the Exp Sim symbol when you enable automatic exposure bracketing (AEB), an exposure tool covered in Chapter 7.
  - *FEB:* This symbol appears next to the Exp Sim symbol if you enable flash exposure bracketing, a function possible only when you shoot with a compatible Canon Speedlite external flash. See the flash unit's manual for help with this option.
- **Touch-control settings:** A symbol surrounded by a rectangular border indicates that tapping that symbol produces a result. In the case of the Q icon in the upper right corner, of course, a tap shifts the screen to Quick Control mode. But during Live View shooting, you also can tap to adjust the following settings, labeled in Figure 4-22:

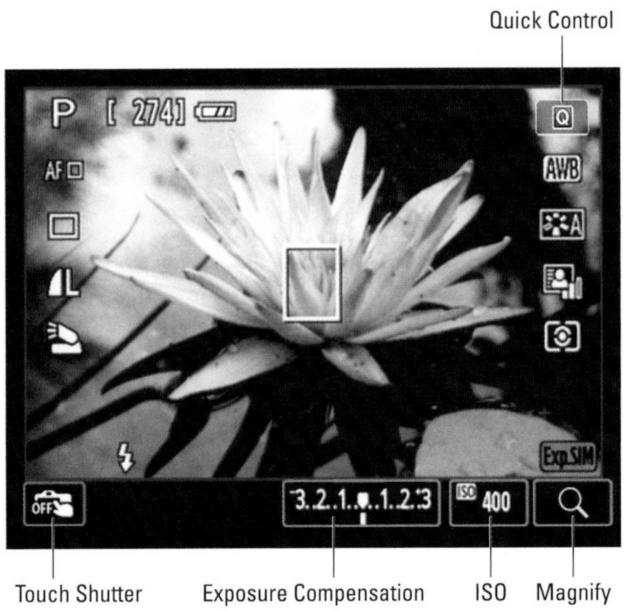

Figure 4-22: A border around a symbol indicates a tappable function.

- *Touch shutter:* This feature enables you to focus the shot and release the shutter simply by tapping your subject on the monitor. When the option is disabled, the word Off appears with the symbol, as in Figure 4-23. Just tap the icon to toggle the feature on and off; see the upcoming section "Using the touch shutter" for details about using it. Make sure this feature is turned off if you want to use the touchscreen to select a focus point without triggering the shutter release.
- *Exposure Compensation:* In the P, Tv, and Av exposure modes, you can apply Exposure Compensation to force a brighter or darker picture than the camera's autoexposure brain thinks is appropriate. After tapping the meter, a scale appears atop the image; drag your finger along the scale to adjust the setting. Or tap the minus and plus signs underneath the scale to raise or lower image brightness a notch at a time. To exit the screen, tap the return arrow in the upper-right corner or press Set.

  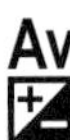

  You also can adjust this setting the old-fashioned way: Press and hold the Exposure Compensation button while rotating the Main dial. (I actually find this option easier.)

Either way, the monitor updates as you change the setting — to a certain limit. The image on the monitor becomes brighter or darker only up to shifts of +/– EV 3.0, even though you can select values as high as +5.0 and as low as –5.0. See Chapter 7 to get a primer on exposure compensation.

- *ISO:* Tapping this option enables you to adjust the ISO setting, an exposure control I cover in Chapter 7. Again, you see a scale on the monitor after you tap the option; this time, drag along the scale or tap the left and right arrows beneath it. Tap the return arrow to exit the screen.

Pressing the ISO button on top of the camera is another route to the same option. After pressing the button, tap the setting you want to use and then tap the return arrow or press Set.

- *Magnified display:* Except when using the Face+Tracking AF mode, you can tap the Zoom icon to magnify the display to verify focus. See the earlier section "Zooming in for a focus check" for details.

- **Settings adjustable via the Quick Control display:** Figure 4-23 labels the settings you can adjust in the P, Tv, Av, and M exposure modes; the following list describes each briefly. To switch to Quick Control mode, press the Quick Control button or tap the Q icon. You then shift to a display like the one shown on the left in Figure 4-24. Just tap a setting to select it and then rotate the Main dial to cycle through the various options or just tap the option you want to use.

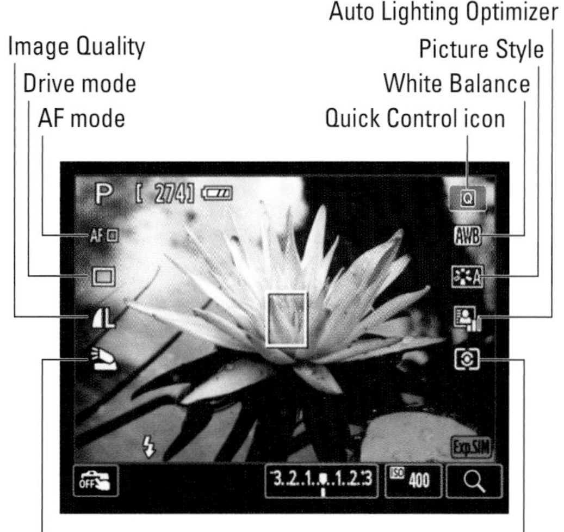

Figure 4-23: You can use the Quick Control screen to modify these settings.

With some settings, the monitor updates the preview to show you the result of your choice. For example, the right side of Figure 4-24 shows the change produced from shifting from the Automatic Picture Style setting to the Landscape setting. To exit Quick Control mode, tap the return arrow or press the Quick Control button.

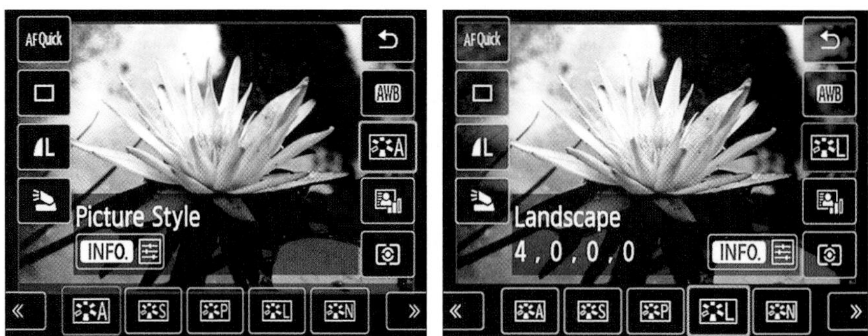

Figure 4-24: When you adjust some settings, such as Picture Style, the preview updates to show you the impact of the change.

- *AF mode:* The AF mode symbol appears regardless of whether you set your lens to manual or autofocus. When manual focus is active, the letters MF appear instead of the AF Mode symbol. See "Focusing in Live View and Movie Modes" for the full story on AF modes and manual focusing.
- *Drive mode:* The icon you see in the figures represents Single Drive mode, in which you capture one image for each press of the shutter button. See Chapter 2 for information about other Drive modes.
- *Image Quality:* This icon tells you the selected Image Quality setting, which Chapter 2 explains. The symbol shown in the figure represents the Large/Fine setting.
- *Built-in Flash Function:* Another of the flash features covered in Chapter 7, this one determines whether the flash fires normally or is used to control off-camera flash units. For normal operation, the icon should look like the one in the figures.
- *White Balance:* This setting, which you can explore in Chapter 8, determines how the camera compensates for the color of the light source that's illuminating your subject. The symbol in the figures represent the Automatic White Balance setting.
- *Picture Style:* Chapter also 8 details Picture Styles, which affect picture color, contrast, and sharpness. The symbol you see in Figure 4-23 and on the left in Figure 4-24 represents the Auto style; the one on the right in Figure 4-24 represents the Landscape style.
- *Auto Lighting Optimizer:* Check out Chapter 7 for help understanding this feature, which aims to accomplish what its name implies: optimize exposure to produce better image contrast. By default, the Standard setting is used; the symbol shown in the figures represent that setting.

In the P, Tv, and Av modes, experiment with disabling Auto Lighting Optimizer if your picture appears too bright even after you've requested a darker photo through the Exposure Compensation setting.

- *Metering mode:* Chapter 7 also explores this option, which determines which part of the frame the camera uses to calculate exposure. By default, the camera uses evaluative metering, which means that exposure is based on the entire frame. The symbol shown in the figures represents that setting.

A couple final tips about using the Quick Control screen in Live View mode:

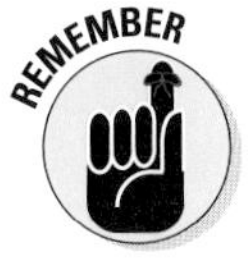

- After you choose some options, additional touch-control icons appear. For example, notice the Info icon on the screens in Figure 4-24. By tapping that icon or pressing the Info button, you can access settings that enable you to modify the characteristics of the current Picture Style. And if you choose the Self-Timer Continuous option for the Drive mode, you see an icon you can tap to set the number of shots you want to record. Again, remember that anything surrounded by a border is a touch-control setting.
- If you're not sure what setting an icon represents, just tap it. A text label appears to show you what option you selected.

Custom Functions and Live View/Movie modes

If you set the Mode dial to P, Tv, Av, or M, you gain access to Custom Functions, a group of advanced camera settings on Setup Menu 4. But when Live View is engaged or the camera is in Movie mode, certain features controlled via Custom Functions are disabled. Specifically:

- *Custom Function 2, ISO Expansion:* In Movie mode, this option is available only if the exposure mode is set to M. See Chapter 7 for more about this Custom Function.
- *Custom Function 4, AF-Assist Beam Firing:* The AF-Assist beam helps illuminate the scene to better enable the camera to find its focusing target. For Movie mode, the beam is disabled. For still photography, the beam is emitted from the built-in flash only if you set the AF mode to Quick. With certain external Canon Speedlite flash units, however, the beam fires normally with any AF mode. Chapter 10 explains this option.
- *Custom Function 5, Mirror Lock-up:* This function, detailed in Chapter 11, is off-limits for both still photography and movie recording.
- *Custom Function 7, Assign Set Button:* For still photography, you can't set the button to option 3 (LCD monitor on/off); for movie recording, that option plus option 2 (Flash exposure compensation) are off limits. Again, see Chapter 10 for details on giving the Set button a work assignment.
- *Custom Function 8, LCD Display When Power On:* This option is also unavailable during Live View and movie shooting. Chapter 10 explains how the option works during viewfinder photography.

Taking a shot in Live View mode

After you digest all the whys and wherefores of the Live View autofocus options and other details about this shooting feature, follow these steps to take a picture.

1. **Turn the Mode dial (on top of the camera) to select an exposure mode.**

   Remember, the exposure mode determines what picture settings you can control. Chapter 3 introduces you to the fully automatic modes and Creative Auto mode; Chapter 7 provides help with the advanced modes (P, Tv, Av, and M).

2. **Set the Live View Shoot option on the Live View menu to Enable.**

   It's set to that option by default, but double-check just in case.

3. **Set the lens switch to your desired focusing method.**

   Move the switch to AF for autofocusing and MF for manual focusing.

4. **For handheld shots, also enable Image Stabilization by setting the Stabilizer switch to On.**

5. **Press the Live View button to switch to Live View mode.**

   The viewfinder pulls the blanket over its head and goes to sleep, and the scene in front of the lens appears on the monitor. What data you see superimposed on top of the scene depends on your display mode; press Info to cycle through the four available display options. (See "Customizing the display," earlier in this chapter, for a look at all your choices.)

6. **Review and adjust picture settings.**

   The preceding section outlines the main options available to you.

7. **If focusing manually, twist the focus ring on the lens to set focus.**

   Be sure that the viewfinder is adjusted to your eyesight so that you can accurately gauge focus. (Chapter 1 has instructions.) Also remember that you can magnify the display to verify focus, as outlined earlier in this chapter.

8. **If autofocusing, follow the techniques outlined for your chosen AF mode, described earlier in this chapter, to choose a focus point if necessary.**

9. **Press and hold the shutter button halfway down to set autofocus.**

   In all exposure modes but M, the camera also sets exposure with your half-press of the button.

10. **Press the shutter button fully to take the shot.**

    You see your just-captured image on the monitor for a few seconds before the Live View preview returns.

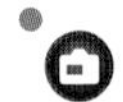

11. **To exit Live View, press the Live View button.**

Using the touch shutter

When touchscreen operation is enabled, you can simply tap your subject on the monitor to tell the camera to set focus on that part of the frame and then snap the photograph immediately after it achieves focus.

Follow these steps to try it out:

1. **Enable the Touch Control option on Setup Menu 3.**
2. **Press the Live View button to engage the Live View display.**
3. **Look for the Touch Shutter icon in the lower-left corner of the monitor.**

   I labeled the icon in the left screen in Figure 4-25. By default, the touch-shutter feature is turned off, so the word Off appears with the icon.

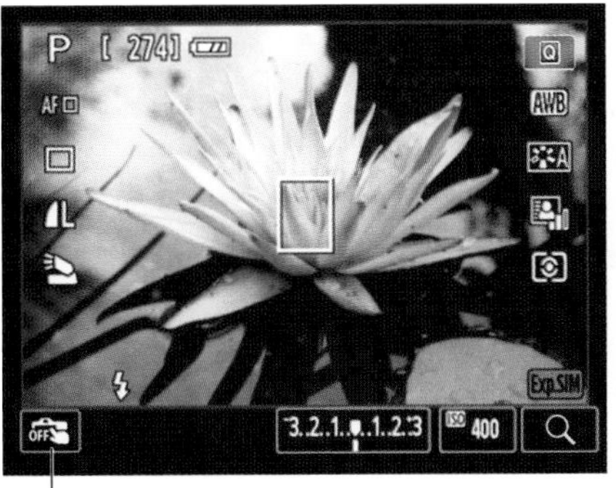

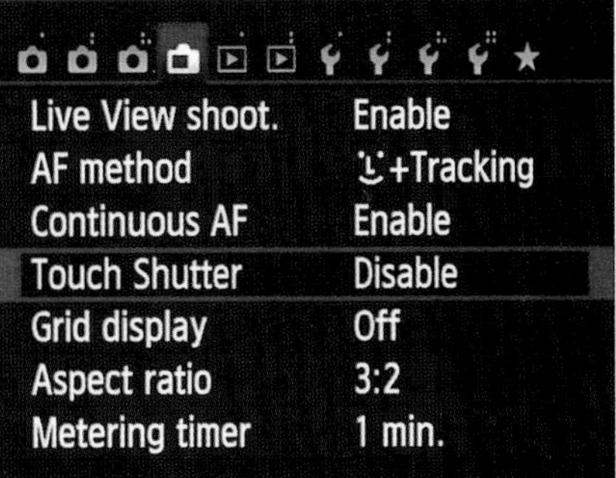

Figure 4-25: Turn the touch-shutter function on and off by tapping its icon (left) or via the Live View menu (right).

4. **Tap the icon to toggle the touch shutter function on.**

   You also can turn the feature on via the Live View menu, as shown on the right in Figure 4-25.

5. **Compose your shot and then tap the subject on the monitor.**

   The camera attempts to focus on the spot you tapped. If it's successful, it releases the shutter to take the picture. If focus can't be achieved, the camera won't record the photo.

   A few fine points: In the FlexiZone-Multi autofocus mode, the camera instead behaves as if FlexiZone-Single mode is active. The Continuous Drive mode doesn't function; you can't shoot a burst of images using the touch shutter. And finally, to shoot a bulb exposure (available in M exposure mode only), tap the screen once to open the shutter and tap again to end the exposure.

Recording Your First Movie

By shifting the On/Off switch to the Movie position, you can record high-definition video, with or without sound. The camera records movies in the MOV format, a popular file format for storing digital video. Movie filenames begin with the characters MVI_. You can play MOV files on your computer with most movie-playback programs. If you want to view your movies on a TV, you can connect the camera to the TV, as explained in Chapter 5. Or if you have the necessary computer software, you can convert the MOV file to a format that a standard DVD player can recognize and then burn the converted file to a DVD. You also can edit your movie in a program that can work with MOV files.

Recording a movie using the default camera settings is a cinch:

1. **To use an external microphone, plug the mic into the port on the left side of the camera, as shown on the left in Figure 4-26.**

   Otherwise, sound is recorded via the internal microphone, positioned in the location shown on the right in the figure. Be careful not to cover up the little microphone holes with your finger, and remember that anything you say during the recording likely will be picked up by the mic.

2. **Set the Mode dial to Scene Intelligent Auto mode (the green A+).**

   In this mode, the camera handles all exposure settings for you, which is the way to go unless you're an experienced videographer.

   If the lens is set to autofocusing, the camera also takes care of focus chores for you. By default, it uses continuous autofocusing (Movie Servo AF) and the Face+Tracking AF mode. If the camera detects a face, it automatically focuses on that face; otherwise, it shifts to FlexiZone-Multi AF mode and typically focuses on the closest object. Focus is continuously adjusted as needed as you pan the camera or your subject moves.

   To use manual focusing, first turn off Movie Servo AF — just tap the Servo AF icon in the lower-left corner of the screen. Then set the lens to the manual focus position and bring the subject into focus using the lens focusing ring.

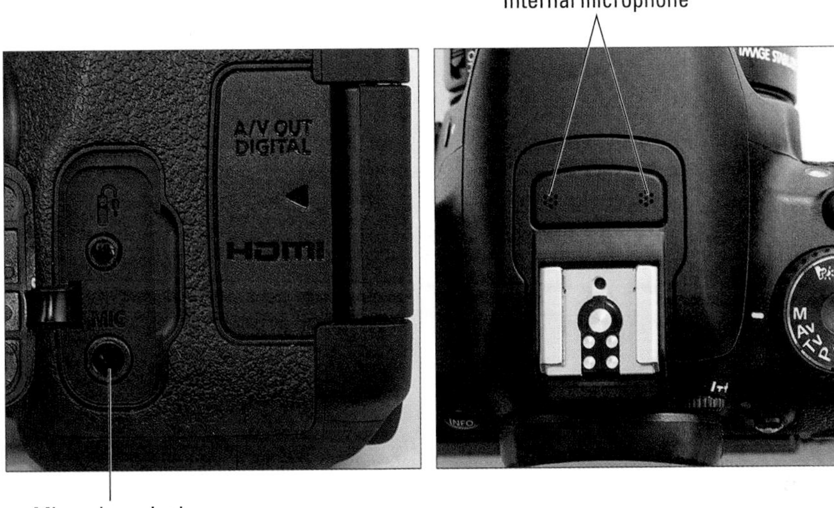

Figure 4-26: You can attach an external microphone (left) or record sound using the internal microphone (right).

3. **Set the On/Off switch to the Movie setting.**

   The viewfinder shuts off, and the live preview appears on the monitor. You also see various data onscreen, as shown on the left in Figure 4-27. The next section explains what each bit of information means. For now, the one critical detail to note is the available recording time, which depends on how much free space exists on your memory card and the Movie Recording Size setting (Movie Menu 2), which determines the resolution, frame rate, and file size of the movie. (I explain this option in detail later in the chapter.)

4. **Focus.**

5. **To start recording, press the Live View button.**

   Most of the shooting data disappears from the screen, and a red "recording" symbol appears, as shown on the right in Figure 4-27. Now, instead of showing you the length of the recording that will fit on your memory card, the display shows the elapsed recording time.

   Depending on the memory card you use, the camera may have trouble moving movie data to the card quickly enough to keep pace with the speed of the recording. A little vertical bar on the right side of the screen, technically named the Data Transfer Alert, shows you how much movie data the camera has in its *buffer* — a temporary data storage tank — awaiting transfer to the memory card. If the indicator level reaches the top, the camera stops recording so that it can finish sending existing data to the card. You can try reducing the Movie Recording Size setting to improve the transfer speed. If the progress indicator keeps hitting the limit, buy a faster memory card. Canon recommends cards with a speed-class rating of 6 or higher.

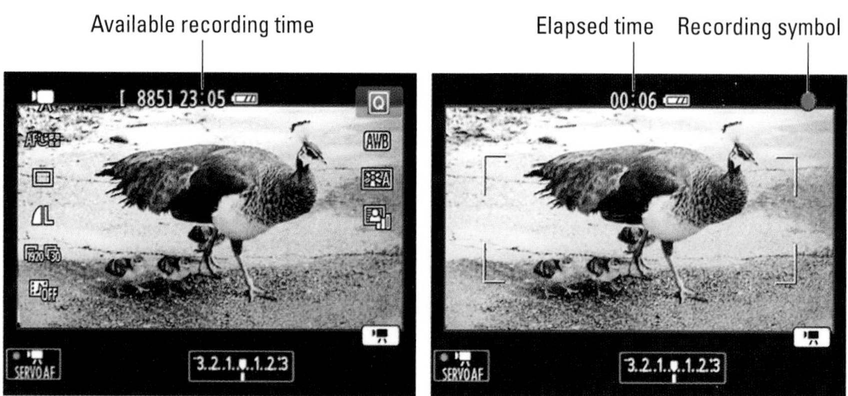

Figure 4-27: The display shows how many minutes of video will fit on your memory card (left) and, after you begin recording, elapsed recording time (right).

The maximum movie length is 11 minutes. When you reach that limit, the camera creates a new movie file to hold the next 11 minutes of video. Recording stops automatically when the recording time reaches 29 minutes and 59 seconds.

6. **To stop recording, press the Live View button again.**

At the default settings, your movie is recorded using the following settings:

- Full HD video quality (1920 x 1080p, or pixels) at 30 frames per second (fps)
- Audio recording enabled
- Evaluative (whole frame) exposure metering
- Automatic white balancing
- Auto Lighting Optimizer applied at the Standard setting
- Auto Picture Style

But of course, you didn't buy this book so that you could remain trapped in the camera's default behaviors. So the upcoming sections explain all your recording options, which range from fairly simply to fairly not.

Customizing Movie Recording Settings

After you set the On/Off switch to the Movie position, you can display critical recording settings on the monitor, shown in Figure 4-28. If you don't see the same data, press the Info button to cycle through different display styles.

You can access the same display options as for Live View shooting, with the exception of the one that adds the histogram.

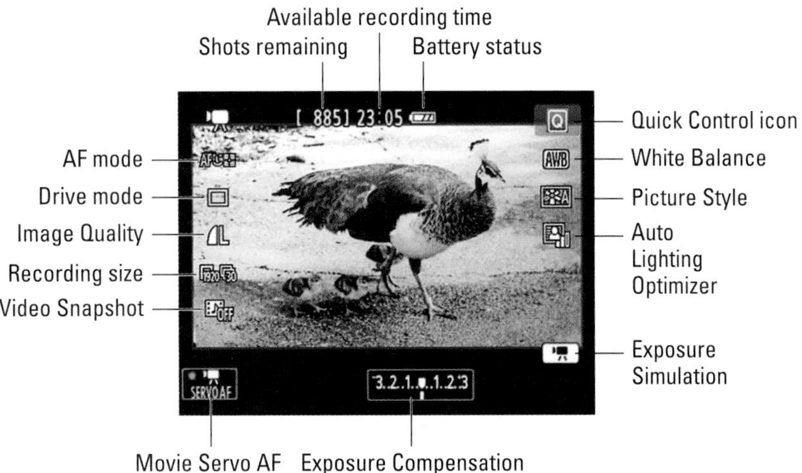

Figure 4-28: Press the Info button to change the data display.

The following list offers some other insights into a few of the screen symbols; upcoming sections provide more details about recording settings.

- **The Drive mode, shots-remaining, and Image Quality settings relate only to still shots you capture during a recording.** See the later section "Snapping a Photo During Movie Recording" for help.
- **By default, the camera controls the aperture, shutter speed, and ISO.** Pressing the shutter button halfway displays the shutter speed, f-stop, and ISO for the still shot, which may be different than for the movie recording. However, you can switch to manual exposure control for the movie by setting the Mode dial to M. This option is best left to experts and involves more details than I have room to cover, so see the camera instruction book for the full story. Regardless of exposure mode, you can't adjust the metering mode; the camera automatically chooses evaluative or center-weighted metering.

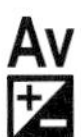

- **In P, Tv, and Av modes, the exposure meter indicates the amount of Exposure Compensation.** Exposure Compensation enables you to adjust the brightness of your next recording. If the little white bar under the meter is at the center position, as shown in Figure 4-27, no compensation has been applied. You can simply tap the setting and then adjust it by dragging your finger along the scale that appears: Drag right for a brighter picture; drag left for a darker picture. Or you can press and hold the Exposure Compensation button while rotating the Main dial.

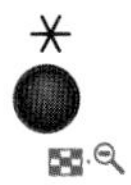

- **In P, Tv, and Av exposure modes, you can press the AE Lock button to disable automatic exposure adjustment.** When you use autoexposure, the camera adjusts exposure during the recording as needed. If you prefer to use the same settings throughout the recording — or to lock in the current settings during the recording — you can use AE (autoexposure) Lock. Just press the AE Lock button. A little asterisk appears in the lower-left corner of the screen.

  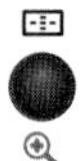

  To cancel AE Lock during recording, press the AF Point Selection button. When recording is stopped, AE Lock is cancelled automatically after 16 seconds by default; this shutoff timing is determined by the Metering Timer option on Movie Menu 1.

- **Focus options:** You select and adjust focus settings just as you do for Live View photography; see the earlier section "Focusing in Live View and Movie Modes" for details. Quick Mode autofocusing isn't available for movie recording, however.

  By default, continuous autofocusing, called Movie Servo AF in Movie mode, is enabled. Toggle continuous autofocusing on and off by tapping the icon in the lower left corner of the screen (refer to Figure 4-28). You also can change this setting via Movie Menu 1.

To adjust other movie recording options, you can go two routes:

- **Movie Menus 1 and 2:** When you set the Mode dial to Movie, you can access two menus of options, which I detail in the next several sections.

- **Quick Control screen:** You can also adjust some recording options via the Quick Control screen. The icons running down the left and right side of the screen represent these settings. Most are the same as for Live View still photography: AF mode, Picture Style, White Balance, Auto Lighting Optimizer, and Image Quality (again, the latter affects only still pictures that you shoot during a recording). You also can change the Movie Recording Size, which affects resolution (frame size) and frames per second (fps), explained later in this chapter.

Movie Menu 1

Start customizing your production with the options on Movie Menu 1, shown in Figure 4-29:

- **AF Method:** This option does the same thing as the AF mode option available via the Quick Control screen. Remember, you can't use Quick mode autofocusing for movie recording.

- **Movie Servo AF:** Here's where to enable or disable continuous autofocusing if you forget that you can do it more quickly by tapping the screen icon (refer to Figure 4-28).

- **AF w/Shutter Button During Movie:** If you enable this option, you can press the shutter button halfway to reset autofocus during movie recording. But understand that doing so can be distracting during playback — the image can drift in and out of focus — and the sound of the lens focusing mechanism might be recorded if you use the internal microphone. In other words, it's best not to use this option if you can avoid it.

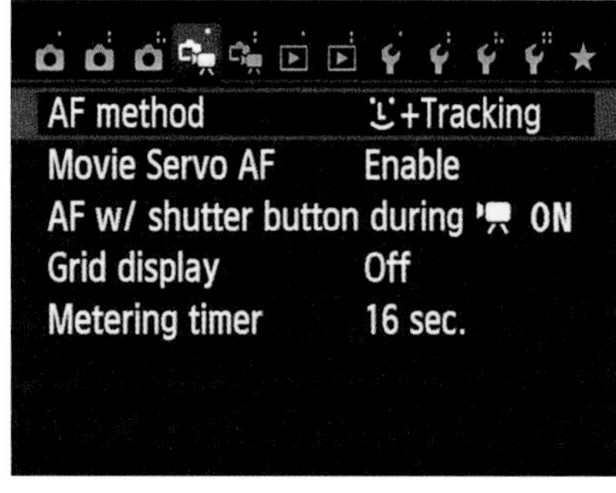

Figure 4-29: Set the Mode dial to Movie to access the Movie menus.

- **Grid Display:** This option is a display customization option. Choose Grid 1 for a loosely spaced grid; choose Grid 2 for a more tightly spaced grid. For no grid, leave the option set to Off, the default. See Figure 4-6 for a look at the grid.
- **Metering Timer:** This option is the one that adjusts the auto shut-off timing of the exposure meter, as explained in the earlier section "Customizing the display." By default, the meter shuts down and disappears from the display after 16 seconds. The setting also controls the automatic cancellation of AE Lock, as explained in the preceding section.

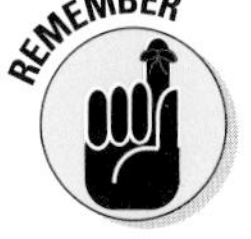

You can access this option and the grid option only in the P, Tv, Av, or M exposure modes; in other modes, it disappears from the menu.

Movie Menu 2

Movie Menu 2, shown in Figure 4-30, includes the following settings:

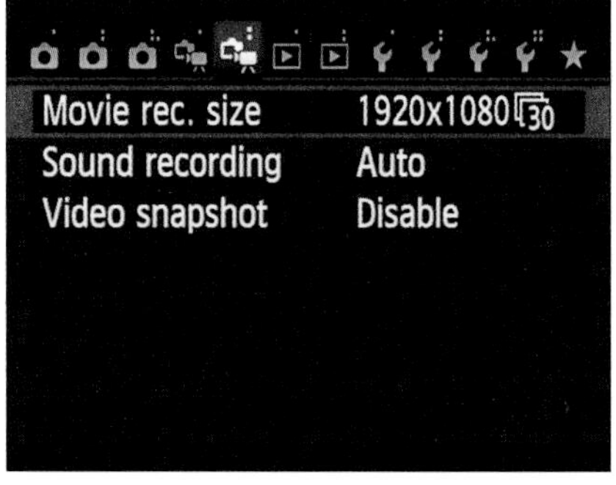

Figure 4-30: Options controlling video quality and sound recording reside on Movie Menu 2.

- **Movie Recording Size:** This option determines movie resolution (frame size, in pixels), frames per second (fps), and frame aspect ratio. This setting is a little complex, so see the next section if you don't know what option to choose.
- **Sound Recording:** Via this menu item, you adjust microphone volume and a couple other sound options. See "Audio recording options," later in this chapter, for help with all the audio settings.

- **Video Snapshot:** This feature enables you to create multiple brief movie clips — each no more than 8 seconds in length — and then combine the clips into one movie. Turn off this feature for regular movie recording and see Chapter 11 for information about creating and playing video snapshots.

Setting the Movie Recording Size option

Through this setting, you set movie resolution and frames per second, or fps. You can access the option via Movie Menu 2, in which case you see the somewhat obtuse screen shown in Figure 4-31.

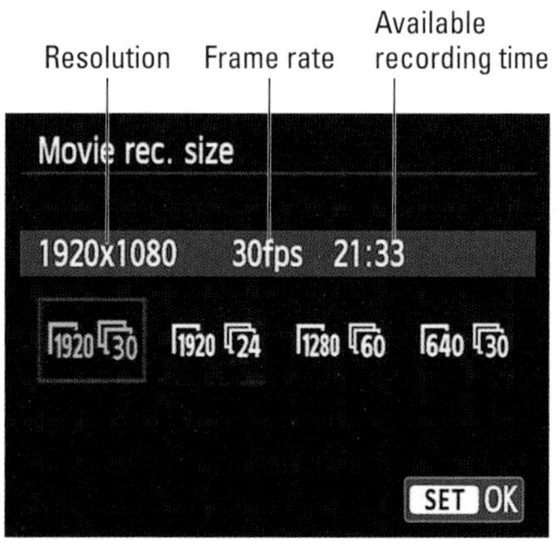

Figure 4-31: After you choose a resolution setting, the screen updates to show the length of the movie that will fit on your memory card.

You also can adjust the resolution and frame rate via the Quick Control screen. After highlighting the setting, as shown in Figure 4-32, rotate the Main dial to cycle through all the settings or just tap the one you want to use. Tap the return arrow in the upper-right corner of the screen to exit the Quick Control screen.

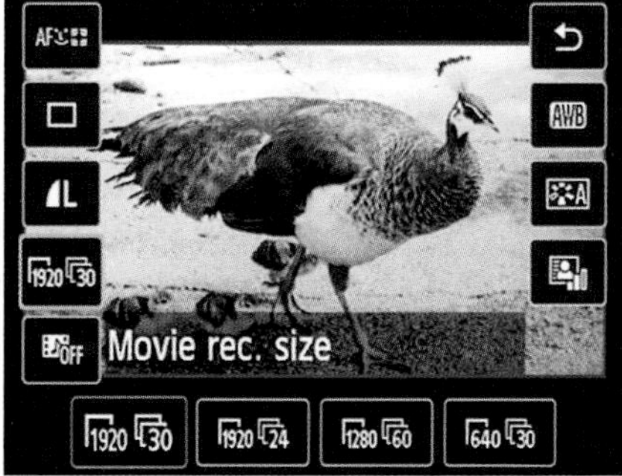

Figure 4-32: You also can access the setting via the Quick Control screen.

Either way, you get the following choices:

- 1920 x 1080 pixels, 30 fps (16:9 aspect ratio)
- 1920 x 1080 pixels, 24 fps (16:9)
- 1280 x 720 pixels, 60 fps (16:9)
- 640 x 480 pixels, 30 fps (4:3)

The frame-rate options depend on the Video System option on Setup Menu 2, which sets the camera to one of two video standards, NTSC or PAL. NTSC is the standard in North America and Japan; PAL is used in Europe, China, and many other countries. If you choose NTSC, you see the recording options shown in Figure 4-31 and in the preceding list. If you select PAL, you can choose frame rates of 24, 25, and 50 instead of 24, 30, and 60.

Here's a bit more information to help you choose the best resolution-and-frame-rate combo:

- **For high-definition (HD) video, choose 1920 x 1080 (Full HD) or 1280 x 720 (Standard HD).** The 640 x 480 setting gives you standard definition (SD) video.
- **Higher resolution means larger data files.** And of course, the larger the file, the more space it eats up on your memory card. An 11-minute movie, shot at either of the HD settings, consumes about 4 GB of space; you can store 46 minutes of footage in that same 4GB closet if you use the SD setting.

- **Resolution helps determine the maximum length of your movie.** The maximum file size for a movie is 4GB, regardless of the capacity of your memory card. So again, at the HD settings, your maximum movie clip length is 11 minutes. However, you can keep shooting until you reach a total time of 29 minutes, 59 seconds — the camera automatically creates a new file to hold your new clip. You have to play back each clip separately or join them together in a movie-editing program if you want one continuous 30-minute (or so) movie.

  At the SD settings, the maximum movie length is still just shy of 30 minutes, even though you can fit more minutes of recording in the 4GB file-size limit. (Don't yell at me — I don't set the limits, I just report them.)

  Either way, when the maximum recording time is up, the camera automatically stops recording. You can always start a new recording, however, and, again, you can join the segments in a movie-editing program later, if you want.
- **Frame rate affects playback quality.** Higher frame rates transfer to smoother playback, especially for fast-moving subjects. But the frame rate also influences the crispness of the picture. To give you some reference, 30 fps is the NTSC standard for television-quality video, and 24 fps is the motion-picture standard. Movies shot at 60 fps tend to appear very sharp and detailed — a look that some people like and others find too harsh. It's hard to explain the difference in words, so experiment to see which look you prefer. The uber-high frame rate is also good for maintaining video quality if you edit your video to create slow-motion effects. Additionally, if you want to "grab" a still frame from a video to use as a photograph, 60 frames per second gives you more frames from which to choose.

Choosing audio recording options

In the fully automatic exposure modes, the Sound Rec. option on Movie Menu 2 gives you just two options: You can enable or disable audio recording. But if you set the Mode dial to P, Tv, Av, or M and select the menu option, you access the audio controls shown on the left in Figure 4-33. The settings apply whether you use the internal microphone or attach an external one.

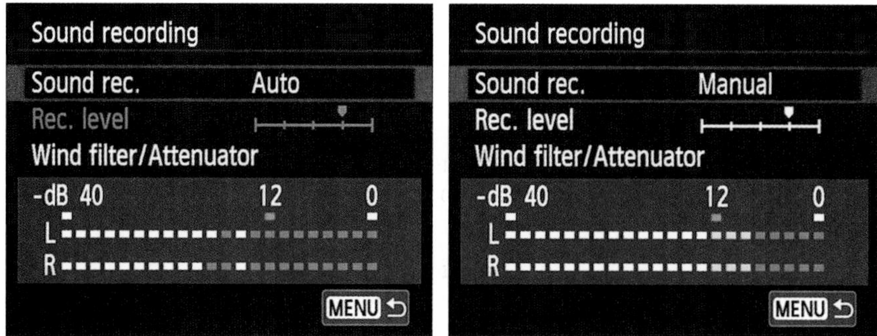

Figure 4-33: The sound meter at the bottom of the screen offers guidance if you choose to set audio recording levels manually.

The audio controls work as follows:

- **Sound Rec.:** At the default setting, Auto, sound is recorded, with the camera automatically adjusting recording volume. If you're an audio expert and want to control recording levels yourself, choose Manual. To record a silent movie, choose Disable.
- **Rec. Level:** If you choose the Manual sound recording option, this option becomes available, as shown on the right in Figure 4-33, enabling you to set the recording volume. To change the setting, tap it or highlight it and press Set. You then see a volume scale; drag along the scale to set the volume. Alternatively, press the right or left cross keys or tap the arrows at either end of the scale. To guide you, a volume-level meter appears at the bottom of the screen, as shown in the figure.

  Audio levels are measured in decibels (dB). Levels on the volume meter range from –40 (very, very soft) to 0 (as much as can be measured digitally without running out of room).

  For best results, adjust the recording level until the sound peaks consistently in the –12 range, as shown on the right in Figure 4-33. The indicators on the meter turn yellow in this range, which is good. (The extra space beyond that level, called *headroom,* gives you both a good signal and a comfortable margin of error.) If the sound is too loud, the volume indicators will peak at 0 and appear red — a warning that the audio may sound distorted.

- **Wind Filter/Attenuator:** Choose this option to access the following two audio options:
  - *Wind Filter:* Ever seen a newscaster out in the field, carrying a microphone that looks like it's covered with a big piece of foam? That foam thing is a wind filter. It's designed to lessen the sounds

that the wind makes when it hits the microphone. You can enable a digital version of the same thing via the Wind Filter menu option. Essentially, the filter works by reducing the volume of noises that are similar to those made by wind. The problem is that some noises *not* made by wind can also be muffled when the filter is enabled. So when you're indoors or shooting on a still day, keep this option set to Disable. Also note that when you use an external microphone, the Wind Filter feature has no effect.

- *Attenuator:* This feature is designed to eliminate distortion that can occur with sudden loud noises. Experiment with enabling this feature if you're shooting in a location where this audio issue is possible.

Snapping a Photo During Movie Recording

You can interrupt your recording to take a still photo without exiting Movie mode. Just press the shutter button as usual to take the shot. The camera records the still photo as a regular image file, using the same Picture Style, White Balance, and Auto Lighting Optimizer settings you chose for your movie. The Image Quality setting determines the picture resolution and file format, as outlined in Chapter 2. The camera uses the Single Drive mode and evaluative (whole frame) exposure metering.

One important note: The status of the AF/w Shutter Button during Movie Recording option, found on Movie Menu 1 and shown in Figure 4-34, determines whether focus is reset when you press the shutter button halfway. If the setting is turned on, as it is by default, focus is reset with your half press. When you disable the feature, you can snap a picture with a quick, one-step press of the shutter button whether or not focus has been achieved.

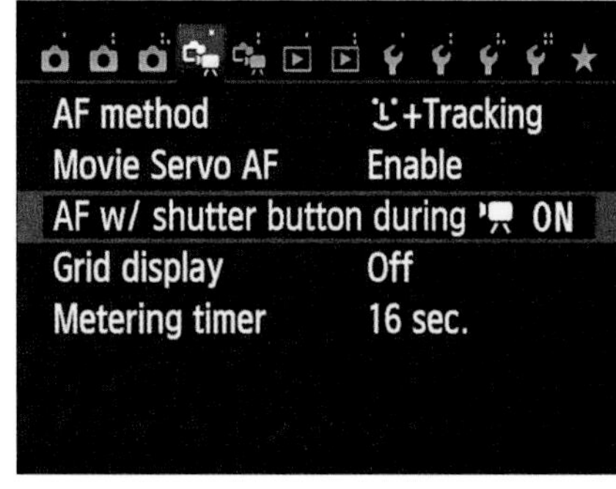

Figure 4-34: This option determines whether a half-press of the shutter button resets autofocus before you take your still picture during recording.

There are a few drawbacks to capturing a still photo during a recording:

- If you're shooting a movie at one of the Movie Recording Size settings that results in the 16:9 aspect ratio, the area included in your still photo is different from what's in the movie shots. All still photos have an aspect ratio of 3:2, so you gain some image area at the top and bottom and lose it from the sides. If the movie size is set to 640 x 480, your still photo still has a 3:2 aspect ratio.

- You can't use flash.
- Perhaps most importantly, your movie will contain a still frame at the point you took the photo; the frame lasts about one second. Ouch. If you're savvy with a video editor, you can edit each still photo out of the video, but if you shoot 50 stills in 5 minutes of video, editing is going to take a while.

Playing Movies

Chapter 5 explains how to connect your camera to a television set for big-screen movie playback. To view movies on the camera monitor, first display the movie in full-frame view. You can spot a movie file by looking for the little movie-camera icon in the upper-left corner of the screen. You also see a big playback symbol in the center of the screen, as shown in Figure 4-35.

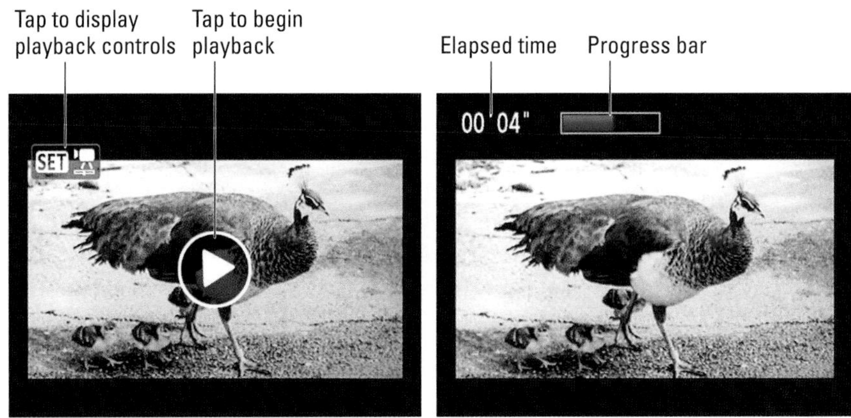

Figure 4-35: To start movie playback, just tap the big playback arrow.

If you see thumbnails instead of a full movie frame on the screen, tap the thumbnail or use the cross keys to highlight it and then press Set to display the file in the full-frame view. You can't play movies in thumbnail view.

Use these techniques to start, stop, and control playback when you're viewing movies on the camera monitor:

- **Start playback:** You can start playback in two ways:
  - *Tap the playback arrow.* I labeled it in Figure 4-35. Your movie begins playing, with a progress bar and time-elapsed value provided at the top of the screen, as shown on the right in Figure 4-35.
  - *Press the Set button or tap the Set icon:* Now you see the first frame of your movie plus a slew of control icons, as shown in Figure 4-36. To start playback, tap the Play icon or use the cross keys to highlight it and then press the Set button.
- **Pause playback:** Just tap the screen or press the Set button. To resume, tap the playback symbol or press Set again.

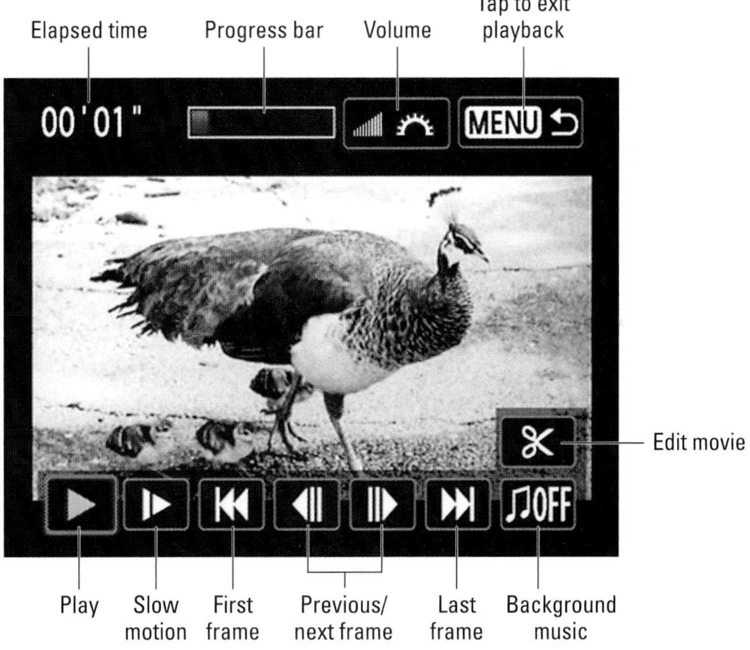

Figure 4-36: If the playback controls disappear, just press the Set button to redisplay them.

- **Play in slow motion:** Tap the slow-motion icon or select it and press Set. Press the right cross key to increase playback speed; press the left cross key to decrease it. You also can adjust the speed by dragging your finger along the little scale that appears in the upper-right corner of the monitor during slo-mo playback.
- **Adjust volume:** Rotate the Main dial. Note the little white wheel and a volume display bar at the top right corner of the display — it reminds you to use the Main dial to adjust volume. Rotating the dial controls volume, but only for the camera speaker during on-camera playback. If you connect the camera to a TV, control the volume using the TV controls instead.

If you recorded a movie without sound, you can enable the Background Music option to play a sound file. In order to use this feature, you must install the Canon EOS Utility found on the software provided with your camera and then use the program to copy music files to your camera memory card. The EOS Utility program's user guide, found on one of the two CDs in your camera box, offers all the details you need to know to copy music files to the card.

- **Fast forward/fast rewind:** To fast-forward, tap or select the Next Frame icon. Then hold down the Set button. To rewind, tap or select the Previous Frame icon and hold down the Set button.
- **Go forward/back one frame while paused:** Highlight or tap the Next Frame or Previous Frame icon, respectively and then press the Set button once. Each time you press the button, you go forward or backward one frame.
- **Skip to the first or last frame of the movie:** Tap the first or last frame icons, respectively, or highlight the icon and press Set.
- **View a still photo you shot during the recording:** If you took this step, the photo is displayed for about one second automatically during playback. You can also view the separate image file after you exit the movie playback; see Chapter 5 for still-photo playback details.
- **Edit the movie:** Tap the Edit icon or highlight it and press Set. Then follow the instructions in Chapter 11 to trim frames from the start or end of the movie — the limits of the editing you can do in-camera.
- **Exit playback:** Tap the Menu icon or press the Menu button.

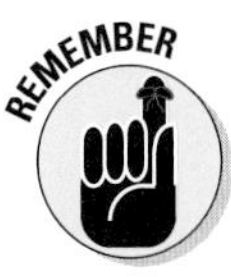

If you connect your camera to a TV or monitor for viewing, you can't use the touch-screen controls; you must use the camera buttons to control playback.

Part II
Working with Picture Files

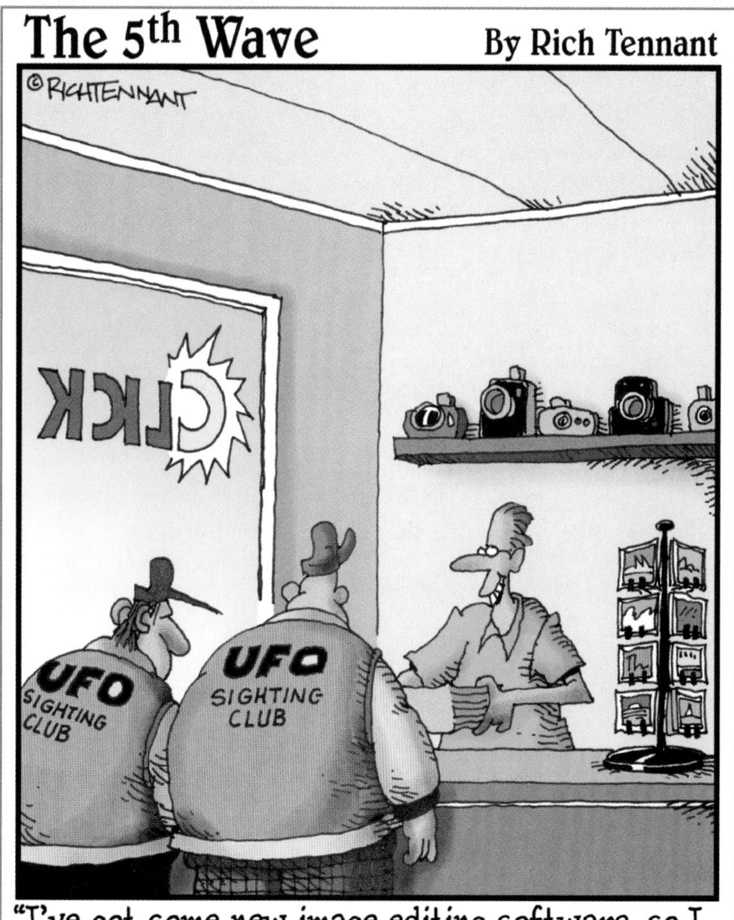

"I've got some new image editing software, so I took the liberty of erasing some of the smudges that kept showing up around the clouds. No need to thank me."

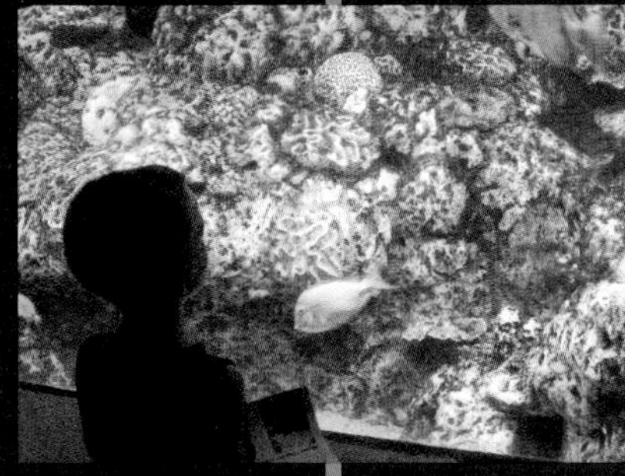

In this part . . .

You have a memory card full of pictures. Now what?

Turn to the two chapters in this part, that's what. The first chapter explains how to review, rate, and delete pictures from your memory card. In addition, you can find out how to connect your camera to your TV so you can display your masterpieces on the big screen instead of just on the camera monitor.

When you're ready to move those pictures from your camera to your computer, the second chapter shows you how. Information on processing Raw (CR2) files, printing pictures, and preparing photos for online sharing also await in this part.

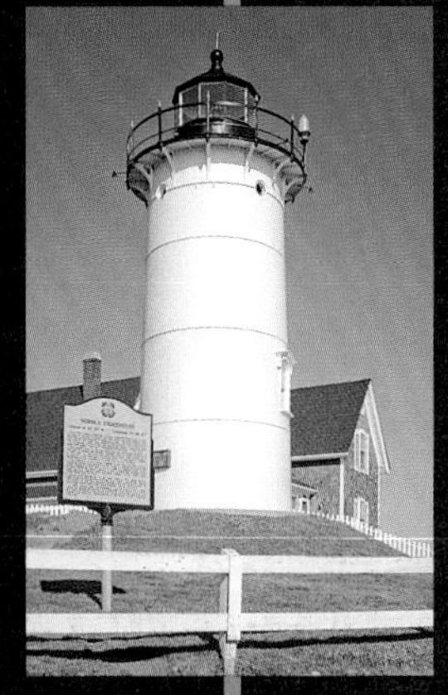

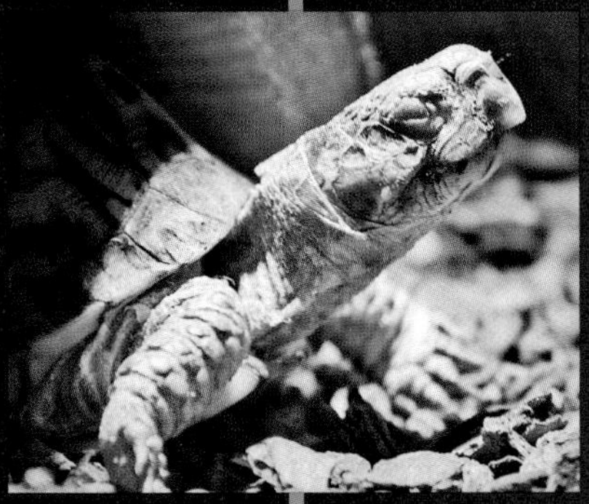

5

Picture Playback

In This Chapter

- Exploring playback functions
- Deciphering the playback displays
- Deleting, protecting, and rating photos and movies
- Connecting your camera to a TV for big-screen playback

Without question, one of the best things about digital photography is being able to view pictures right after you shoot them. No more guessing whether you got the shot you want or need to try again; no more wasting money on developing and printing pictures that stink. But seeing your pictures is just the start of the things you can do when you switch your camera to playback mode. You also can review the settings you used to take the picture, display graphics that alert you to exposure problems, and add file markers that protect the picture from accidental erasure. This chapter tells you how to use all these playback features and more.

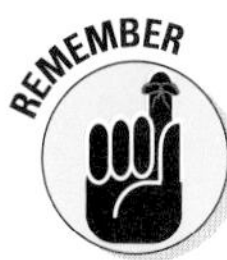

Many features discussed in this chapter apply to still photos, movies, and video snapshots. But for some playback functions that apply only to movies, see Chapter 4. Chapter 11 covers video snapshots.

Disabling and Adjusting Image Review

After you take a picture, it automatically appears briefly on the camera monitor. By default, the instant-review period lasts two seconds. You can customize this behavior via the Image Review option on Shooting Menu 1, as shown in Figure 5-1.

You can select from the following options:

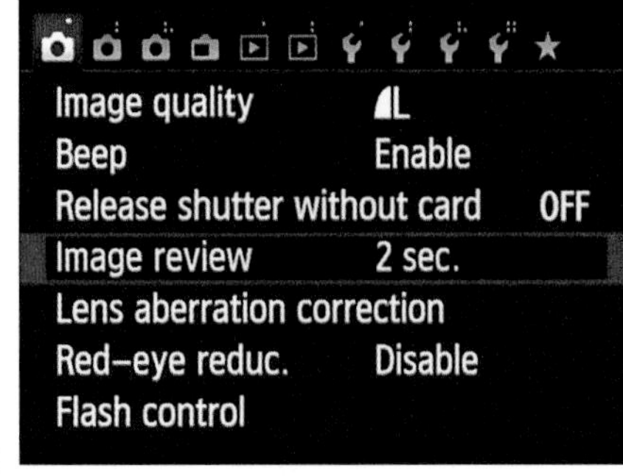

Figure 5-1: Use this option to control the timing of instant picture review.

- **Select a specific review period:** Pick 2, 4, or 8 seconds.
- **Off:** Disables automatic instant review. Turning off the monitor saves battery power, so keep this option in mind if the battery is running low. You can still view pictures by pressing the Playback button.
- **Hold:** Displays the current image until you return to shooting or until the camera automatically shuts off to save power. See the Chapter 1 section about Setup Menu 2 to find out about the Auto Power Off feature.

Note that the Image Review feature doesn't work for movies or video snapshots; you must put the camera in playback mode to view those masterpieces.

Exploring Playback Mode

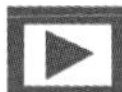

To switch your camera to Playback mode, just press the Playback button, labeled in Figure 5-2.

Here are the absolute basics of playback mode:

- **Scrolling through pictures:** You can go old-school or high-tech: Either press the right or left cross key or swipe your fingertip horizontally across the touchscreen.
- **Return to shooting:** Press the Playback button or give the shutter button a quick half-press and release it.

For still photos, you may see your image only, as in Figure 5-2, or see a little or a lot of shooting data along with the image. For a movie or video snapshot, you always see at minimum a big playback arrow that you can tap to start playback. For any type of file, you can press the Info button to change how much data appears; see "Viewing Picture Data," later in this chapter, for help deciphering what you see. You can also display multiple images at a time; the next section tells all.

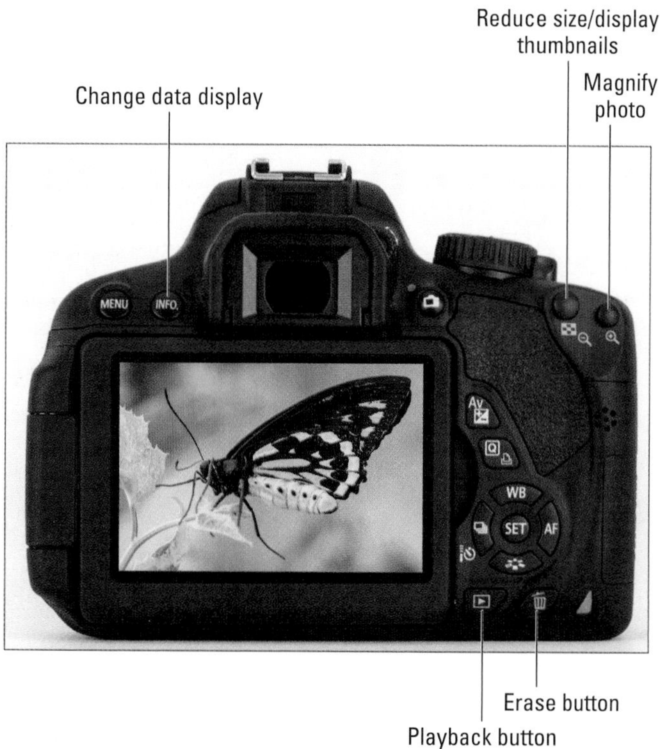

Figure 5-2: The default Playback mode displays one picture at a time.

Switching to Index (thumbnails) view

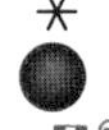

To switch from full-frame view to thumbnails view — called Index view in Canon parlance — press the AE Lock button — labeled "Reduce size/display thumbnails" in Figure 5-2. Your first press displays four thumbnails, as shown on the left in Figure 5-3; press again to display nine thumbnails, as shown on the right.

Note the little blue checkerboard and magnifying glass icons under the button. Blue labels are reminders that the button serves a function in Playback mode. In this case, the checkerboard indicates the Index function, and the minus sign in the magnifying glass tells you that pressing the button reduces the size of the thumbnail.

You don't have to use the button, though, to switch to Index view. Instead, use the touchscreen approach: Pinch inward to shift from full-frame to four-thumbnail view; pinch inward again to display nine thumbnails. See Chapter 1 for details about using the touchscreen.

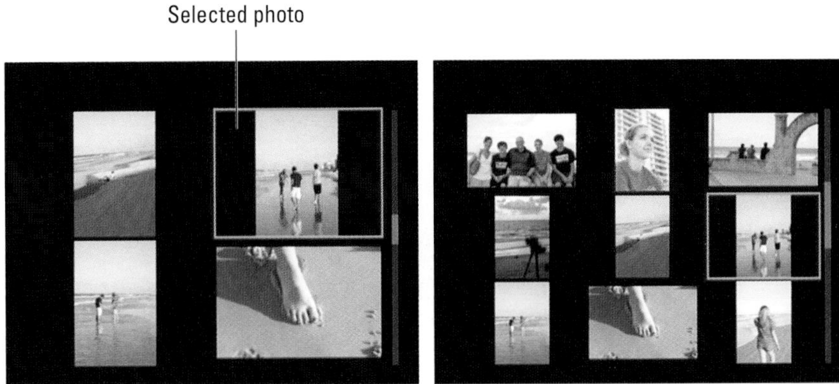

Figure 5-3: You can view four or nine thumbnails at a time.

Remember these other factoids about Index display mode:

- **Select a thumbnail.** For some playback operations, you start by selecting the photo, movie, or video snapshot thumbnail. A highlight box surrounds the currently selected thumbnail; for example, in Figure 5-3, the upper-right photo is selected. To select a different file, tap its thumbnail or press the cross keys to move the highlight box over it.
- **Scroll from one screen of thumbnails to another.** Swipe your finger up or down the screen, rotate the Main dial, or press the up or down cross keys.
- 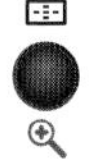 **Reduce the number of thumbnails.** Press the AF Point Selection button, labeled *Magnify photo* in Figure 5-2. This button also has a blue magnifying glass icon, this time with a plus sign in the center to indicate that pressing it enlarges the thumbnail. Press once to switch from nine thumbnails to four; press again to switch from four thumbnails to single-image view. You also can pinch outward on the touchscreen to reduce the number of thumbnails and return to full-frame view.

  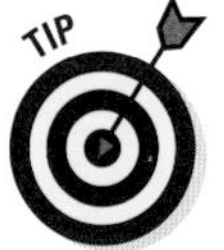
  For a quicker way to shift from Index view to full-frame view, select a photo and then press Set or tap the thumbnail.

Using the Quick Control screen during playback

During playback, you can access a handful of playback functions via the Quick Control screen. Here's how it works:

1. **Press the Quick Control button.**

   If you were viewing pictures in Index mode, the camera shifts temporarily to full-frame playback. Then various icons appear on the screen, as shown in Figure 5-4.

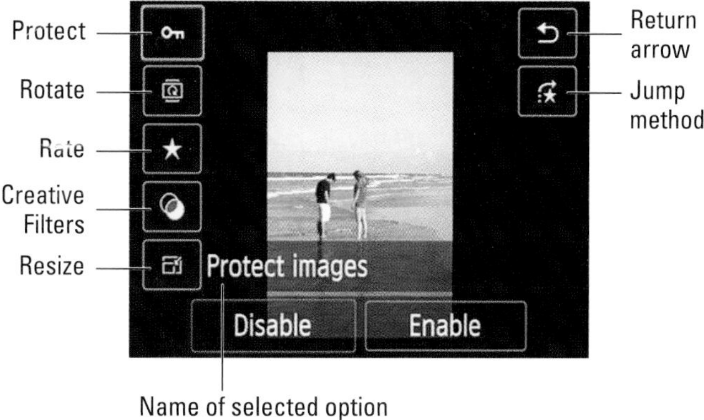

Figure 5-4: You can control these playback features via the Quick Control screen.

2. **Select one of the playback function icons.**

   Either tap the icon or use the up and down cross keys to select it. The selected icon is surrounded by the yellow box; for example, in the figure, the Protect feature is active.

   The name of the selected feature appears at the bottom of the screen, along with symbols that represent the available settings for that option. For example, in Figure 5-4, you see the two options available for the Protect feature (Disable and Enable).

   You can read more about rotating, rating, protecting, and jumping through images in other sections of this chapter. See Chapter 11 for a look at the Creative Filters, and visit Chapter 6 for information about the Resize feature.

3. **Select the setting you want to use.**

   Either tap the option or use the left/right cross keys to select it.

4. **To exit the Quick Control screen, tap the return arrow (labeled in Figure 5-4) or press the Quick Control button again.**

Jumping through images

If your memory card contains scads of files, here's a trick you'll love: By using the Jump feature, you can rotate the Main dial to leapfrog through them rather than scrolling through them one by one to get to the file you want to see. You also can search for the first photo, movie, or video snapshot taken on a specific date, tell the camera to display only movies and video snapshots or only stills, or display images with a specific rating or stored in a certain folder. (See the upcoming section "Rating Photos" for details on the rating feature.)

You can choose from the following jumping options:

- **1 Image:** This option, in effect, disables jumping, restricting you to browsing pictures one at a time. So what's the point? You can use this setting to scroll pictures using the Main dial instead of swiping across the touchscreen or pressing the right/left cross keys.
- **10 Images:** Select this option to advance 10 images at a time.
- **100 Images:** Select this option to advance 100 images at a time.
- **Date:** If your card contains files shot on different dates, you can jump between dates with this option. For example, if you're looking at the first of 30 pictures taken on June 1, you can jump past all others from that day to the first file created on, say, June 5.
- **Folder:** If your memory card contains multiple folders — as it might if you create custom folders as outlined in Chapter 10 — this option jumps you from the current folder to the first photo in a different folder.
- **Movies:** Does your memory card contain both still photos and movies? If you want to view only the movie files, select this option. Then you can rotate the Main dial to jump from one movie to the next without seeing any still photos. (Video snapshots are considered movies, so they're included in the playback lineup as well.)
- **Stills:** This one is the opposite of the Movies option: Your movies and video snapshots are hidden when you jump through files.
- **Image Rating:** This Jump mode relates to the Rating feature covered later in this chapter. You can choose to view all rated photos, movies, or video snapshots; only those with a specific rating; or those without any rating at all.

Use one of these two methods to specify which type of jumping you want to do:

- **Quick Control screen:** After displaying the Quick Control screen, select the Jump option, as shown on the left in Figure 5-5. You see a row of icons across the bottom of the screen, each one representing a different jump method. (I labeled the more cryptic icons in the figure.) Tap the method you want to use or use the left/right cross keys to highlight its icon.

  If you select the Rating mode, as I did in Figure 5-5, tap the Info icon or press the Info button to display the second screen in the figure. Then select the rating option that applies to the files you want to view when jumping. Again, you can choose files that have no rating; files that have any rating; or select a certain rating (one star, five stars, and so on). Tap the return arrow or press the Menu button to exit the rating selection screen and return to the screen on the left in the figure.

  To exit the Quick Control screen, tap the return arrow or press the Quick Control button again.

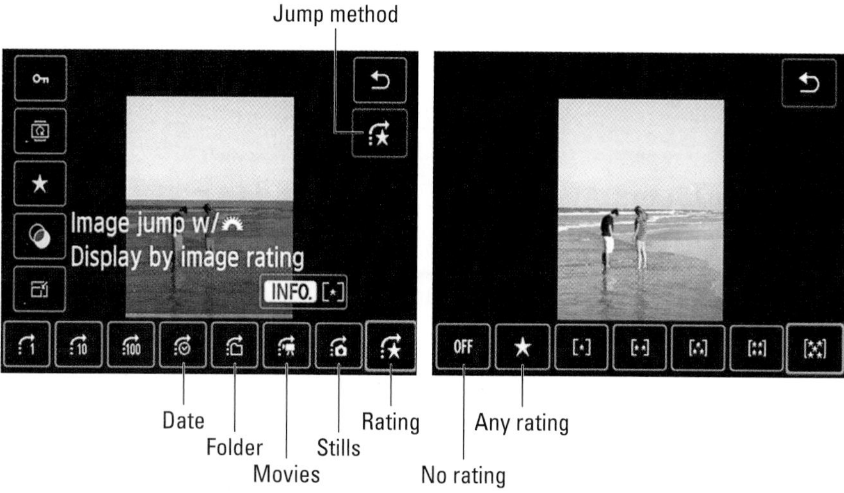

Figure 5-5: You can specify a Jump mode by using the Quick Control screen.

- **Playback Menu 2:** Choose the Image Jump option, highlighted on the left in Figure 5-6, to display the right screen in the figure, which presents the Jump settings. Tap your choice or highlight it by using the cross keys. If you choose the Rating option, as I did in the figure, rotate the Main dial to select the rating of the files you want to see. You also can tap the little arrows next to the selected rating symbol, labeled in the figure. For example, in the figure, I set the rating level to five stars. After making your choice, tap Set or press the Set button.

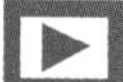

Press the Playback button to exit the menus and return to playback mode.

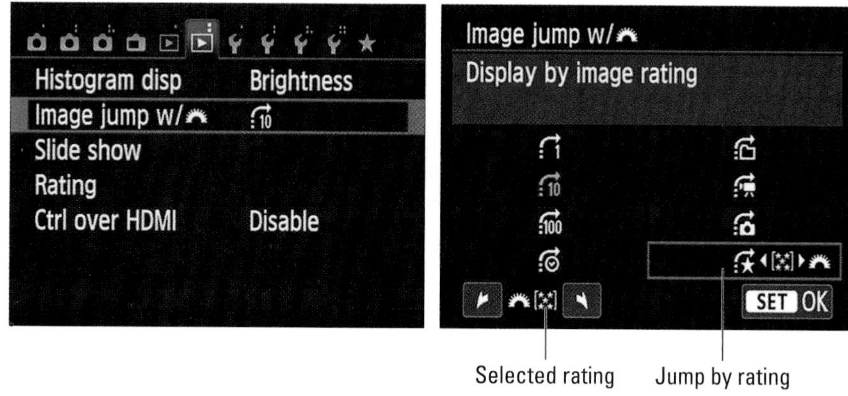

Figure 5-6: Or select the Jump method from Playback Menu 2.

After selecting a Jump mode, take the following steps to jump through your photos during playback:

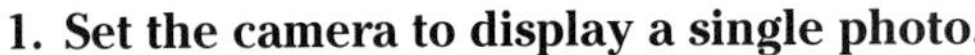

1. **Set the camera to display a single photo.**

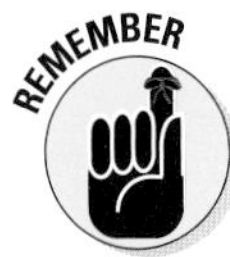

   You can use jumping only when viewing a single photo at a time. To leave Index mode, just press the Set button or tap the selected thumbnail.

2. **Rotate the Main dial or swipe two fingers across the screen.**

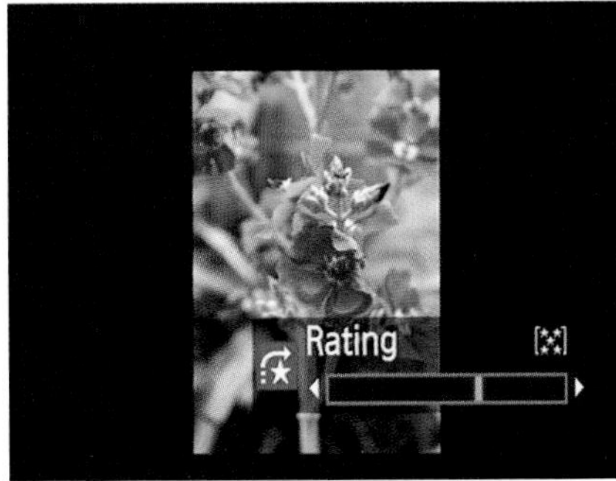

Figure 5-7: Rotate the Main dial to start jumping through pictures.

   The camera jumps to the next image, movie, or video snapshot according to the jump method you selected.

   If you select any Jump setting except 1 Image, a *jump bar* appears for a few seconds at the bottom of the monitor, as shown in Figure 5-7, indicating the current Jump setting. For the Rating Jump mode, you also see the number of stars you specified — in Figure 5-7, for example, the five tiny stars above the jump bar indicate that I asked the camera to show me only five-star photos.

3. **To exit Jump mode, just start scrolling through pictures using the cross keys or touchscreen.**

   Now you're back to regular Playback mode, in which each press of the right or left cross key or left/right swipe of the touchscreen advances to the next or previous picture.

Rotating pictures

When you take a picture, the camera can record the image *orientation:* that is, whether you held the camera horizontally or on its side to shoot vertically. This bit of data is added into the picture file. Then when you view the picture, the camera reads the data and rotates the image so that it appears upright in the monitor, as shown on the left in Figure 5-8, instead of on its side, as shown on the right. The image is also rotated automatically when you view it in the Canon photo software that shipped with your camera (as well as in some other programs that can read the rotation data).

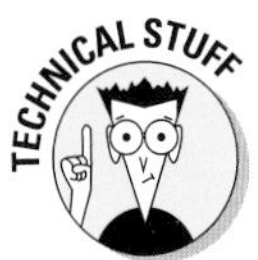

Official photo lingo uses the term *portrait orientation* to refer to vertically oriented pictures and *landscape orientation* to refer to horizontally oriented pictures. The terms stem from the traditional way that people and places are captured in painting and photographs — portraits, vertically; landscapes, horizontally.

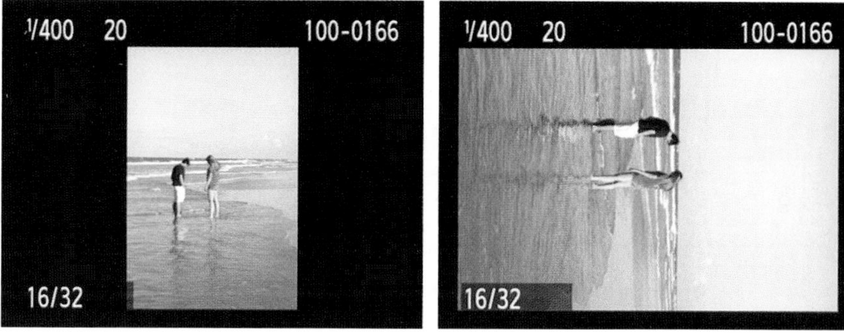

Figure 5-8: Display a vertically oriented picture upright (left) or sideways (right).

By default, the camera tags the photo with the orientation data and rotates the image automatically both on the camera and on your computer screen. But you have other choices, as follows:

- **Disable or adjust automatic rotation:** Select Auto Rotate on Setup Menu 1, as shown on the left in Figure 5-9. Then choose from these options, listed in the order they appear on the menu:
  - *On, camera and computer:* This option is the default.
  - *On, computer only:* Pictures are tagged with orientation data but rotated only on your computer monitor.
  - *Off:* New pictures aren't tagged with the orientation data, and existing photos aren't rotated during playback on the camera, even if they are tagged.

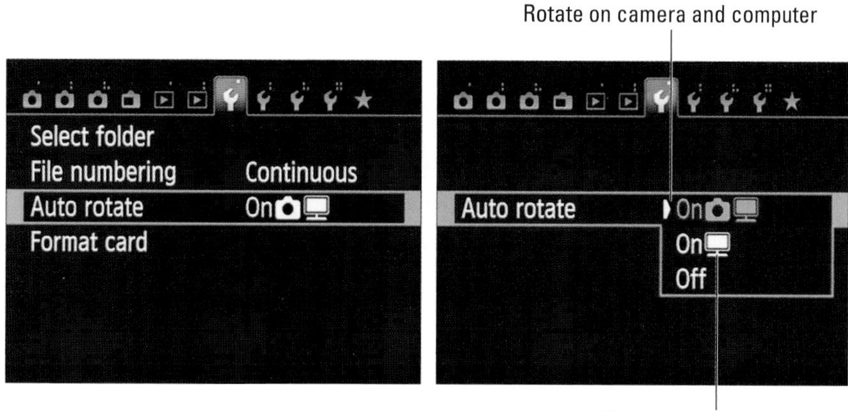

Figure 5-9: Go to Setup Menu 1 to disable or adjust automatic image rotation.

- **Rotate pictures during playback:** If you stick with the default Auto Rotate setting, you can rotate pictures during playback via the Quick Control screen. Tap the Rotate option (labeled on the left screen in Figure 5-10), and then tap one of the three orientation icons at the bottom of the screen. You also can use the up/down cross keys to select the Rotate icon and the left/right keys to select the orientation icons. Either way, the display updates as you select an orientation icon. Tap the return arrow (upper-right corner of the screen) or press the Quick Control button a second time to exit the Quick Control screen.

  If the Auto Rotate menu option is set to Off or computer-rotation only, the Quick Control technique only adds the rotation data to the image file — your picture doesn't rotate on the camera monitor. However, you can still rotate pictures for on-camera display via the Rotate option on Playback Menu 1, shown on the right in the figure.

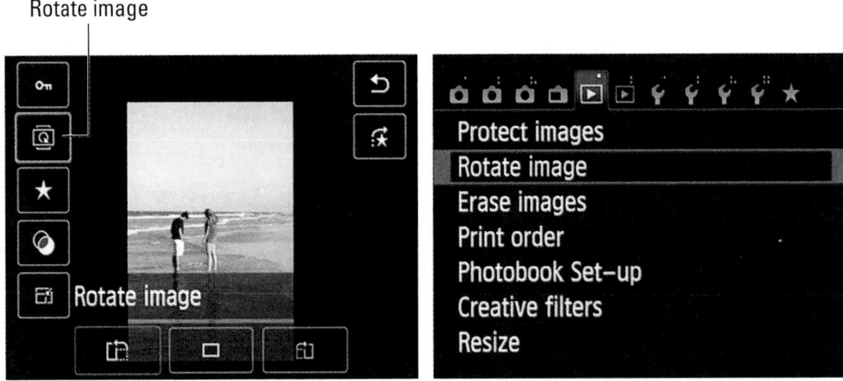

Figure 5-10: The fastest way to rotate individual images is to use the Quick Control screen (left); you also can get the job done via Playback Menu 1 (right).

  Choose the menu option to display your photos. In Index display mode, use the touchscreen or cross keys to select the image that needs rotating. In full-frame display, just scroll to the photo. Either way, press Set or tap the Set icon once to rotate the image 90 degrees; press or tap again to rotate 180 degrees from the first press (270 total degrees); press or tap once more to return to 0 degrees, or back where you started. Press the Playback button to return to viewing pictures. The photo remains in its rotated orientation only if the Auto Rotate option is set to the default.

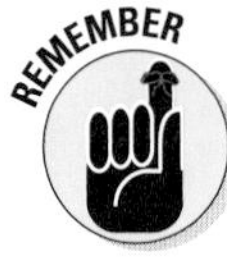

These steps apply only to still photos; you can't rotate movies or video snapshots during playback.

Zooming in for a closer view

During playback, you can magnify a photo to inspect small details, as shown in Figure 5-11. As with image rotating, zooming works only for still photos and only when you're displaying photos one at a time, though. So if you're viewing pictures in Index display mode, press Set or tap the thumbnail to return to full-frame view.

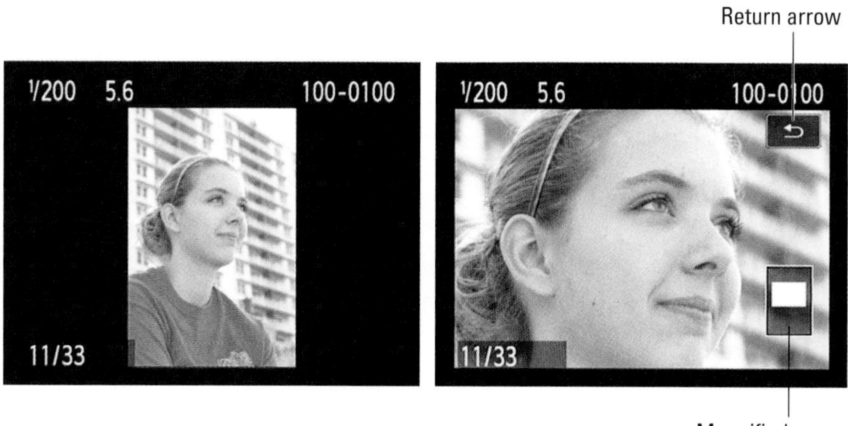

Figure 5-11: After displaying your photo in full-frame view (left), you can magnify the image for a closer view (right).

When the image is magnified, a little thumbnail representing the entire image appears in the lower-right corner of the monitor, as shown in the right image in Figure 5-11. The white box indicates the area of the image that's visible.

To take advantage of this feature, you can use either of these approaches:

- **Touchscreen zooming:** Using your thumb and forefinger, pinch outward from the center of the screen to magnify the display; pinch inward to zoom out. To scroll the magnified display, just drag your finger in the direction you want to scroll. To exit to full-image view, tap the return arrow (labeled on the right in Figure 5-11).
- **Button zooming:** Use these navigation techniques to operate the display via buttons instead of the touchscreen:

  - *Zoom in.* Press and hold the AF Point Selection button until you reach the magnification you want. You can enlarge the image up to ten times its normal display size. (Again, note the blue magnifying glass label under the button — the plus sign reminds you that you use the button to magnify the view.)

- *View another part of the picture.* Press the cross keys to scroll the display to see another portion of the image.

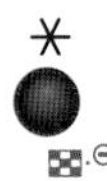

- *Zoom out.* To zoom out to a reduced magnification, press the AE Lock button. (Note that the magnifying glass label contains a minus sign, for zoom out.) Continue holding down the button until you reach the magnification you want.

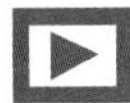

- *Return to full-frame view when zoomed in.* When you're ready to exit the magnified view, you don't need to keep pressing the AE Lock button until you zoom out all the way. Instead, press the Playback button, which quickly returns you to full-frame view.

Here's an especially neat trick you can use no matter which zoom approach you prefer: While the display is zoomed, you can rotate the Main dial to display the same area of the next photo at the same magnification. For example, if you shot a group portrait several times, you can easily check each one for shut-eye problems.

Viewing Picture Data

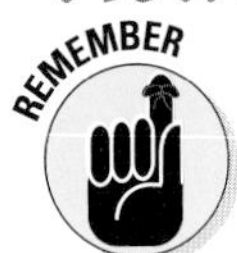

When you review still photos, you can press the Info button to change the type and amount of shooting data that appear with the photo in the monitor. Choose from the following four display styles, shown in Figure 5-12:

- **No Information:** True to its name, this display option shows just your picture, with no shooting or file data.
- **Basic Information:** What's this? Two settings with clear-cut names? Holy cannoli, pretty soon you won't need me at all. Well, at least check out the next section, which explains the basic data that appears in this display mode.
- **Shooting Information:** This mode gives you a slew of tiny symbols and numbers, all representing various shooting settings, plus a histogram (the graph in the upper-right corner of the screen). If you need help deciphering all the data, it's presented two sections from here.
- **Histogram:** This mode gives you a Brightness histogram plus an RGB histogram. Head to "Understanding Histogram display mode," later in this chapter, to find out what wisdom you can glean from these little graphs.

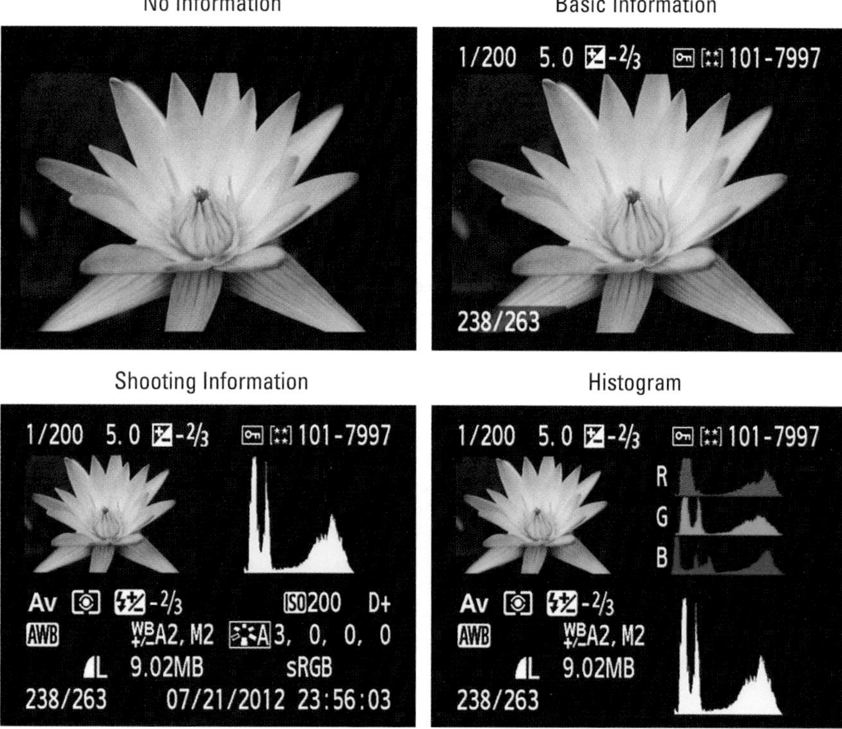

Figure 5-12: Press the Info button to change the amount of picture data displayed with your photo.

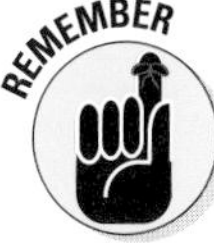

A couple of notes before you start exploring each display mode:

- When you view images on your camera monitor, some data is actually overlaid on the image instead of appearing above the photo, as it does in the figures in this book. The difference is due to the process used to capture the camera screens for publication. Don't worry about it — the data itself is the same; only the positioning varies.
- Also, if you shot your picture using Scene Intelligent Auto, Flash Off, Creative Auto, or a scene mode, you see less data in Shooting Information and Histogram display modes than appears in Figure 5-12. You get the full complement of data only if you took the picture in P, Tv, Av or M modes.
- You can access the various display modes for movies and video snapshots, but the data displayed will relate to the movie or snapshot. Also, the histograms relate to the first frame of the movie or snapshot and go blank as soon as you start movie playback. You can't change the display mode while the movie or snapshot is playing.

Basic Information display data

In Basic Information mode, you see the following bits of information (labeled in Figure 5-13):

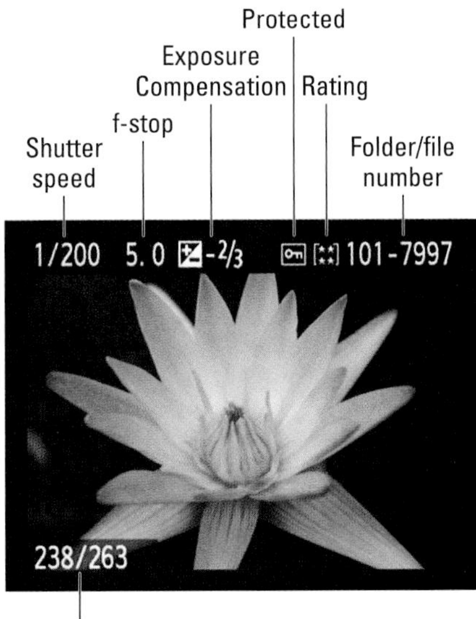

Figure 5-13: You can view basic exposure and file data in this display mode.

- **Shutter speed, f-stop (aperture), and Exposure Compensation setting:** Chapter 7 explains these exposure settings, the last of which appears in the display only if you enabled it when you took the shot.

  For movies and video snapshots, the movie length takes the place of the shutter speed and f-stop values.

- **Protected status:** A little key icon appears if you used the Protect feature to prevent the file from being erased when you use the normal file-deleting feature. You can find out how to protect files later in this chapter. The key doesn't appear for unprotected files.
- **Rating:** If you rated the file, you can see how many stars you assigned it. For example, I gave the picture in Figure 5-13 four stars. See the section "Rating Photos" for details about image ratings.
- **Folder number and last four digits of file number:** See Chapter 1 for information about how the camera assigns folder and file numbers. And visit Chapter 10 for details on how you can create custom folders if you're into that sort of organizational control.
- **Frame number/total frames:** Displayed in the bottom-left corner of the screen, this pair of values shows you the current frame number and the total number of frames on the memory card. For example, in Figure 5-13, you see frame 238 of 263.

Shooting Information display mode

In Shooting Information display mode, the camera presents a thumbnail of your image along with scads of shooting data. You also see a *Brightness histogram* — the chart-like thingy on the top-right side of the screen. You can get schooled in the art of reading histograms in the next section. (Remember, just press the Info button to cycle through the other display modes to this one.)

How much data you see, though, depends on the exposure mode you used to take the picture, as illustrated in Figure 5-14. The screen on the left shows the data dump that occurs when you shoot in the advanced exposure modes, where you can control all the settings indicated on the playback screen. When you shoot in the other exposure modes, you get a far-less detailed playback screen. For example, the right screen in Figure 5-14 shows the data that appears for a picture taken in Close-up mode. Here, you can view the Shoot by Ambience and Shoot by Lighting and Scene Type settings you used, but not all the individual exposure and color settings that appear for pictures shot in the advanced exposure modes.

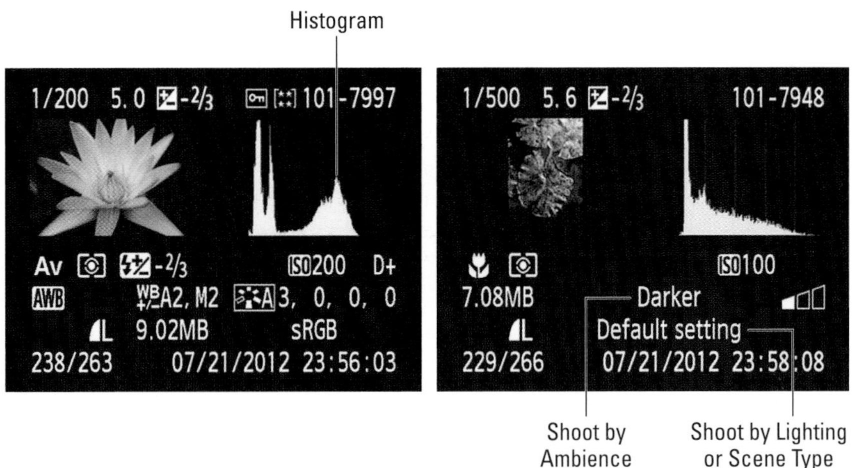

Figure 5-14: How much data appears depends on which exposure mode you used to shoot the picture.

I'm going to go out on a limb here and assume that if you're interested in the Shooting Information display mode, you're shooting in the advanced exposure modes, so the rest of this section concentrates on that level of playback data. To that end, it helps to break the display shown on the left in Figure 5-14 into five rows of information: the row along the top of the screen and the four rows that appear under the image thumbnail and histogram. Here's what appears in the five rows:

- **Row 1 data:** You see the same data that appears in the Basic Information display mode explained in the preceding section.
- **Row 2 data:** For photos, this row contains the exposure settings labeled in Figure 5-15. You can find details about all of them in Chapter 7.

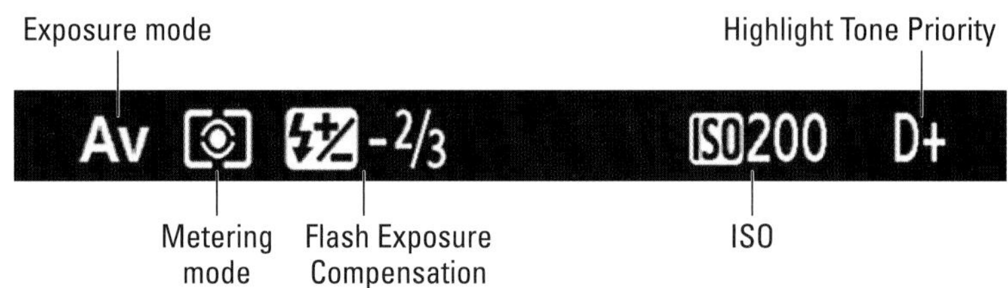

Figure 5-15: This row contains additional exposure information.

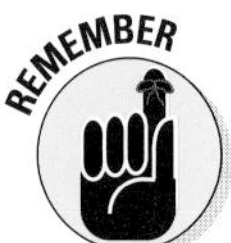

Note that in Figures 5-15 through 5-17, I show all possible shooting data for the purpose of illustration. If a data item doesn't appear on your monitor, it simply means that the feature wasn't enabled when you captured the photo.

For movies, you see a little movie camera symbol plus the letter A (for movies taken in the fully automatic modes) or M (for movies shot in Manual exposure mode). No letter means that you used the P, Tv, or Av exposure mode. In Manual mode, you also see the f-stop and shutter speed used to record the movie.

- **Row 3 data:** Information on this row of the display, labeled in Figure 5-16, relates to color settings that you can explore in Chapter 8.

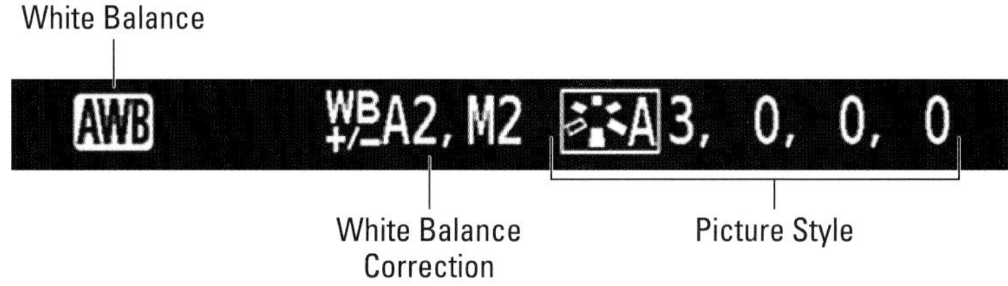

Figure 5-16: Look to this row for details about advanced color settings.

- **Row 4 data:** Figure 5-17 labels the data found in this row. For movies, the Image Quality symbol (explained in Chapter 2) is swapped out for data showing the Movie Recording Size option (Chapter 4). You can read about the Color Space option in Chapter 10.

What are these blinking spots?

When you view photos in the Shooting Information or Histogram display modes, you may notice some areas of the photo thumbnail blinking black and white. Those blinking spots indicate pixels that are completely white. Depending on the number and location of the "blinkies," you may or may not want to adjust exposure settings and retake the photo. For example, if someone's face contains the blinking spots, you should take steps to correct the problem. But if the blinking occurs in, say, a bright window behind the subject, and the subject looks fine, you may choose to simply ignore it.

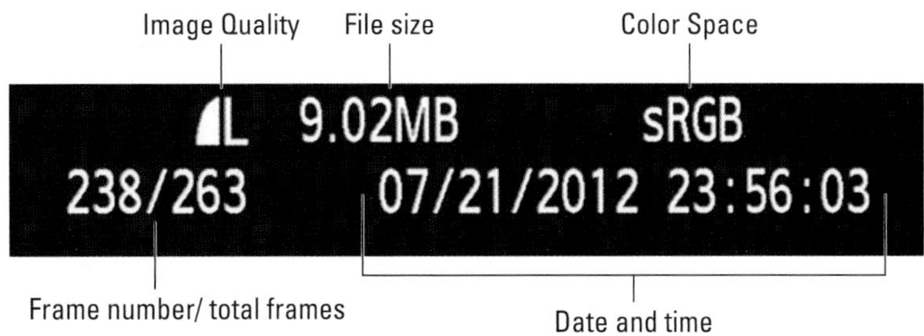

Figure 5-17: The bottom two rows of the display offer this data.

- **Row 5 data:** Wrapping up the smorgasbord of shooting data, the bottom row of the playback screen holds the information labeled along the bottom of Figure 5-17. If you use Eye-Fi memory cards, you also see a small icon depicting the card's wireless connection status. See Chapter 1 for more information about Eye-Fi cards and setting the current date and time.

Understanding Histogram display mode

A variation of the Shooting Information display, the Histogram display offers the data you see in Figure 5-18. Again, you see an image thumbnail, but some of the detailed color and exposure information that you see in Shooting Information display is left out, making room for an additional histogram, called an RGB histogram. Again, remember that this figure shows you the playback screen for pictures taken in the advanced exposure modes; in the other exposure modes, you see slightly different data, but you still get two histograms. For movies and video snapshots, the histograms relate to the first frame of the movie and go blank after playback begins.

The next two sections explain what information you can gain from both types of histograms.

Interpreting a Brightness histogram

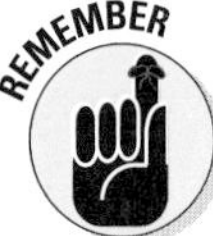

One of the most difficult photo problems to correct in a photo-editing program is known as *blown highlights,* or *clipped highlights.* In plain English, both terms mean that *highlights* — the brightest areas of the image — are so overexposed that areas that should include a variety of light shades are instead totally white. For example, in a cloud image, pixels that should be light to very light gray become white because of overexposure, resulting in a loss of detail in those clouds.

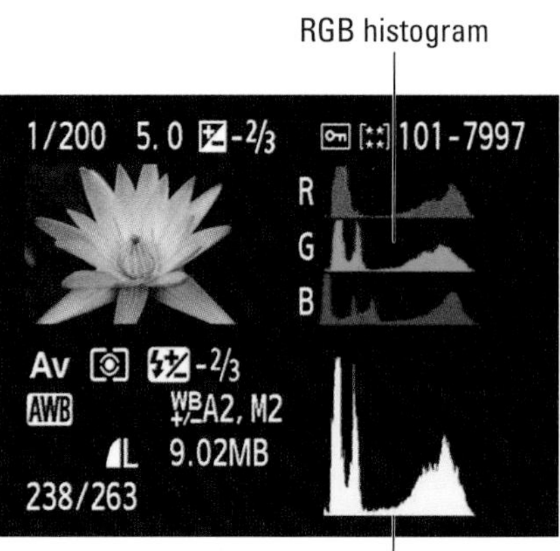

Figure 5-18: Histogram display mode replaces some shooting data with an RGB histogram.

In Shooting Information and Histogram display modes, areas that fall into this category blink in the image thumbnail. This warning is a helpful feature because simply viewing the image on the camera monitor isn't always a reliable way to gauge exposure. The relative brightness of the monitor and the ambient light in which you view it affect the appearance of the image onscreen.

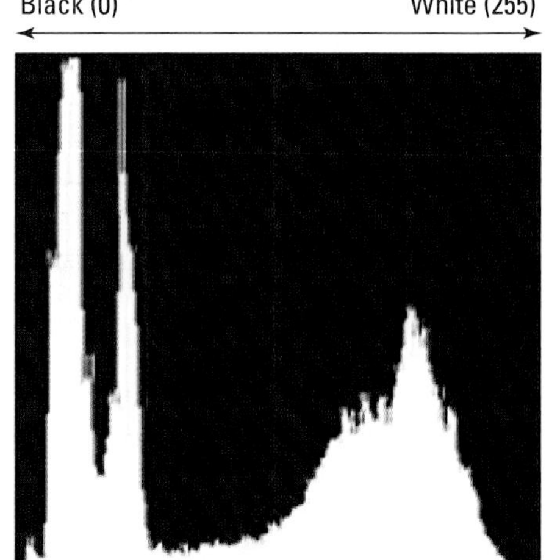

Figure 5-19: The Brightness histogram indicates the tonal range of an image.

The *Brightness histogram,* found in both display modes, offers another analysis of image exposure. This graph, featured in Figure 5-19, indicates the distribution of shadows, highlights, and *midtones* (areas of medium brightness) in an image. Photographers use the term *tonal range* to describe this aspect of their pictures.

The horizontal axis of the graph represents the possible picture brightness values, from black, which has a value of 0, to white, which has a value of 255. And the vertical axis shows you how many pixels fall at a particular brightness value. A spike indicates a heavy concentration of pixels. For example, in Figure 5-19, which shows the histogram for the water lily image you see in Figure 5-18, the histogram indicates a broad range of brightness values but with very few at either end of the brightness spectrum.

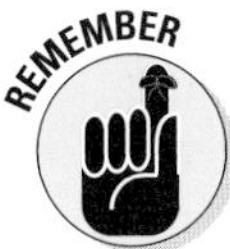

Keep in mind that there is no "perfect" histogram that you should try to duplicate. Instead, interpret the histogram with respect to the amount of shadows, highlights, and midtones that make up your subject. For example, don't expect to see lots of shadow pixels in a photo of a white polar bear standing amid a snowy landscape. Pay attention, however, if you see a very high concentration of pixels at the far right or left end of the histogram, which can indicate a seriously overexposed or underexposed image, respectively.

In Figure 5-19, the lack of white pixels may seem odd for the water lily photo — after all, the petals contain a lot of light tones. But I purposely underexposed the image just a hair to avoid the possibility of blowing out the highlights. So, the histogram offered reassurance that I hadn't overshot the exposure, which can be difficult to determine from just looking at the image itself.

Reading an RGB histogram

In Histogram display mode, you see two histograms: the Brightness histogram and an RGB histogram, shown in Figure 5-20.

To make sense of an RGB histogram, you need to know that digital images are known as *RGB images* because they're created from three primary colors of light: red, green, and blue. The brightness values of each of the three colors are stored in separate data vats called *channels.* Whereas the Brightness histogram reflects the brightness of all three channels rolled into one, RGB histograms let you view the values for each channel.

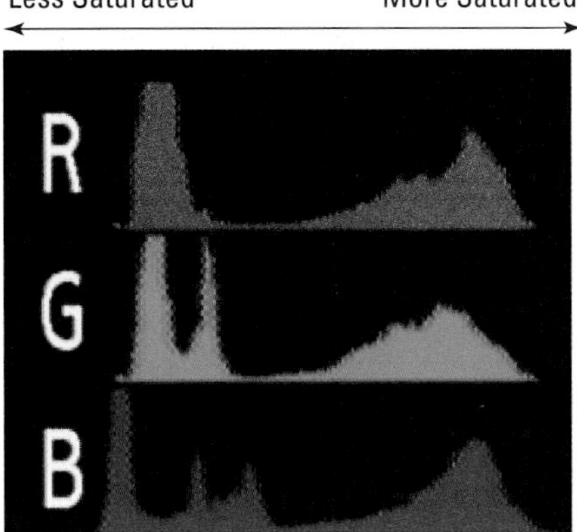

Figure 5-20: The RGB histogram can indicate problems with color saturation.

When you look at the brightness data for a single channel, though, you glean information about *color saturation* rather than image brightness. I don't have space in this book to provide a full lesson in RGB color theory, but the short story is that when you mix red, green, and blue light, and each component is at maximum brightness, you create white. Zero brightness in all three channels creates black. If you have maximum red and no blue or green, though, you have fully saturated red. If you mix two channels at maximum brightness, you also create full saturation. For example, maximum red and blue produce fully saturated magenta.

Where colors are fully saturated, you can lose picture detail. For example, a rose petal that should have a range of tones from medium to dark red may instead be a flat blob of dark red. So the upshot is that if all the pixels for one or two channels are slammed to the right end of the histogram, you may be losing picture detail because of overly saturated colors. If all three channels show a heavy pixel population at the right end of the histogram, you may have blown highlights — again, because the maximum levels of red, green, and blue create white. Either way, you may want to adjust the exposure settings and try again.

A savvy RGB histogram reader can also spot color balance issues by looking at the pixel values. But frankly, color balance problems are fairly easy to notice just by looking at the image on the camera monitor.

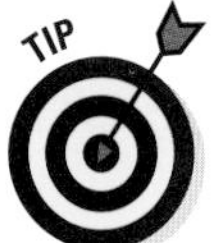

If you're a fan of RGB histograms, however, you may be interested in another possibility: You can swap the standard Brightness histogram that appears in Shooting Information playback mode with the RGB histogram. Just set the Histogram Disp option on Playback Menu 2 to RGB instead of Brightness.

For information about manipulating color, see Chapter 8.

Deleting Photos

When you spot a clunker during your picture review, you can erase it in a few ways, as outlined in the next three sections.

Erasing single images

To delete photos one at a time, display the photo (in single image view) or select it (in Index view). Then press the Erase button. The words *Cancel* and *Erase* appear at the bottom of the screen, as shown in Figure 5-21. To zap that photo into digital oblivion, either tap Erase or press the right cross key to highlight it and press the Set button.

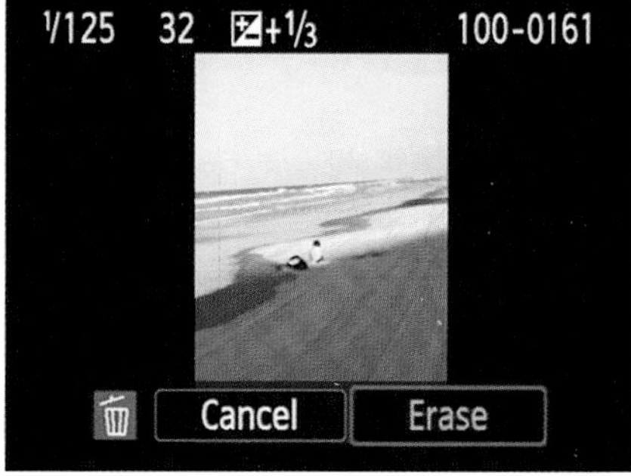

Figure 5-21: Press the Erase button and then tap Erase to delete the current image.

Erasing all images

To erase all images on the memory card — with the exception of those you locked by using the Protect feature discussed later in this chapter — take the following steps:

1. **Display Playback Menu 1, shown on the left in Figure 5-22.**

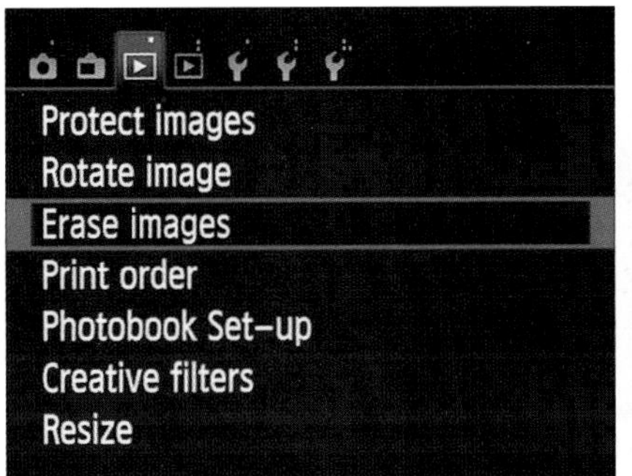

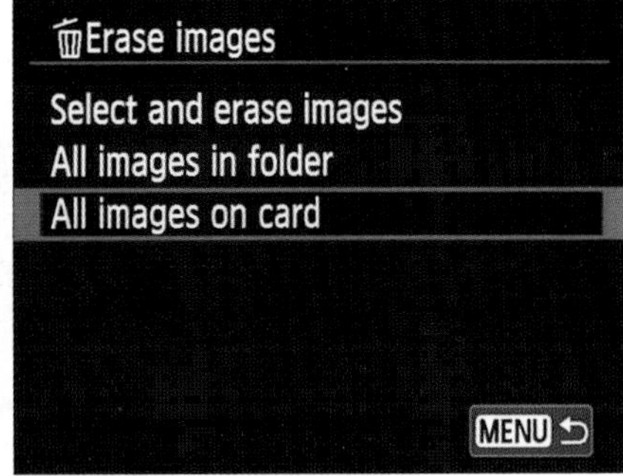

Figure 5-22: Use the Erase option on Playback Menu 1 to delete multiple images quickly.

2. **Choose Erase Images to display the screen shown on the right in Figure 5-22.**
3. **Choose All Images on Card.**

   You then see a confirmation screen.
4. **Choose OK to go ahead and dump the photos.**

If your card contains multiple folders, you can limit the card-wide image dump to just the images in a specific folder. Take these same steps but choose All Images in Folder in Step 3. You then display a list of folders; choose the folder you want to empty and then tap Set or press the Set button.. (See Chapter 10 to find out how to create folders in addition to the ones the camera creates by default.)

Erasing selected images

To erase more than a few but not all images on your memory card, save time and trouble by using this alternative to deleting photos one by one:

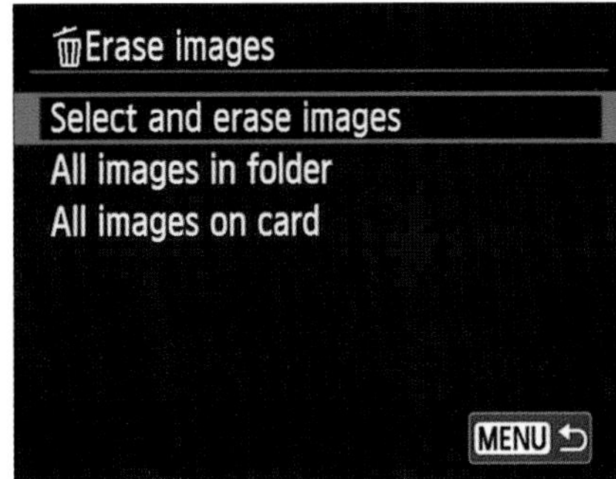

Figure 5-23: You can delete multiple selected images at once.

1. **On Playback Menu 1, choose Erase Images.**

   You see the main Erase Images screen, shown in Figure 5-23.
2. **Choose Select and Erase Images.**

   You see the current image in the monitor. At the top of the screen, a little check box appears, as shown on the left in Figure 5-24.

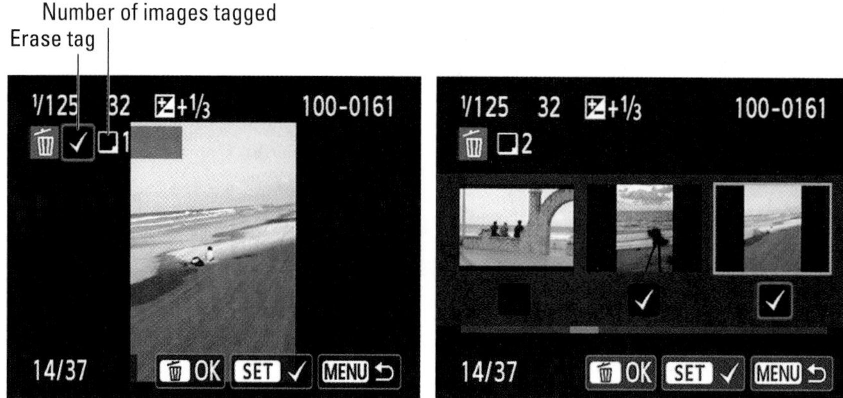

Figure 5-24: Tap the check box or press the Set button to tag images you want to delete.

3. **Tag the image for deletion.**

   Tap the check box, press the Set button, or tap the Set icon to put a check mark in the box, thereby declaring it ready for the trash. If you change your mind, tap the box or the icon or press the Set button again to remove the check mark.

4. **Scroll to the next image.**

5. **Keep repeating Steps 3 and 4 until you mark all images you want to trash.**

   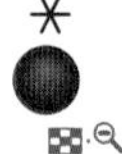

   If you don't need to inspect each image closely, you can display up to three thumbnails per screen. (Refer to the image on the right in Figure 5-24.) Just press the AE Lock button to shift into this display. Use the same methods to tag images for erasure and to scroll through photos as you do when viewing them one at a time.

   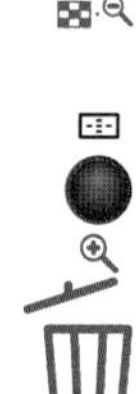

   To return to full-frame view, press the AF Point Selection button.

6. **After tagging all the photos you want to delete, press the Erase button or tap the OK icon.**

   You see a confirmation screen asking whether you really want to get rid of the selected images.

7. **Tap OK or highlight it and press Set.**

   The selected images are deleted, and you return to the Erase Images menu.

8. **Tap the Menu icon or press the Menu button to return to Playback Menu 1.**

   Or, to continue shooting, press the shutter button halfway and release it.

Protecting Photos

You can protect pictures from accidental erasure by giving them protected status. After you take this step, the camera doesn't allow you to delete a picture from your memory card, whether you press the Erase button or use the Erase Images option on Playback Menu 1.

I also use the protection feature when I want to keep a handful of pictures on the card but delete the rest. Instead of using the Select and Erase Images option, which requires that you tag each photo you want to delete, I protect the handful I want to preserve. Then I use the Erase All Images option to dump the rest — the protected photos are left intact.

Although the Erase functions don't touch protected pictures, formatting your memory card *does* erase them. For more about formatting, see the Chapter 1 section related to Setup Menu 1, which contains the Format Card tool.

Also note that when you download protected files to your computer, they show up as read-only files, meaning that the photo can't be altered. So if you want to be able to edit your photos, be sure to remove the protected status before downloading.

Anyway, protecting a picture on the camera is easy. You can use either of the techniques outlined in the next two sections.

Protecting a single photo

To apply protection to just one or two photos, the Quick Control screen offers the fastest option. Display the photo you want to protect in full-frame view. Or in Index view, select the photo by moving the highlight box over it. Then press the Quick Control button and tap or highlight the Protect symbol, labeled in Figure 5-25. Choose Enable at the bottom of the screen, and a little key symbol appears at the top of the frame, as shown in the figure. Tap the return arrow (upper right corner of the screen) or press the Quick Control button again to exit the Quick Control display.

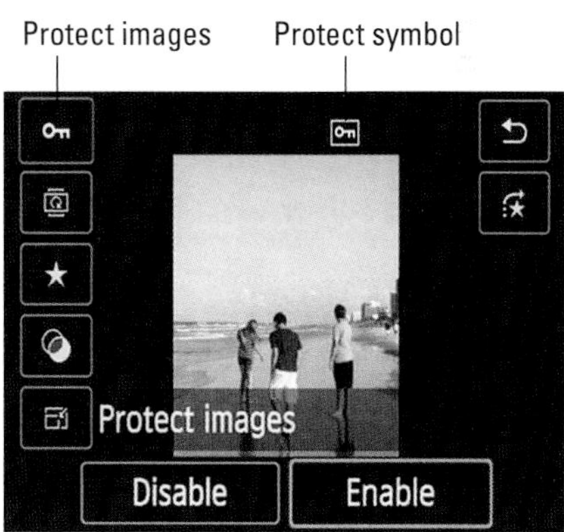

Figure 5-25: You can use the Quick Control screen to protect the current photo.

If you later want to remove the protected status, follow the same steps but choose Disable on the Quick Control screen.

Protecting (or unprotecting) multiple photos

When you want to apply protected status — or remove it — from more than a couple photos, going through Playback Menu 1 is faster than using the Quick Control screen. Take these steps:

1. **Display Playback Menu 1 and choose Protect Images, as shown on the left in Figure 5-26.**

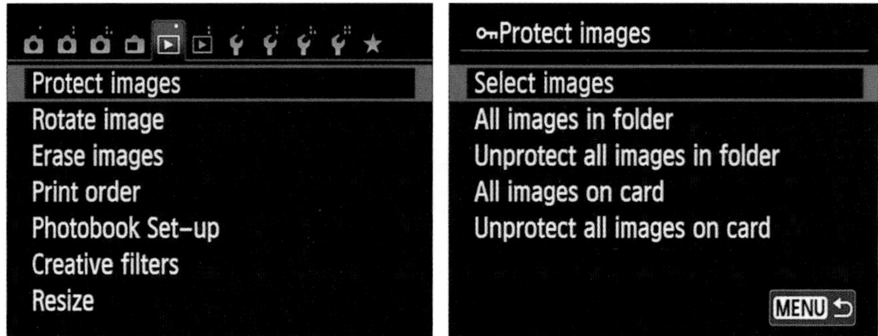

Figure 5-26: This option prevents you from erasing pictures using the normal picture-deletion techniques.

   You then see the options shown on the right in the figure:

   - *Select Images:* This option enables you to choose the photos you want to protect.
   - *All Images in Folder:* Protects all the photos in a folder. Unless your memory card contains multiple folders, this option protects all your pictures. If you do have multiple folders, you can select a folder in the next step.
   - *Unprotect All Images in Folder:* This does the opposite, in case you protected those images and no longer need them locked down.
   - *All Images on Card:* This is a handy option to protect all photos on the card.
   - *Unprotect All Images on Card:* Removes protected status from all pictures on the card.

2. **Choose an option from the list.**

   What happens now depends on which option you chose:

   - *Select Images:* An image appears on the monitor, along with a little key icon in the upper-left corner of the screen, as shown on the left in Figure 5-27. Scroll to the first picture you want to protect and then tap the Set icon or press the Set button. Now a key icon appears with the data at the top of the screen, as shown in the right image of the figure. After you finish protecting photos, press the Menu button or tap the Menu icon to exit the protection screens.

- *All Images in Folder* or *Unprotect All Images in Folder:* You see a screen where you can select a specific folder. Select that folder, tap Set or press the Set button, and then tap OK or press the Set button again.
- *All Images on Card* or *Unprotect All Images on Card:* Choose OK on the confirmation screen.

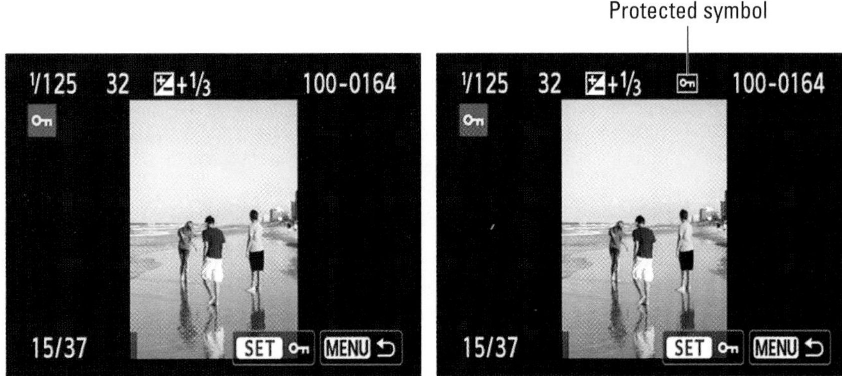

Figure 5-27: The key icon indicates that the picture is protected.

To remove protection from individual pictures, follow these same steps, choosing Select Images in Step 2. When you display the locked picture, just press or tap Set to turn off the protection. The little key icon disappears from the top of the screen to let you know that the picture is no longer protected.

Rating Photos

Many image browsers provide a tool that you can use to assign a rating to a picture: five stars for your best shots, one star for those you wish you could reshoot, and so on. But you don't have to wait until you make it to your computer, because your camera offers the same feature. If you later view your pictures in the Canon image software, as detailed in the next chapter, you can see the ratings you assigned and even sort pictures according to rating.

You assign a rating to a photo either via the Quick Control screen or Playback Menu 2. For rating just a photo or two, either works fine, but for rating a batch of photos, using the menu is fastest. Here's how the two options work:

- **Quick Control screen:** Display your photo in full-screen view and then press the Quick Control button and choose the Rating icon, as shown in Figure 5-28. Along the bottom of the screen, tap or highlight the icon representing the number of stars you want to give the photo and then tap the return arrow or press the Quick Control button to return to the normal playback screen. You must exit the Quick Control screen before rating a second photo — there's no way to advance to another image while the Quick Control screen is active. To remove a rating, choose the Off option.

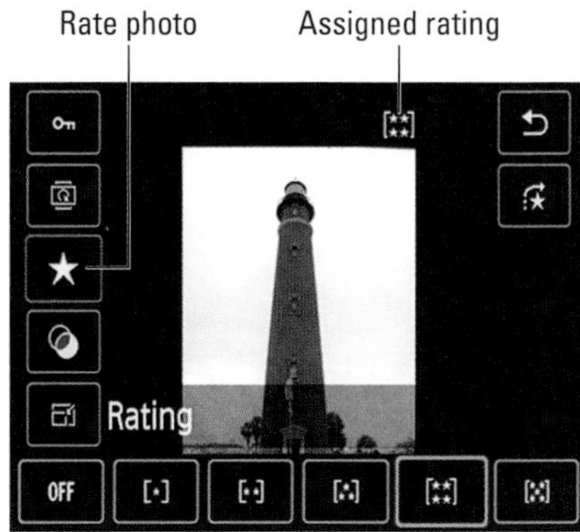

Figure 5-28: You can rate photos via the Quick Control screen.

- **Playback Menu 2:** Choose the Rating option, as shown in Figure 5-29, to access the screen shown on the left in Figure 5-30. Above the image, you get a control box for setting the rating of the current picture — just press the up or down cross keys to give the photo anything from one to five stars. You also can tap the up/down arrows at the bottom of the thumbnail to set the rating level.

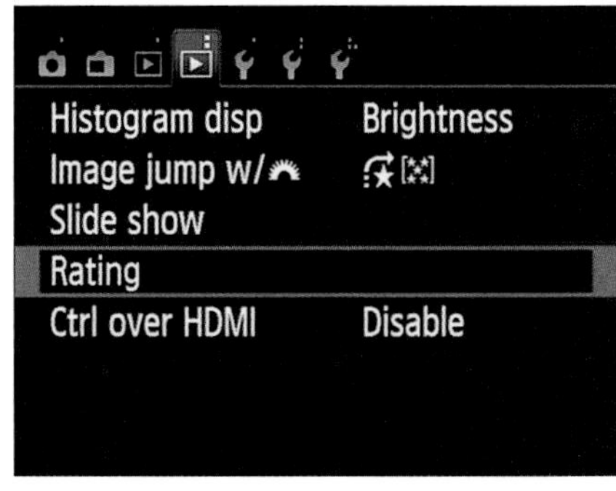

Figure 5-29: Rating photos is a great organizational tool.

  The values next to the control box indicate how many other photos on the card have been assigned each of the ratings. For example, in the figure, the numbers tell me that I have one two-star photo, one four-star photo, and four five-star photos. (I grade myself on a curve.)

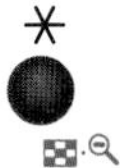

  You can press the AE Lock button to display three thumbnails at a time, as shown on the right in Figure 5-30. Use the right/left cross keys to highlight a thumbnail — or just give the thumbnail a tap to select it. Its rating appears in the box right below the thumbnail. A value of Off simply means you haven't rated the photo yet. You can raise or lower the rating by pressing the up/down cross keys or by tapping the arrows at the bottom of the screen.

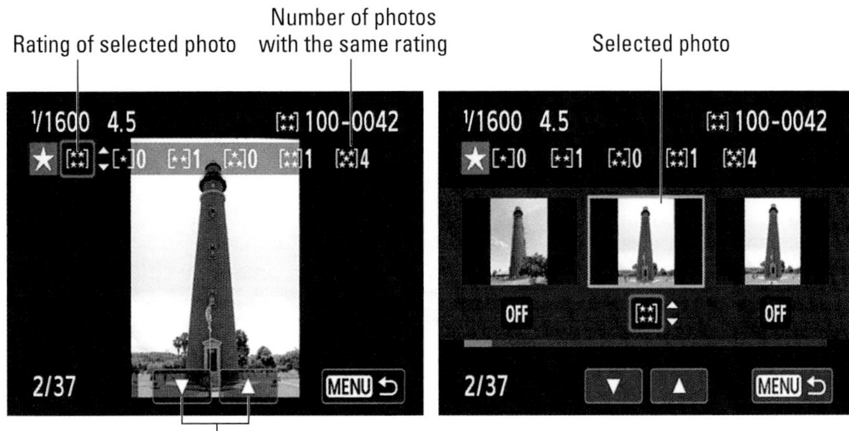

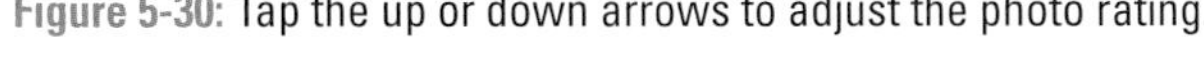

Figure 5-30: Tap the up or down arrows to adjust the photo rating.

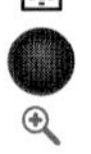

To go back to the one-image display, press the AF Point Selection button.

After rating your photos, press Menu or tap the Menu icon to return to the Playback Menu 2.

Viewing Your Photos on a Television

Your camera is equipped with a feature that allows you to play your pictures and movies on a television screen. In fact, you have three playback options:

- **Regular video playback:** Haven't made the leap yet to HDTV? No worries: You can set the camera to send a regular standard-definition audio and video signal to the TV. You'll need to purchase the Canon AVC-DC400ST cable to do so.
- **HDTV playback:** If you have a high-definition television, you can set the camera to high-def playback. However, you need to purchase an HDMI cable to connect the camera and television; the Canon part number you need is HDMI cable HTC-100. Do *not* use the HDMI port with anything other than the HDMI HTC-100 cable or a quality equivalent.
- **For HDMI CEC TV sets:** If your television is compatible with HDMI CEC, your camera enables you to use the TV's remote control to rule your playback operations. You can put the camera on the coffee table and sit back with your normal remote in hand to entertain family and friends with your genius. To make this operation work, you must enable it on Playback Menu 2, as shown in Figure 5-31.

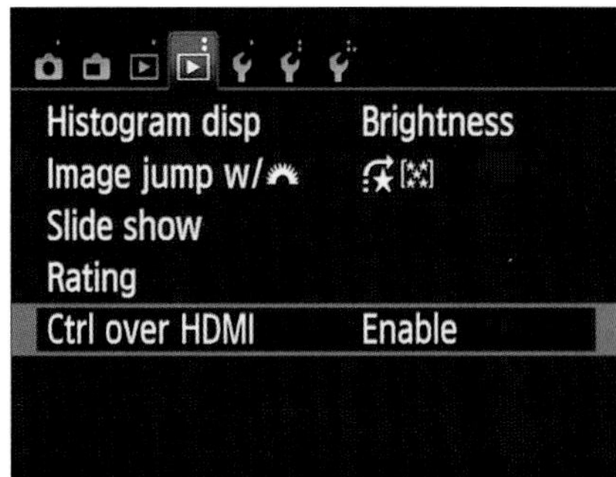

Figure 5-31: To use your HDTV's remote to control playback, enable this option.

Before you begin connecting your camera to your TV, you may need to adjust one camera setting, Video System, which is found on Setup Menu 2. You have just two options: NTSC and PAL. Select the video mode used by your part of the world. (In the United States, Canada, and Mexico, NTSC is the standard.) The camera should have shipped from the factory with the right setting selected, but it never hurts to double-check.

With the right cable in hand and the camera turned off, open the little rubber door that covers the video-out ports — it's the door closest to the back of the camera — as shown in Figure 5-32. The camera has two *ports* (connection slots): one for a standard audio/video (A/V) signal and one for the HDMI signal. The A/V port is the same one you use to connect the camera via USB for picture download, as explained in Chapter 6.

The smaller plug on the A/V cable attaches to the camera. For A/V playback, your cable has three plugs at the other end: Put the yellow one into your TV's video jack and the red and white ones into your TV's stereo audio jacks. For HDMI playback, a single plug goes to the TV.

At this point, I need to point you to your specific TV manual to find out exactly which of its jacks to use to connect your camera. You also need to consult your manual to find out which channel to select for playback of signals from auxiliary input devices.

After you sort out that issue, turn on your camera to send the signal to the TV set. If you don't have the latest and greatest HDMI CEC capability (or lost your remote), you can control playback using the same camera controls as you normally do to view pictures on your camera monitor.

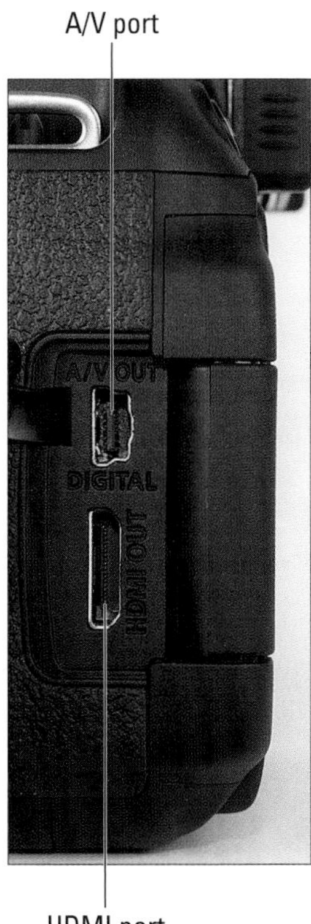

Figure 5-32: You can connect your camera to a television via the A/V port or HDMI port.

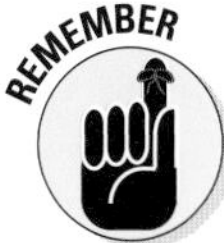

Understand that as soon as you plug your camera into a TV, the camera monitor goes dark — which means touchscreen operations are no longer possible. So you must use the camera buttons (or remote control) to operate any playback functions.

6

Downloading, Printing, and Sharing Your Photos

In This Chapter

- Choosing photo software
- Transferring pictures to your computer
- Processing Raw (CR2) files
- Preparing pictures for print
- Creating low-resolution copies for online sharing

For many digital photographers, the task of moving pictures from camera to computer — *downloading* — is one of the more confusing aspects of the art form. Unfortunately, providing you with detailed downloading instructions is impossible because the steps vary widely depending on which computer software you use to do the job.

To give you as much help as possible, however, this chapter starts with a quick review of photo software, in case you aren't happy with your current solution. Following that, you can find general information about downloading images, converting pictures that you shoot in the Raw format to a standard format, and preparing your pictures for print and e-mail.

Choosing the Right Photo Software

Programs for downloading, archiving, and editing digital photos abound, ranging from beginner-level software to high-end options geared to professionals. The good news is that if you don't need serious photo-editing capabilities, you can find free programs (including two from Canon) that provide all the basic tools you require. The next section takes a look at the Canon programs along with a couple other freebies; following that, I offer advice on a few programs to consider when the free options don't meet your needs.

Four free photo programs

If you don't plan on doing a lot of retouching or other manipulation of your photos and simply want a tool for downloading, organizing, printing, and sharing photos online, one of the following free programs may be a good solution:

- **Canon ImageBrowser EX:** The CD that comes with your camera includes this program, shown in Figure 6-1. It's a capable image organizer and offers a few basic photo-editing features as well.

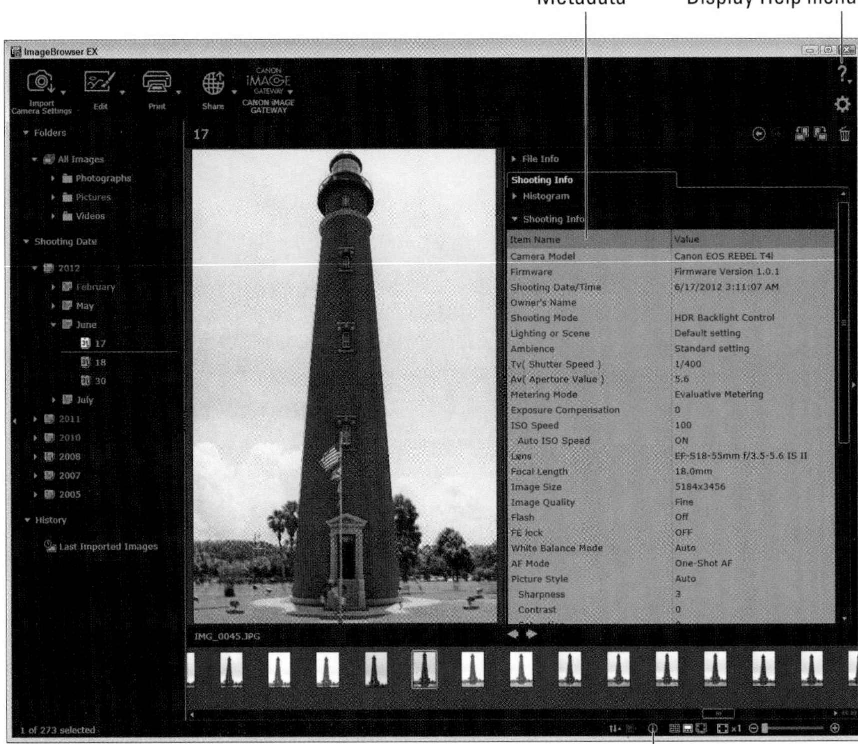

Figure 6-1: Canon ImageBrowser EX provides easy-to-use photo viewing and organizing tools.

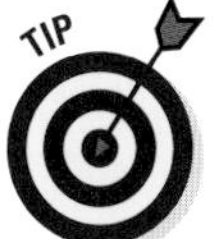

I don't have room to tell you much about using this software, but if you click the Help icon (labeled in Figure 6-1) and choose User Guide from the drop-down Help menu that appears, you can access the program's electronic user manual.

- **Canon Digital Photo Professional:** Designed for more advanced users, this product (see Figure 6-2) offers a higher level of control over certain photo functions. But its most important difference from ImageBrowser EX is that it offers a tool to convert photos that you shoot in the Raw (CR2) format into a standard format (JPEG or TIFF). The upcoming section "Processing Raw (CR2) Files" shows you how. This program, too, has a built-in help system, which you access via the Help menu.

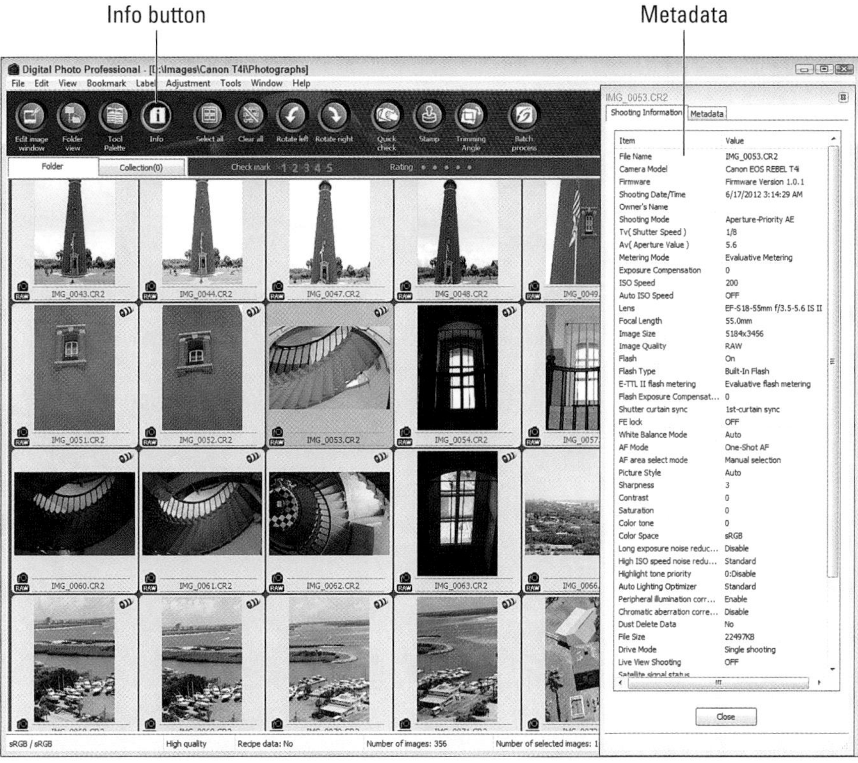

Figure 6-2: Canon Digital Photo Professional offers more advanced features, including a tool for converting Raw files to a standard picture format.

- **Apple iPhoto:** Most Mac users are familiar with this photo browser, built in to the Mac operating system. Apple provides great tutorials on using iPhoto at its website (`www.apple.com`) to help you get started.
- **Windows Photo Gallery:** Some versions of Microsoft Windows also offer a free photo downloader and browser. In Windows 7 and Vista, the tool is Windows Photo Gallery.

After downloading photos, you can view image *metadata* — the data that records the settings you used to take the picture as well as the date and time you shot the photo. In the Canon programs, display the metadata as follows:

- **ImageBrowser EX:** Click the Show Image Properties icon, labeled in Figure 6-1, to display the metadata on the right side of the screen.
- **Canon Digital Photo Professional:** Click the Info button, labeled in Figure 6-2. In this case, the information appears in a separate window, as shown in the figure.

Many other programs also can display camera metadata but sometimes can't display data that's very camera specific, such as the Picture Style. Every camera manufacturer records metadata differently, so it's a little difficult for software companies to keep up with each new model.

Four advanced photo-editing programs

Here are a few popular options for photographers who need more powerful tools than are provided by the free options mentioned in the preceding section:

- **Adobe Photoshop Elements (**`www.adobe.com`**, about $100):** With a full complement of retouching tools, onscreen guidance for beginners, and an assortment of templates for creating photo projects such as scrapbooks, Elements offers all the features that most consumers need.
- **Apple Aperture (**`www.apple.com`**, about $80 through Mac App store):** Aperture is geared to shooters who need to organize and process lots of images but typically do only light retouching work — wedding photographers and school portrait photographers, for example.
- **Adobe Photoshop Lightroom (**`www.adobe.com`**, about $150):** Lightroom is the Adobe counterpart to Aperture. In its latest version, it offers some fairly powerful retouching tools as well, however.
- **Adobe Photoshop (**`www.adobe.com`**, about $700, or available as a monthly subscription via Adobe Cloud services):** Geared to photo pros, Photoshop offers the industry's most sophisticated retouching tools, including features for producing HDR (High Dynamic Range) and 3D images.

Of these programs, only Elements is designed with the novice in mind, and even using Elements involves a bit of a learning curve. So it's a good idea to buy (and read!) a guidebook or take some classes to help you maximize your software investment.

Not sure which tool you need, if any? Good news: You can download 30-day free trials of all these programs from the manufacturers' websites.

Sending Pictures to the Computer

Whatever photo software you choose, you can take the following approaches to downloading images to your computer:

- **Connect the camera to the computer via a USB cable.** The cable is supplied in the camera box.
- **Use a memory-card reader.** With a card reader, you pop the memory card out of your camera and into the card reader instead of hooking the camera to the computer. Many computers and printers now have card readers, and you also can buy standalone readers for under $30. ***Note:*** If you use SDHC (Secure Digital High-Capacity) or SDXC (Secure Digital Extended-Capacity) cards, the reader must specifically support that type. Many older card readers — including some still on the market — do not.
- **Invest in Eye-Fi memory cards and transfer images via a wireless network.** You can find out more about these special memory cards, and how to set up the card to connect with your computer, at the manufacturer's website, `www.eye.fi`. Your computer must be connected to a wireless network for the transfer technology to work.

For most people, I recommend a card reader. Sending pictures directly from the camera, whether via cable or wirelessly, requires that the camera be turned on during the download process, wasting battery power. Additionally, not all devices can use Eye-Fi memory cards, meaning that you're spending money on cards that may have limited use beyond serving as storage on your camera. Card readers, on the other hand, can accept cards from any device that uses SD cards, which are fast becoming the standard storage medium for portable devices.

That said, I include information about both cable and card-reader transfer in the next sections. Again, go to `www.eye.fi` for help with downloading from Eye-Fi cards.

Connecting your camera and computer

You need to follow a specific set of steps when connecting the camera to your computer. Otherwise, you can damage the camera or the memory card. Here's the suggested process:

1. **Make sure the camera battery is fully charged.**

   Running out of battery power during the transfer process can cause problems, including lost picture data. Alternatively, if you have an AC adapter, use it to power the camera during picture transfers.

2. **Turn your computer on and give it time to finish its normal startup routine.**
3. **Turn the camera off.**
4. **Insert the smaller of the two plugs on the USB cable into the A/V Out/Digital port on the side of the camera.**

   This port is hidden behind the little rubber door that's just around the corner from the left side of the monitor, as shown in Figure 6-3.

5. **Plug the other end of the cable into a USB port on the computer.**
6. **Turn on the camera.**

   What happens next depends on what software you use to download photos. As for the camera itself, it doesn't give you any indications that it's in transfer mode, aside from a brief flicker of the card access lamp. If you try to focus or take a photo, the word "Busy" appears in the viewfinder.

   For details about the next step in the downloading routine, move on to the next section.

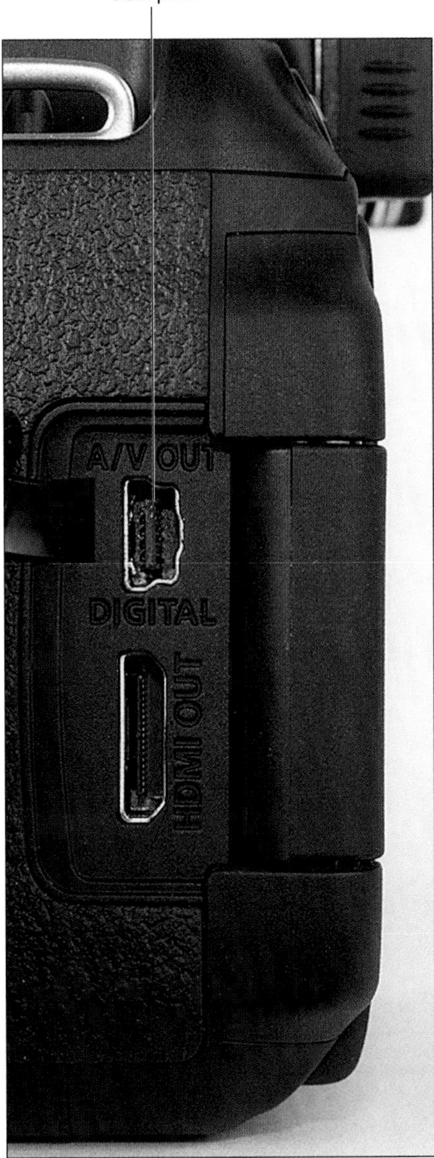

Figure 6-3: Connect the smaller end of the USB cable here to download pictures.

Reviewing the transfer process

After you connect the camera to the computer or insert a memory card into the card reader, your next step depends on the software installed on your computer and on the computer's operating system. Here are the most common possibilities and how to move forward:

- **On a computer running Microsoft Windows, a message box similar to the one in Figure 6-4 appears.** The figure shows the dialog box as it appears in Windows 7. By default, clicking the Import Pictures and Videos icon starts image transfer using the Windows picture-transfer utility, but you can click the Change program link to choose some other program as your preferred transfer tool. If you installed Canon ImageBrowser EX, you may see a link to Canon EOS Utility, the downloader associated with that program, as in the figure.

  In older versions of Windows, you typically see a dialog box listing all the installed programs that can handle the transfer; click the one you want to use.

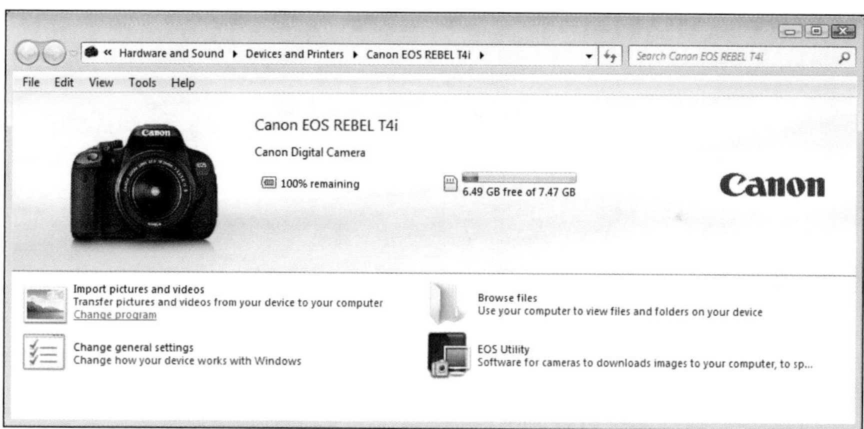

Figure 6-4: Windows 7 may display this initial boxful of transfer options.

- **An installed photo program automatically displays a photo download wizard.** Again, if you installed the Canon software, the EOS Utility window may leap to the forefront. Or, if you installed another program (such as Photoshop Elements), its downloader may pop up instead. On a Mac, the iPhoto downloader may take over. Usually, the downloader that appears is associated with the software you most recently installed. Each new program you add to your system tries to wrestle away control over your image downloads from the previous program.

If you don't want a particular program's auto downloader to launch whenever you insert a memory card or connect your camera, you should be able to turn off that feature. Check the software manual to find out how to disable the auto-launch.

- **Nothing happens.** Don't panic; assuming that your card reader or camera is properly connected, all is probably well. Someone simply may have disabled all automatic downloaders on your system. Just launch your photo software and then transfer your pictures using whichever command starts that process.

As another option, you can use Windows Explorer or the Mac Finder to drag and drop files from your memory card to your computer's hard drive. You connect the card through a card reader, the computer sees the card as just another drive on the system. Windows Explorer also shows the camera as a storage device when you cable the camera directly to the computer. So the process of transferring files is exactly the same as when you move any other file from a CD, DVD, or other storage device onto your hard drive. (With some versions of the Mac OS, including the most recent ones, the Finder doesn't recognize cameras in this way.)

Downloading images with Canon ImageBrowser EX

The process of using ImageBrowser EX to download images is a little different depending on whether you're sending photos directly from the camera or from a card reader. The next two sections provide the details.

Note: Figures here show the Windows version of the software, but the Mac version contains the same options, although sometimes with a slightly different visual design.

Downloading from the camera

The launching pad for downloading from the camera is Canon EOS Utility, shown in Figure 6-5. This window may pop up automatically after you connect your camera to the computer, or your operating software may offer a link to launch the tool. If neither of those things happens, start ImageBrowser EX, click the Import Settings icon at the top of the window, and choose Connect to EOS Camera, as shown in Figure 6-6.

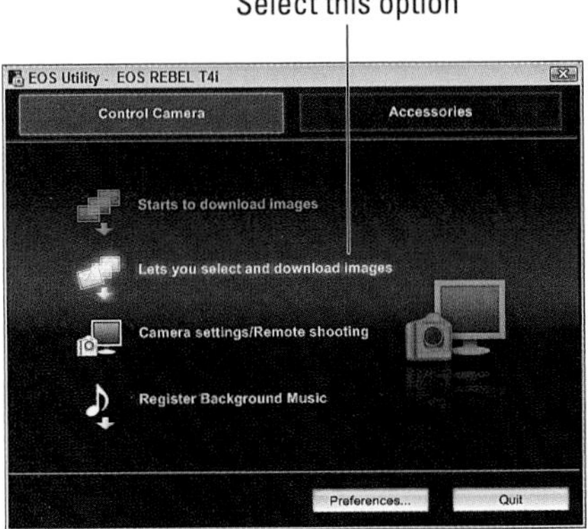

Figure 6-5: Canon EOS Utility is the key to downloading pictures directly from your camera.

Click to open menu

Select to download from camera

Figure 6-6: If the EOS Utility doesn't appear automatically, you can access it from this ImageBrowser EX menu.

After the utility screen opens, take these steps:

1. **Click the Lets You Select and Download Images option.**

   You see a browser window that looks similar to the one in Figure 6-7, with thumbnails of the images on your memory card. Click the magnifying glass icons in the lower-right corner of the window to enlarge or reduce the thumbnail size.

2. **Select the images you want to copy to the computer.**

   Each thumbnail contains a check box in its lower-left corner. To select an image for downloading, click the box to put a check mark in it.

3. **Click the Download button.**

   A screen appears that tells you where the program wants to store your downloaded pictures, as shown in Figure 6-8.

   By default, pictures are stored in the Pictures or My Pictures folder in Windows (depending on the version of Windows you use) and in the Pictures folder on a Mac. You can put images anywhere you like; however, most photo-editing programs look first for photos in those folders, so sticking with this universally accepted setup makes some sense.

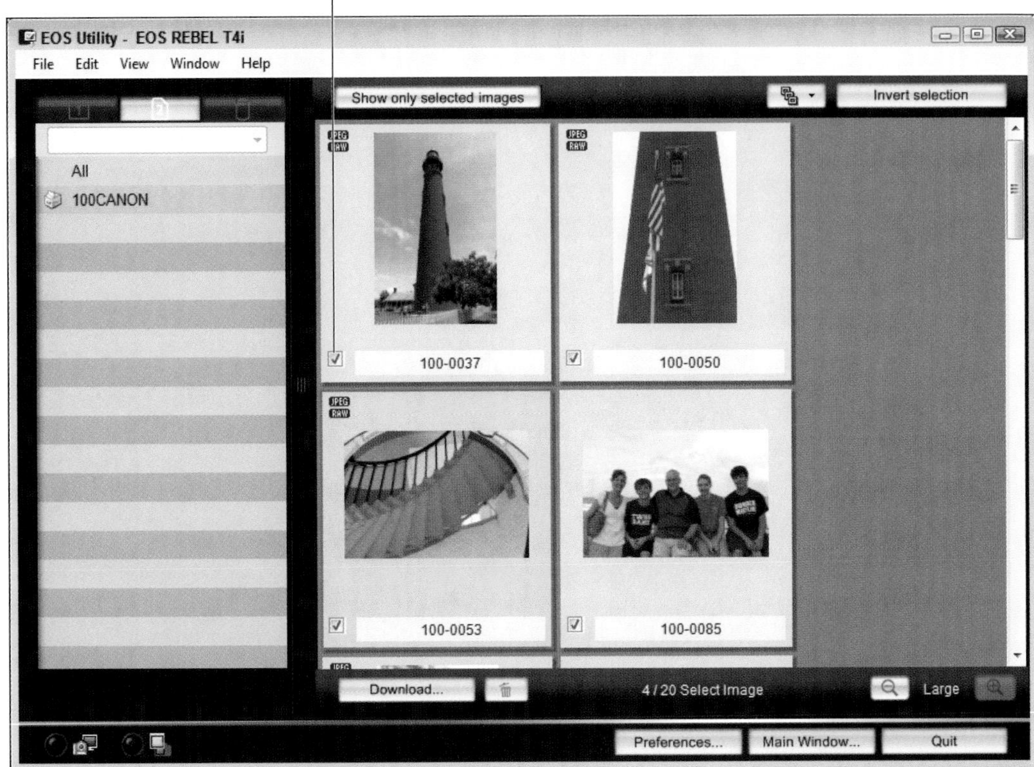

Figure 6-7: Select the thumbnails of the images you want to transfer.

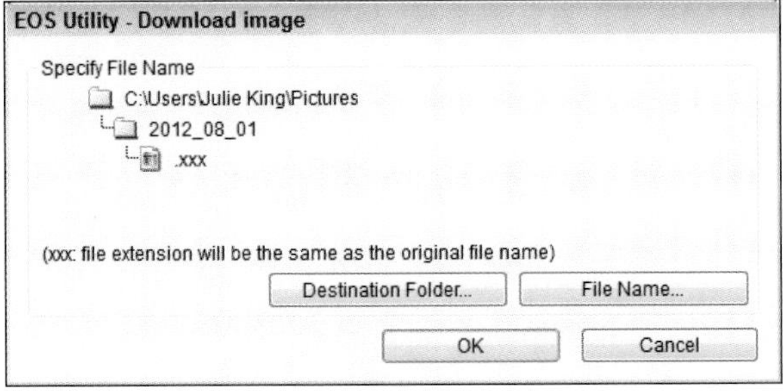

Figure 6-8: You can specify where you want to store the photos.

4. **Verify or change the storage location for your pictures.**

   If you want to put the pictures in a location different from the one the program suggests, click the Destination Folder button and then select the storage location and folder name you prefer.

5. **Click OK to begin the download.**

   A progress window appears, showing you the status of the download.

6. **When the download is complete, turn off the camera.**

   You can then safely remove the cable connecting it to the computer.

A couple of fine points here:

- **Setting download preferences:** While the camera is connected and turned on, click the Preferences button at the bottom of the EOS Utility browser (refer to Figure 6-7) to open the Preferences dialog box, where you can specify many aspects of the transfer process.
- **Auto-launching the other Canon programs:** After the download is complete, the EOS Utility may automatically launch Canon Digital Photo Professional or ImageBrowser EX so that you can immediately start working with your pictures. (You must have installed the programs for this to occur.) Visit the Linked Software panel of the EOS Utility's Preferences dialog box to specify which software you want to use or choose None to disable auto-launch altogether.
- **Closing the EOS Utility:** The browser window doesn't close automatically after the download is complete. You must return to it and click the Quit button in the lower-right corner to shut it down.

Using ImageBrowser EX to download from a card reader

After you put your camera memory card into a card reader, the dialog box shown in Figure 6-9 may appear automatically. This window is the jump-off point for memory-card transfers. If you don't see it after a few moments, you can access it by opening ImageBrowser EX, opening the Import Camera Settings menu (refer to Figure 6-6), and selecting Import Images from Memory Card. Note that depending on your operating system and the program preferences you install, the dialog box shown in Figure 6-9 may also have an option to print directly from the memory card (not shown in the figure).

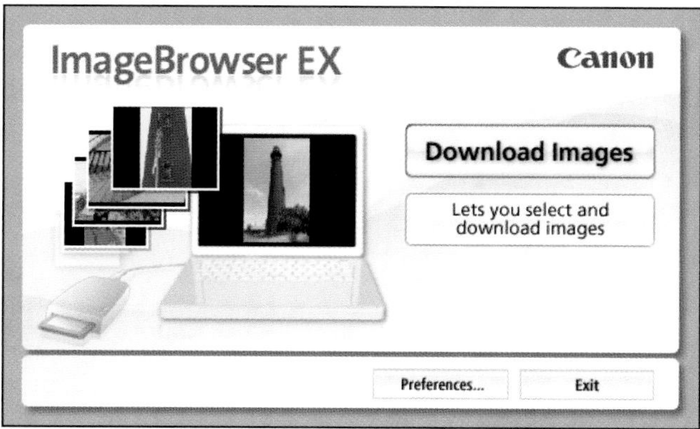

Figure 6-9: Choose Lets You Select and Download images option to choose which pictures get transferred to the computer.

After the window appears, take these steps:

1. **Click the Lets You Select and Download Images option.**

   You see the browser window shown in Figure 6-10. (The figure shows the Windows version of the window; on a Mac, the controls you see at the top of the screen in the figure appear at the bottom of the window. Go figure.)

2. **Select the images you want to download.**

   - *To select the first photo:* Click its thumbnail.
   - *To select additional pictures:* Ctrl+click (Windows) or ⌘+click (Mac) their thumbnails.
   - *To quickly select all images:* Press Ctrl+A in Windows or ⌘+A on a Mac.

3. **Click the Image Download button.**

   A new window opens to show you where the downloader wants to put your files and the name it plans to assign the storage folder, as shown in Figure 6-11.

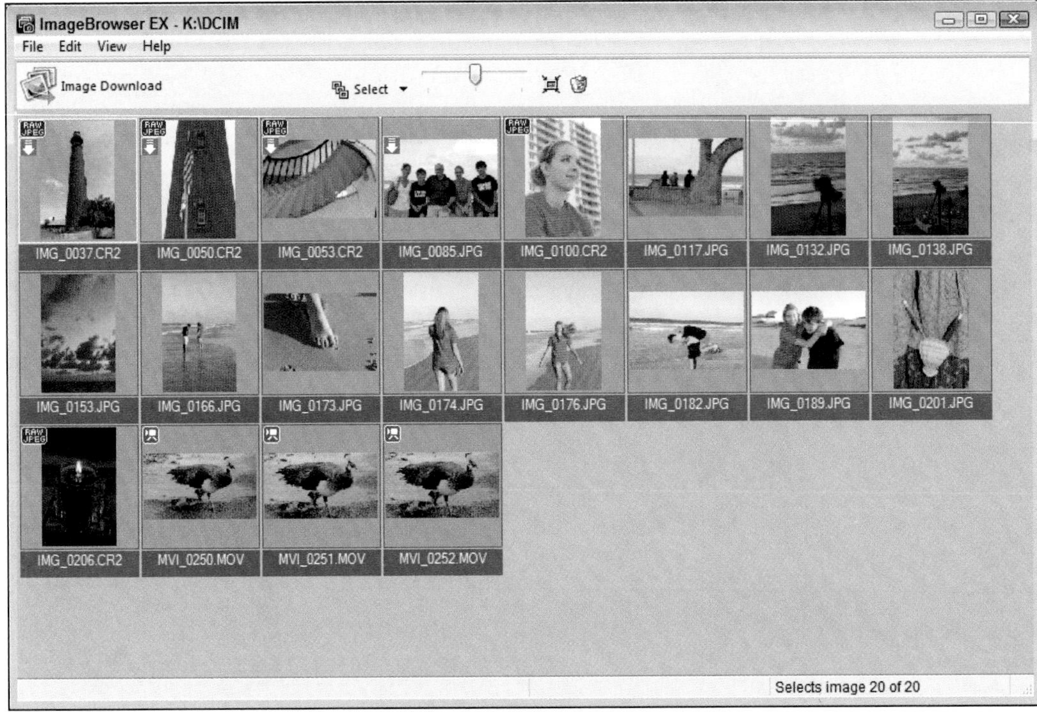

Figure 6-10: Select images to download from the browser window.

If you're not happy with the program's choices, click the Change Settings button to open a dialog box where you can select a different storage location. In the same dialog box, you can also choose to have the files renamed when they're copied. Click OK to close the Change Settings dialog box.

4. **Click the Starts Download button.**

   Your files start making their way to your computer. When the download is finished, your pictures appear in ImageBrowser EX. You must close the downloader windows yourself; they don't automatically disappear.

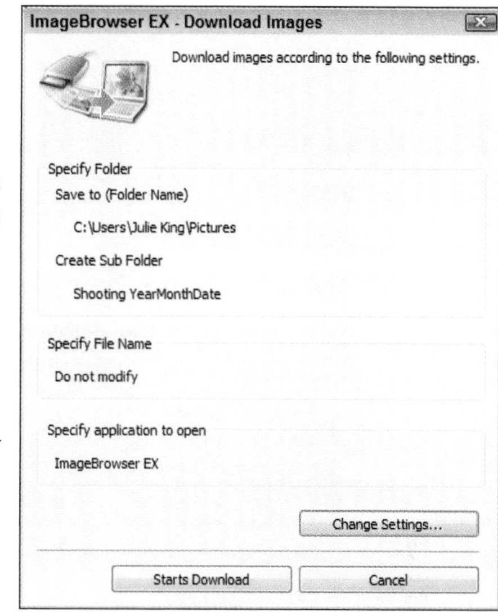

Figure 6-11: Tell the software where you want it to store the downloaded photos via this dialog box.

Processing Raw (CR2) Files

Chapter 2 introduces you to the Raw file format, which enables you to capture images as raw data. Although you can print Raw files immediately if you use the Canon software, you can't take them to a photo lab for printing, share them online, or edit them in your photo software until you process them using a raw converter tool. You can do the job using Digital Photo Professional, the Canon software that shipped with your camera.

After downloading photos to your computer, follow these steps:

1. **Open Digital Photo Professional, click the thumbnail of the image you want to process, and choose View⇨Edit in Edit Image Window.**

   Your photo appears inside an editing window, as shown in Figure 6-12. The exact appearance of the window may vary depending on your program settings. If you don't see the Tool palette on the right side of the window, choose View⇨Tool Palette or click the Tool Palette icon to display it. (Other View menu options enable you to customize the window display.)

2. **Choose Adjustment⇨Work Color Space to choose the color space.**

   By default, the program uses the color space selected when you shot the picture (sRGB or Adobe RGB, Shooting Menu 2). But you can select from a couple of other options if you prefer. The color space determines the spectrum of colors your image can contain; sRGB is the best option if you're not yet schooled in this subject, which I cover in Chapter 10.

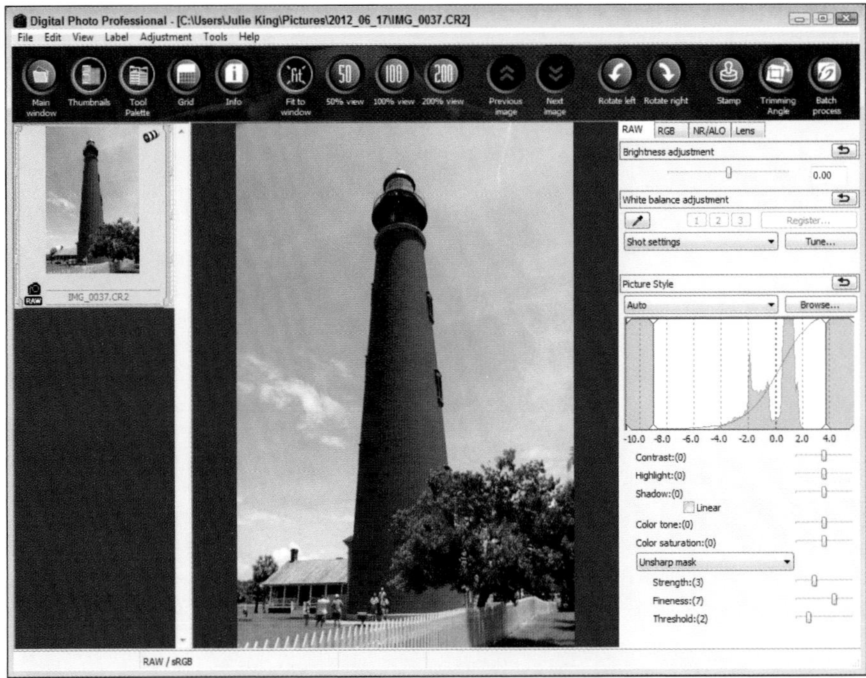

Figure 6-12: You can convert Raw images using Digital Photo Professional.

3. **Adjust the image using controls in the Tool palette.**

   The Tool palette offers four tabs of controls for adjusting photos. You can find complete details in the program's Help system, but here are some tips for a couple critical options:

   - *Raw tab:* On this tab, shown in Figure 6-12, you find controls for tweaking exposure, white balance, color, and sharpness. For white balance, you can choose a specific setting, as shown in the figure (in this case, the current White Balance value is Shot Settings, which means the camera setting is preserved), or click the little eyedropper and then click an area of the image that should be white, black, or gray to remove any color cast. Using the Picture Style option, you can apply one of the camera's Picture Style options to the photo.

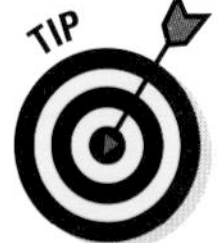

     If you captured the picture in Live View and set the aspect ratio to anything other than 3:2, the thumbnail image at the bottom of the Raw tab (not shown in the figure) shows a border over the image to indicate how the photo will be cropped to achieve that ratio. Remember, Raw images are captured using the 3:2 aspect ratio — and then the Raw processing function crops the original to the aspect ratio you chose. To change the aspect ratio or crop area, choose Tools⇨Start Trimming/Angle Adjustment tool, which displays your picture in a separate editing window. Drag inside the crop box to reposition it; click the Clear button to remove the crop box. Then use the Aspect Ratio option to set a new aspect ratio for the picture and drag in the window to create a new crop box. Click OK to close the window. (The program's built-in Help system, available via the Help menu, has details.)

- *RGB tab:* From this tab, you adjust exposure further by using Tone Curve adjustment, a tool that may be familiar to you if you've done any advanced photo editing. You can make additional color and sharpness adjustments here as well, but make those changes using the controls on the Raw tab instead. (The RGB tab options are provided primarily for manipulating JPEG and TIFF photos and not for Raw conversion.)
- *NR/ALO tab:* On this tab, you find controls for softening image noise and can apply the Auto Lighting Optimizer effect here instead of using the in-camera correction.
- *Lens tab:* Click the Tune button to access the options that enable you to access certain lens correction options, including the Peripheral Illumination and Chromatic Aberration features discussed in Chapters 7 and 8, respectively.

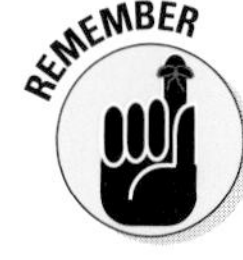

At any time, you can revert the image to the original settings by choosing Adjustment⇨Revert to Shot Settings.

4. **Choose File⇨Convert and Save.**

   You see the standard file-saving dialog box with a few additional controls. Here's the rundown of critical options:

   - *Save as type:* Choose Exif-TIFF (8bit). This option saves your image in the TIFF file format, which preserves all image data. Don't choose the JPEG format; doing so is destructive to the photo because of the lossy compression that's applied. (Chapter 2 explains JPEG compression.)

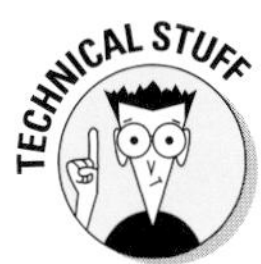

   A *bit* is a unit of computer data; the more bits you have, the more colors your image can contain. Some photo-editing programs can't open 16-bit files, or else they limit you to a few editing tools, so stick with the standard, 8-bit image option unless you know that your software can handle the higher bit depth. If you prefer 16-bit files, you can select TIFF 16bit as the file type.

   - *Output Resolution:* This option sets the default output resolution to be used if you send the photo to a printer. The final resolution will depend on the print size you choose, however. See the next section for more information about printing and resolution.

- *Embed ICC Profile in Image:* Select this check box to include the color-space data in the file. If you then open the photo in a program that supports color profiles, the colors are rendered more accurately. *ICC* refers to the International Color Consortium, the group that created color-space standards.
- *Resize*: Clear this check box so that your processed file contains all its original pixels.

5. **Enter a filename, select the folder where you want to store the image, and then click Save.**

   A progress box appears, letting you know that the conversion and file saving is going forward. Click the Exit button (Windows) or the Terminate button (Mac) to close the progress box when the process is complete.

6. **Click the Main Window button (upper-right corner of program window) to return to the image browser.**
7. **Close Digital Photo Professional.**

   You see a dialog box that tells you that your Raw file was edited and asks whether you want to save the changes.

8. **Click Yes to store your raw-processing "recipe" with the Raw file.**

   The Raw settings you used are then kept with the original image so that you can create additional copies of the Raw file easily without having to make all your adjustments again.

Again, these steps give you only a basic overview of the process. If you regularly shoot in the Raw format, take the time to explore the Digital Photo Professional Help system so that you can take advantage of its other features.

If you prefer, you can jump from ImageBrowser EX directly to the Digital Photo Professional Raw processing window. In ImageBrowser EX, open the Edit menu and choose Process Raw Images to do so.

Planning for Perfect Prints

Images from your camera can produce dynamic prints, and getting those prints made is easy and economical, thanks to an abundance of digital printing services in stores and online. For home printing, today's printers are better and less expensive than ever, too.

That said, getting the best prints from your picture files requires a little bit of knowledge and prep work on your part, regardless of whether you decide to do the job yourself or use a retail lab. The next three sections offer tips to help you avoid the most common causes of printing problems.

Check the pixel count before you print

Resolution — the number of pixels in your digital image — plays a huge role in how large you can print your photos and still maintain good picture quality. You can get the complete story in Chapter 2, but here's a quick resolution recap as it relates to printing:

- **Choose the right resolution before you shoot.** Set resolution via the Image Quality option on Shooting Menu 1 or, in the P, Tv, Av, or M exposure modes, via the Quick Control display.

  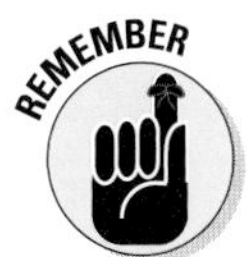

  You must select the Image Quality option *before* you capture an image, which means that you need some idea of the ultimate print size before you shoot. When you do the resolution math, remember to consider any cropping you plan to do.

- **Aim for a minimum of 200 pixels per inch (ppi).** You'll get a wide range of recommendations on this issue, even among professionals. In general, if you aim for a resolution in the neighborhood of 200 ppi, you should be pleased with your results. If you want a 4 x 6–inch print, for example, you need at least 800 x 1200 pixels.

  Depending on your printer, you may get even better results at a slightly lower resolution. On the other hand, some printers do their best work when fed 300 ppi, and a few request 360 ppi as the optimum resolution. However, using a resolution higher than that typically doesn't produce any better prints.

  Unfortunately, because most printer manuals don't bother to tell you what image resolution produces the best results, finding the right pixel level is a matter of experimentation. Don't confuse *ppi* with the manual's statements related to the printer's dpi. *Dots per inch (dpi)* refers to the number of dots of color the printer can lay down per inch; many printers use multiple dots to reproduce one image pixel.

  If you're printing photos at a retail kiosk or at an online site, the software you use to order prints should determine the resolution of your files and then suggest appropriate print sizes. If you're printing on a home printer, though, you need to be the resolution cop.

What do you do if you find that you don't have enough pixels for the print size you have in mind? Well, if you can't compromise on print size, you have two choices:

- **Keep the existing pixel count and accept lowered photo quality.** In this case, the pixels simply get bigger to fill the requested print size. When pixels grow too large, they produce *pixelation:* The picture starts to appear jagged, or stair-stepped, along curved or oblique lines. Or (at worst), your eye can make out the individual pixels and your photo begins to look more like a mosaic than, well, like a photograph.

- **Add more pixels and accept lowered photo quality.** In some photo programs, you can use a process called *resampling* to add pixels to an existing image. Some other photo programs even resample the photo automatically for you, depending on the print settings you choose.

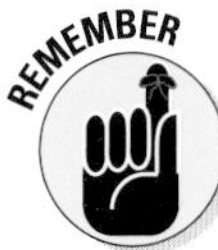

Although adding pixels might sound like a good option, it actually doesn't help. You're asking the software to make up photo information out of thin air, and the resulting image usually looks worse than the original. You don't see pixelation, but details turn muddy, giving the image a poorly rendered appearance.

Just to hammer home the point and show you the impact of resolution picture quality, Figures 6-13 and 6-14 show you the same image as it appears at 300 ppi (the resolution required by the publisher of this book), at 50 ppi, and then resampled from 50 ppi to 300 ppi. As you can see, there's just no way around the rule: If you want the best-quality prints, you need the right pixel count from the get-go.

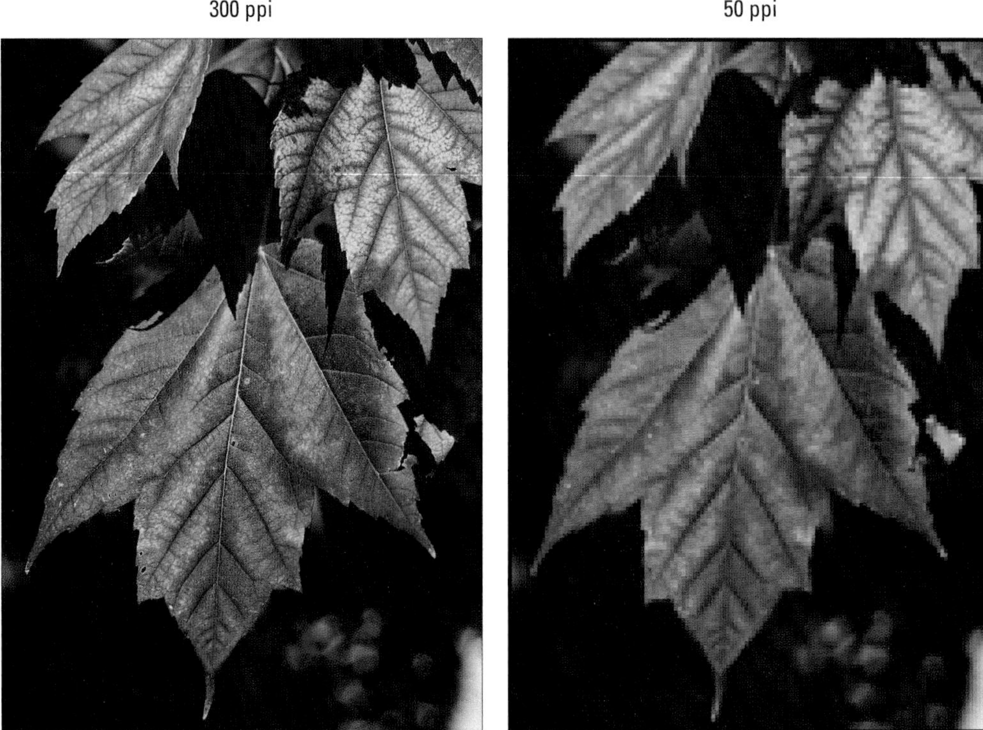

Figure 6-13: A high-quality print depends on a high-resolution original.

Allow for different print proportions

By default, your camera produces images that have a 3:2 aspect ratio, which means that they translate perfectly to the standard 4-x-6-inch print size.

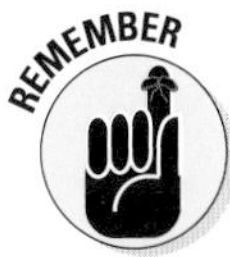

To print at other standard sizes — 5 x 7, 8 x 10, 11 x 14, and so on — you need to crop the photo to match those proportions. Alternatively, you can reduce the photo size slightly and leave an empty margin along the edges of the print as needed.

As a point of reference, both images in Figure 6-15 are original, 3:2 images. The blue outlines indicate how much of the original can fit within a 5-x-7-inch frame and an 8-x-10-inch frame, respectively.

50 ppi resampled to 300 ppi

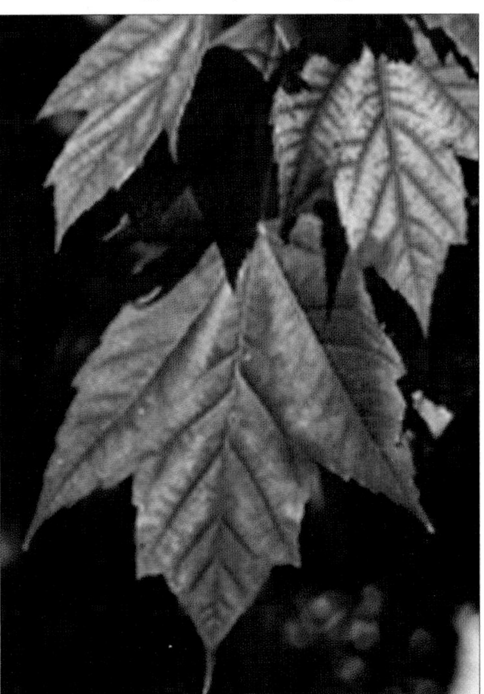

Figure 6-14: Adding pixels in a photo editor doesn't rescue a low-resolution original.

To allow yourself some printing flexibility, leave at least a little margin of background around your subject when you shoot, as I did when shooting the photo in Figure 6-15. That way you don't clip off the edges of the subject, no matter what print size you choose. (Some people refer to this margin padding as *head room,* especially when describing portrait composition.)

Note that all these tips also apply if you use the Live View option that lets you change the photo aspect ratio from 3:2 to 4:3, 16:9, or 1:1. In fact, you'll have to crop or shrink your photos to fit even a 4 × 6 snapshot in that case.

Get print and monitor colors in sync

Your photo colors look perfect on your computer monitor, but when you print the picture, the image is too red or too green or has another nasty color tint. This problem, which is probably the most prevalent printing issue, can occur because of any or all of the following factors:

- **Your monitor needs to be calibrated.** If the monitor isn't accurately calibrated, chances are that it's not displaying an accurate rendition of image colors. The same caveat applies to monitor brightness: You can't accurately gauge the exposure of a photo if the brightness of the monitor is cranked way up or down. Many of today's new monitors are very bright, providing ideal conditions for web browsing and watching movies but not necessarily for photo editing. So you may need to turn the brightness way, way down to get to a true indication of image exposure.

To ensure that your monitor is displaying photos on a neutral canvas, you can start with a software-based *calibration utility,* which is just a small program that guides you through the process of adjusting your monitor.

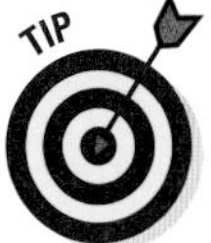

If you use a Mac, its operating system (OS) offers a built-in calibration utility, the Display Calibrator Assistant; Windows 7 offers a similar tool: Display Color Calibration. You also can find free calibration software for both Mac and Windows systems online; just enter the term *free monitor calibration software* into your favorite search engine.

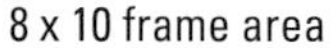

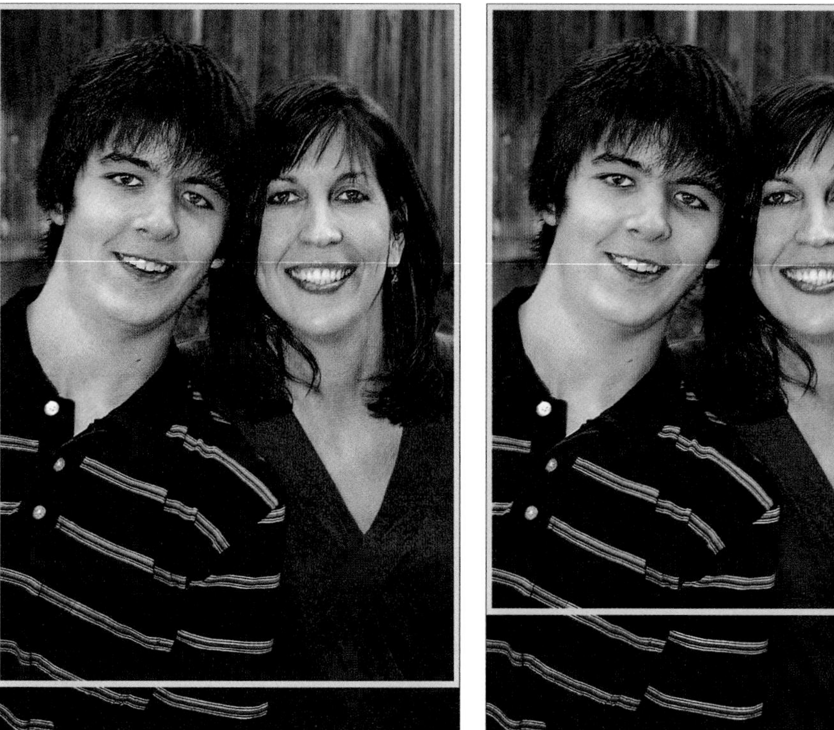

Figure 6-15: Composing shots with a little head room enables you to crop to different frame sizes.

Software-based tools, though, depend on your eyes to make decisions during the calibration process. For a more reliable calibration, you may want to invest in a hardware solution, such as the Pantone huey PRO ($99, `www.pantone.com`) or the Datacolor Spyder3Express ($89, `www.datacolor.com`) or X-Rite ColorMunki Display ($190, `www.colormunki.com`). These products use a device known as a *colorimeter* to accurately measure display colors.

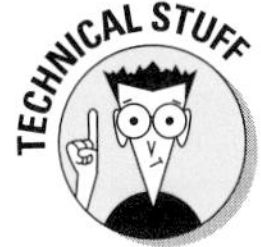

Whichever route you take, the calibration process produces a monitor *profile,* which is simply a data file that tells your computer how to adjust the display to compensate for any monitor color casts or brightness and contrast issues. Your Windows or Mac operating system loads this file automatically when you start your computer. Your only responsibility is to perform the calibration every month or so because monitor colors drift over time.

- **One of your printer cartridges is empty or clogged.** If your prints look great one day but are way off the next, the number-one suspect is an empty ink cartridge or a clogged print nozzle or head. Check your manual to find out how to perform the necessary maintenance to keep the nozzles or print heads in good shape.

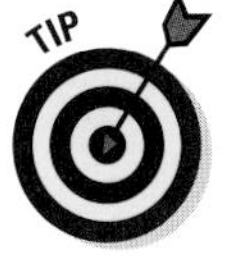

If black-and-white prints have a color tint, a logical assumption is that your black ink cartridge is to blame, if your printer has one. The truth is that images from a printer that doesn't use multiple black or gray cartridges always have a slight color tint because to create gray, the printer has to mix yellow, magenta, and cyan in perfectly equal amounts, which is difficult for a typical inkjet printer to pull off. If your black-and-white prints have a strong color tint, however, a color cartridge might be empty, and replacing it may help somewhat. Long story short: Unless your printer is marketed for producing good black-and-white prints, you'll probably save yourself some grief by simply having your black-and-whites printed at a retail lab.

When you buy replacement ink, by the way, keep in mind that third-party brands (although perhaps cheaper) may not deliver the same performance as cartridges from your printer manufacturer. A lot of science goes into getting ink formulas to mesh with the printer's ink-delivery system, and the printer manufacturer obviously knows most about that delivery system.

- **You chose the wrong paper setting in your printer software.** When you set up a print job, be sure to select the right setting from the paper type option: glossy or matte, for example. This setting affects the way the printer lays down ink on the paper.
- **Your photo paper is low quality.** Sad but true: Cheap, store-brand photo papers usually don't render colors as well as the higher-priced,

name-brand papers. For best results, try papers from your printer manufacturer; again, those papers are engineered to provide top performance with the printer's specific inks and ink-delivery system.

TIP

Some paper manufacturers, especially those that sell fine-art papers, offer downloadable *printer profiles*, which are simply little bits of software that tell your printer how to manage color for the paper. Refer to the manufacturer's website for information on how to install and use the profiles. And note that a profile mismatch can also cause incorrect colors in your prints, including the color tint in black-and-white prints alluded to earlier.

- **Your printer and photo software are fighting over color management duties.** Some photo programs offer *color management* tools, which enable you to control how colors are handled as an image passes from camera to monitor to printer. Most printer software also offers color management features. The problem is, if you enable color management controls in both your photo software and printer software, you can create conflicts that lead to wacky colors. Check your photo software and printer manuals for color management options and ways to turn them on and off.

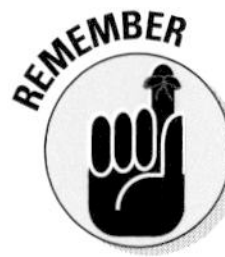

Even if all the aforementioned issues are resolved, however, don't expect perfect color matching between printer and monitor. Printers simply can't reproduce the entire spectrum of colors that a monitor can display. In addition, monitor colors always appear brighter because they are, after all, generated with light.

Finally, be sure to evaluate print colors and monitor colors in the same ambient light — daylight, office light, whatever — because that light source has its own influence on the colors you see. Also allow your prints to dry for 15 minutes or so before you make any final judgments.

Preparing Pictures for Online Sharing

Have you ever received an e-mail message containing a photo so large that you can't view the whole thing on your monitor without scrolling the e-mail window? This annoyance occurs because monitors can display only a limited number of pixels. The exact number depends on the screen resolution setting, but suffice it to say that most of today's digital cameras produce photos with pixel counts in excess of what the monitor can handle.

Thankfully, the newest e-mail programs incorporate features that automatically shrink the photo display to a viewable size. In Windows Live Mail, for example, photos arrive with a thumbnail link to a slide show viewer that can handle even gargantuan images. But that still doesn't change the fact that a large photo file means longer downloading times and, if recipients choose to hold onto the picture, a big storage hit on their hard drives.

Sending a high-resolution photo *is* the thing to do if you want the recipient to be able to generate a good print. But it's polite practice to ask people if they *want* to print 11 x 14 glossies of your new puppy before you send them a dozen 18-megapixel shots.

For simple onscreen viewing, I limit my photos to about 800 pixels across and 600 pixels down. That ensures that people who use an e-mail program that doesn't offer the latest photo-viewing tools can see the entire picture without scrolling the viewer window.

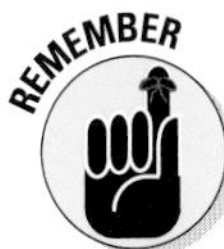

At the lowest Image Quality setting on your camera, S3, pictures contain 720 x 480 pixels. But recording your originals at that tiny size isn't a good idea because if you want to print the photo, you won't have enough pixels to produce a good result. Instead, shoot your originals at a resolution appropriate for print and then create a low-res copy of the picture for e-mail sharing or for other online uses, such as posting to Facebook. (Posting only low-res photos to Facebook and online photo-sharing sites also helps dissuade would-be photo-thieves looking for free images for use in their company's brochures and other print materials.)

In addition to resizing high-resolution images, also check their file types; if the photos are in the Raw or TIFF format, you need to create a JPEG copy for online use. Web browsers and e-mail programs can't display Raw or TIFF files.

You have a couple ways to tackle both bits of photo prep. You can use Canon Digital Photo Professional to convert Raw and TIFF files to the JPEG format and then use ImageBrowser EX's Share⇨E-mail Images feature to size your JPEG copy and ship it off through the innertubes. Check the programs' Help systems for assistance with both tasks.

For JPEG pictures, though, you can create a small-size copy right in the camera. The only exceptions are pictures captured using the S3 Quality setting — at 740 x 480 pixels, they're already the smallest images the camera can create.

Use either of these approaches to use the in-camera shrink ray:

- **Playback Menu 1:** Choose the Resize option, as shown on the left in Figure 6-16. You see a photo along with a Resize icon in the upper-left corner and a Set icon in the lower-right corner.

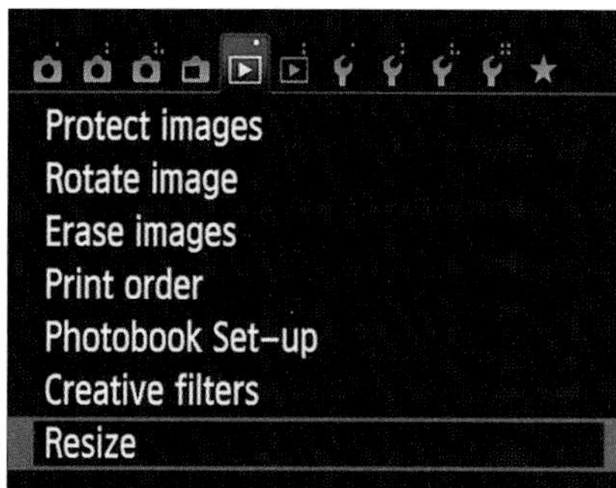

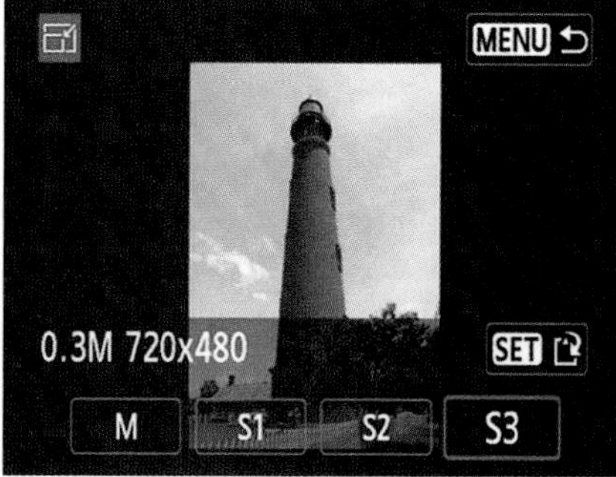

Figure 6-16: Choose the Resize command to make a low-resolution copy of an existing image.

Scroll to the picture you want to resize and then tap the Set icon or press the Set button. You see display size options available for the photo, as shown on the right in Figure 6-16. Which sizes appear depends on the size of the original photo; you're offered only sizes that produce a smaller picture. The text label above the options indicates the file size and pixel count of the selected setting.

Tap the setting you want to use (or highlight it and press Set) to display a confirmation screen. Choose OK, and the camera creates your low-res copy and displays a text message along with a 7-digit number. The first three numbers indicate the folder number where the copy is stored and the last four numbers are the last four numbers of the image filename. Be sure to note the filename of the small copy so that you can tell it apart from its high-pixel sibling later. Choose OK one more time to wrap up.

- **Quick Control screen:** Display the photo you want to resize, shift to Quick Control mode (press the Quick Control button), and then highlight the Resize icon, as shown in Figure 6-17. Size options appear at the bottom of the screen; tap the one you want to use or highlight it and press Set. From that point, things work the same as just described.

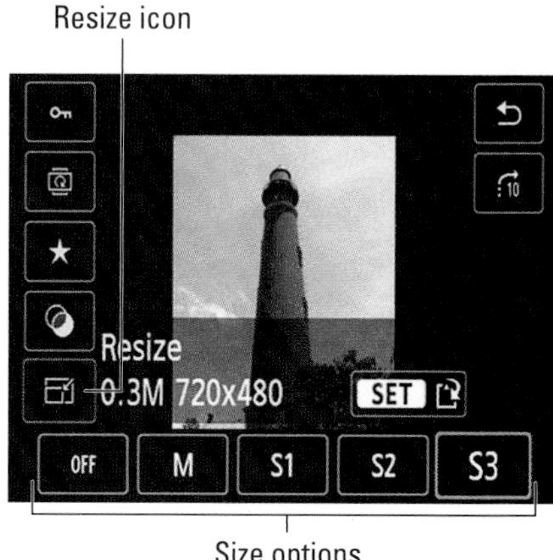

Figure 6-17: You also can resize photos from the Quick Control screen during playback.

Part III
Taking Creative Control

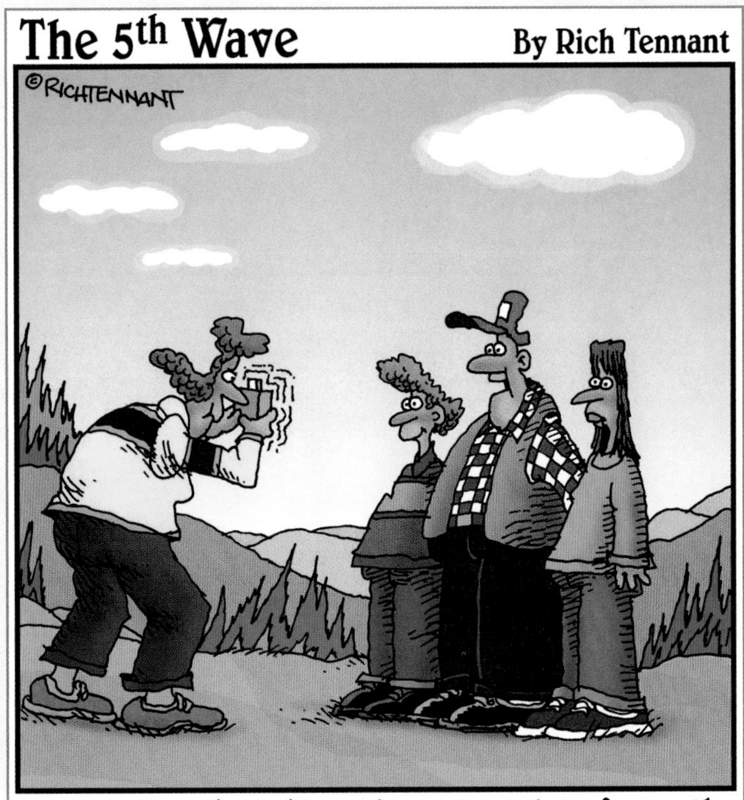

"Remember, when the subject comes into focus, the camera makes a beep. But that's annoying, so I set it on vibrate."

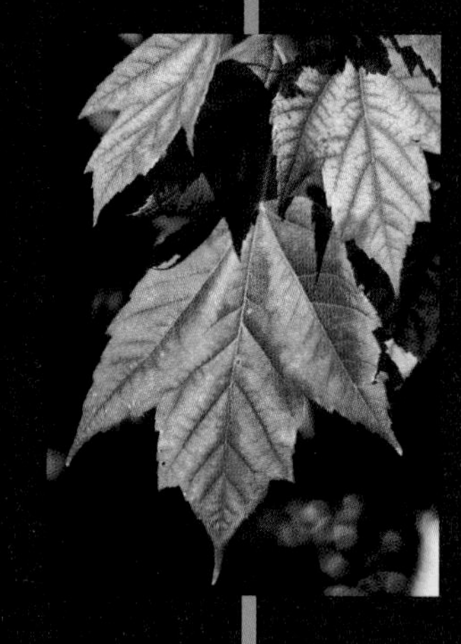

In this part . . .

As nice as it is to rely on the point-and-shoot exposure modes and let the camera handle all decisions for you, I encourage you to explore the advanced exposure modes (P, Tv, Av, and M) as well. In these modes, you control settings that affect exposure, focus, and color, which is key to capturing an image as you see it in your mind's eye. And don't think that you have to be a genius or spend years in study to be successful — adding just a few simple techniques to your photographic repertoire can make a huge difference in how happy you are with the pictures you take.

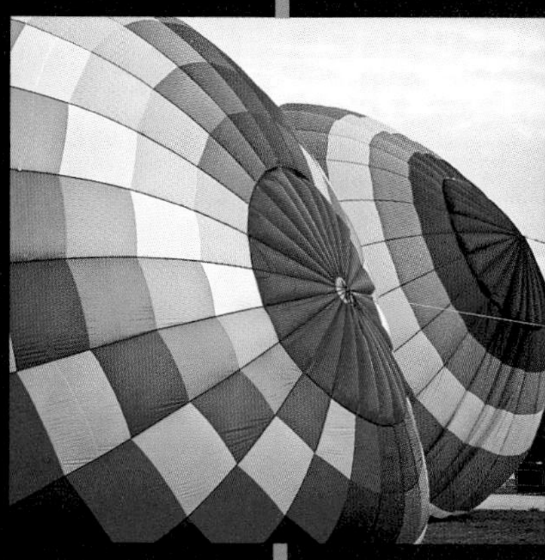

The first two chapters in this part explain everything you need to know to do just that, providing some necessary photography fundamentals and details about using the advanced exposure modes. Following that, Chapter 9 helps you draw together all the information presented earlier in this book, summarizing the best camera settings and other tactics to use when capturing portraits, action shots, landscapes, and close-up shots.

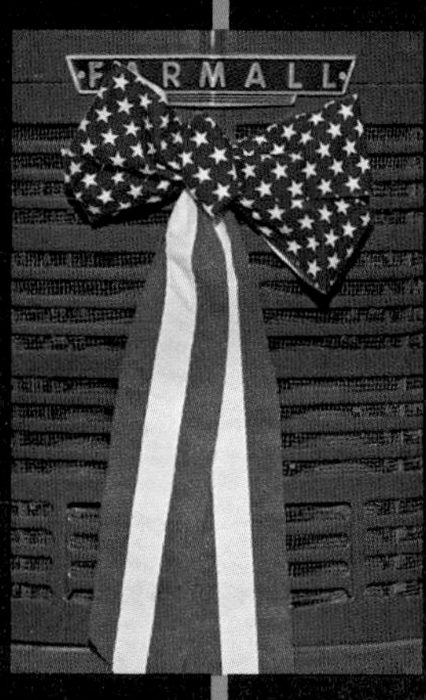

7

Getting Creative with Exposure

In This Chapter

- Exploring advanced exposure modes: P, Tv, Av, and M
- Getting a grip on aperture, shutter speed, and ISO
- Choosing an exposure metering mode
- Tweaking exposure results
- Taking advantage of automatic exposure bracketing (AEB)
- Using advanced flash options

By using the simple exposure modes I cover in Chapter 3, you can take good pictures with your Rebel T4i/650D. But to fully exploit your camera's capabilities — and, more importantly, to exploit *your* creative capabilities — you need to explore your camera's advanced exposure modes, represented on the Mode dial by the letters P, Tv, Av, and M.

This chapter explains everything you need to know to start taking advantage of these modes. First, you get an introduction to three critical exposure controls: aperture, shutter speed, and ISO. Adjusting these settings enables you to not only fine-tune image exposure but also affect other aspects of your image, such as *depth of field* (the zone of sharp focus) and motion blur. In addition, this chapter explains other advanced exposure features, such as exposure compensation and metering modes, and discusses the flash options available to you in the advanced exposure modes. (For movie-recording exposure information, see Chapter 4.)

Kicking Your Camera into Advanced Gear

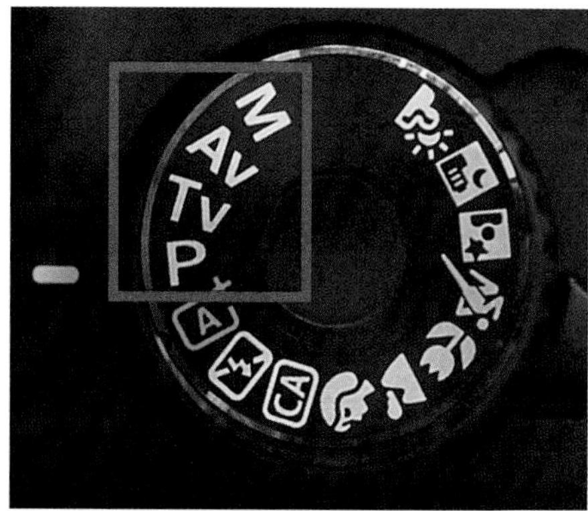

Figure 7-1: To fully control exposure and other picture properties, choose one of these exposure modes.

With your camera in Creative Auto mode, covered in Chapter 3, you can affect picture brightness and depth of field to some extent by using the Shoot by Ambience and Background Blur features. The scene modes let you request a slightly brighter or darker exposure via the Shoot by Ambience setting, but that's pretty much it. So if you're really concerned with these picture characteristics – and you should be – set the Mode dial to one of its advanced exposure modes, highlighted in Figure 7-1: P, Tv, Av, or M.

Using these modes lets you manipulate two critical exposure controls, *aperture* and *shutter speed.* That's not a huge deal in terms of exposure — the camera typically gets that part of the picture right in the fully automatic modes. But changing the aperture setting also affects the distance over which focus is maintained *(depth of field),* and shutter speed determines whether movement of the subject or camera creates blur. The next part of the chapter explains the details; for now, just understand that having input over these two settings provides you with a whole range of creative options that you don't enjoy in the fully automatic modes.

Each of the advanced modes offers a different level of control over aperture and shutter speed, as follows:

- **P (programmed autoexposure):** The camera selects both the aperture and shutter speed for you, but you can choose from different combinations of the two.
- **Tv (shutter-priority autoexposure):** You select a shutter speed, and the camera chooses the aperture setting that produces a good exposure.

  Why *Tv?* Well, shutter speed controls exposure time; *Tv* stands for *t*ime *v*alue.
- **Av (aperture-priority autoexposure):** The opposite of shutter-priority autoexposure, this mode asks you to select the aperture setting — thus *Av,* for *a*perture *v*alue. The camera then selects the appropriate shutter speed to properly expose the picture.

- **M (manual exposure):** In this mode, you specify both shutter speed and aperture. Although that prospect may sound intimidating, it's actually the fastest and least complicated way to dial in exactly the exposure settings you want to use. And even in M mode, the camera assists you by displaying a meter that tells you whether your exposure settings are on target.

A quick reminder about a point that is often misunderstood: Setting the Mode dial to M has *no effect* on whether autofocusing or manual focusing is enabled. To choose your focusing method, use the switch on the lens. You can focus manually or use autofocus no matter what your exposure mode.

Again, these modes won't make much sense to you if you aren't schooled in the basics of exposure. To that end, the next several sections provide a quick lesson in this critical photography subject.

Introducing the Exposure Trio: Aperture, Shutter Speed, and ISO

Any photograph, whether taken with a film or digital camera, is created by focusing light through a lens onto a light-sensitive recording medium. In a film camera, the film negative serves as the medium; in a digital camera, it's the image sensor, which is an array of light-responsive computer chips.

Between the lens and the sensor are two barriers, the *aperture* and *shutter,* which together control how much light makes its way to the sensor. The actual design and arrangement of the aperture, shutter, and sensor vary depending on the camera, but Figure 7-2 offers an illustration of the basic concept.

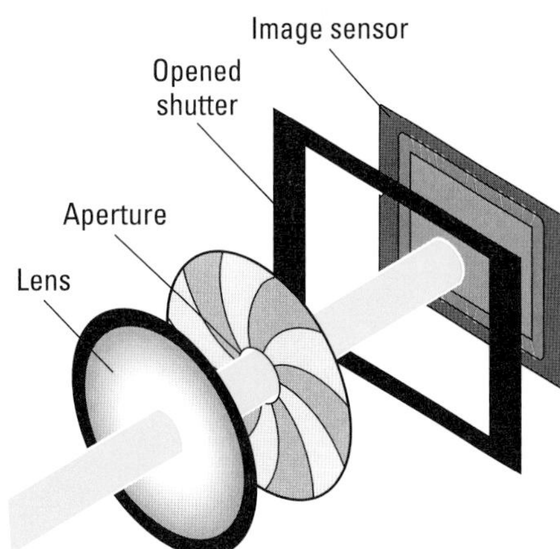

Figure 7-2: The aperture size and shutter speed determine how much light strikes the image sensor.

The aperture and shutter, along with a third feature, ISO, determine exposure — what most of us would describe as picture brightness. This three-part exposure formula works as follows:

- **Aperture (controls amount of light):** The *aperture* is an adjustable hole in a diaphragm set inside the lens. By changing the size of the aperture, you control the size of the light beam that can enter the camera. Aperture settings are stated as *f-stop numbers,* or simply *f-stops,* and are expressed with the letter *f* followed by a number: f/2, f/5.6, f/16, and so on. The lower the f-stop number, the larger the aperture opening, as illustrated in Figure 7-3.

  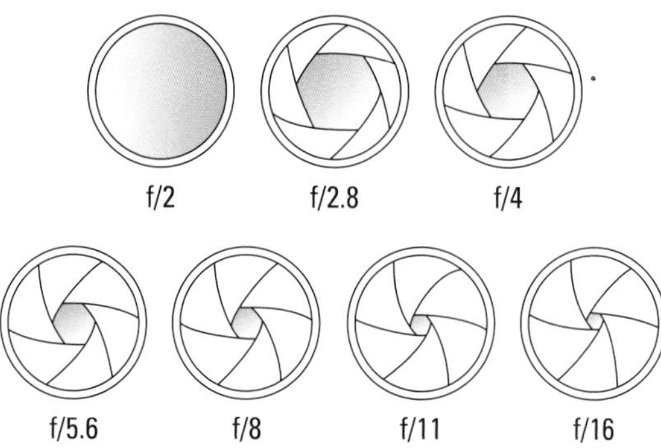

  Figure 7-3: The smaller the f-stop number, the larger the aperture opening.

  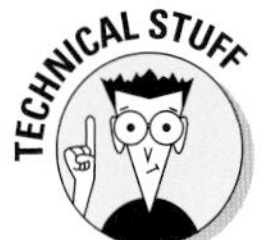

  The range of possible f-stops depends on your lens and, with most zoom lenses, on the zoom position (focal length) of the lens. For the 18–55mm kit lens sold with the Rebel T4i/650D, for example, you can select apertures from f/3.5 to f/22 when zoomed all the way out to the shortest focal length (18mm). When you zoom in to the maximum focal length (55mm), the aperture range is from f/5.6 to f/36. (See Chapter 8 for a discussion of focal lengths.)

- **Shutter speed (controls duration of light):** Set behind the aperture, the shutter works something like, er, the shutters on a window. When you aren't taking pictures, the camera's shutter stays closed, preventing light from striking the image sensor. When you press the shutter button, the shutter opens briefly to allow light that passes through the aperture to hit the image sensor. The exception to this scenario is when you compose in Live View mode — the shutter remains open so that your image can form on the sensor and be displayed on the camera's monitor. In fact, when you press the shutter release in Live View mode, the shutter first closes and then reopens for the actual exposure.

  The length of time that the shutter is open is the *shutter speed* and is measured in seconds: 1/60 second, 1/250 second, 2 seconds, and so on. Shutter speeds on your camera range from 30 seconds to 1/4000 second when you shoot without flash. If you want a shutter speed longer than 30 seconds, manual exposure mode also provides the *bulb* exposure feature. At this setting, the shutter stays open indefinitely as long as you press the shutter button.

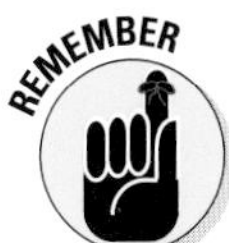

If you use the built-in flash, the fastest available shutter speed is 1/200 second; the slowest ranges from 1/60 second to 30 seconds, depending on the exposure mode. See the section "Understanding your camera's approach to flash," later in this chapter, for details.

- **ISO (controls light sensitivity):** ISO, which is a digital function rather than a mechanical structure on the camera, enables you to adjust how responsive the image sensor is to light. The term *ISO* is a holdover from film days, when an international standards organization rated each film stock according to light sensitivity: ISO 100, ISO 200, ISO 400, ISO 800, and so on. A higher ISO rating means greater light sensitivity.

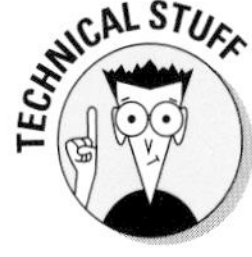

On a digital camera, the sensor itself doesn't actually get more or less sensitive when you change the ISO — rather, the light "signal" that hits the sensor is either amplified or dampened through electronics wizardry, sort of like how raising the volume on a radio boosts the audio signal. But the upshot is the same as changing to a more light-reactive film stock: A higher ISO means that less light is needed to produce the image, enabling you to use a smaller aperture, faster shutter speed, or both. (In other words, from now on, don't worry about the technicalities and just remember that ISO equals light sensitivity.)

On your camera, you can select ISO settings ranging from 100 to a whopping 25600 when you shoot in the advanced exposure modes. (You're restricted to an ISO range of 200 to 12800, however, if you enable the Highlight Tone Priority function, which you can explore later in this chapter.) For the fully automatic modes, you have no control over ISO; the camera chooses a setting automatically.

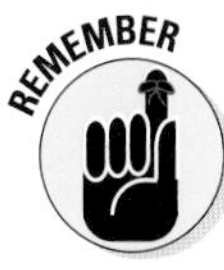

Distilled to its essence, the image-exposure formula is this simple:

- Aperture and shutter speed together determine the quantity of light that strikes the image sensor.
- ISO determines how much the sensor reacts to that light.

The tricky part of the equation is that aperture, shutter speed, and ISO settings affect your pictures in ways that go *beyond* exposure. You need to be aware of these side effects, explained in the next section, to determine which combination of the three exposure settings will work best for your picture.

Understanding exposure-setting side effects

You can create the same exposure with different combinations of aperture, shutter speed, and ISO, which Figure 7-4 illustrates. Although the figure shows only two variations of settings, your choices are pretty much endless — you're limited only by the aperture range the lens allows and the shutter speeds and ISO settings the camera offers.

f/13, 1/25 second, ISO 200

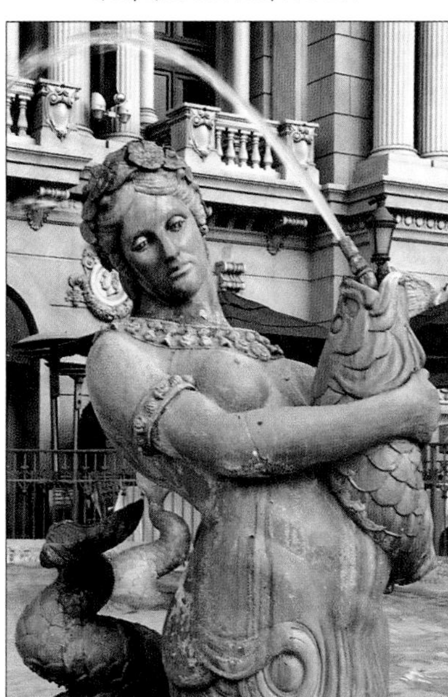

f/5.6, 1/125 second, ISO 200

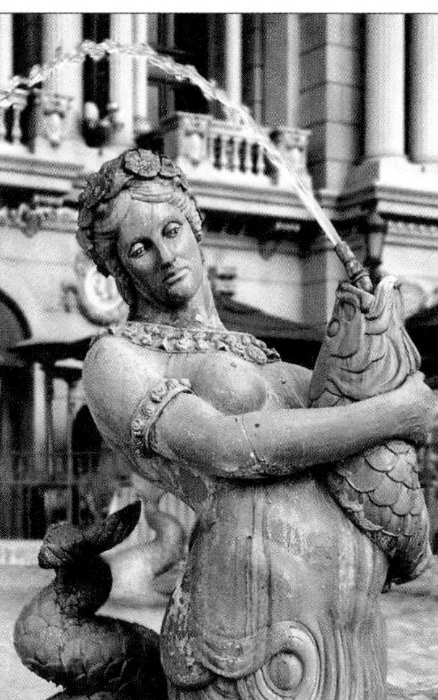

Figure 7-4: Aperture and shutter speed affect depth of field and motion blur.

But the settings you select impact your image beyond mere exposure, as follows:

- Aperture affects *depth of field,* or the distance over which focus remains acceptably sharp.
- Shutter speed determines whether moving objects appear blurry or sharply focused.
- ISO affects the amount of image *noise,* which is a defect that looks like specks of sand.

The next three sections explore these exposure side effects in detail.

Aperture and depth of field

The aperture setting, or f-stop, affects *depth of field,* or the distance over which acceptable focus is maintained. I introduce this concept in Chapter 3, but here's a quick recap: With a shallow depth of field, your subject appears more sharply focused than faraway objects; with a large depth of field, the sharp-focus zone spreads over a greater distance from the lens.

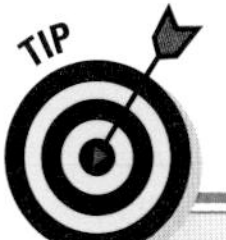

Putting the f (stop) in focus

One way to remember the relationship between f-stop and depth of field, or the distance over which focus remains sharp, is simply to think of the *f* as *focus:* The higher the *f*-stop number, the larger the zone of sharp *focus.*

Please *don't* share this tip with photography elites, who will roll their eyes and inform you that the *f* in *f-stop* most certainly does *not* stand for focus but, rather, for the ratio between aperture size and lens focal length — as if *that's* helpful to know if you aren't an optical engineer. (Chapter 8 explains focal length, which *is* helpful to know.)

When you reduce the aperture size — "stop down the aperture," in photo lingo — by choosing a higher f-stop number, you increase depth of field. For example, notice that the background in the left image in Figure 7-4, taken at f/13, appears sharper than the right image, taken at f/5.6.

Aperture is just one contributor to depth of field, however. The camera-to-subject distance and the focal length of your lens also play a role in this characteristic of your photos. Depth of field is reduced as you move closer to the subject or increase the focal length of the lens (moving from a wide-angle lens to a telephoto lens, for example). See Chapter 8 for the complete story on how these three factors combine to determine depth of field.

Shutter speed and motion blur

At a slow shutter speed, moving objects appear blurry, whereas a fast shutter speed captures motion cleanly. Compare the water motion in the photos in Figure 7-4, for example. At a shutter speed of 1/25 second (left photo), the water blurs, giving it a misty look. At 1/125 second (right photo), the splashing water appears more sharply focused. The shutter speed you need in order to freeze action depends on the speed of your subject.

If your picture suffers from overall image blur, like you see in Figure 7-5, where even stationary objects appear out of focus, the camera moved during the exposure — which is always a danger when you handhold the camera at slow shutter speeds. The longer the exposure time, the longer you have to hold the camera still to avoid the blur caused by camera shake.

How slow is too slow? It depends on your physical capabilities and your lens. For reasons that are too technical to get into, camera shake affects your picture more when you shoot with a lens that has a long focal length. For example, you may be able to use a much slower shutter speed when you shoot with a lens that has a maximum focal length of 55mm than if you switch to a 200mm telephoto lens. The best idea is to do your own tests to see where your handholding limit lies. Check out the first section of Chapter 6 to find out how to see each picture's shutter speed when you view your test images using the Canon software.

To avoid the issue altogether, use a tripod or otherwise steady the camera. If you need to handhold (and face it — no one can carry a tripod *all* the time), improve your odds of capturing a sharp photo by turning on image stabilization, if your lens offers it. (On the kit lenses, turn the Stabilizer switch on the side of the lens to On.) See Chapter 8 for tips on solving other focus problems and Chapter 9 for more help with action photography.

f/29, 1/5 second, ISO 200

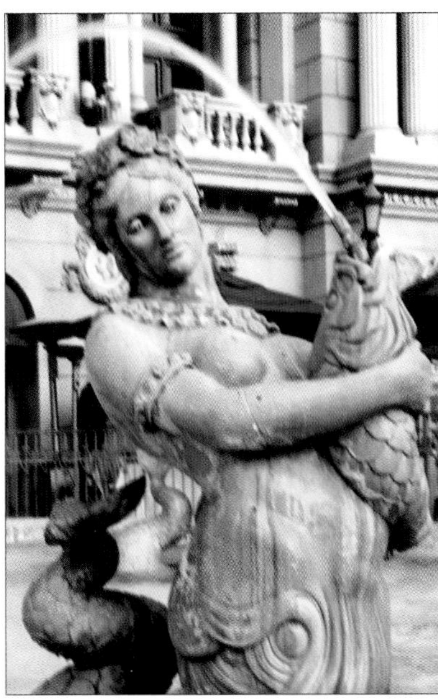

Figure 7-5: Slow shutter speeds increase the risk of allover blur caused by camera shake.

ISO and image noise

As ISO increases, making the image sensor more reactive to light, you increase the risk of *noise*. Noise looks like bits of sand and is similar in appearance to film *grain,* a defect that often mars pictures taken with high-ISO film. Figure 7-6 offers an example.

Ideally, then, you should always use the lowest ISO setting on your camera to ensure top image quality. But sometimes, the lighting conditions don't permit you to do so. Take my rose image as an example. On my first attempt, taken at ISO 100, f/6.3, and 1/40 second, the flower was slightly blurry, as shown on the left in Figure 7-7. I was using a tripod, so camera shake wasn't the problem. But a very slight breeze was moving the flower just enough that 1/40 second wasn't fast enough to freeze the action. My aperture already was at the maximum opening the lens offered, so the only way to be able to use a faster shutter speed was to raise the ISO. By increasing the ISO to 200, I was able to use a shutter speed of 1/80 second, which captured the flower cleanly, as shown on the right.

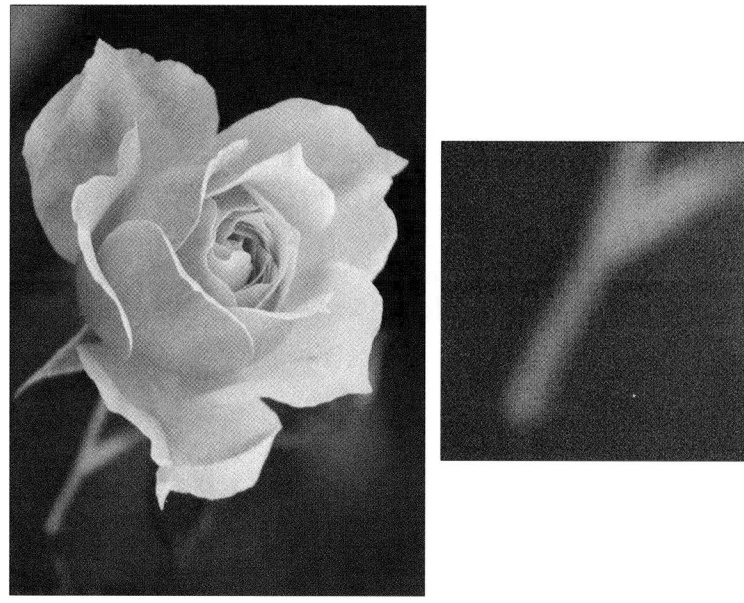

Figure 7-6: Caused by a very high ISO or long exposure time, noise becomes more visible as you enlarge the image.

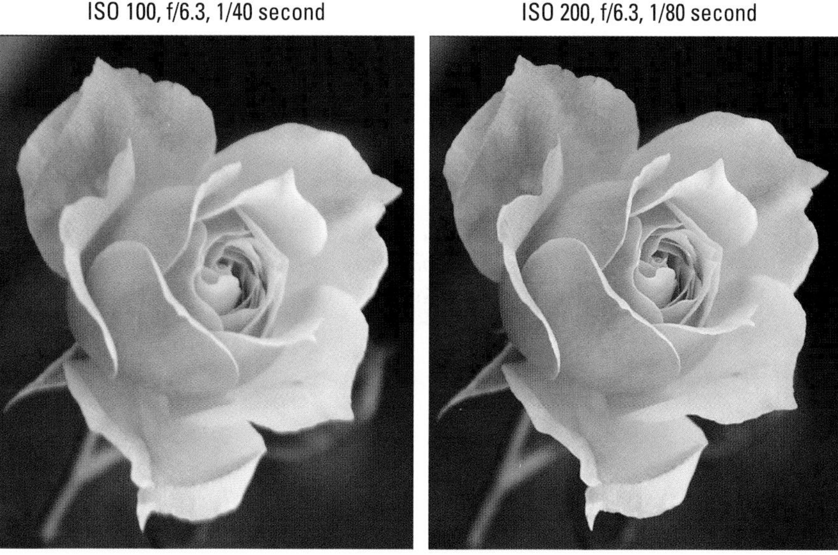

Figure 7-7: Raising the ISO enabled me to bump the shutter speed up enough to permit a blur-free shot of the flower, which was moving slightly in the breeze.

Fortunately, you don't encounter serious noise on the T4i/650D until you really crank up the ISO. In fact, you may even be able to get away with a fairly high ISO if you keep your print or display size small. Some people probably wouldn't even notice the noise in the left image in Figure 7-6 unless they were looking for it, for example. But as with other image defects, noise becomes more apparent as you enlarge the photo, as shown on the right in that same figure. Noise is also easier to spot in shadow areas of your picture and in large areas of solid color.

How much noise is acceptable, and, therefore, how high an ISO is safe, is a personal choice. Even a little noise isn't acceptable for pictures that require the highest quality, such as images for a product catalog or a travel shot that you want to blow up to poster size.

It's also important to know that a high ISO isn't the only cause of noise: A long exposure time (slow shutter speed) can also produce the defect. So how high you can raise the ISO before the image gets ugly varies depending on shutter speed. I can pretty much guarantee, though, that your pictures will exhibit visible noise at the camera's highest ISO setting, 25600. In fact, that's why Canon doesn't make that setting available until you enable it via a Custom Function menu option, ISO Expansion, and names the setting H (for high). It's a way to let you know that you should use that setting only if the light is so bad that you have no other way to get the shot. If you do need the maximum ISO, see the section "Controlling ISO" to find out how to enable the H (ISO 25600) setting.

Doing the exposure balancing act

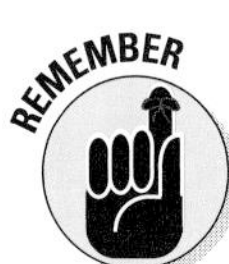

When you change any of the three exposure settings — aperture, shutter speed, or ISO — one or both of the others must also shift to maintain the same image brightness.

Say you're shooting a soccer game and you notice that although the overall exposure looks great, the players appear slightly blurry at the current shutter speed. If you raise the shutter speed, you have to compensate with either a larger aperture, to allow in more light during the shorter exposure, or a higher ISO setting, to make the camera more sensitive to the light. Which way should you go? Well, it depends on whether you prefer the shorter depth of field that comes with a larger aperture or the increased risk of noise that accompanies a higher ISO. Of course, you can also adjust both settings if you choose to get the exposure results you need.

All photographers have their own approaches to finding the right combination of aperture, shutter speed, and ISO, and you'll no doubt develop your own system when you become more practiced at using the advanced exposure modes. In the meantime, here are some handy recommendations:

- Use the lowest possible ISO setting unless the lighting conditions are so poor that you can't use the aperture and shutter speed you want without raising the ISO.
- If your subject is moving (or might move, as with a squiggly toddler or an excited dog), give shutter speed the next highest priority in your exposure decision. Choose a fast shutter speed to ensure a blur-free photo or, on the flip side, select a slow shutter speed to intentionally blur that moving object, an effect that can create a heightened sense of motion. When shooting waterfalls, for example, consider using a slow shutter speed to give the water that blurry, romantic look.
- For images of nonmoving subjects, make aperture a priority over shutter speed, setting the aperture according to the depth of field you have in mind. For portraits, for example, try using a wide-open aperture (a low f-stop number) to create a short depth of field and a nice, soft background for your subject.

Be careful not to go too shallow with depth of field when shooting a group portrait, though — unless all the subjects are the same distance from the camera, some may be outside the zone of sharp focus. A short depth of field also makes action shots more difficult because you have to be absolutely spot-on with focus. With a larger depth of field, the subject can move a greater distance toward or away from you before leaving the sharp-focus area, giving you a bit of a focusing safety net.

Keeping all this information straight is a little overwhelming at first, but the more you work with your camera, the more the whole exposure equation will make sense to you. You can find tips in Chapter 9 for choosing exposure settings for specific types of pictures; keep moving through this chapter for details on how to monitor and adjust aperture, shutter speed, and ISO settings.

Monitoring Exposure Settings

When you press the shutter button halfway, the current f-stop, shutter speed, and ISO speed appear in the viewfinder display, as shown in Figure 7-8. Or if you're looking at the Shooting Settings display, the settings appear as shown in Figure 7-9. In Live View mode, the exposure data appears at the bottom of the monitor and takes a form similar to what you see in the viewfinder. (See Chapter 4 for details about this and other Live View exposure issues.)

In the viewfinder and on the monitor in Live View mode, shutter speeds are presented as whole numbers, even if the shutter speed is set to a fraction of a second. For example, for a shutter speed of 1/500 second, you see just the number 500 in the display. (Refer to Figure 7-8.) When the shutter speed slows to 1 second or more, you see quote marks after the number in both displays — 1" indicates a shutter speed of 1 second, 4" means 4 seconds, and so on.

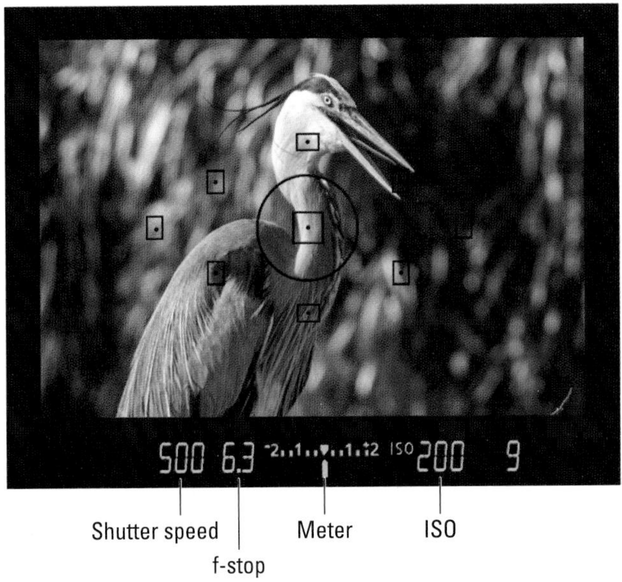

Figure 7-8: The shutter speed, f-stop, and ISO speed appear in the viewfinder.

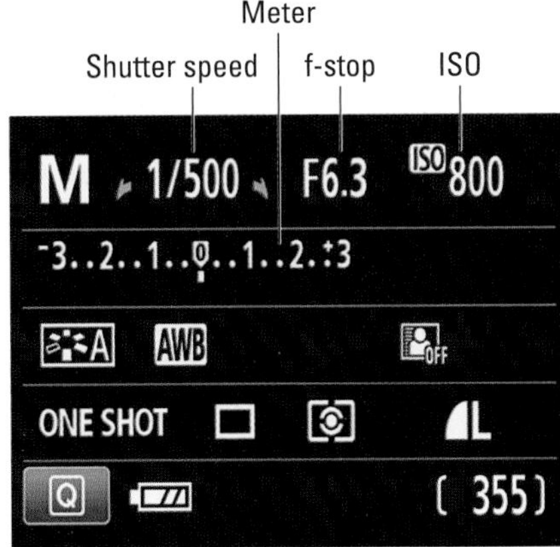

Figure 7-9: You also can view the settings in the Shooting Settings display.

The viewfinder, Shooting Settings display, and Live View display also offer an *exposure meter,* labeled in Figures 7-8 and 7-9. This little graphic serves two different purposes, depending on which of the advanced exposure modes you're using:

- **In manual exposure (M) mode, the meter acts in its traditional role, which is to indicate whether your settings will properly expose the image.** Figure 7-10 gives you three examples. When the *exposure indicator* (the bar under the meter) aligns with the center point of the meter, as shown in the middle example, the current settings will produce a proper exposure. If the indicator moves to the left of center, toward the minus side of the scale, as in the left example in the figure, the camera is alerting you that the image will be underexposed. If the indicator moves to the right of center, as in the right example, the image will be overexposed. The farther the indicator moves toward the plus or minus sign, the greater the potential exposure problem.

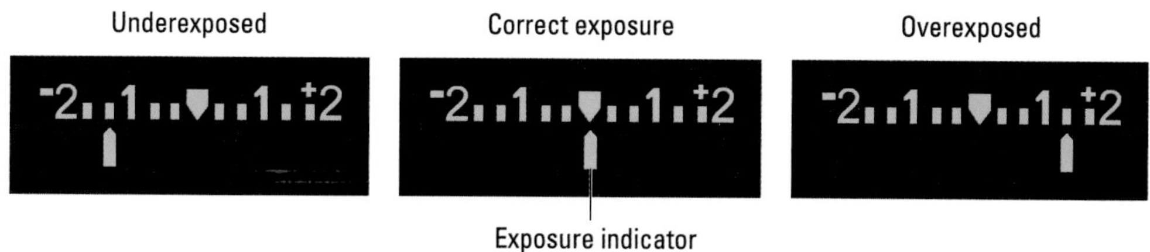

Figure 7-10: In manual exposure (M) mode, the meter indicates whether exposure settings are on target.

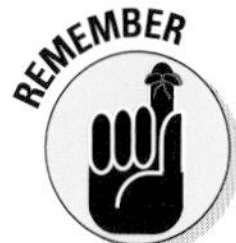

Keep in mind that the information reported by the meter is dependent on the *metering mode,* which determines what part of the frame the camera uses to calculate exposure. You can choose from four metering modes, as covered in the next section. But regardless of metering mode, consider the meter a guide, not a dictator — the beauty of manual exposure is that *you* decide how dark or bright an exposure you want, not the camera.

- **In the other advanced exposure modes (P, Tv, and Av), the meter displays the current Exposure Compensation setting.** Remember, in those modes the camera sets either the shutter speed or aperture, or both, to produce a good exposure — again, depending on the current metering mode. Because you don't need the meter to tell you whether exposure is okay, the meter instead indicates whether you enabled *Exposure Compensation,* a feature that forces a brighter or darker exposure than the camera thinks is appropriate. (Look for details later in this chapter.) When the exposure indicator is at 0, no compensation is being applied. If the indicator is to the right of 0, you applied compensation to produce a brighter image; when the indicator is to the left, you asked for a darker photo.

In some lighting situations, the camera *can't* select settings that produce an optimal exposure in the P, Tv, or Av mode, however. Because the meter indicates the Exposure Compensation amount in those modes, the camera alerts you to exposure issues as follows:

- **Av mode (aperture-priority autoexposure):** The shutter speed value blinks to let you know that the camera can't select a shutter speed that will produce a good exposure at the aperture you selected. Choose a different f-stop or adjust the ISO.
- **Tv mode (shutter-priority autoexposure):** The aperture value blinks to tell you that the camera can't open or stop down the aperture enough to expose the image at your selected shutter speed. Your options are to change the shutter speed or ISO.
- **P mode (programmed autoexposure):** In P mode, both the aperture and shutter speed values blink if the camera can't select a combination that will properly expose the image. Your only recourse is either to adjust the lighting or change the ISO setting.

Choosing an Exposure Metering Mode

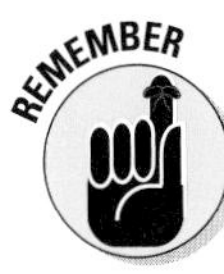

The *metering mode* determines which part of the frame the camera analyzes to calculate the proper exposure. Your camera offers four metering modes, described in the following list and represented in the Shooting Settings display by the icons you see in the margin. However, you can access all four modes only in the advanced exposure modes (P, Tv, Av, and M).

- **Evaluative metering:** The camera analyzes the entire frame and then selects exposure settings designed to produce a balanced exposure.
- **Partial metering:** The camera bases exposure only on the light that falls in the central 9 percent of the frame. The left image in Figure 7-11 provides a rough approximation of the area that factors into the exposure equation.
- **Spot metering:** This mode works like Partial metering but uses a smaller region of the frame to calculate exposure. For Spot metering, exposure is based on just the central 4 percent of the frame, as indicated by the illustration on the right in Figure 7-11.
- **Center-Weighted Average metering:** The camera bases exposure on the entire frame but puts extra emphasis — or *weight* — on the center.

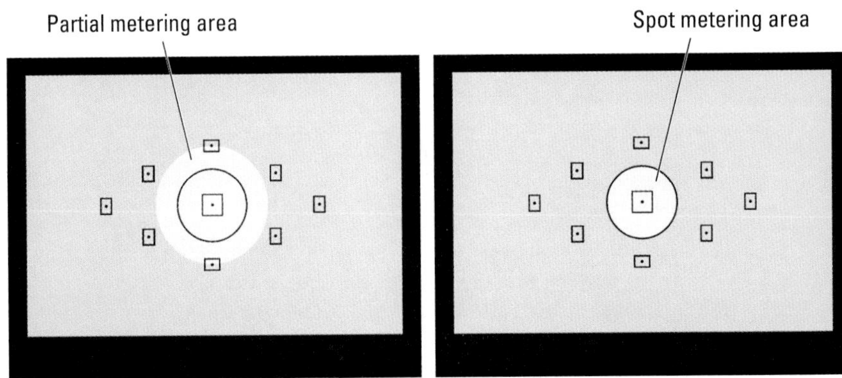

Figure 7-11: The spotlights indicate the metered area for Partial metering and Spot metering.

Note that for Live View photography, the areas metered for Partial and Spot metering are slightly different than what you see in Figure 7-11, and the metering circle and focus points don't appear onscreen. Don't worry about the discrepancy too much — the key words here are "slightly different."

In most cases, Evaluative metering does a good job of calculating exposure. But it can get thrown off when a dark subject is set against a bright background or vice versa. For example, in the left image in Figure 7-12, the amount of bright background caused the camera to select exposure settings that underexposed the statue, which was the point of interest for the photo. Switching to Partial metering properly exposed the statue. (Spot metering would produce a similar result for this particular subject.)

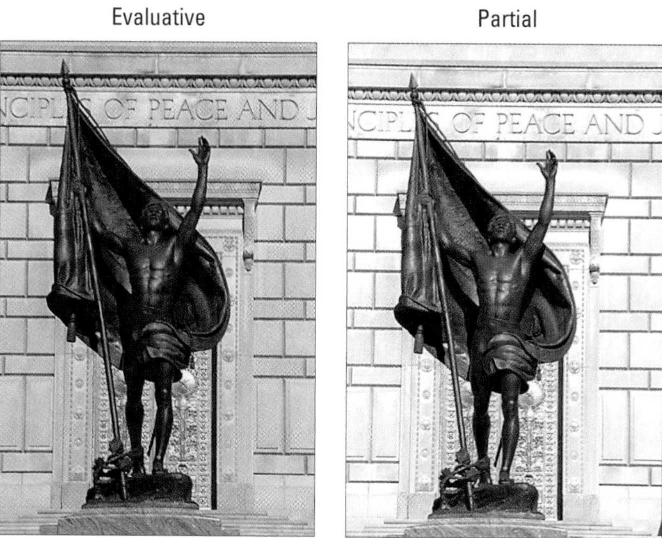

Figure 7-12: In Evaluative mode, the camera underexposed the statue; switching to Partial metering produced a better result.

Of course, if the background is very bright and the subject is very dark, the exposure that does the best job on the subject typically overexposes the background. You may be able to reclaim some lost highlights by turning on Highlight Tone Priority, a Custom Function explored later in this chapter, or, if you want to shoot in a fully automatic mode, by trying the HDR Backlight Control scene mode, covered in Chapter 3.

As for metering mode, use either of these two options to make your selection:

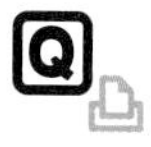

- **Quick Control screen:** Choose the icon labeled in Figure 7-13 and rotate the Main dial to cycle through the four modes. Or tap the icon or press Set to display a list of all four modes, as shown on the right in the figure. If you take the second route, choose the icon representing the mode you want to use and then press Set or tap the return arrow to lock in your decision.

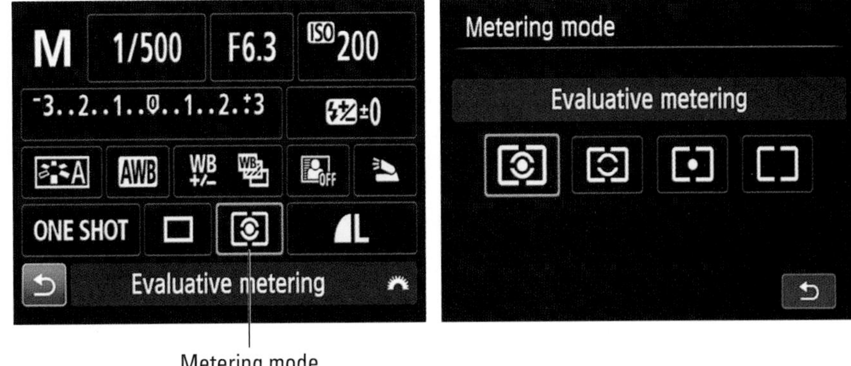

Figure 7-13: You can quickly adjust the Metering mode from the Quick Control screen.

- **Shooting Menu 2:** You also can find the metering mode option at the menu address shown in Figure 7-14.

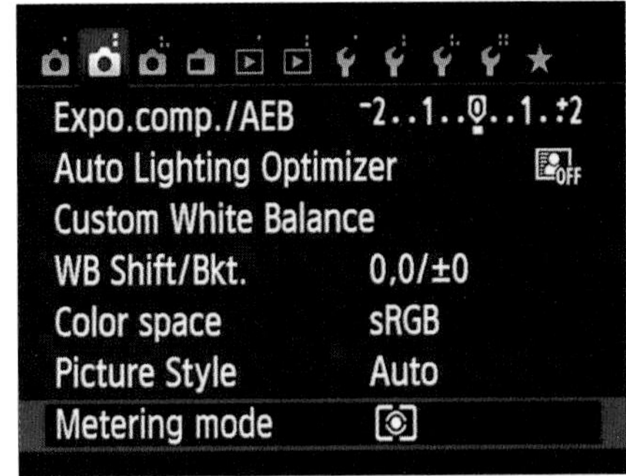

Figure 7-14: You also can access the Metering mode from Shooting Menu 2.

In theory, the best practice is to check the metering mode before each shot and choose the mode that best matches your exposure goals. But in practice, it's a pain, not just in terms of having to adjust yet one more setting but also in terms of having to *remember* to adjust one more setting. So until you're comfortable with all the other controls on your camera, just stick with Evaluative metering. It produces good results in most situations, and after all, you can see in the monitor whether you like your results and, if not, adjust exposure settings and reshoot. This option makes the whole metering mode issue a lot less critical than it is when you shoot with film.

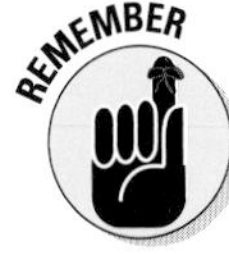

However — and this is an important however — for viewfinder photography, your choice of metering mode determines when the camera sets the final exposure for your picture. In Evaluative mode, exposure is locked when you press the shutter button halfway, but in the other modes, exposure is adjusted up to the time you press the button all the way to take the picture. Should you want to lock exposure before that point, you can use the technique outlined in the later section "Locking Autoexposure Settings."

For Live View photography, exposure is always set at the moment you snap the picture, regardless of the metering mode.

Setting ISO, f-stop, and Shutter Speed

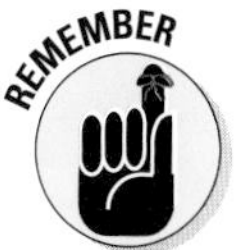

If you want to control ISO, aperture (f-stop), or shutter speed, set the camera to one of the advanced exposure modes: P, Tv, Av, or M. Then check out the next several sections to find the exact steps to follow in each of these modes.

Controlling ISO

To recap the ISO information presented at the start of this chapter, your camera's ISO setting controls how sensitive the image sensor is to light. At a camera's higher ISO values, you need less light to expose an image correctly. Remember the downside to raising ISO, however: The higher the ISO, the greater the possibility of noisy images. Refer to Figure 7-6 for a reminder of what that defect looks like.

In Scene Intelligent Auto, Creative Auto, Flash Off, and the scene modes (Portrait, Landscape, and so on), the camera controls ISO. But in the advanced exposure modes, you have the following ISO choices:

- **Select a specific ISO setting.** Normally, you can choose ISO settings ranging from 100 to ISO 12800. Or if you really want to push things, you can amp ISO up to 25600. In order to take advantage of that option, set Custom Function 2, ISO Expansion, to On, as shown in Figure 7-15. Now when you adjust ISO, an H (for High) appears as a possible setting; select that setting for ISO 25600.

  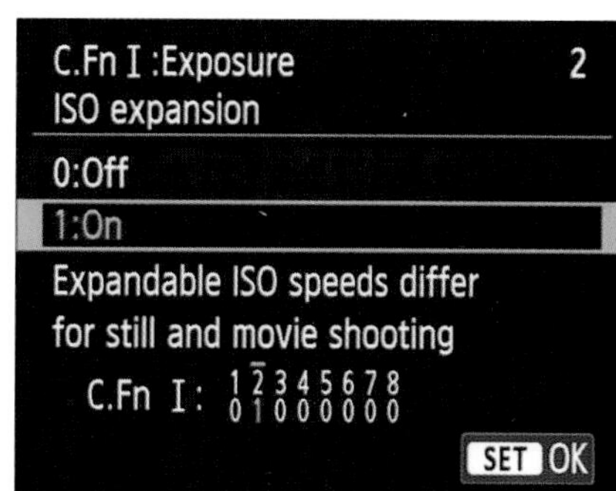

  Figure 7-15: By enabling Custom Function 2, you can push the available ISO range to 25600.

  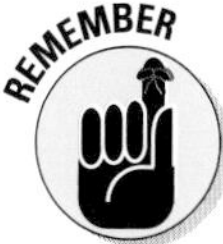

  A few complications to note: If you enable Highlight Tone Priority, an exposure feature covered later in this chapter, you lose the option of using ISO 100 as well as the expanded ISO setting (H, 26500).

  In addition, choosing ISO 12800 or 25600 slows the maximum burst rate the camera can achieve in Continuous Drive mode. Finally, in Movie mode, the top ISO speed is 6400 when ISO Expansion is turned off; when it's enabled, the top (H) speed is 12800. See Chapter 4 for more about exposure issues related to shooting movies.

- **Let the camera choose (Auto ISO).** You can ask the camera to adjust ISO for you if you prefer. And you can specify the highest ISO setting that you want the camera to use, but only within a range of ISO 400 to ISO 6400. Set the top ISO limit via the ISO Auto setting on Shooting Menu 3, as shown in Figure 7-16.

I like to use Auto ISO when the light is changing fast or my subject is moving from light to dark areas quickly. In these situations, Auto ISO can save the day, giving you properly exposed images without any ISO futzing on your part.

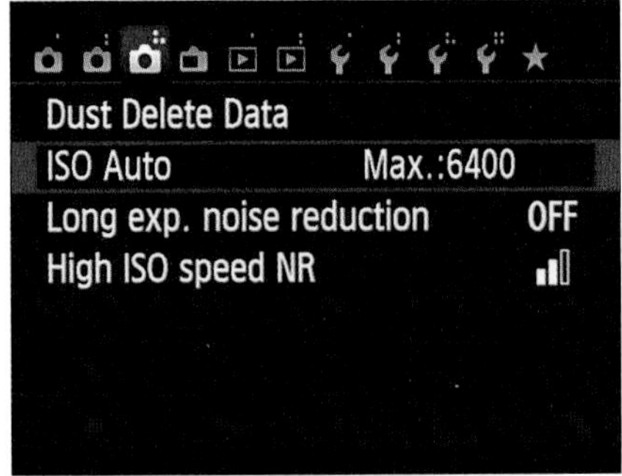

Figure 7-16: This setting enables you to specify the maximum ISO setting the camera can use in Auto ISO mode.

You can view the current ISO setting in the upper-right corner of the Shooting Settings screen, as shown on the left in Figure 7-17. You can also monitor the ISO in the viewfinder display. (Refer to Figure 7-8.) During Live View shooting, the setting appears at the bottom of the screen unless you choose the display mode that hides all the shooting data. (See Chapter 4 for details on the Live View display.)

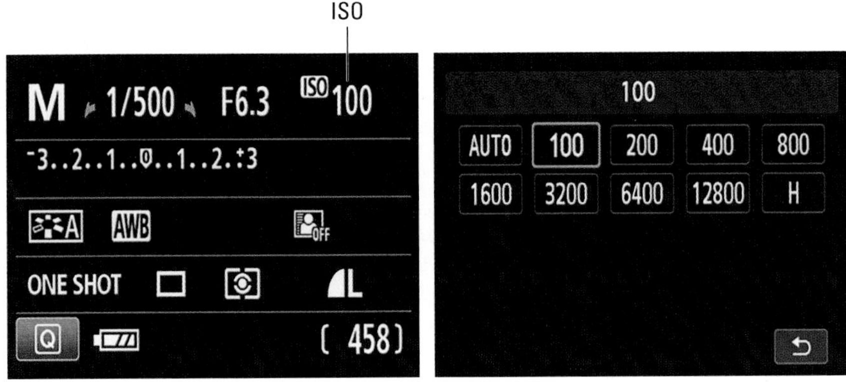

Figure 7-17: Press the ISO button on top of the camera to access the ISO setting.

To adjust the setting, you have two options:

- **Press the ISO button (on top of the camera).** You then see the screen shown on the right in Figure 7-17, where you can choose your desired setting.

- **Use the Quick Control screen.** After choosing the ISO option, rotate the Main dial to cycle through the available ISO settings. You also can tap the icon or press Set to display the same screen you see on the right in Figure 7-17 and select your choice there.

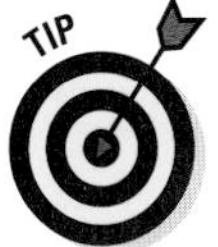

In Auto ISO mode, the Shooting Settings display and Live View display initially show Auto as the ISO value, as you would expect. But when you press the shutter button halfway, which initiates exposure metering, the value changes to show you the ISO setting the camera has selected. You also see the selected value rather than Auto in the viewfinder. ***Note:*** When you view shooting data during playback, you may see a value reported that isn't on the list of "official" ISO settings — ISO 320, for example. This happens because in Auto mode, the camera can select values all along the available ISO range, whereas if you select a specific ISO setting, you're restricted to specific notches within the range.

Adjusting aperture and shutter speed

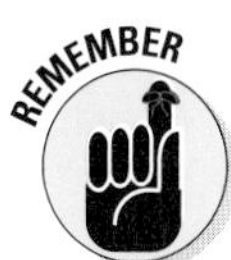

You can adjust aperture and shutter speed only in P, Tv, Av, and M exposure modes. To see the current exposure settings, press the shutter button halfway. The following actions then take place:

- The exposure meter comes to life. If autofocus is enabled, focus is also established at this point.
- The aperture and shutter speed appear in the viewfinder or the Shooting Settings display, if you have it enabled. In Live View mode, the settings appear under the image preview on the monitor, assuming that you're using a display mode that reveals shooting data. (Press the Info button to cycle through the available Live View display modes.)
- In manual exposure (M) mode, the exposure meter lets you know whether the current settings will expose the image properly. In the other modes, the camera indicates an exposure problem by flashing the shutter speed or the f-stop value. (See the section "Monitoring Exposure Settings," earlier in this chapter, for details.)

The technique you use to change the exposure settings depends on the exposure mode:

- **P (programmed auto):** The camera displays its recommended combination of aperture and shutter speed. To select a different combination, rotate the Main dial. But note that your change applies only to the current shot.
- **Tv (shutter-priority autoexposure):** Rotate the Main dial to change the shutter speed. As you do, the camera automatically adjusts the aperture as needed to achieve the proper exposure.

  Changing the aperture also changes depth of field. So even though you're working in shutter-priority mode, keep an eye on the f-stop, too, if depth of field is important to your photo. ***Note:*** In extreme lighting conditions, the camera may not be able to adjust the aperture enough to produce a good exposure at the current shutter speed — again, possible aperture settings depend on your lens. So you may need to compromise on shutter speed (or, in dim lighting, raise the ISO).

- **Av (aperture-priority autoexposure):** Rotate the Main dial to set the f-stop. The camera automatically adjusts the shutter speed.

  If you're handholding the camera, be careful that the shutter speed doesn't drop so low when you stop down the aperture that you run the risk of camera shake. If your scene contains moving objects, make sure that when you dial in your preferred f-stop, the shutter speed that the camera selects is fast enough to stop action (or slow enough to blur it, if that's your creative goal).

- **M (manual exposure):** In this mode, you select both aperture and shutter speed, like so:
  - *To adjust shutter speed:* Rotate the Main dial.

  - *To adjust aperture:* Press and hold the Exposure Compensation button while you rotate the Main dial. (See the *Av* label at the top of the Exposure Compensation button? That's your clue to the aperture-related function of the button — *Av* stands for *aperture value.*) Don't let up on the button when you rotate the Main dial — if you do, you instead adjust the shutter speed.

You also can use the Quick Control method of adjusting the settings in the M, Tv, and Av modes. After shifting to Quick Control mode, choose the setting you want to adjust. For example, in Figure 7-18, the aperture setting is highlighted, and a text label shows the name of the option at the bottom of the screen. Now, rotate the Main dial to adjust the setting. You also can tap the f-stop or shutter speed to display a screen with a setting scale; drag your finger along the scale or tap the arrows above it to adjust the setting.

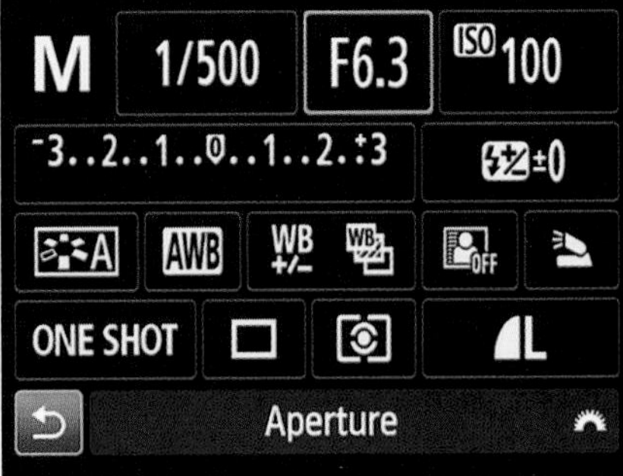

Figure 7-18: You can also use the Quick Control screen to adjust aperture and shutter speed in the M, Tv, and Av exposure modes.

Keep in mind that when you use P, Tv, and Av modes, the settings that the camera selects are based on what it thinks is the proper exposure. If you don't agree with the camera, you have two options. Switch to manual exposure (M) mode and simply dial in the aperture and shutter speed that deliver the exposure you want, or if you want to stay in P, Tv, or Av mode, tweak the autoexposure settings by using Exposure Compensation, one of the exposure-correction tools described in the next section.

Sorting through Your Camera's Exposure-Correction Tools

In addition to the normal controls over aperture, shutter speed, and ISO, your Rebel offers a collection of tools that enable you to solve tricky exposure problems. The next sections give you the lowdown on these features.

Overriding autoexposure results with Exposure Compensation

When you set your camera to the P, Tv, or Av exposure modes, you can enjoy the benefits of autoexposure support but retain some control over the final exposure. If you think that the image the camera produced is too dark or too light, you can use *Exposure Compensation,* sometimes called *EV Compensation.* (The *EV* stands for *exposure value.*)

Whatever you call it, this feature enables you to tell the camera to produce a darker or lighter exposure than its autoexposure mechanism thinks is appropriate. Here's how it works:

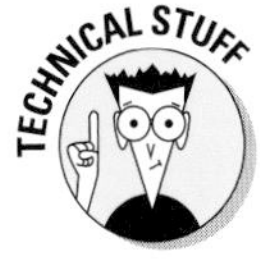

- Exposure compensation is stated in EV values, as in +2.0 EV. Possible values range from +5.0 EV to –5.0 EV.
- Each full number on the EV scale represents an exposure shift of one *full stop.* In plain English, it means that if you change the Exposure Compensation setting from EV 0.0 to EV –1.0, the camera adjusts exposure settings to result in half as much light as the current settings. If you instead raise the value to EV +1.0, the settings are adjusted to double the light.

  By default, you can adjust this and other exposure settings in increments of 1/3 stop. To find out how to switch to 1/2-stop increments, visit Chapter 10.
- A setting of EV 0.0 results in no exposure adjustment.
- For a brighter image, raise the EV value. The higher you go, the brighter the image becomes.
- For a darker image, lower the EV value. The picture becomes progressively darker with each step down the EV scale.

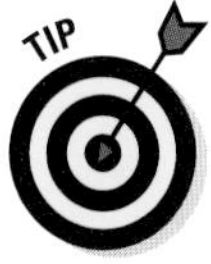

Exposure compensation is especially helpful when your subject is much lighter or darker than the background. For example, take a look at the first image in Figure 7-19. Because of the very bright sky, the camera chose an exposure that made the tree too dark. Setting the Exposure Compensation value to EV +1.0 resulted in a properly exposed tree.

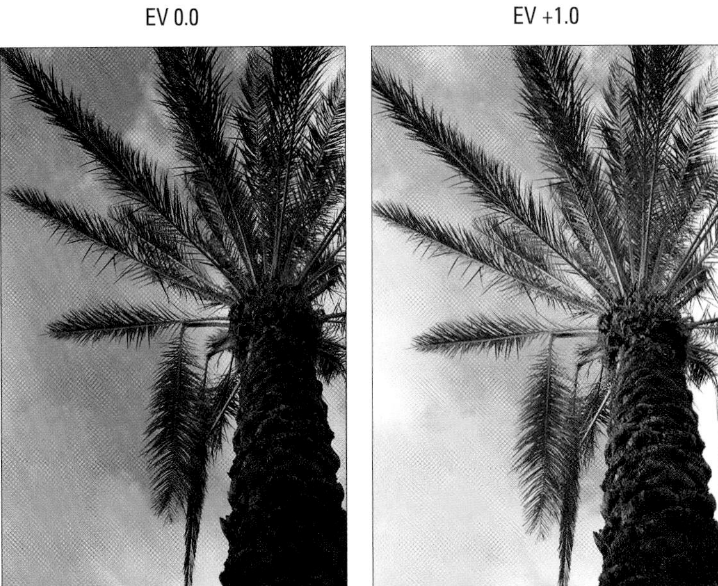

Figure 7-19: For a brighter exposure than the autoexposure mechanism chooses, dial in a positive Exposure Compensation value.

Sometimes you can cope with situations like this one by changing the Metering mode setting, as discussed earlier in this chapter. The images in Figure 7-19 were metered in Evaluative mode, for example, which meters exposure over the entire frame. Switching to Partial or Spot metering probably wouldn't have helped in this case because the center of the frame was bright. In any case, I find it easier to simply adjust Exposure Compensation than to experiment with metering modes.

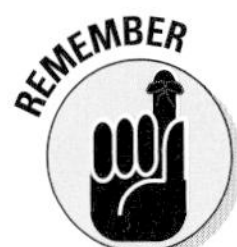

You can take several different roads to applying exposure compensation. Here are the two most efficient options:

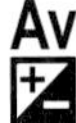

- **Exposure Compensation button:** Press and hold the Exposure Compensation button while rotating the Main dial. Note the little plus/minus sign on the button label — that's your reminder that you use the button to raise or lower the Exposure Compensation amount. (The Av label, as explained in the preceding section, refers to the button's role in adjusting aperture when you shoot in M exposure mode.)

If the Shooting Settings screen is displayed, the meter becomes active while the button is pressed, as shown on the left in Figure 7-20. As you rotate the dial, the little notch under the meter moves to show the current Exposure Compensation value. For example, in Figure 7-20, the amount of adjustment is +1.0. The viewfinder meter also displays the amount of adjustment.

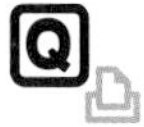

- **Quick Control screen:** Select the exposure meter, as shown on the right in Figure 7-20, and rotate the Main dial to move the exposure indicator left or right along the meter.

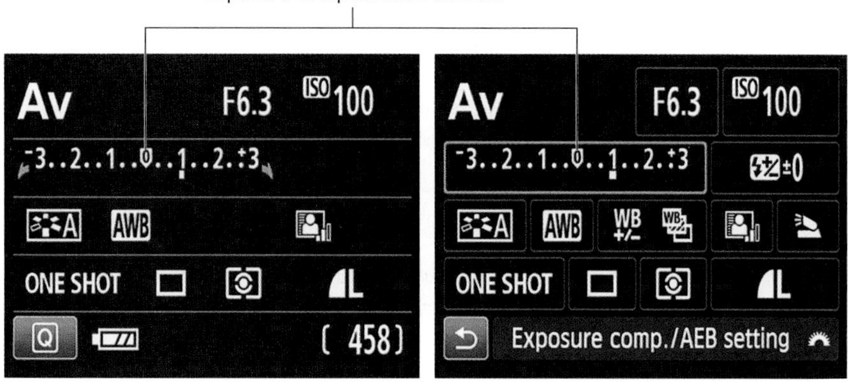

Figure 7-20: You can apply Exposure Compensation by rotating the Main dial while holding the Exposure Compensation button (left) or by using Quick Control screen (right).

You can also follow one of these two paths instead:

- **Shooting Menu 2:** Select Expo. Comp/AEB, as shown in Figure 7-21.
- **Quick Control screen:** Tap the exposure meter or highlight it and then press Set.

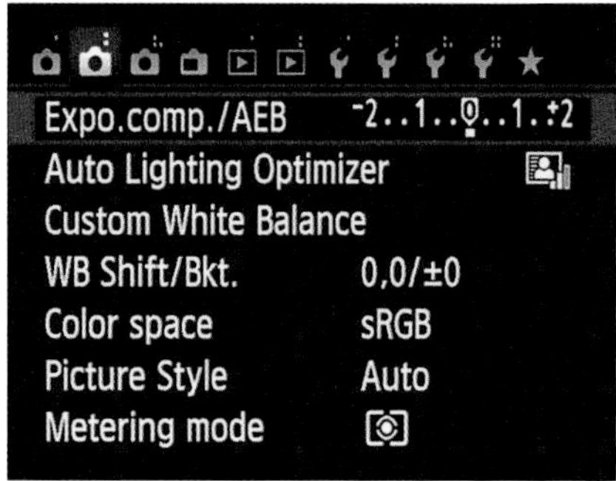

Figure 7-21: You also can apply the adjustment via this menu option.

Either way, you see the screen shown in Figure 7-22. This is a tricky screen, so pay attention:

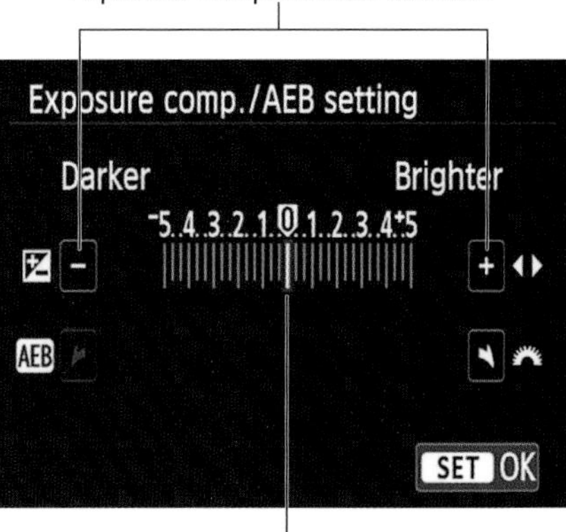

Figure 7-22: Be careful that you adjust Exposure Compensation and not AEB (Auto Exposure Bracketing).

- The screen has a double purpose: You use it to enable automatic exposure bracketing (AEB) as well as exposure compensation. So if you're not careful, you can wind up changing the wrong setting.
- To apply exposure compensation, move the exposure indicator (labeled *current setting* in the figure) along the scale by pressing the left or right cross keys or tapping the plus or minus signs, labeled *Exposure Compensation controls* in the figure. If you rotate the Main dial, you adjust the AEB setting instead.
- Tap Set or press the Set button to lock in the amount of exposure compensation and exit the screen.

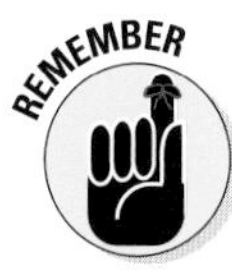

When you dial in an adjustment of greater than two stops, the notch under the viewfinder meter disappears and is replaced by a little triangle at one end of the meter — at the right end for a positive Exposure Compensation value and at the left for a negative value. However, the meter on the Shooting Information screen and on Shooting Menu 2 adjust to show the proper setting.

Whatever setting you select, the way that the camera arrives at the brighter or darker image you request depends on the exposure mode:

- In Av (aperture-priority) mode, the camera adjusts the shutter speed but leaves your selected f-stop in force. Be sure to check the resulting shutter speed to make sure that it isn't so slow that camera shake or blur from moving objects is problematic.
- In Tv (shutter-priority) mode, the opposite occurs: The camera opens or stops down the aperture, leaving your selected shutter speed alone.
- In P (programmed autoexposure) mode, the camera decides whether to adjust aperture, shutter speed, or both to accommodate the Exposure Compensation setting.

These explanations assume that you have a specific ISO setting selected rather than Auto ISO. If you do use Auto ISO, the camera may adjust that value instead.

Keep in mind, too, that the camera can adjust the aperture only so much, according to the aperture range of your lens. The range of shutter speeds is limited by the camera. So if you reach the end of those ranges, you have to compromise on either shutter speed or aperture or adjust ISO.

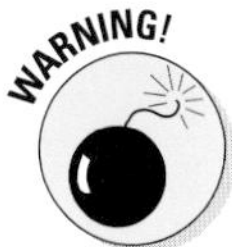

A final, and critical, point about exposure compensation: When you power off the camera, it doesn't return you to a neutral setting (EV 0.0). The setting you last used remains in force for the P, Tv, and Av modes until you change it.

Improving high-contrast shots with Highlight Tone Priority

When a scene contains both very dark and very bright areas, achieving a good exposure can be difficult. If you choose exposure settings that render the shadows properly, the highlights are often overexposed, as in the left image in Figure 7-23. Although the dark lamppost in the foreground looks fine, the white building behind it has become so bright that all detail has been lost. The same thing occurred in the highlight areas of the green church steeple.

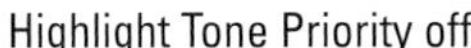

Highlight Tone Priority on

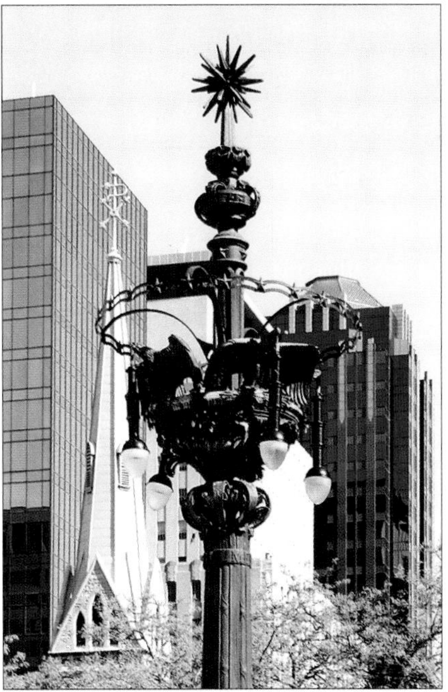

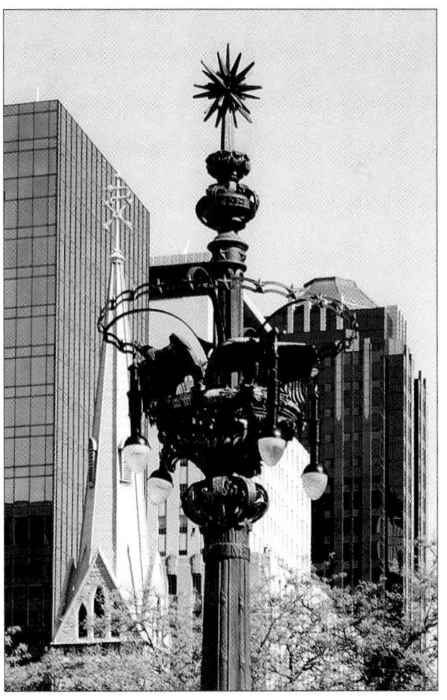

Figure 7-23: The Highlight Tone Priority feature can help prevent overexposed highlights.

One tool to try is the HDR Backlight Control scene mode, covered in Chapter 3. But that setting, while it can improve exposure, prevents you from accessing all the other options available in the advanced exposure modes. So when you want to stick with P, Tv, Av, or M exposure mode, turn to the Highlight Tone Priority option instead, as I did to produce the second image in Figure 7-23. The difference is subtle, but if you look at that white building and steeple, you can see that the effect does make a difference. Now the windows in the building are at least visible, the steeple has regained some of its color, and the sky, too, has a bit more blue.

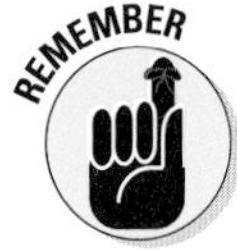

This feature is turned off by default, which may seem like an odd choice after looking at the improvement it made to the scene in Figure 7-23. What gives? The answer is that in order to do its thing, Highlight Tone Priority needs to play with a few other camera settings, as follows:

- **The ISO range is reduced to ISO 200–12800.** The camera needs the more limited range in order to favor the image highlights. (The whys and wherefores aren't important.) Losing the highest ISO is no big deal — the noise level at that setting can make your photo unattractive anyway. But in bright light, you may miss the option of lowering the ISO to 100 because you may be forced to use a smaller aperture or a faster shutter speed than you like.
- **Auto Lighting Optimizer is disabled.** This feature, which attempts to improve image contrast, is incompatible with Highlight Tone Priority. So read the next section, which explains Auto Lighting Optimizer, to determine which of the two exposure tweaks you want to use.
- **Shadows may exhibit slightly more noise.** Again, noise is the defect that looks like speckles in your image.

To try Highlight Tone Priority, head for the Custom Function options on Setup Menu 4. You turn the feature on and off via Custom Function 3, as shown in Figure 7-24.

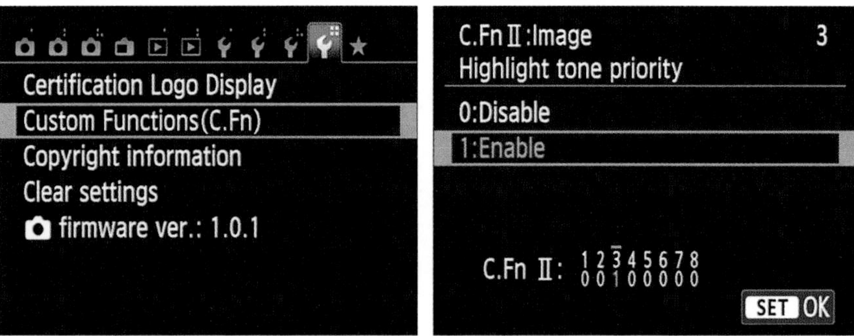

Figure 7-24: Enable Highlight Tone Priority from Custom Function 3 on Setup Menu 4.

As a reminder that Highlight Tone Priority is enabled, a D+ symbol appears near the ISO value in the Shooting Settings display, as shown in Figure 7-25. The same symbol appears with the ISO setting in the viewfinder and in the shooting data that appears onscreen in Live View mode and Playback mode. (See Chapter 5 to find out more about picture playback.) Notice that the symbol that represents Auto Lighting Optimizer is dimmed because that feature is now disabled.

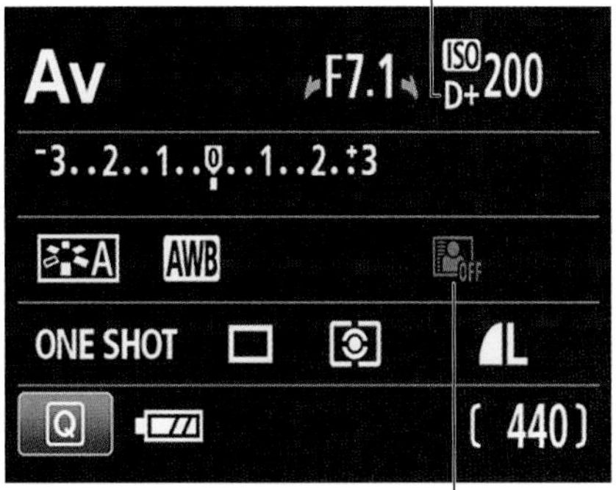

Highlight Tone Priority on

Auto Lighting Optimizer off

Figure 7-25: These symbols indicate that Highlight Tone Priority is enabled and Auto Lighting Optimizer is disabled.

Experimenting with Auto Lighting Optimizer

When you select an Image Quality setting that results in a JPEG image file — that is, any setting other than Raw — the camera tries to enhance your photo while it's processing the picture. Unlike Highlight Tone Priority, which concentrates on preserving highlight detail only, Auto Lighting Optimizer adjusts both shadows and highlights to improve the final image tonality (range of darks to lights). In other words, it's a contrast adjustment.

In the fully automatic exposure modes as well as in Creative Auto, you have no control over how much adjustment is made. But in the P, Tv, Av, and M modes, you can decide whether to enable Auto Lighting Optimizer. You also can request a stronger or lighter application of the effect than the default setting. Figure 7-26 offers an example of the type of impact of each Auto Lighting Optimizer setting.

Given the level of improvement that the Auto Lighting Optimizer correction made to this photo, you may be thinking that you'd be crazy to ever disable the feature. But it's important to note a few points:

- The level of shift that occurs between each Auto Lighting Optimization setting varies dramatically depending on the subject. This particular example shows a fairly noticeable difference between the High and Off settings. But you don't always see this much impact from the filter. Even in this example, it's difficult to detect much difference between Off and Low.
- Although the filter improved this particular scene, at times you may not find it beneficial. For example, maybe you're purposely trying to shoot a backlit subject in silhouette or produce a low-contrast image. Either way, you don't want the camera to insert its opinions on the exposure or contrast you're trying to achieve.

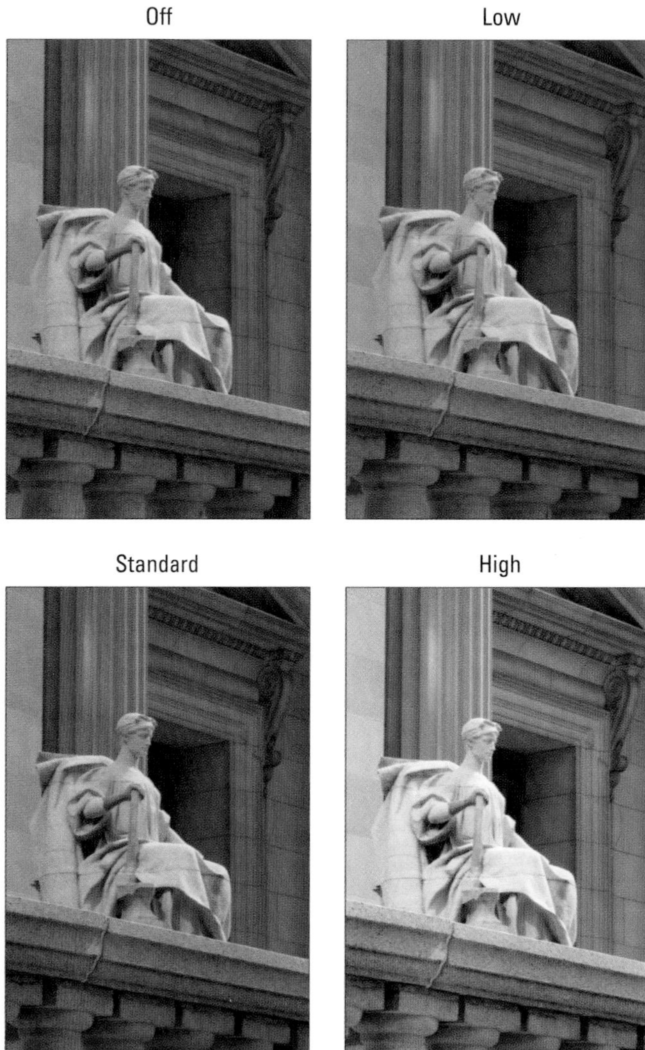

Figure 7-26: For this image, Auto Lighting Optimizer brought more life to the shot by increasing contrast.

- Because the filter is applied after you capture the photo, while the camera is writing the data to the memory card, it can slow your shooting rate.
- In some lighting conditions, Auto Lighting Optimizer can produce an increase in image noise.

- The corrective action taken by Auto Lighting Optimization can make some other exposure-adjustment features less effective. So turn it off if you don't see the results you expect when you're using the following features:
    - Exposure compensation, discussed earlier in this chapter
    - Flash compensation, discussed later in this chapter
    - Automatic exposure bracketing, also discussed later in this chapter

By default, the camera applies the Auto Lighting Optimizer feature at the Standard level *except* in Manual exposure mode, in which case the feature is turned *off* by default. Here's how to choose a different setting:

- **Quick Control screen:** Choose the option, labeled on the left in Figure 7-27, and rotate the Main dial to adjust the level of adjustment. To access the option that enables you to turn the shift on and off for Manual exposure mode, tap the Auto Lighting Optimizer icon or highlight it and press Set; you then see the second screen in the figure. Tap the check box or press the Info button to toggle the adjustment on and off for Manual exposure mode. Exit the screen by tapping the Return arrow or pressing Set.

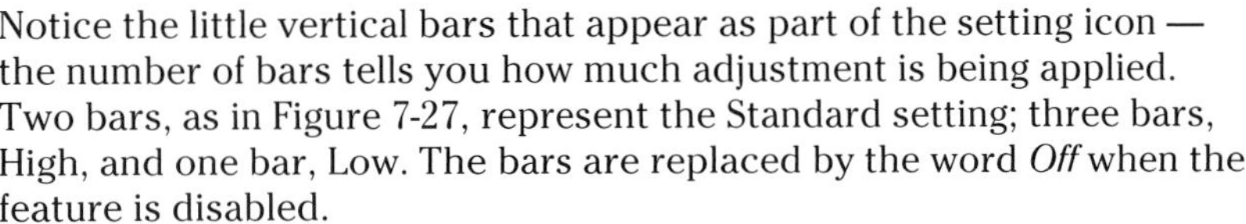

  Notice the little vertical bars that appear as part of the setting icon — the number of bars tells you how much adjustment is being applied. Two bars, as in Figure 7-27, represent the Standard setting; three bars, High, and one bar, Low. The bars are replaced by the word *Off* when the feature is disabled.

- **Shooting Menu 2:** You also can adjust the Auto Lighting Optimizer setting via Shooting Menu 2, as illustrated in Figure 7-28.

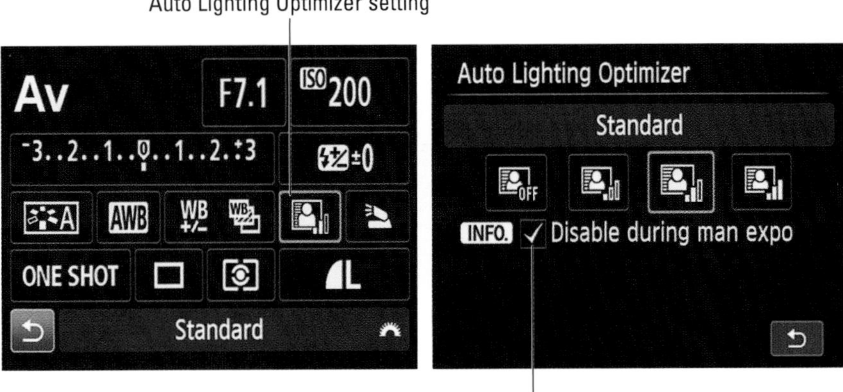

Figure 7-27: To toggle the adjustment on and off for M exposure mode, tap the check box or press the Info button.

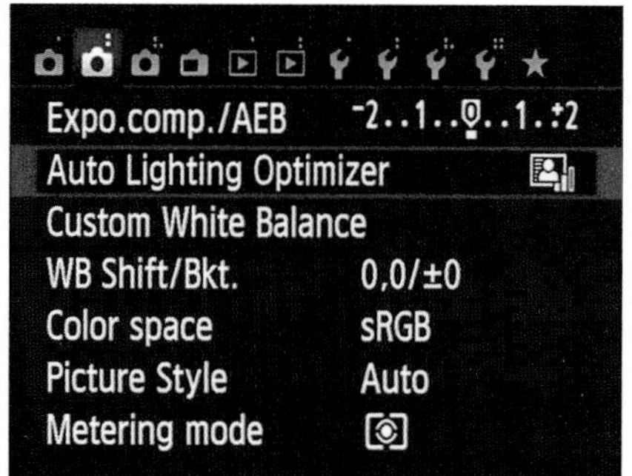

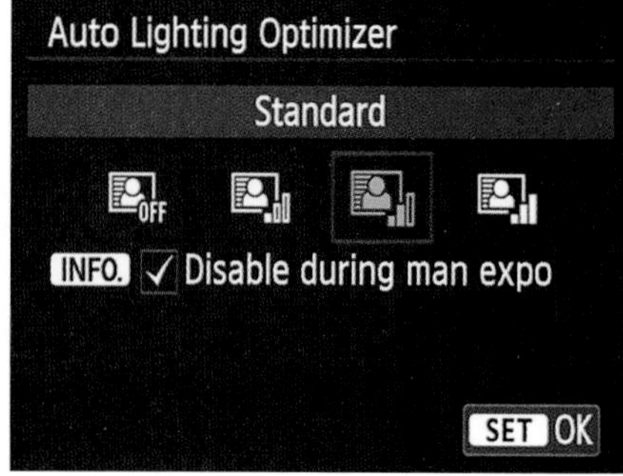

Figure 7-28: Shooting Menu 2 also offers access to the setting.

If you're not sure what level of Auto Lighting Optimization might work best or you're concerned about the other drawbacks of enabling the filter, consider shooting the picture in the Raw file format. For Raw pictures, the camera applies no post-capture tweaking, regardless of whether this filter or any other one is enabled. Then, by using Canon Digital Photo Professional, the software provided free with the camera, you can apply the Auto Lighting Optimizer effect when you convert your Raw images to a standard file format. (See Chapter 6 for details about processing Raw files.)

Correcting vignetting with Peripheral Illumination Correction

Because of some optical science principles that are too boring to explore, some lenses produce pictures that appear darker around the edges of the frame than in the center, even when the lighting is consistent throughout. This phenomenon goes by several names, but the two heard most often are *vignetting* and *light fall-off.* How much vignetting occurs depends on the lens, your aperture setting, and the lens focal length. (Chapter 8 explains focal length.)

To help compensate for vignetting, your camera offers Peripheral Illumination Correction, which adjusts image brightness around the edges of the frame. Figure 7-29 shows an example. In the left image, just a slight amount of light fall-off occurs at the corners, most noticeably at the top of the image. The right image shows the same scene with Peripheral Illumination Correction enabled.

Now, this "before" example hardly exhibits serious vignetting — it's likely that most people wouldn't even notice if it weren't shown next to the "after" example. But if you're a stickler for this sort of thing or your lens suffers from stronger vignetting, it's worth trying Peripheral Illumination Correction.

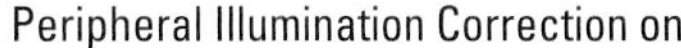

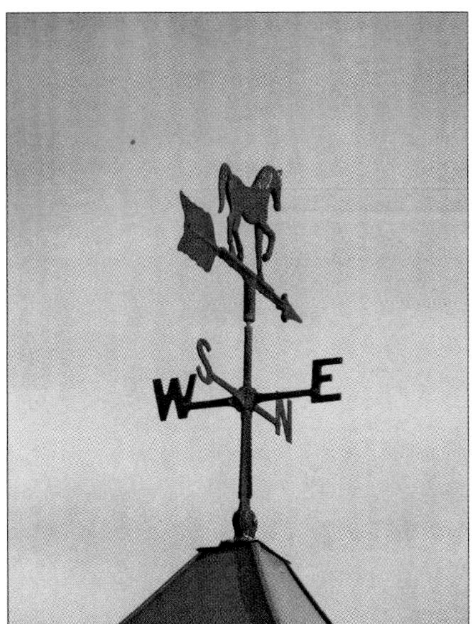

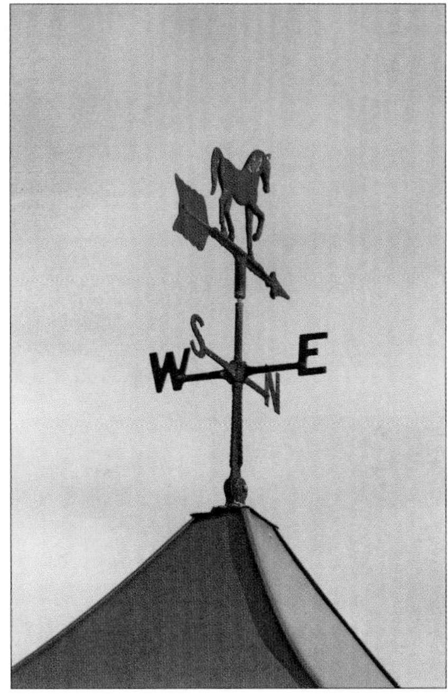

Figure 7-29: Peripheral Illumination Correction tries to correct the corner darkening that can occur with some lenses.

The adjustment is available in all your camera's exposure modes. But a few factoids need spelling out:

- **The correction is available only for photos captured in the JPEG file format.** For Raw photos, you can choose to apply the correction and vary its strength if you use Canon Digital Photo Professional to process your Raw images. Chapter 6 talks more about Raw processing.
- **For the camera to apply the proper correction, data about the specific lens must be included in the camera's *firmware* (internal software).** You can determine whether your lens is supported by opening Shooting Menu 1 and selecting Lens Aberration Correction, as shown on the left in Figure 7-30. Press Set to display the right screen in the figure. If the screen reports that correction data is available, as in the figure, the Peripheral Illumination Correction feature is enabled by default. (See Chapter 8 for information about the Chromatic Aberration feature, which deals with a lens-related color defect.)

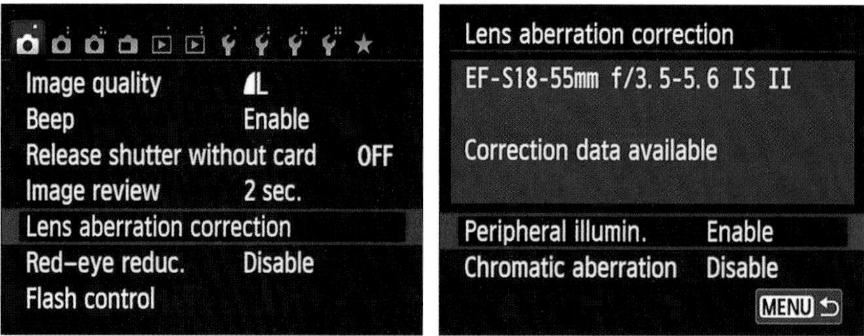

Figure 7-30: If the camera has information about your lens, you can enable the feature.

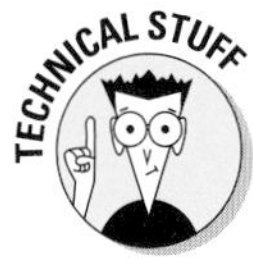

If your lens isn't supported, you may be able to add its information to the camera; Canon calls this step *registering your lens.* You do this by cabling the camera to your computer and then using some tools included with the free EOS Utility software, also provided with your camera. I must refer you to the software manual for help on this bit of business because of the limited number of words that can fit in these pages. (The manuals for all the software are located on one of the two CDs that ship in the camera box.)

- **For non-Canon lenses, Canon recommends disabling Peripheral Illumination Correction even if correction data is available.** To turn off the feature, select the Disable setting. You can still apply the correction in Digital Photo Professional when you shoot in the Raw format.

- **In some circumstances, the correction may produce increased noise at the corners of the photo.** This problem occurs because exposure adjustment can make noise more apparent. Also, at high ISO settings, the camera applies the filter at a lesser strength — presumably to avoid adding even more noise to the picture. (See the first part of this chapter for an understanding of noise and its relationship to ISO.)

Dampening noise

Noise, the digital defect that gives your pictures a speckled look (refer to Figure 7-6), can occur for two exposure-related reasons: a long exposure time and a high ISO setting. Your camera offers two noise-removal filters, one to address each cause of noise. However, you can control whether and how they're applied only in the P, Tv, Av, and M modes; in other modes, the camera makes the call for you.

The next two sections explain a little more about these two filters. But before you explore them, realize that many photo editing programs have pretty good noise-removal filters also, so the in-camera noise filters aren't your only solution to the problem. Especially if you shoot in the Raw file format, you can often get excellent anti-noise results when you process the Raw files. (See Chapter 6 for help with processing of your camera's Raw files.)

Long Exposure Noise Reduction

This filter, found on Shooting Menu 3 and featured in Figure 7-31, goes after the type of noise that's caused by a slow shutter speed. The settings work as follows:

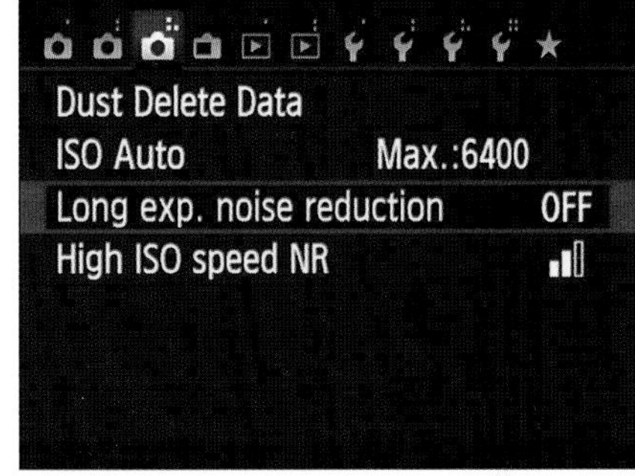

Figure 7-31: This filter attacks noise that can occur when you use a very slow shutter speed.

- **Off:** No noise reduction is applied. This setting is the default.
- **Auto:** Noise reduction is applied when you use a shutter speed of 1 second or longer, but only if the camera detects the type of noise that's caused by long exposures.
- **On:** Noise reduction is always applied at exposures of 1 second or longer. (*Note:* Canon suggests that this setting may result in more noise than either Off or Auto when the ISO setting is 1600 or higher.)

Long Exposure Noise Reduction can be fairly effective at reducing noise but it has a pretty significant downside because of the way it works. Say that you make a 30-second exposure at night. After the shutter closes at the end of the exposure, the camera takes a *second* 30-second exposure to measure the noise by itself, and then subtracts that noise from your *real* exposure. So your shot-to-shot wait time is twice what it would normally be. For some scenes, that may not be a problem, but for shots that feature action, such as fireworks, you definitely don't want that long wait time between shutter clicks.

High ISO Noise Removal

This filter, also found on Shooting Menu 3 and spotlighted in Figure 7-32, attempts to do just what its name implies: eradicate the kind of noise that's caused by using a very high ISO setting. You can select from these settings:

- **Low:** Applies a little noise removal
- **Standard:** Applies a more pronounced amount of noise removal; this setting is the default
- **High:** Goes after noise in a more dramatic way
- **MultiShot:** Tries to achieve a better result than High by capturing four frames in a quick burst and then merging them together into a single JPEG shot. (More about this option momentarily.)
- **Disable:** Turns off the filter

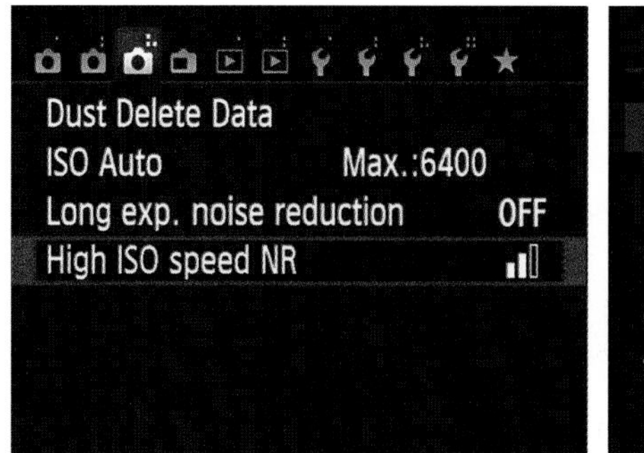

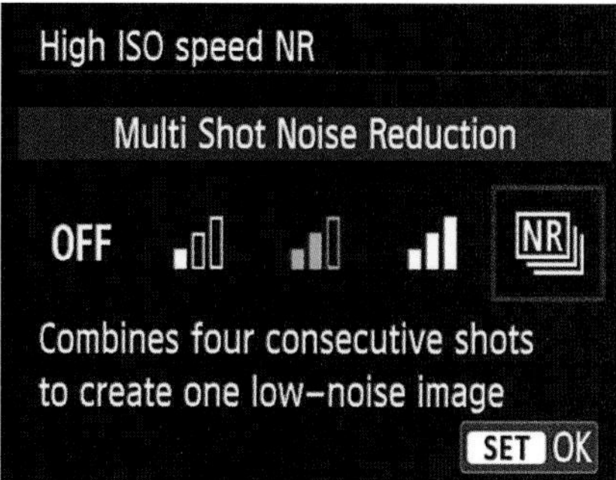

Figure 7-32: The MultiShot setting captures four images and merges them into a single JPEG file.

As with the Long Exposure Noise Reduction filter, this one is applied after you take the shot, slowing your capture rate. In fact, using the High or MultiShot setting for High ISO noise removal reduces the maximum frame rate (shots per second) that you can click off.

It's also important to know that High ISO noise-reduction filters work primarily by applying a slight blur to the image. Don't expect this process to eliminate noise entirely, and expect some resulting image softness. You may be able to get better results by using the blur tools or noise-removal filters found in many photo editors because then you can blur just the parts of the image where noise is most noticeable — usually in areas of flat color or little detail, such as skies.

So what about this mysteriously named MultiShot setting? Canon promises that this setting delivers a better result than the High setting by capturing a burst of four images and merging them into a single JPEG frame, similar to the result of using the Handheld Night Scene mode detailed in Chapter 3. But choosing the option has so many caveats that you may find it not worth the trouble:

- Flash is not possible.
- The feature is off limits when any of the following are enabled: Long Exposure Noise Reduction, Auto Exposure Bracketing, or White Balance Bracketing.
- You can't use the feature with the Bulb exposure setting (the manual exposure shutter speed that keeps the shutter open as long as you press the shutter button).
- The merged images may not align properly, resulting in ghosting or blurring, if there's any camera shake during the exposures. So for best results, use a tripod. In addition, any moving objects may also appear blurry, so this feature works best with still life and landscape shots.

- The setting automatically reverts to Standard if you turn off the camera, switch to a fully automatic exposure mode or Movie mode, or set the shutter speed to Bulb.
- Direct printing of shots taken with this setting isn't possible. Okay, so that's not a biggie for most folks; see Chapter 11 for more information about direct printing nonetheless.
- Your end result is a JPEG photo, even if the Image Quality setting is set to Raw or Raw+JPEG. So if you're a Raw fan, don't use this setting.

My take is this: If you have a tripod and you want to experiment with the MultiShot setting, it's worth a try if you don't need fast shot-to-shot capture time and your scene doesn't include moving objects. Otherwise, I'd stick with High or even Standard and either live with the resulting noise or clean it up using my photo software after downloading.

If you do opt for the MultiShot setting, you see a little multi-box symbol during playback next to the Metering Mode symbol when you set the Playback mode to the Shooting Information or Histogram modes. See Chapter 5 for help with the playback display modes.

Locking Autoexposure Settings

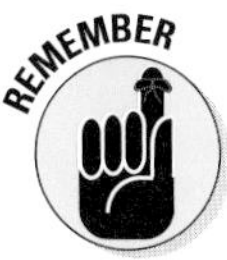

When you combine Spot, Partial, or Center-weighted metering with the P, Tv, or Av exposure modes, your camera continually meters the light until the moment you press the shutter button fully to shoot the picture. The same thing happens with Evaluative metering if you use Live View.

For most situations, this approach works great, resulting in the right settings for the light that's striking your subject when you capture the image. But on occasion, you may want to lock in a certain combination of exposure settings. For example, perhaps you want your subject to appear at the far edge of the frame. If you were to use the normal shooting technique, you would place the subject under a focus point, press the shutter button halfway to lock focus and set the initial exposure, and then reframe to your desired composition to take the shot. The problem is that exposure is then recalculated based on the new framing, which can leave your subject under- or overexposed.

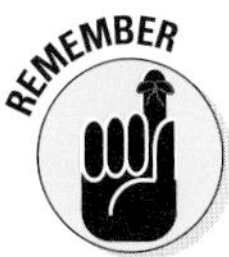

The easiest way to lock in exposure settings is to switch to M (manual exposure) mode and use the same f-stop, shutter speed, and ISO settings for each shot. In manual exposure mode, the camera never overrides your exposure decisions; they're locked until you change them.

But if you prefer to use autoexposure, you can lock the current exposure settings by pressing the AE (autoexposure) Lock button while holding the shutter button halfway down.

Exposure is locked and remains locked for four seconds, even if you release the AE Lock button and the shutter button. To remind you that AE Lock is in force, the camera displays a little asterisk in the viewfinder. If you need to relock exposure, just press the AE Lock button again.

Note: If your goal is to use the same exposure settings for multiple shots, you must keep the AE Lock button pressed during the entire series of pictures. Every time you let up on the button and press it again, you lock exposure anew based on the light that's in the frame.

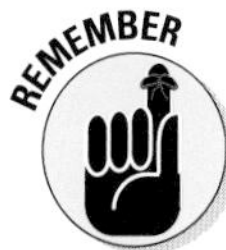

One other critical point to remember about using AE Lock: The camera establishes and locks exposure differently depending on the metering mode, the focusing mode (automatic or manual), and on an autofocusing setting called AF Point Selection mode. (Chapter 8 explains this option thoroughly.) Here's the scoop:

- **Evaluative metering and automatic AF Point Selection:** Exposure is locked on the focusing point that achieved focus.
- **Evaluative metering and manual AF Point Selection:** Exposure is locked on the selected autofocus point.
- **All other metering modes:** Exposure is based on the center autofocus point, regardless of the AF Point Selection mode.
- **Manual focusing:** Exposure is based on the center autofocus point.

Again, if this focusing lingo sounded like gibberish, check out Chapter 8 to get a full explanation.

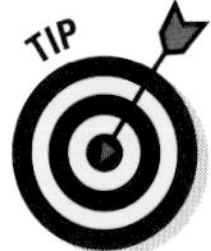

By combining autoexposure lock with Spot metering, you can ensure a good exposure for photographs in which you want your subject to be off-center, and that subject is significantly darker or lighter than the background. Imagine, for example, a dark statue set against a light blue sky. First, select Spot metering so that the camera considers only the object located in the center of the frame. Frame the scene initially so that your statue is located in the center of the viewfinder. Press and hold the shutter button halfway to establish focus and then lock exposure by pressing the AE Lock button. Now reframe the shot to your desired composition and take the picture.

These bits of advice assume that you haven't altered the function of the AE Lock button, which you can do via Custom Function 6. You can swap the tasks of the shutter button and AE Lock button, for example, so that pressing the shutter button halfway locks exposure and pressing the AE Lock button locks focus. Chapter 10 offers details on the relevant Custom Function.

Bracketing Exposures Automatically

Many photographers use a strategy called *bracketing* to ensure that at least one shot of a subject is properly exposed. They shoot the same subject multiple times, slightly varying the exposure settings for each image.

To make bracketing easy, your camera offers *automatic exposure bracketing* (AEB). When you enable this feature, your only job is to press the shutter button to record the shots; the camera automatically adjusts the exposure settings between each image.

Aside from cover-your, uh, "bases" shooting, bracketing is useful for *HDR imaging.* HDR stands for *high dynamic range,* with dynamic range referring to the spectrum of brightness values in a photograph. The idea behind HDR is to capture the same shot multiple times, using different exposure settings for each image. You then use special imaging software, called *tone mapping software,* to combine the exposures in a way that uses specific brightness values from each shot. By using this process, you get a shot that contains more detail in both the highlights and shadows than a camera could ever record in a single image.

With the HDR Backlight Control scene mode, covered in Chapter 3, you can create limited HDR effects; that scene mode captures three frames and merges the result into a single JPEG image. But for a greater dynamic range in your final image, you need to start with more than three frames and a greater variation between the brightest and darkest frames. Doing the job yourself also gives you more control over how the brightness values are merged in the composite image.

Figure 7-33 shows an example of what you can achieve by bracketing and merging frames yourself. To create the final, HDR version shown on the right in the figure, I captured the shot at five different exposures. The first two images in the figure show you the brightest and darkest of those five frames. The result contains much more detail in the shadows and the highlights than the HDR Backlight Control feature can deliver with its three-exposure series.

When applied to its extreme limits, HDR produces images that have something of a graphic-novel look. My example is pretty tame; some people might not even realize that any digital trickery has been involved. To me, it has the look of a hand-tinted photo. That, too, is an important difference between the automated HDR Backlight Control feature and manual HDR — the automated HDR feature isn't designed to have an HDR "look" but rather to subtly enhance the dynamic range. So it's all a matter of what result you're after — and how much work you're willing to do to achieve it.

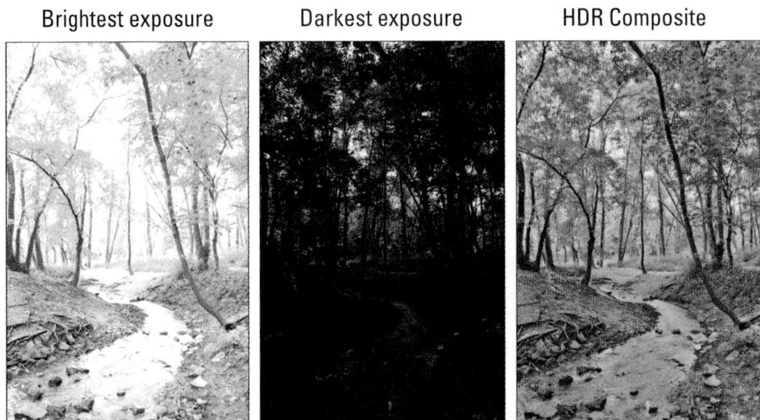

Figure 7-33: Using HDR software tools, I merged the brightest and darkest exposures along with several intermediate exposures, to produce the composite image.

Whether you're interested in automatic exposure bracketing for HDR or just want to give yourself an exposure safety net, keep these points in mind:

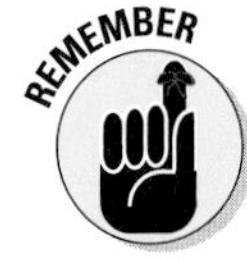

- **Exposure mode:** AEB is available only in the P, Tv, Av, and M exposure modes.
- **Flash:** AEB isn't available when you use flash. You can still bracket your shots and use flash — you just have to change the exposure settings between frames yourself.
- **Bracketing amount:** You can request an exposure change of up to two stops from the auto bracketing system.
- **Exposure Compensation:** You can combine AEB with Exposure Compensation if you want. The camera simply applies the compensation amount when it calculates the exposure for the three bracketed images.
- **Auto Lighting Optimizer:** Because that feature is designed to automatically adjust images that are underexposed or lacking in contrast, it can render AEB ineffective. So it's best to disable the feature when bracketing. See the section "Experimenting with Auto Lighting Optimizer," earlier in this chapter, for information on where to find and turn off the feature.

The next two sections explain how to set up the camera for automatic bracketing and how to actually record a series of bracketed shots.

Turning auto bracketing on and off

The following steps show you how to turn on automatic exposure bracketing via Shooting Menu 2. (More about another option for enabling the feature momentarily.)

1. **Display Shooting Menu 2 and choose Expo. Comp./AEB, as shown on the left in Figure 7-34.**

   After you tap the menu option (or highlight it and press Set), you see the screen shown on the right in the figure. This is the same dual-natured screen that appears when you apply exposure compensation, as explained earlier in this chapter. The figure shows the screen as it appears in the P, Tv, or Av modes.

   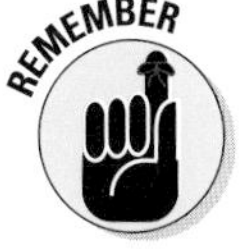

   In M mode, exposure compensation isn't relevant — if you want a darker or brighter image, you just adjust the f-stop, shutter speed, or ISO. So the Exposure Compensation controls are dimmed on the AEB/Exp. Comp screen if the Mode dial is set to M.

2. **Rotate the Main dial to establish the amount of exposure change you want between images.**

   What you see onscreen after you rotate the dial depends on your exposure mode.

   - *P, Tv, or Av modes:* For these modes, both the Exposure Compensation and AEB features are enabled. And the meter expands, as shown on the left in Figure 7-35, to represent the total 7-stop adjustment you can make in bracketed shots if you also enable the maximum amount of Exposure Compensation. (The meter expands after you rotate the Main dial; otherwise it just shows the 5-stop range for Exposure Compensation.)

     Where does the 7-stop thing come from? Well, you're still limited to adjusting exposure a total of two stops between bracketed shots, but if you turn on Exposure Compensation and set that value to +5.0 and then set the bracketed amount to +2.0, your brightest shot in the bracketed series is captured at +7.0. Your darkest shot is captured at +3.0, and the "neutral" shot is captured at +5.0.

   - *M mode:* The screen changes to look similar to the one on the right in Figure 7-35, with only the AEB setting active.

   Either way, each whole number on the meter represents one stop of exposure shift. The little red lines under the meter show you the amount of shift that will occur in your bracketed series of shots. For example, the settings in Figure 7-35 represent the maximum two stops of adjustment.

Keep rotating the dial until you get the exposure indicators to reflect the amount of adjustment you want between each bracketed shot. If you want to adjust the Exposure Compensation setting, press the right/left cross keys or tap the plus/minus signs at the end of the meter.

3. **Tap Set or press the Set button.**

   AEB is now enabled. To remind you of that fact, the exposure meter in the Shooting Settings display and on Shooting Menu 2 shows the three exposure indicators to represent the exposure shift you established in Step 2, as shown in Figure 7-36. You see the same markers on the viewfinder meter. When you snap your three pictures, the first image is captured at the actual exposure settings; the second, at settings that produce a darker image; and the third, at settings that produce a brighter photo.

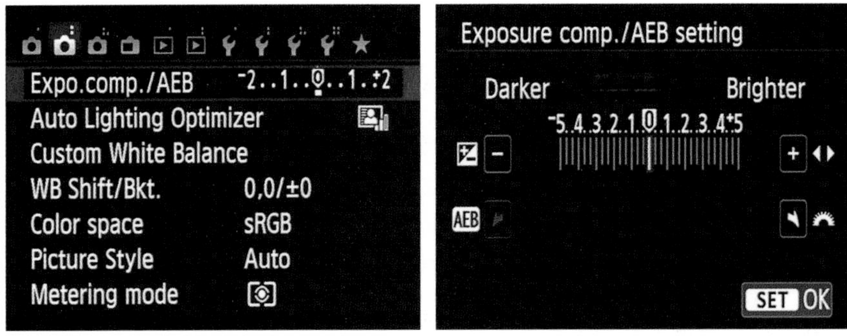

Figure 7-34: Automatic exposure bracketing records your image at three exposure settings.

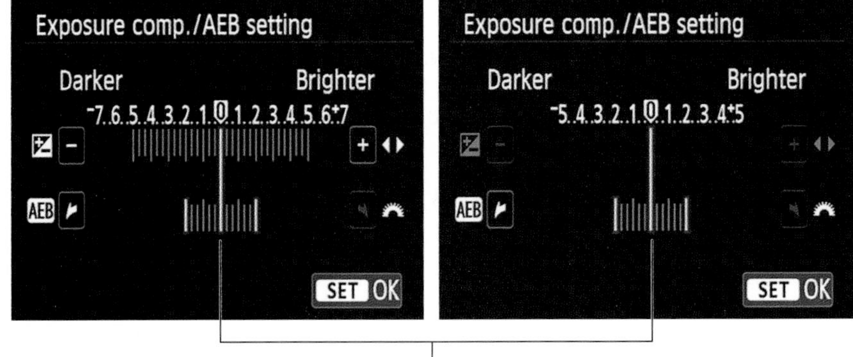

Figure 7-35: The bracketing control appears different in P, Tv, and AV modes (left) than in M mode (right). But in all modes, rotate the Main dial to adjust the setting.

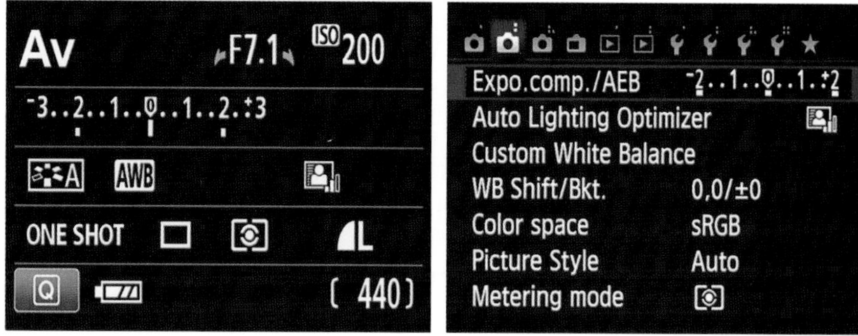

Figure 7-36: The three bars under the meter remind you that automatic exposure bracketing is enabled.

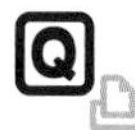

If you prefer, you can also enable AEB through the Quick Control screen. Just tap the exposure meter (or highlight it and press Set) to access the screens you see in Figure 7-35, where you can set the amount of bracketing.

To turn off auto exposure bracketing, just revisit Shooting Menu 2 or the Quick Control screen and use the Main dial to change the AEB setting back to 0, so that you see only one meter indicator instead of three.

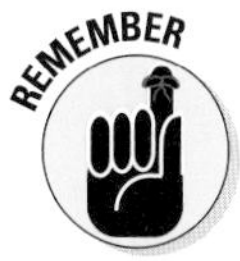

AEB is also turned off when you power down the camera, enable the flash, replace the camera battery, or replace the memory card. You also can't use the feature in manual exposure (M) mode if you set the shutter speed to the Bulb option. (At that setting, the camera keeps the shutter open as long as you press the shutter button.)

Shooting a bracketed series

After you enable auto bracketing, the way you record your trio of bracketed exposures depends on whether you set the Drive mode to Single or Continuous. Drive mode, which is described in Chapter 2, determines whether the camera records a single image or multiple images with each press of the shutter button. (Press the left cross key for the fastest way to access the screen that enables you to change this setting.)

- **AEB in Single mode:** You take each exposure separately, pressing the shutter button fully three times to record your trio of images.

  If you forget which exposure you're taking, look at the exposure meter. After you press the shutter button halfway to lock focus, the meter shows just a single indicator bar instead of three. If the bar is at 0, you're ready to take the first capture. If it's to the left of 0, you're on capture two, which creates the darker exposure. If it's to the right of 0, you're on capture three, which produces the brightest image. This assumes that you haven't also applied exposure compensation, in which case the starting point is at a notch other than zero. (And yes, all these possible combinations make my head spin, too.)

- **AEB in Continuous mode:** The camera records all three exposures with one press of the shutter button. To record another series, release and then press the shutter button again. In other words, when AEB is turned on, the camera doesn't keep recording images until you release the shutter button as it normally does in Continuous mode — you can take only three images with one press of the shutter button.
- **Self-Timer/Remote modes:** All three exposures are recorded with a single press of the shutter button, as with Continuous mode.

Using Flash in Advanced Exposure Modes

Sometimes, no amount of fiddling with aperture, shutter speed, and ISO produces a bright enough exposure — in which case you simply have to add more light. The built-in flash on your camera offers the most convenient solution.

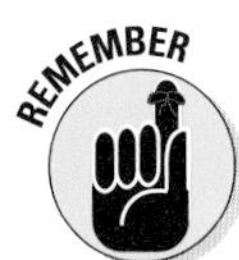

Chapter 2 offers a primer in flash basics, but here's a quick recap:

- In Scene Intelligent Auto and the scene modes, the camera decides when flash is needed.
- In Creative Auto mode, you can either let the camera retain flash control (auto flash) or set the flash to always fire or never fire. You make the selection via the Quick Control screen.
-  The advanced exposure modes leave flash decisions entirely up to you. There's no automatic flash mode that lets you hand the reins over to the camera. Instead, when you want to use the built-in flash, just press the Flash button on the left side of the camera. The flash pops up and fires on your next shot. To turn off the flash, just press down on the flash assembly to close it.
- For normal flash operation in the advanced modes, set the Built-in Flash Function to Normal. The fastest way to adjust the setting is via the Quick Control screen. I labeled the icon that represents the Normal setting in Figure 7-37. (You don't see the icon until you raise the flash.)

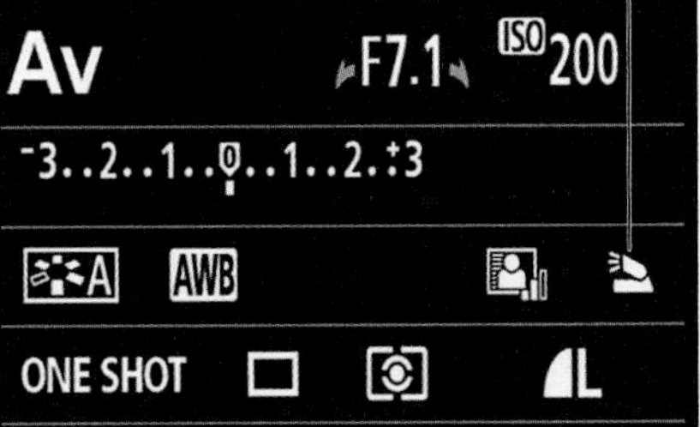

Figure 7-37: Set the Built-in Flash Function to Normal for regular flash photography.

- When you use the built-in flash, the fastest shutter speed possible is 1/200 second. The limitation is needed for the camera to synchronize the timing of the flash with the opening and closing of the shutter. So fast-action photography and the built-in flash really aren't compatible. (If you use some compatible external flash units, you can access the entire range of shutter speeds.)
- Pay careful attention to your results when you use the built-in flash with a telephoto lens that is very long. You may find that the flash casts an unwanted shadow when it strikes the lens. For best results, try switching to an external flash head.

The next section goes into a little background detail about how the camera calculates the flash power that's needed to expose the image. This stuff is a little technical, but it will help you to better understand how to get the results you want because the flash performance varies depending on the exposure mode.

Following that discussion, the rest of the chapter covers advanced flash features.

Getting more help with flash

In order to keep this book from being exorbitantly large (and expensive), I can cover only the basics of flash photography. But I can point you toward a couple of my favorite resources for delving more deeply into the subject:

- Canon's USA website (`www.usa.canon.com`) offers some great tutorials on flash photography (as well as other subjects). Under the Consumer and Home Office menu, click the Resources and Learning Link and then the Learning Station links to find resources related to Canon Speedlite flash technology.
- A website completely dedicated to flash photography, www.strobist.com, enables you to learn from and share with other photographers.
- You can find many good books detailing the art of flash photography — and trust me, when you're working with the harsh and narrowly focused light that a flash emits, it *is* an art to produce great pictures. A seasoned portrait photographer, for example, knows where to place and modify the light to produce soft, beautiful images that look as though no artificial light at all was used. That's why wedding pictures taken by a professional photographer look so nice and the snapshots taken by most wedding guests look so, um, not. (That's also why a good wedding photographer costs money.)
- Chapter 9 of this book offers additional flash and lighting tips related to portraits and other specific types of photographs.

Understanding your camera's approach to flash

When you use flash, your camera automatically calculates the flash power needed to illuminate the subject. This process is sometimes referred to as *flash metering.* Your camera uses a flash-metering system that Canon calls E-TTL II. The *E* stands for *evaluative, TTL* stands for *through the lens,* and *II* refers to the fact that this system is an update to the first version of the system.

It isn't important that you remember what the initials stand for or even the flash system's official name. What is helpful to keep in mind is how the system is designed to work.

First, you need to know that a flash can be used in two basic ways: as the primary light source or as a *fill flash.* When flash is the primary light source, both the subject and background are lit by the flash. In dim lighting, this typically results in a brightly lit subject and a dark background, as shown on the left in Figure 7-38. This assumes that the background is far enough from the subject that it's beyond the reach of the flash, of course.

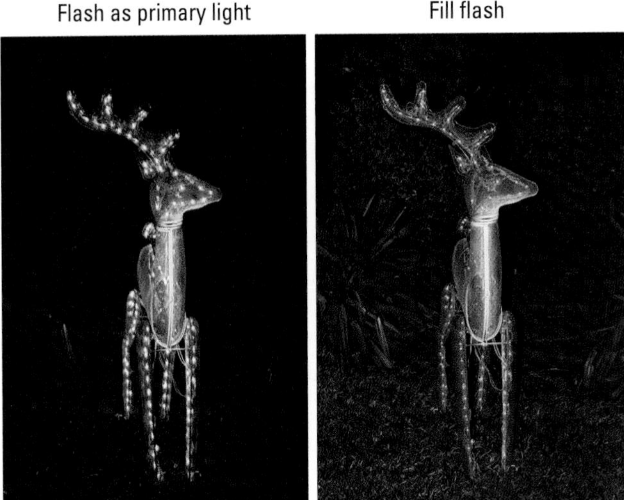

Figure 7-38: Fill flash produces brighter backgrounds.

With fill flash, the background is exposed primarily by ambient light, and the flash adds a little extra illumination to the subject. Fill flash typically produces brighter backgrounds and, often, softer lighting of the subject because not as much flash power is needed. The downside is that if the ambient light is dim, as in this nighttime example, you need a slow shutter speed to properly expose the image, and both the camera and the subject must remain still to avoid blurring. The shutter speed for the fill-flash image, shown on the right in Figure 7-38, was 1/30 second. Fortunately, I had a tripod, and the deer was happy to stay perfectly still as long as I needed. Well, at least until the wind whipped up later that night and, sadly, blew him a few feet down the driveway.

At any rate, neither flash approach is necessarily right or wrong. Whether you want a dark background depends on the scene and your artistic interpretation. If you want to diminish the background, you may prefer the darker background you get when you use flash as your primary light source. But if the background is important to the context of the shot, allowing the camera to absorb more ambient light and adding just a small bit of fill flash may be more to your liking.

So how does this little flash lesson relate to your camera? Well, the exposure mode you use (P, Tv, Av, or M) determines whether the flash operates as a fill flash or as the primary light source. The exposure mode also controls the extent to which the camera adjusts the aperture and shutter speed in response to the ambient light in the scene.

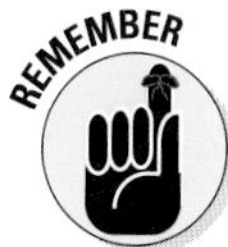

In all modes, the camera analyzes the light both in the background and on the subject. Then it calculates the exposure and flash output as follows:

- **P:** In this mode, the shutter speed is automatically set between 1/60 and 1/200 second. If the ambient light is sufficient, the flash output is geared to providing fill-flash lighting. Otherwise, the flash is determined to be the primary light source, and the output is adjusted accordingly. In the latter event, the image background may be dark, as in the left example in Figure 7-38, depending on its distance from the flash.
- **Tv:** In this mode, the flash defaults to fill-flash behavior. After you select a shutter speed, the camera determines the proper aperture to expose the background with ambient light. Then it sets the flash power to provide fill-flash lighting to the subject.

You can select a shutter speed between 30 seconds and 1/200 second. If the aperture (f-stop) setting blinks, the camera can't expose the background properly at the shutter speed you selected. You can adjust either the shutter speed or ISO to correct the problem.

- **Av:** Again, the flash is designed to serve as fill-flash lighting. After you set the f-stop, the camera selects the shutter speed needed to expose the background using only ambient light. The flash power is then geared to fill in shadows on the subject.

Depending on the ambient light and your selected f-stop, the camera sets the shutter speed at anywhere from 30 seconds to 1/200 second. So be sure to note the shutter speed before you shoot — at slow shutter speeds, you may need a tripod to avoid camera shake. Your subject also must remain still to avoid blurring.

If you want to avoid the possibility of a slow shutter altogether, you can: Visit Shooting Menu 1, choose Flash Control, and then choose the Flash Sync Speed in AV mode option, as shown in Figure 7-39. At the default setting, Auto, the camera operates as just described. You also have two other choices (not shown in the figure): 1/200-1/60 second Auto, which tells the camera to choose any shutter speed between 1/60 and 1/200 second; and 1/200 second, which restricts the camera to *always* setting the shutter speed to 1/200 second when you use flash in Av mode.

The latter two options both ensure that you can handhold the camera without blur, but obviously, in dim lighting, it can result in a dark background because the camera doesn't have time to soak up much ambient light. At the 1/200 to 1/60 setting, the backgrounds are usually brighter than the 1/200 fixed setting, of course, because the camera at least has the latitude to slow the shutter to 1/60 second.

- **M:** In this mode, the shutter speed, aperture, and ISO setting you select determine how brightly the background will be exposed. The camera takes care of illuminating the subject with fill flash. The maximum shutter speed you can select is 1/200 second; the slowest normal shutter speed is 30 seconds.

You also can set the shutter speed to the Bulb setting — which keeps the shutter open as long as you keep the shutter button pressed, however. In Bulb mode, the flash fires at the beginning of the exposure if the Shutter Sync setting is set to the 1st Curtain setting; with the 2nd Curtain setting, the flash fires at the beginning of the exposure and again at the end. See the upcoming section "Exploring more flash options" for details about the Shutter Sync setting.

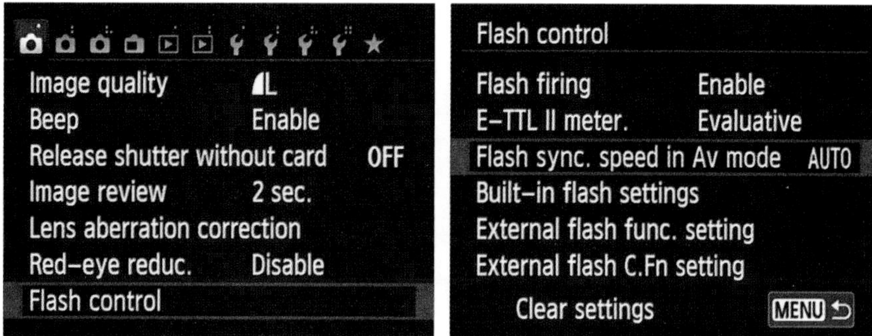

Figure 7-39: You can limit the camera to a fast shutter when using Av mode with flash.

If the flash output in any mode isn't to your liking, you can adjust it by using flash exposure compensation, explained a little later in this chapter. Also check out the upcoming section "Locking the flash exposure" for another trick to manipulate flash results. In any autoexposure mode, you can also use exposure compensation, discussed earlier, to tweak the ambient exposure — that is, the brightness of your background. So you have multiple points of control: exposure compensation to manipulate the background brightness, and flash compensation and flash exposure lock to adjust the flash output.

Again, these guidelines apply to the camera's built-in-flash. If you use certain Canon external flash units, you not only have more flash control but can also select a faster shutter speed than the built-in flash permits.

Using flash outdoors

Although most people think of flash as a tool for nighttime and low-light photography, adding a bit of light from the built-in flash can improve close-ups and portraits that you shoot outdoors during the day. After all, your main light source — the sun — is overhead, so although the top of the subject may be adequately lit, the front typically needs some additional illumination. And if your subject is in the shade, getting no direct light, using flash is even more critical. For example, the two photos in Figure 7-40 show you the same scene, captured with and without fill flash. The fruit stand was shaded by an awning, so even though it was a bright, cloudless day, I popped up the built-in flash to bring just a smidge more light to the scene and produce a better result.

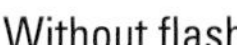

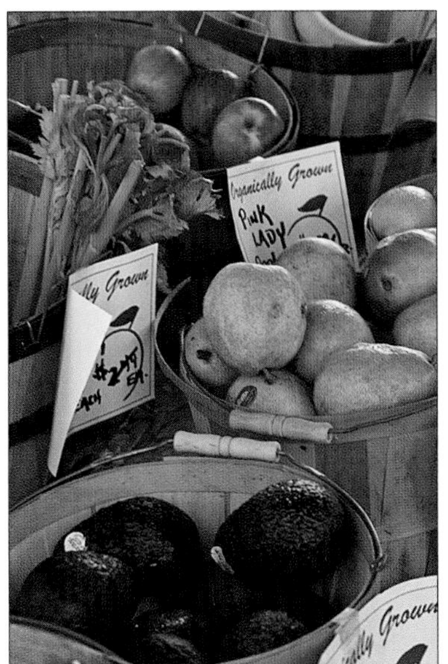

With flash

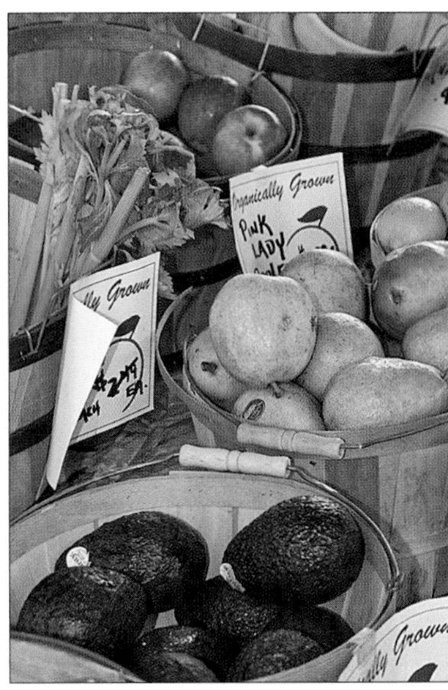

Figure 7-40: Flash often improves daytime pictures outdoors.

You do need to be aware of a couple issues that can arise when you supplement the sun with the built-in flash:

- **You may need to make a White Balance adjustment.** Adding flash may result in colors that are slightly warmer (more yellow/red), as in the flash example here, or cooler (bluish) because the camera's white balancing system can get tripped up by mixed light sources. If you don't appreciate the shift in colors, see Chapter 8 to find out how to make a white balance adjustment to solve the problem.
- **You may need to stop down the aperture or lower ISO to avoid overexposing the photo.** The top shutter speed for the built-in flash, 1/200 second, may not be fast enough to produce a good exposure in very bright light when you use a wide-open aperture, even if you use the lowest possible ISO setting. If you want both flash *and* the short depth of field that comes with an open aperture, you can place a neutral density filter over your lens. This accessory reduces the light that comes through the lens without affecting colors. In addition, some Canon external flash units enable you to access the entire range of shutter speeds on the camera.

Adjusting flash power with Flash Exposure Compensation

When you shoot with your built-in flash, the camera attempts to adjust the flash output as needed to produce a good exposure in the current lighting conditions. On some occasions, you may find that you want a little more or less light than the camera thinks is appropriate.

You can adjust the flash output by using the feature called *Flash Exposure Compensation.* Similar to exposure compensation, discussed earlier in this chapter, flash exposure compensation affects the output level of the flash unit, whereas exposure compensation affects the brightness of the background in your flash photos. As with exposure compensation, flash exposure compensation is stated in terms of EV *(exposure value)* numbers. A setting of 0.0 indicates no flash adjustment; you can increase the flash power to +2.0 or decrease it to –2.0.

Figure 7-41 shows an example of the benefit of this feature — again, available only when you shoot in the advanced exposure modes. The first image shows you a flash-free shot. Clearly, a little more light was needed, but at normal flash power, the flash was too strong, blowing out the highlights in some areas, as shown in the middle image. Reducing the flash power to EV –1.3, resulted in a softer flash that straddled the line perfectly between no flash and too much flash.

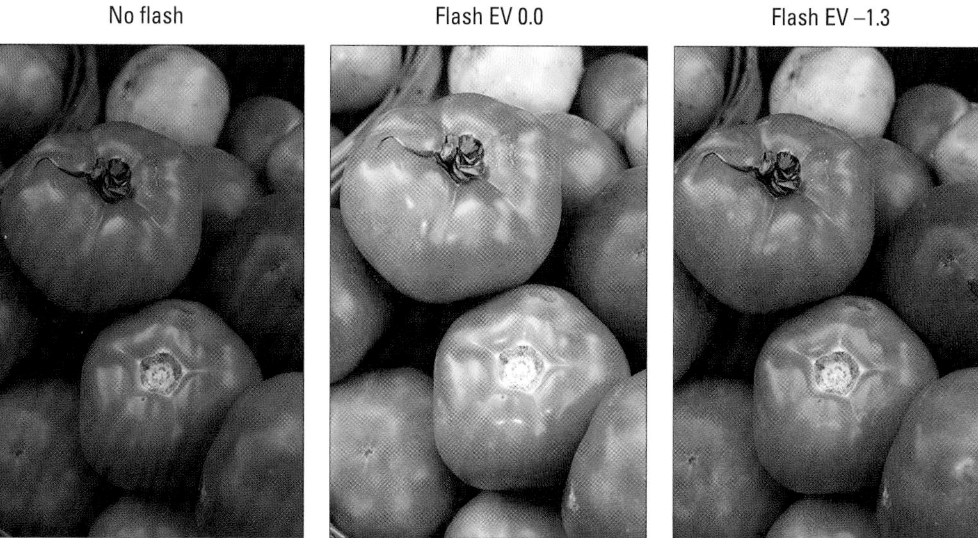

Figure 7-41: When normal flash output is too strong, lower the Flash Exposure Compensation value.

As for boosting the flash output, well, you may find it necessary on some occasions, but don't expect the built-in flash to work miracles even at a Flash Exposure Compensation of +2.0. Any built-in flash has a limited range, so the light simply can't reach faraway objects.

Whichever direction you want to go with flash power, you have two ways to do so:

- **Quick Control screen:** This path is by far the easiest way to travel. After shifting to the Quick Control display, highlight the Flash Exposure Compensation value, as shown on the left in Figure 7-42. Rotate the Main dial to raise or lower the amount of flash adjustment. Or if you need more help, tap the icon or press Set to display the second screen in the figure, which contains a little meter along with a text note that tells you that if you use an external flash, any compensation you dial in via the flash itself overrides the on-camera setting. Press the right/left cross keys or tap the arrows at the end of the meter to adjust the flash power on this screen. You also can drag your finger along the scale to adjust the setting. Tap the return arrow or press Set when you finish.

  When flash compensation is in effect, the value appears in the Shooting Settings screen, in the area occupied by the icon in the left screen in Figure 7-42. You see the same plus/minus flash symbol in the viewfinder and Live View display, although in both cases without the actual Flash Exposure Compensation value. If you change the Flash Exposure Compensation value to zero, the flash-power icon disappears from all the displays until you enter Quick Control mode again.

- **Shooting Menu 1:** The menu route to flash power is a little more tedious. Display Shooting Menu 1, select Flash Control, and press Set. You then see the left screen in Figure 7-43. Choose Built-in Flash Settings to display the right screen. Now choose Flash Exp. Comp. to display a flash meter like the one shown on the right in Figure 7-42. You can then use the right or left cross keys drag along the scale, or tap the Brighter and Darker arrows to adjust the setting. Tap the return arrow or press Set when you finish. (In other words, learn the Quick Control method and save yourself a bunch of button presses!)

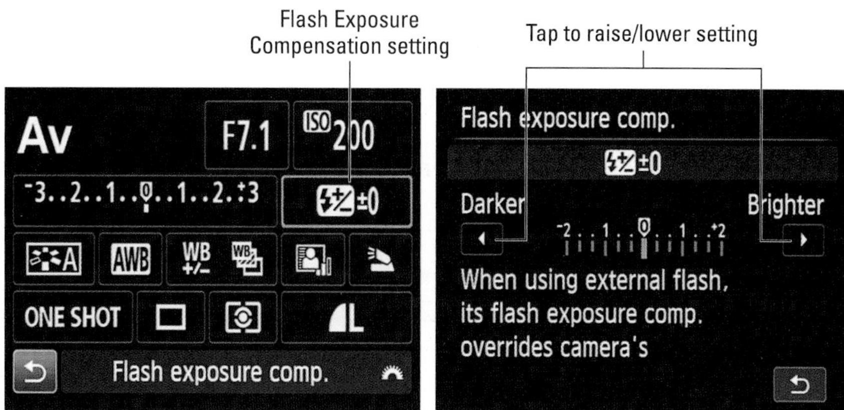

Figure 7-42: The quickest way to adjust flash power is via the Quick Control screen.

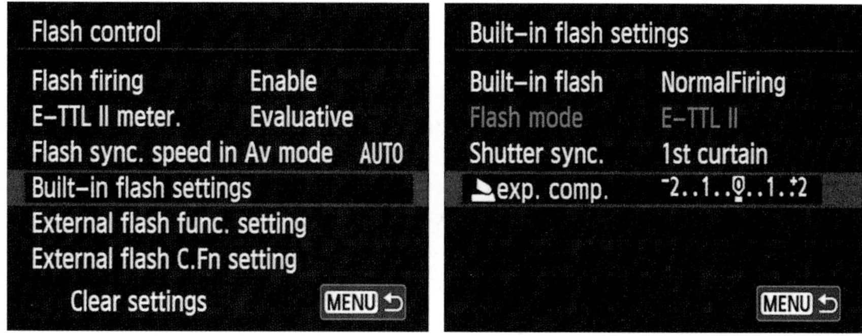

Figure 7-43: You can also change flash power by using the menus, but it's a tedious task.

You also have the option of customizing the Set button to whisk you directly to the Flash Exposure Compensation setting. You make this change via Custom Function 7. (Chapter 10 shows you how.)

As with exposure compensation, any flash-power adjustment you make remains in force until you reset the control, even if you turn off the camera. So be sure to check the setting before using your flash. Additionally, the Auto Lighting Optimizer feature, covered earlier in this chapter, can interfere with the effect produced by flash exposure compensation, so you might want to disable it.

Locking the flash exposure

You might never notice it, but when you press the shutter button to take a picture with flash enabled, the camera emits a brief *preflash* before the actual flash. This preflash is used to determine the proper flash power needed to expose the image.

Occasionally, the information that the camera collects from the preflash can be off-target because of the assumptions the system makes about what area of the frame is likely to contain your subject. To address this problem, your camera has a feature called *Flash Exposure Lock,* or FE Lock. This tool enables you to set the flash power based on only the center of the frame.

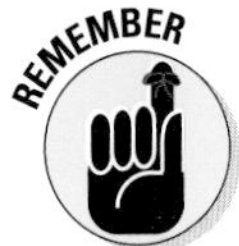

Unfortunately, FE Lock isn't available in Live View mode. If you want to use this feature, you must abandon Live View and use the viewfinder to frame your images.

Follow these steps to use FE Lock:

1. **Frame your photo so that your subject falls under the center autofocus point.**

   You want your subject smack in the middle of the frame. You can reframe the shot after locking the flash exposure, if you want.

2. **Press the shutter button halfway.**

   The camera meters the light in the scene. If you're using autofocusing, focus is set on your subject. (If focus is set on another spot in the frame, see Chapter 8 to find out how to select the center autofocus point.) You can now lift your finger off the shutter button, if you want.

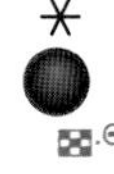

3. **While the subject is still under the center autofocus point, press and release the AE Lock button.**

You can see the button in the margin here. The camera emits the preflash, and the letters FEL display for a second in the viewfinder. (FEL stands for *flash exposure lock.*) You also see the asterisk symbol — the one that appears above the AE Lock button on the camera body — next to the flash icon in the viewfinder. (Of course, the flash must be in the open position for this to work.)

4. **If needed, reestablish focus on your subject.**

   In autofocus mode, press and hold the shutter button halfway. (Take this step only if you released the shutter button after Step 2.) In manual focus mode, twist the focusing ring on the lens to establish focus.

5. **Reframe the image to the composition you want.**

   While you do, keep the shutter button pressed halfway to maintain focus if you're using autofocusing.

6. **Press the shutter button the rest of the way to take the picture.**

   The image is captured using the flash output setting you established in Step 3.

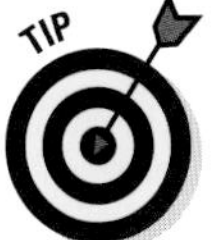

Flash exposure lock is also helpful when you're shooting portraits. The preflash sometimes causes people to blink, which means that with normal flash shooting, in which the actual flash and exposure occur immediately after the preflash, their eyes are closed at the exact moment of the exposure. With flash exposure lock, you can fire the preflash and then wait a second or two for the subject's eyes to recover before you take the actual picture.

Better yet, the flash exposure setting remains in force for about 16 seconds, meaning that you can shoot a series of images using the same flash setting without firing another preflash at all.

Exploring more flash options

When you set the Mode dial to P, Tv, Av, or M, Shooting Menu 1 offers a Flash Control option. Using this menu item, you can adjust flash power, as explained a couple of sections earlier (although using the Quick Control screen is easier). The Flash Control option also enables you to customize a few other aspects of the built-in flash as well as control an external flash head.

To explore your options, choose Flash Control, as shown on the left in Figure 7-44, to access the screen shown on the right in the figure. Here's the rundown of the available options:

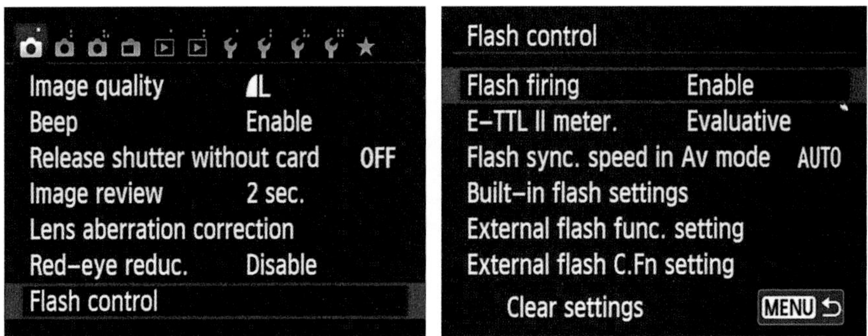

Figure 7-44: You can customize additional flash options via Setup Menu 1.

- **Flash Firing:** Normally, this option is set to Enable. If you want to disable the flash, you can choose Disable instead. However, you don't have to take this step in most cases — just close the pop-up flash head on top of the camera if you don't want to use flash.

  What's the point of this option, then? Well, if you use autofocusing in dim lighting, the camera may need some help finding its target. To that end, it sometimes emits an *AF-assist beam* from the flash head — the beam is a series of rapid pulses of light. If you want the benefit of the AF-assist beam but you don't want the flash to fire, you can disable flash firing. Remember that you have to pop up the flash unit to expose the lamp that emits the beam. You also can take advantage of this option when you attach an external flash head.

- **E-TTL II Metering:** This option enables you to switch from the default flash metering approach, called Evaluative. In this mode, the camera operates as described in the earlier section, "Understanding your camera's approach to flash." That is, it exposes the background using ambient light when possible and then sets the flash power to serve as fill light on the subject.

  If you instead select the Average option, the flash is used as the primary light source, meaning that the flash power is set to expose the entire scene without relying on ambient light. Typically, this results in a more powerful (and possibly harsh) flash lighting and dark backgrounds.

- **Flash Sync. Speed in Av Mode:** This is the option that prevents the shutter speed from dropping beyond a certain level when you shoot in the Av exposure mode. See "Understanding your camera's approach to flash," earlier in this chapter, for details.
- **Built-in Flash Settings:** If you highlight this option and press Set, you display the screen shown in Figure 7-45.

  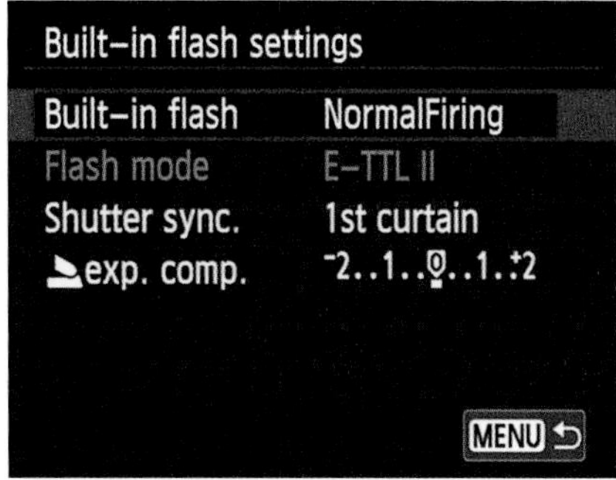

  Figure 7-45: These advanced flash options affect only the built-in flash.

  Which options are adjustable depends on whether you set the first option, Built-in Flash, to Normal Firing, as in the figure, or to one of the two settings that set the built-in flash to trigger off-camera flash units. See the sidebar "Using one flash to control others" for details on that possibility.

  The other options available for normal flash operation work like so:

  - *Shutter Sync:* By default, the flash fires at the beginning of the exposure. This flash timing, known as *1st curtain sync,* is the best choice for most subjects. However, if you use a very slow shutter speed and you're photographing a moving object, 1st curtain sync causes the blur that results from the motion to appear in front of the object, which doesn't make much visual sense.

    To solve this problem, you can change the Shutter Sync option to *2nd curtain sync,* also known as *rear-curtain sync.* In this flash mode, the motion trails appear behind the moving object. The flash fires twice in this mode: once when you press the shutter button and again at the end of the exposure.
  - *Flash Exposure Compensation:* This setting adjusts the power of the built-in flash; again, see the earlier section "Adjusting flash power with Flash Exposure Compensation" for details.
- **External Flash controls:** The last two options on the Flash Control list (refer to the right screen in Figure 7-44) relate to external flash heads; they don't affect the performance of the built-in flash. However, they apply only to Canon EX-series Speedlites that enable you to control the flash through the camera. If you own such a flash, refer to the flash manual for details.

- **Clear Settings:** Choose this option to access three settings that restore flash defaults. The first one, Clear Built-in Flash Set, restores the settings for the built-in flash. Sorry, you probably could have figured that out for yourself. The second option restores defaults for external flash settings, and the third restores the external flash head's Custom Function menu settings.

Using one flash to control others

If you're ready to try some multiple-light shooting, you can use your built-in flash as a *master* to wirelessly trigger off-camera flash units, which are called *slaves.* (I know, but don't write me any nasty letters — I'm here to tell you what the current terminology is, no matter how politically insensitive.) You can even set the power of the external units through the camera's flash options and specify whether you want the built-in flash to simply trigger the other flash heads or add its own flash power to the scene.

Using a master/slave flash setup can provide you with great added lighting flexibility without requiring you to spend lots of money (although you certainly can) or carrying around lots of bulky, traditional lighting equipment. In fact, I rely on this lighting option to shoot most of my product and still-life shots, using the on-board flash to trigger two off-camera flashes.

In order to use this camera function, your external flash units must support wireless control, of course. You can find a list of compatible Canon flash products that fit the bill in the camera manual. You also have to change the Built-in Flash option to one of the two wireless modes, as shown in the figures here. (You get to this option via the Flash Control option on Shooting Menu 1.)

With the Easy Wireless option, the camera handles most of the flash-firing settings for you, although you do have to take a couple simple setup steps. To really control the lighting, choose the Custom Wireless setting instead. It enables you to adjust the output of each flash unit separately to fine-tune the way your subject is lit.

Your camera manual offers complete details on setting up the camera and your flash units for wireless operation.

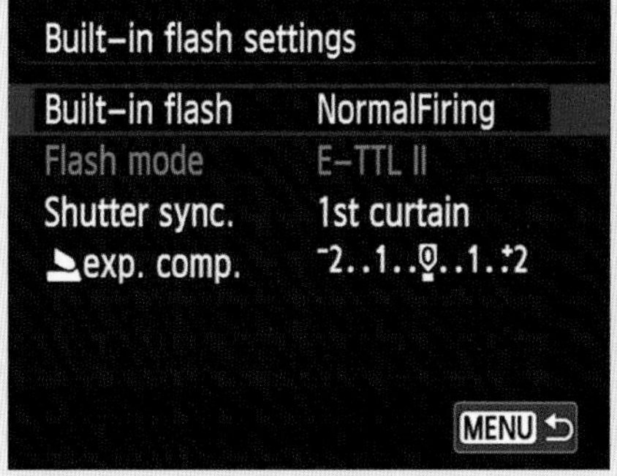

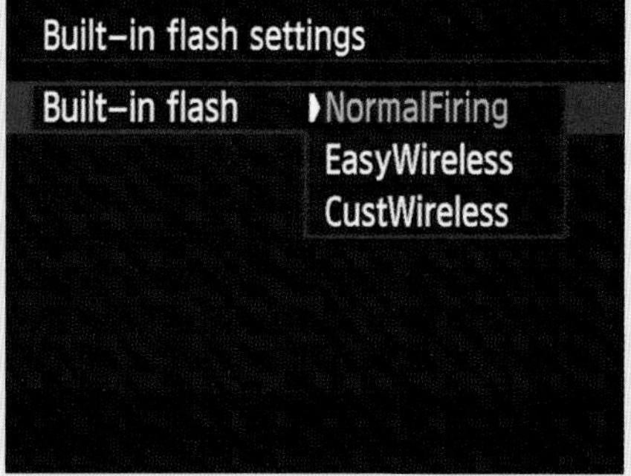

You can probably discern from these descriptions that most of these features are designed for photographers schooled in flash photography who want to mess around with advanced flash options. If that doesn't describe you, don't worry about it. The default settings selected by Canon will serve you well in most every situation — the exception is flash exposure compensation, which you can just as easily adjust via the Quick Control screen instead of digging through the menus.

8

Manipulating Focus and Color

In This Chapter

- Controlling the camera's focusing performance
- Sorting through autofocusing options
- Understanding focal length and depth of field
- Exploring white balance and Picture Styles

To many people, the word *focus* has just one interpretation when applied to a photograph: Either the subject is in focus or it's blurry. But an artful photographer knows that there's more to focus than simply getting a sharp image of a subject. You also need to consider *depth of field,* or the distance over which focus appears acceptably sharp. This chapter explains all the ways to control depth of field and also discusses how to use your Rebel's advanced autofocus options.

In addition, this chapter dives into the topic of color, explaining *White Balance,* a feature that compensates for the varying color casts created by different light sources, and *Picture Styles,* which affect image sharpness and contrast as well as color.

Reviewing Focus Basics

Chapters 1, 3, and 7 touch on various focus issues. But in case you're not reading this book from front to back, the following steps provide a recap of the basic process of focusing using the default focusing options. (The next section explains how to stray from these default settings.)

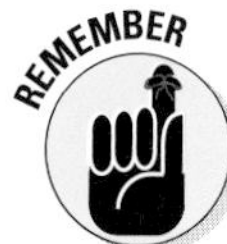

These steps relate only to viewfinder photography; look for details on autofocusing in Live View and Movie modes in Chapter 4. Also, the instructions assume that you're using the 18–55mm lens (shown in Figure 8-1) or its sibling, the 18–135mm lens, sold in T4i/650D kits. If you use another lens, check its instruction manual for focusing assistance.

1. **If you haven't done so, adjust the viewfinder to your eyesight.**

   Chapter 1 explains how to take this critical step.

2. **Set the focusing switch on the lens to manual or automatic focusing.**

   To focus manually, set the switch to the MF position. For autofocusing, set the switch to the AF position, as in Figure 8-1.

3. **For handheld shooting, turn on Image Stabilization.**

   For sharper handheld shots, set the Stabilizer switch to On. (Refer to Figure 8-1.) If you use another lens that offers image stabilization (it may go by a different name, depending on the manufacturer), check the lens manual to find out how to turn on the feature.

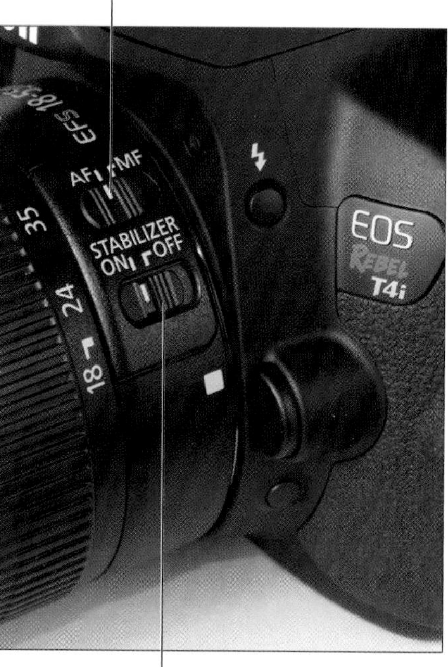

Figure 8-1: Select AF for autofocus or MF for manual focus.

   For a non-Canon lens, the manufacturer may suggest turning off stabilization when you use a tripod, so again, check the lens manual. You don't need to turn off the feature for most Canon IS lenses, but you can save battery power by doing so.

4. **Set focus:**

   - *To autofocus:* In Sports mode, frame your subject under the center focus point and press the shutter button halfway. You hear a series of beeps, indicating that the camera is adjusting focus as needed to track the subject's movement up to the time you take the shot.

     In the other scene modes as well as in P, Tv, Av, and M exposure modes, frame your subject so that it appears under one of the nine autofocus points. (The center point usually provides fastest performance.) Then press and hold the shutter button halfway. The focus lamp in the viewfinder lights, one or more of the focus points turns red, as shown in Figure 8-2, and you hear a tiny beep. A red dot indicates that the area under the focus point is in focus. Focus is locked as long as you hold down the shutter button halfway.

The same thing happens in Scene Intelligent Auto, Creative Auto, and Flash Off modes unless the camera senses motion in front of the lens, in which case it adjusts focus as needed to track the moving subject.

For the P, Tv, Av, and M exposure modes, you can vary this autofocusing behavior; see the next section for how-to's. In all modes, you can silence the focus beep by setting the Beep option on Shooting Menu 1 to disable.

- *For manual focus:* Twist the focusing ring on the lens.

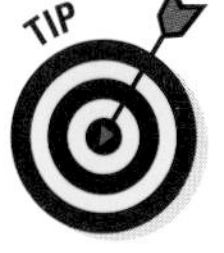

Even in the camera's manual mode, you can confirm focus by pressing the shutter button halfway. The autofocus point or points that achieved focus flash for a second or two, the viewfinder's focus lamp lights up, and you hear the focus-achieved beep.

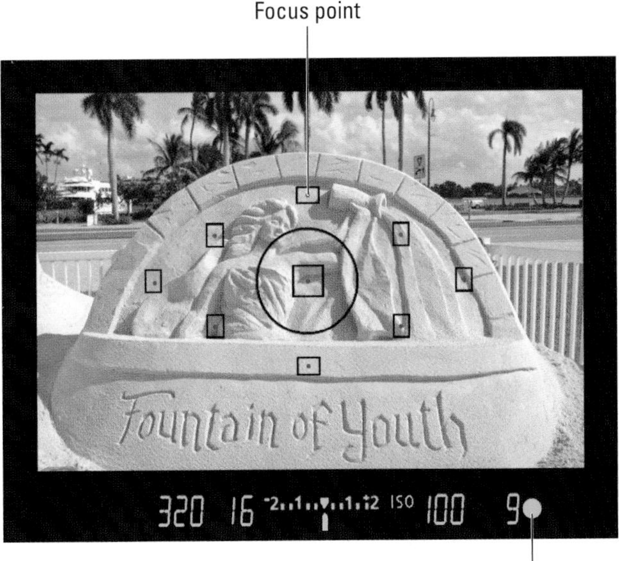

Figure 8-2: The viewfinder offers these focusing aids.

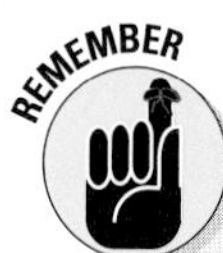

Shutter speed and blurry photos

A poorly focused photo isn't always related to the issues discussed in this chapter. Any movement of the camera or subject can also cause blur. Both problems are related to shutter speed, an exposure control I cover in Chapter 7. Be sure to also visit Chapter 9, which provides additional tips for capturing moving objects without blur.

Adjusting Autofocus Performance

In the point-and-shoot photography modes that I cover in Chapter 3, you're stuck with the choices the camera makes for each exposure mode. (The individual descriptions of the modes in Chapter 3 tell you what to expect.) But in P, Tv, Av, and M modes, you can tweak autofocusing behavior through two controls:

- **AF (autofocus) mode:** This option determines whether the camera locks focus when you press the shutter button halfway or continues to adjust focus from the time you press the shutter button halfway until you press it the rest of the way to take the shot.
- **AF Point Selection:** This setting determines which autofocus points the camera uses to establish focusing distance. At the default setting, all nine points are in play, and the camera typically focuses on the closest object. But you can choose to base focus on a single point that you select instead.

The next few sections explain both options in detail. But two notes before you dig in:

- Information in this chapter assumes that you haven't changed the default functions of camera buttons (such as the AE Lock button and the shutter button). I detail those customization options in Chapter 10, but leave the buttons at their default settings until you're fully acquainted with the camera — otherwise the instructions given here (and those you find in the camera manual) aren't going to work.
- Again, the settings and techniques described here relate to viewfinder photography. Autofocusing works differently in Live View and Movie modes; Chapter 4 covers those topics.

AF Selection Point: One focus point or many?

In Sports mode, the camera bases focus on the center focus point. In the other fully automatic exposure modes (Scene Intelligent Auto, Portrait, Landscape, and so on) as well as in Creative Auto mode, the autofocusing system looks at all nine autofocus points when trying to establish focus. Typically the camera sets focus on the point that falls over the object closest to the lens.

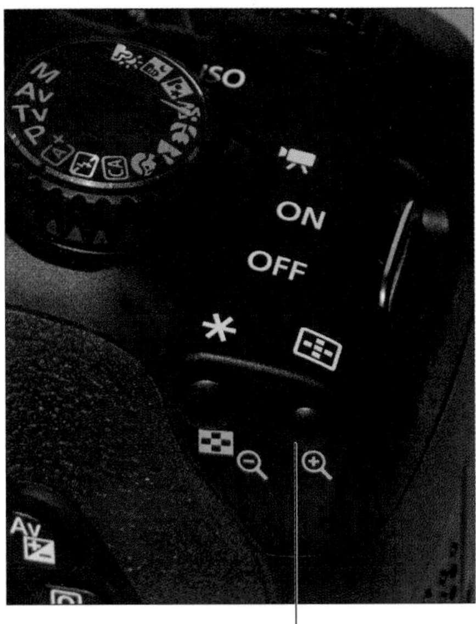

Figure 8-3: Press and release the AF Point Selection button to select an autofocus point.

In the P, Tv, Av, and M exposure modes, however, you can tell the camera to base focus on a specific autofocus point. Here's how to switch from automatic point selection (the default setting) to single-point selection:

1. **Set the Mode dial to P, Tv, Av, or M.**

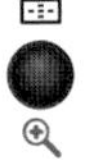

2. **Press and release the AF Point Selection button, highlighted in Figure 8-3.**

   When you do, you see the AF Point Selection screen on the monitor. From this screen, you can choose one of two modes: Automatic AF Point Selection, in which all focus points are considered, or Manual AF Point Selection, in which you choose a single focus point.

   In Automatic AF Point Selection mode, all autofocus points appear in color, as shown in Figure 8-4. In Manual AF Point Selection mode, only one point is selected and appears in color, as shown in Figure 8-5. In the figure, the center AF point is selected.

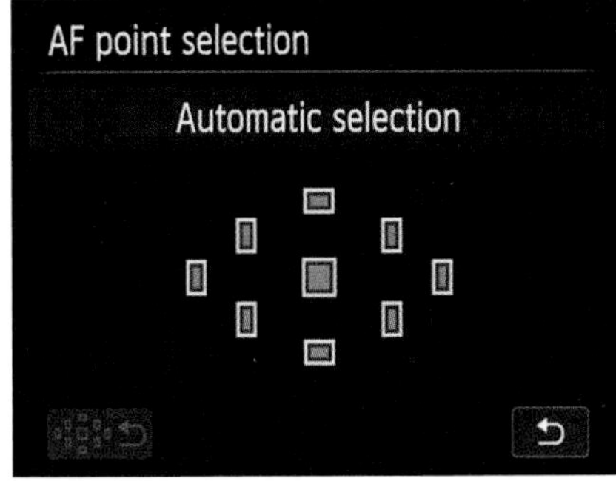

Figure 8-4: In Automatic mode, all nine autofocus points are active.

You can check the current mode by looking through the viewfinder, too. When you press and release the AF Point Selection button, all nine autofocus points turn red in the viewfinder if you're in Automatic AF Point Selection mode. A single point turns red if you're in Manual AF Point Selection mode.

3. **Use one of these techniques to switch to Manual AF Point Selection and select your focus point.**

   - *Touchscreen:* Tap the point you want to use.
   - *Main dial:* Rotate the dial to shift from Automatic AF Point Selection mode to Manual mode; keep rotating the dial to cycle through all the points until the one you want is highlighted. After you cycle through all the points, you return to auto-point mode; just rotate the dial again to switch back to single-point selection.
   - *Set button:* Press the Set button to immediately select the center focus point. Then rotate the Main dial to select a focus point.

   After you switch to manual point selection, you also can use the cross keys to select a point. However, if you're looking through the viewfinder, that method's kind of cumbersome; using the Main dial is easier.

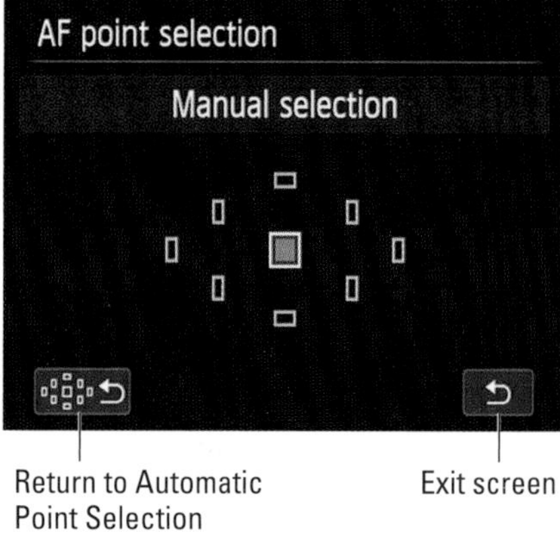

Figure 8-5: You also can base autofocus on a single point; here the center point is selected.

That's all there is to it. After you select the autofocus point, just frame your shot so that your subject falls under that point, and then press the shutter button halfway to focus.

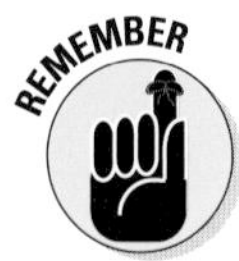

To return to automatic point selection, tap the Return to Auto Point Selection arrow, labeled in Figure 8-5, or rotate the Main dial until all nine points light up. Or, if the center point is selected, press the Set button.

Changing the AF (autofocus) mode

Your camera offers three different autofocusing schemes, which you select through the AF mode control. The three choices work like so:

- **One Shot:** This mode, geared to shooting stationary subjects, locks focus when you press and hold the shutter button halfway down. This setting is used for all scene modes except Sports. It's also the default mode for P, Tv, Av, and M exposure modes.

  Note that if you pair One Shot autofocusing with the Continuous Drive mode, detailed in Chapter 2, focus for all frames in a burst is based on the focus point used for the first shot.

- **AI Servo:** In this mode (the *AI* stands for *artificial intelligence,* if you care), the camera adjusts focus continually as needed from when you press the shutter button halfway to the time you take the picture. This mode is designed to make focusing on moving subjects easier, and it's the one the camera uses when you shoot in the Sports scene mode.

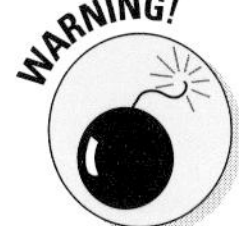

  For AI Servo to work properly, you must reframe as needed to keep your subject under the active autofocus point if you're working in Manual AF Point Selection mode. If the camera is set to Automatic AF Point Selection, the camera initially bases focus on the center focus point. If the subject moves away from the point, focus should still be okay as long as you keep the subject within the area covered by one of the other nine autofocus points. (The preceding section explains these two modes.)

  In either case, the green focus dot in the viewfinder blinks rapidly if the camera isn't tracking focus successfully. If all is going well, the focus dot doesn't light up, nor do you hear the beep that normally sounds when focus is achieved. (You can hear the autofocus motor whirring a little when the camera adjusts focus.)

  If you use this AF mode with the Continuous Drive mode, focus is adjusted as needed between frames, which may slow the maximum shots-per-second rate. However, it's still the best option for shooting a moving subject.

- **AI Focus:** This mode automatically switches the camera from One Shot to AI Servo as needed. When you first press the shutter button halfway, focus is locked on the active autofocus point (or points), as in One Shot mode. But if the subject moves, the camera shifts into AI Servo mode and adjusts focus as it thinks is warranted. AI Focus is the setting used when you shoot in the Scene Intelligent Auto, Flash Off, and Creative Auto modes.

I prefer not to use AI Focus because I don't want to rely on the camera to figure out whether I'm interested in a moving or stationary subject. So I stick with One Shot for stationary subjects and AI Servo for focusing on moving subjects.

One way to remember which mode is which: For still subjects, you only need *one shot* at setting focus. For moving subjects, think of a tennis or volleyball player *serving* the ball — so AI *Servo* for action shots.

You can the view current AF mode in the Shooting Settings screen, as shown in Figure 8-6. To change the mode, you have two options:

- **AF mode button (right cross key):** Your fastest move is to press this button. It takes you directly to the screen shown in Figure 8-7. Choose a setting and then tap Set or press the Set button.

- **Quick Control screen:** Use the cross keys to highlight the AF Mode icon, as shown in Figure 8-8. The selected AF mode setting appears at the bottom of the screen. Rotate the Main dial to cycle through the three mode options.

  If you prefer, you can tap the icon or press Set after highlighting it to display the screen shown in Figure 8-7, where all the mode choices appear.

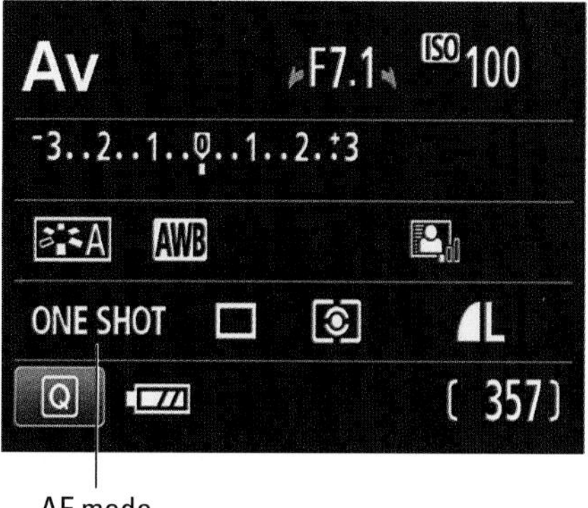

Figure 8-6: The current AF mode appears here.

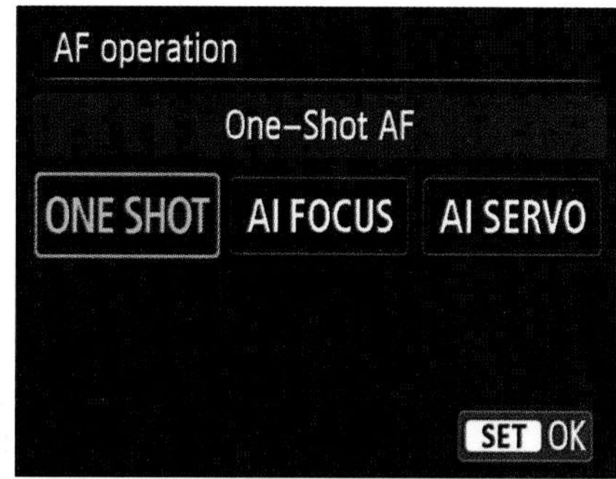

Figure 8-7: The fastest way to access the AF mode setting is to press the right cross key.

Choosing the right autofocus combo

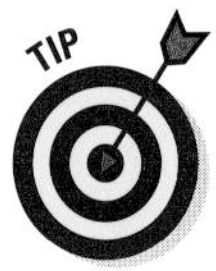

You'll get the best autofocus results if you pair your chosen AF mode with the most appropriate AF Point Selection mode, because the two settings work in tandem. Here are the combinations that I suggest:

- **For still subjects: One Shot and Manual AF Point Selection.** You then select a specific focus point, and the camera locks focus on that point at the time you press the shutter button halfway. Focus remains locked on your subject even if you reframe the shot after you press the button halfway.

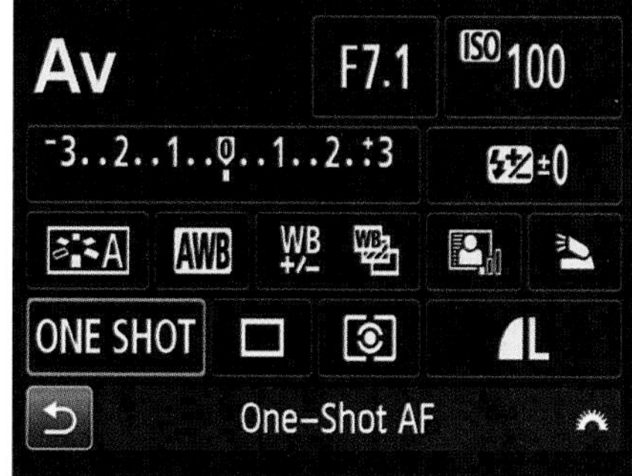

Figure 8-8: But you also can adjust the setting via the Quick Control screen.

- **For moving subjects: AI Servo and Automatic AF Point Selection.** Begin by framing your subject so that it's under the center focus point — remember, when you combine AI Servo with Automatic AF Point Selection, the camera chooses the center point to establish the initial focusing distance when you press the shutter button halfway. But the camera adjusts focus as needed if your subject moves within the frame before you take the shot. All you need to do is reframe as needed to keep your subject within the boundaries of the autofocus points.

Keeping these two combos in mind should greatly improve your autofocusing accuracy. But in some situations, no combination will enable speedy or correct autofocusing. For example, if you try to focus on a very reflective subject, the camera may hunt for an autofocus point forever. And if you try to focus on a subject behind a fence, the autofocus system may continually insist on focusing on the fence instead of your subject. In such scenarios, don't waste time monkeying with the autofocus settings — just switch to manual focusing.

Manipulating Depth of Field

Getting familiar with the concept of depth of field is one of the biggest steps you can take to becoming a more artful photographer. *Depth of field* simply refers to the distance over which objects in a photograph appear acceptably sharp. Chapters 3 and 7 provide an introduction to depth of field, but here's a quick summary just to hammer home the lesson:

- **Shallow (small) depth of field:** Only your subject and objects at the same (or nearly the same) distance from the lens appear sharp. Objects at a distance appear blurry.
- **Large depth of field:** The zone of apparent focus extends to include distant objects.

Which arrangement works best depends on your creative vision. In portraits, for example, a classic technique is to use a shallow depth of field, as in Figure 8-9. This approach increases emphasis on the subject while diminishing the impact of the background. But for the photo shown in Figure 8-10, the goal was to give the historical marker, the lighthouse, and the cottage equal weight in the scene, so I used settings that produced a large depth of field to keep them all in focus.

Shallow depth of field

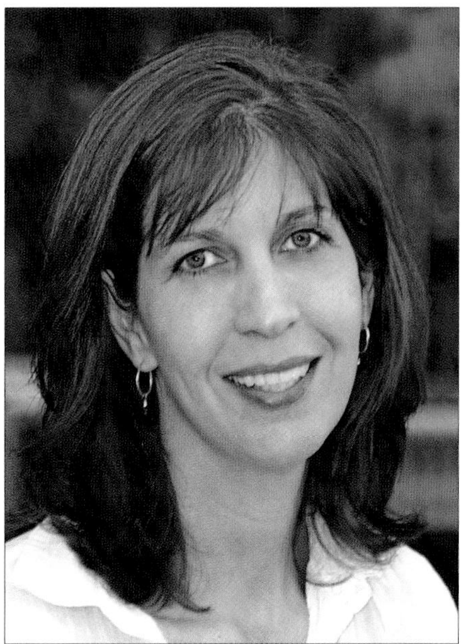

Figure 8-9: A shallow depth of field blurs the background and draws added attention to the subject.

Large depth of field

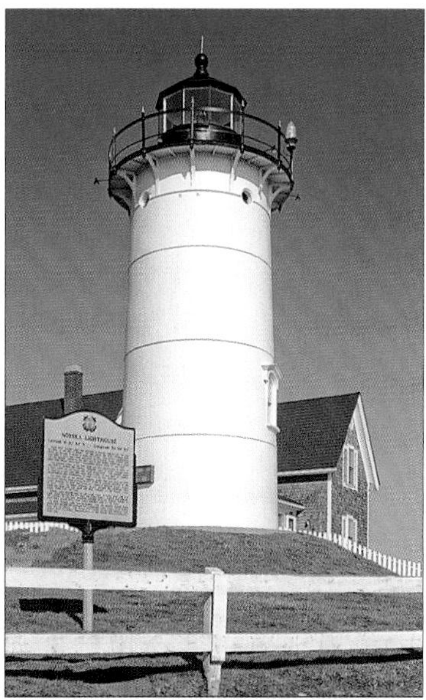

Figure 8-10: A large depth of field keeps both near and far subjects in sharp focus.

Note, though, that with a shallow depth of field, which part of the scene appears blurry depends on the spot at which you establish focus. In the lighthouse scene, for example, had I used settings that produce a short depth of field and set focus on the lighthouse, both the historical marker in the foreground and the cottage in the background might be outside the zone of sharp focus.

So how do you adjust depth of field? You have three points of control:

- **Aperture setting (f-stop):** The aperture is one of three main exposure settings, all explained fully in Chapter 7. Depth of field increases as you stop down the aperture (by choosing a higher f-stop number). For shallow depth of field, open the aperture (by choosing a lower f-stop number).

Figure 8-11 offers an example. Notice that the trees in the background are much more softly focused in the f/5.6 example than in the f/11 version. Of course, changing the aperture requires adjusting the shutter speed or ISO to maintain the equivalent exposure; for these images, I adjusted shutter speed.

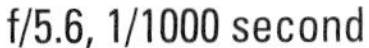

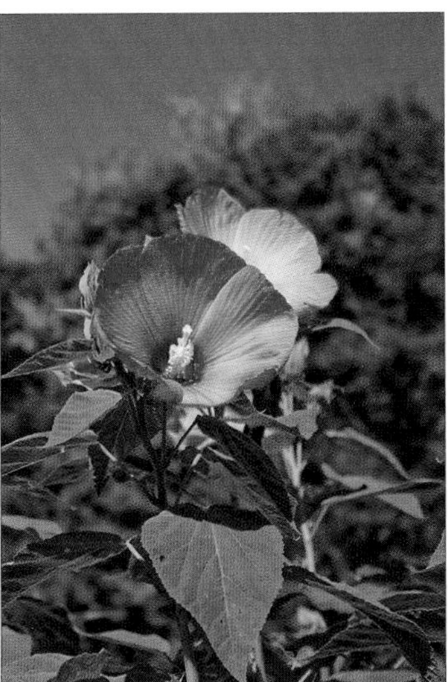

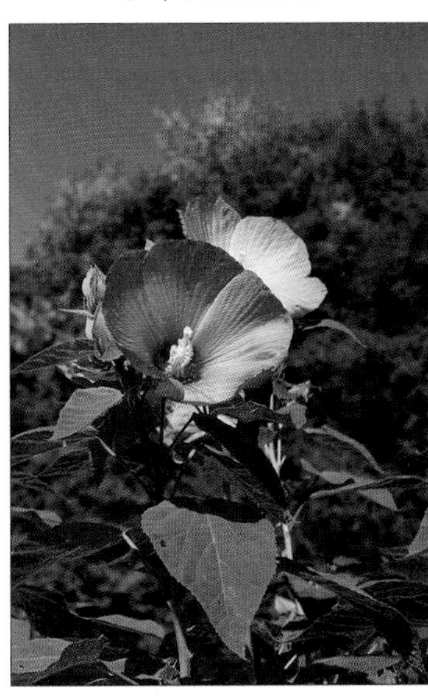

Figure 8-11: Raising the f-stop value increases depth of field.

- **Lens focal length:** In lay terms, *focal length,* which is measured in millimeters, determines what the lens "sees." As you increase focal length (use a "longer" lens, in photography-speak) the angle of view narrows, objects appear larger in the frame, and — the important point in this discussion — depth of field decreases. Additionally, the spatial relationship of objects changes as you adjust focal length.

  For example, Figure 8-12 compares the same scene shot at focal lengths of 138mm and 255mm. The aperture was set to f/22 for both examples.

Whether you have any focal-length flexibility depends on your lens: If you have a zoom lens, you can adjust the focal length by zooming in or out. If your lens offers only a single focal length — a *prime* lens in photo-speak — scratch this means of manipulating depth of field (unless you want to change to a different prime lens, of course).

For more technical details about focal length and your camera, see the later sidebar "Focal length and the crop factor."

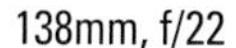

255mm, f/22

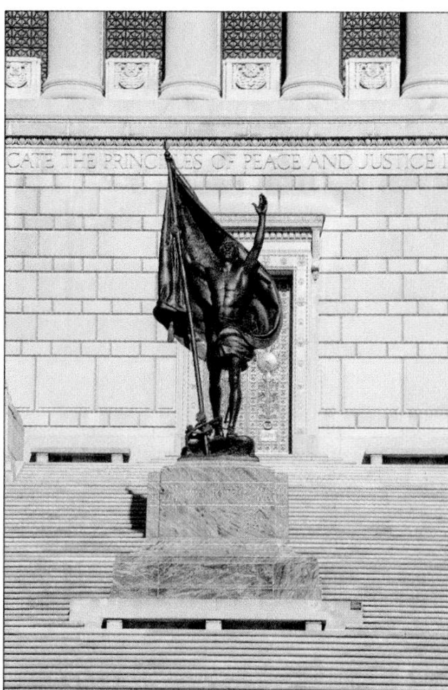

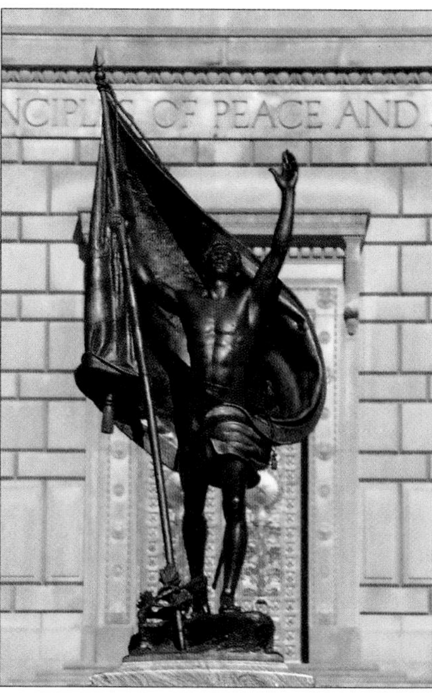

Figure 8-12: Using a longer focal length also reduces depth of field.

- **Camera-to-subject distance:** When you move the lens closer to your subject, depth of field decreases. This statement assumes that you don't zoom in or out to reframe the picture, thereby changing the focal length. If you do, depth of field is affected by both the camera position and focal length.

Together, these three factors determine the maximum and minimum depth of field you can achieve, as illustrated by Figure 8-13 and summed up in the following list:

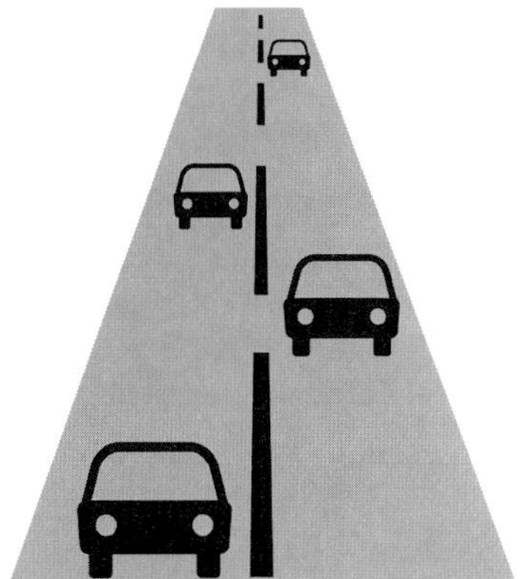

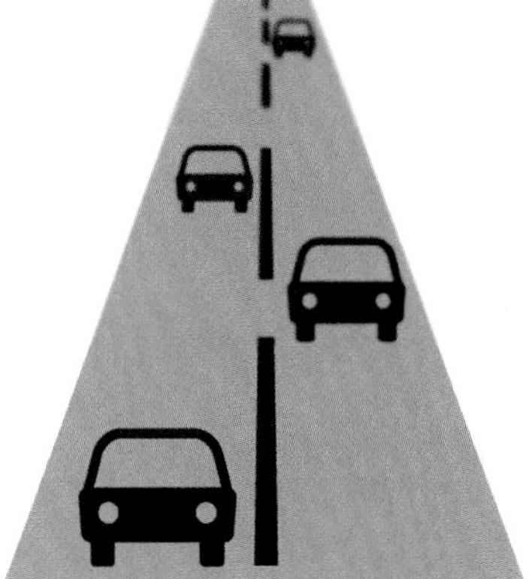

Figure 8-13: Aperture, focal length, and your shooting distance determine depth of field.

- **To produce the shallowest depth of field:** Open the aperture as wide as possible (select the lowest f-stop number), zoom in to the maximum focal length of your lens, and move as close as possible to your subject.
- **To produce maximum depth of field:** Stop down the aperture to the highest possible f-stop setting, zoom out to the shortest focal length your lens offers, and move farther from your subject.

Here are a few additional tips and tricks related to depth of field:

- **Subject to camera distance:** The extent to which background focus shifts as you adjust depth of field also is affected by the distance between the subject and the background. For increased background blurring, move the subject farther away from the background.

- **Aperture-priority autoexposure (Av) mode:** When depth of field is a primary concern, try using aperture-priority autoexposure (Av). In this mode, detailed fully in Chapter 7, you set the f-stop, and then the camera selects the appropriate shutter speed to produce a good exposure.
- **Creative Auto mode:** Creative Auto mode also gives you some control over depth of field via the Background Blur slider. Chapter 3 has details.
- **Scene modes:** Some of the scene modes are designed with depth of field in mind. Portrait and Close-up modes produce shortened depth of field; Landscape mode produces a greater depth of field. You can't adjust aperture in these modes, however, so you're limited to the setting the camera chooses. And in certain lighting conditions, the camera may not be able to choose an aperture that produces the depth of field you expect from the selected mode.

- **Depth of field preview:** When you look through your viewfinder and press the shutter button halfway, you can see only a partial indication of the depth of field that your current camera settings will produce. You can see the effect of focal length and the camera-to-subject distance, but because the aperture doesn't actually stop-down to your selected f-stop until you take the picture, the viewfinder doesn't show you how that setting will affect depth of field.

  By using the Depth-of-Field Preview button on your camera, however, you can do just that when you shoot in the advanced exposure modes. Almost hidden away on the front of your camera, the button is labeled in Figure 8-14.

  To use this feature, just press and hold the shutter button halfway and then press and hold the Depth-of-Field Preview button with a finger on the other hand. Depending on the selected f-stop, the scene in the viewfinder may then get darker. Or in Live View mode, the same thing happens in the monitor preview. Either way, this effect doesn't mean that your picture will be darker; it's just a function of how the preview works.

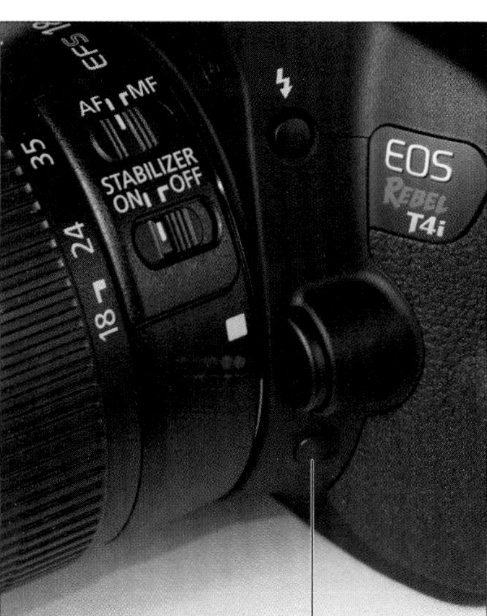

Figure 8-14: Press this button to see how the aperture setting will affect depth of field.

Focal length and the crop factor

The angle of view that a lens can capture is determined by its *focal length,* or in the case of a zoom lens, the range of focal lengths it offers. Focal length is measured in millimeters.

According to photography tradition, a focal length of 50mm is described as a "normal" lens. Most point-and-shoot cameras feature this focal length, which is a medium-range lens that works well for the type of snapshots that users of those kinds of cameras are likely to shoot.

A lens with a focal length under 35mm is characterized as a *wide-angle* lens because at that focal length, the camera has a wide angle of view, making it good for landscape photography. A short focal length also has the effect of making objects seem smaller and farther away. At the other end of the spectrum, a lens with a focal length longer than 80mm is considered a *telephoto* lens and often referred to as a *long lens.* With a long lens, angle of view narrows, and faraway subjects appear closer and larger, which is ideal for wildlife and sports photographers.

Note, however, that the focal lengths stated here and elsewhere in the book are *35mm-equivalent* focal lengths. Here's the deal: For reasons that aren't really important, when you put a standard lens on most digital cameras, including your T4i/650D, the available frame area is reduced, as if you took a picture on a camera that uses 35mm film negatives and then cropped the photo.

This so-called *crop factor* varies depending on the camera, which is why the photo industry adopted the 35mm-equivalent measuring stick as a standard. With your camera, the crop factor is roughly 1.6. So the 18–55mm lens featured in this book, for example, captures the approximate area you would get from a 29–88mm lens on a 35mm film camera. (Multiply the crop factor by the actual focal length to get the actual angle of view.) In the following figure, the red outline indicates the image area that results from the 1.6 crop factor.

When shopping for a lens, it's important to remember this crop factor to make sure that you get the focal length designed for the type of pictures you want to take. Most camera stores have a lens chart to guide you as to the angle of view that you can get at different focal lengths.

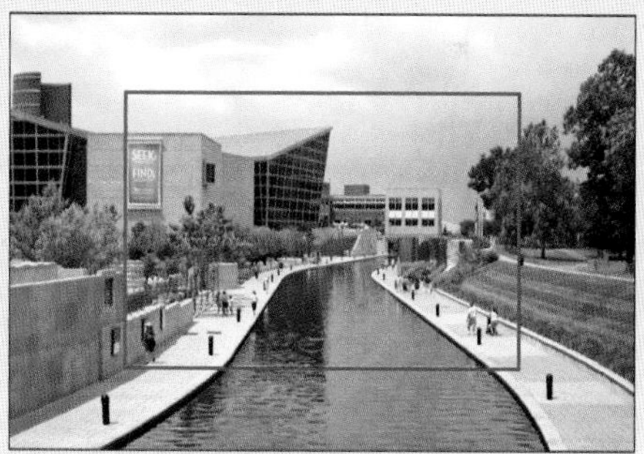

Note that the preview doesn't engage in P, Tv, or Av mode if the aperture and shutter speed aren't adequate to expose the image properly. You have to solve the exposure issue before you can use the preview.

- **Shutter speed:** If you adjust aperture to affect depth of field, be sure to always keep an eye on shutter speed as well. To maintain the same exposure, shutter speed must change in tandem with aperture, and you may encounter a situation where the shutter speed is too slow to permit handholding a camera. Lenses that offer optical image stabilization enable most people to handhold the camera at slower shutter speeds than nonstabilized lenses, but double-check your results. You can also consider raising the ISO setting to make the image sensor more reactive to light, but remember that higher ISO settings can produce noise. (Chapter 7 has details.)

Controlling Color

Compared with understanding some aspects of digital photography — resolution, aperture, shutter speed, and depth of field, for example — making sense of your camera's color options is easy-breezy. First, color problems aren't all that common, and when they are, they're usually simple to fix with a quick shift of your camera's White Balance control. Second, getting a grip on color requires learning only a couple of new terms, an unusual state of affairs for an endeavor that often seems more like high-tech science than art.

The rest of this chapter explains a couple of options that enable you to fine-tune the way your camera renders colors. Be sure to also check out Chapter 10, which explains an option that affects the color space of your photos (sRGB or Adobe RGB), found on Shooting Menu 2. Stick with the default, sRGB, for now.

Correcting colors with white balance

Every light source emits a particular color cast. The old-fashioned fluorescent lights found in most public restrooms, for example, put out a bluish-green light, which is why our reflections in the mirrors in those restrooms always look so sickly. And if you think that your beloved looks especially attractive by candlelight, you aren't imagining things: Candlelight casts a warm, yellow-red glow that's flattering to the skin.

Science-y types measure the color of light, officially known as *color temperature,* on the Kelvin scale, which is named after its creator. You can see an illustration of the Kelvin scale in Figure 8-15.

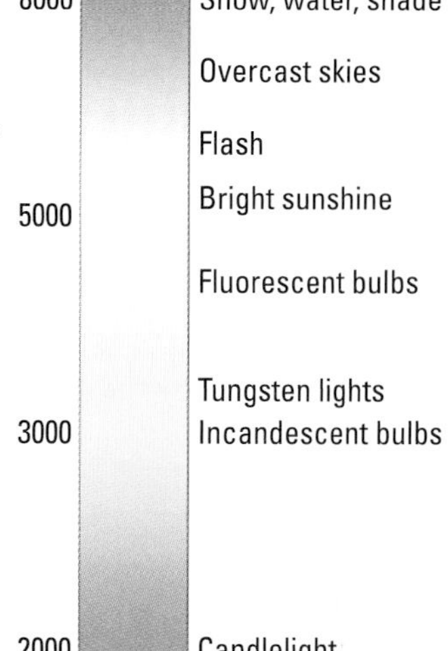

Figure 8-15: Each light source emits a specific color.

When photographers talk about "warm light" and "cool light," though, they aren't referring to the position on the Kelvin scale — or at least not in the way we usually think of temperatures, with a higher number meaning hotter. Instead, the terms describe the visual appearance of the light. Warm light, produced by candles and incandescent lights, falls in the red-yellow spectrum you see at the bottom of the Kelvin scale in Figure 8-15; cool light, in the blue-green spectrum, appears at the top of the scale.

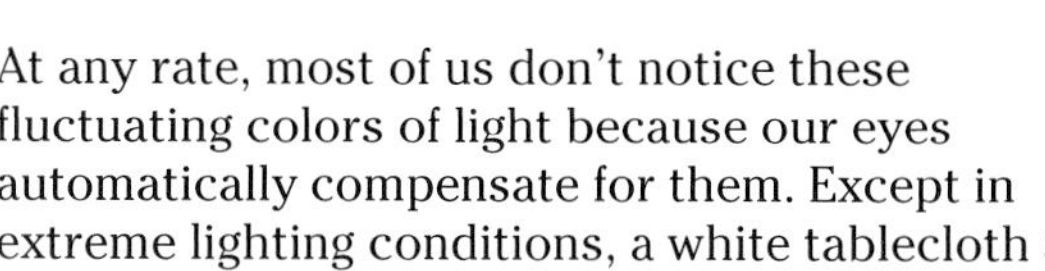

At any rate, most of us don't notice these fluctuating colors of light because our eyes automatically compensate for them. Except in extreme lighting conditions, a white tablecloth appears white to us no matter whether we view it by candlelight, fluorescent light, or regular house lights.

Similarly, a digital camera compensates for different colors of light through a feature known as *white balancing.* Simply put, white balancing neutralizes light so that whites are always white, which in turn ensures that other colors are rendered accurately. If the camera senses warm light, it shifts colors slightly to the cool side of the color spectrum; in cool light, the camera shifts colors in the opposite direction.

The good news is that your camera's Automatic White Balance setting, which carries the label AWB, tackles this process remarkably well in most situations. In some lighting conditions, though, the AWB adjustment doesn't quite do the trick, resulting in an unwanted color cast like the one you see in the left image in Figure 8-16.

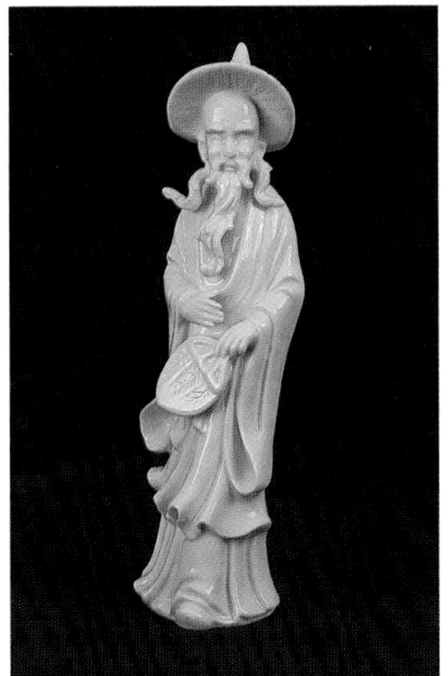
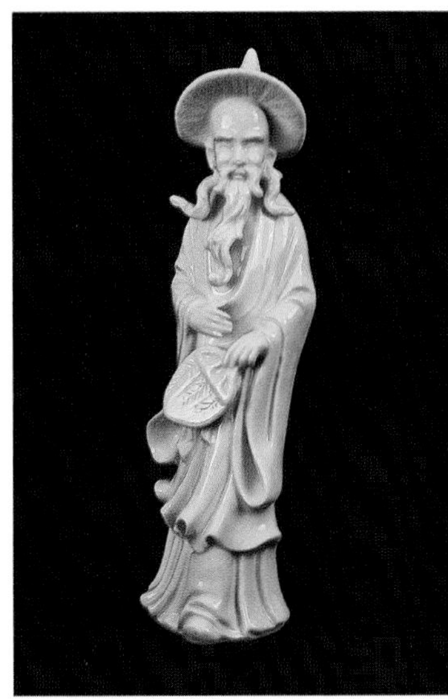

Figure 8-16: Multiple light sources resulted in a color cast in Auto White Balance mode (left); switching to manual White Balance control solved the problem (right).

Serious AWB problems most often occur when your subject is lit by a variety of light sources. For example, I shot the figurine in Figure 8-16 under a mix of tungsten photo lights along with strong window light. The photo lights are similar in color temperature to regular household incandescent bulbs; the daylight is very blue by comparison. In Automatic White Balance mode, the camera reacted to that daylight and applied too much warming, giving the original image a yellow tint. No problem: Switching the White Balance mode from AWB to the Tungsten Light setting did the trick. The right image in Figure 8-16 shows the corrected colors.

Unfortunately, you can't access the White Balance setting in any of the point-and-shoot exposure modes, although you can sometimes address color issues via the Shoot by Lighting or Scene Type setting when you shoot in a couple of the scene modes. (Chapter 3 has details on that setting and its relative, Shoot by Ambience.) So your best bet is to shift to P, Tv, Av, or M mode, where you can not only choose different White Balance settings but also fine-tune each setting to precisely match the light that's illuminating your subject.

Changing the White Balance setting

An icon representing the current White Balance setting appears in the Shooting Settings screen, as shown in Figure 8-17. To adjust the setting, you have several options:

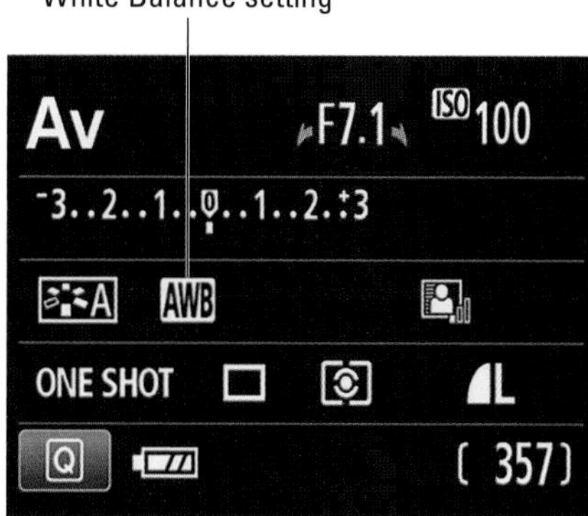

Figure 8-17: This symbol represents the Automatic White Balance setting.

- **WB button (top cross key):** Press the WB button to display the screen shown in Figure 8-18. Choose the setting you want to use and then tap Set or press the Set button.

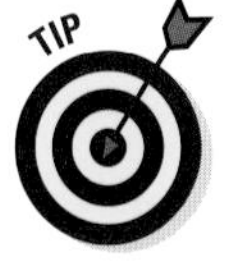

On this screen, as in the Shooting Settings and Quick Control displays, the White Balance settings are represented by the icons listed in Table 8-1. You don't need to memorize them, however, because as you scroll through the list of options, the name of the selected setting appears on the screen. For some settings, the camera also displays the approximate Kelvin temperature (K) of the selected light source, as shown in the figure. (Refer to Figure 8-15 for a look at the Kelvin scale.)

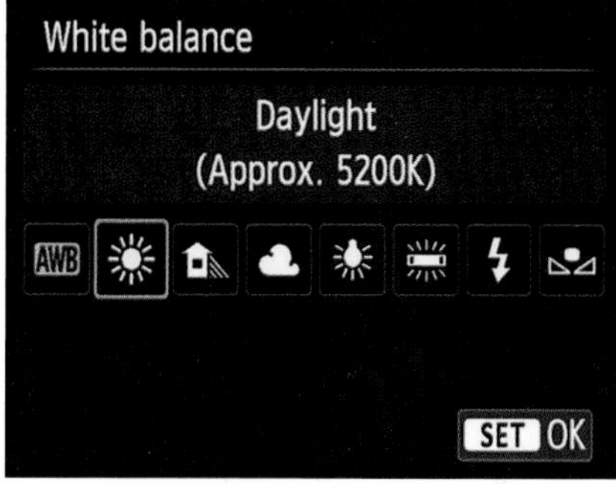

Figure 8-18: The WB button (top cross key) takes you directly to the White Balance setting.

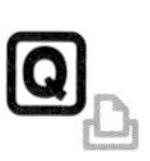

- **Quick Control screen:** After you highlight the White Balance icon, the selected setting appears at the bottom of the screen, as shown in Figure 8-19, and you can then rotate the Main dial to cycle through the various options.

  If you want to see all settings at one time, tap the icon or press Set to display the screen similar to the one shown in Figure 8-18. Choose your desired setting and tap the return arrow (not shown in the figure) or press the Set button to exit the screen.

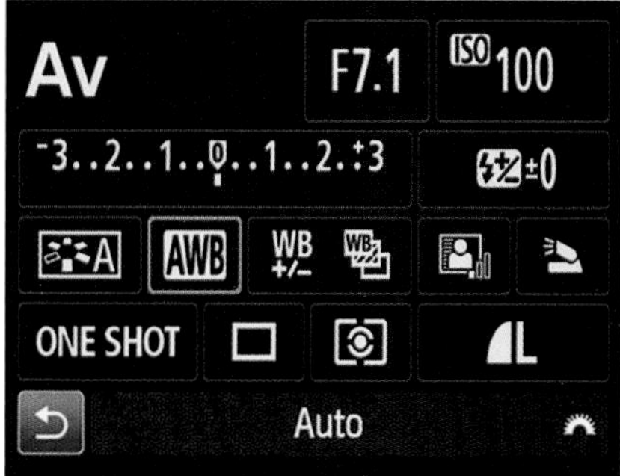

Figure 8-19: When using the Quick Control screen, rotate the Main dial to change the setting.

Table 8-1	White Balance Settings
Symbol	*Setting*
AWB	Auto
	Daylight
	Shade
	Cloudy
	Tungsten
	White Fluorescent
	Flash
	Custom

A couple of quick tips related to white balance:

- If the scene is lit by several sources, choose the setting that corresponds to the strongest one. The Tungsten Light setting is usually best for regular incandescent household bulbs, by the way. Selecting the right setting for the new energy-saving CFL (compact fluorescent) bulbs can be a little tricky because the color temperature varies depending on the bulb you buy.

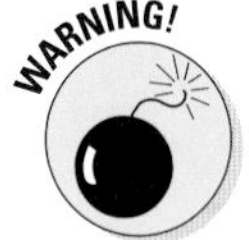

- Your selected White Balance setting remains in force until you change it. To avoid accidentally using an incorrect setting later, get in the habit of resetting the option to the automatic setting (AWB) after you finish shooting whatever subject it was that caused you to switch from automatic to manual white balancing.
- Not sure which setting to choose? Try switching to Live View temporarily. As you adjust the White Balance setting, the live preview shows you the impact on your scene. See Chapter 4 for details on using Live View. Then use the Quick Control screen to adjust the White Balance setting (the WB button doesn't work in Live View mode).

- If none of the settings produce neutral colors, you can tweak the selected setting or even create a custom setting, as outlined in the next sections.

Creating a custom White Balance setting

If none of the preset white balance options produces the right amount of color correction, you can create your own, custom setting. To use this technique, you need a piece of card stock that's either neutral gray or absolute white — not eggshell white, sand white, or any other close-but-not-perfect white. (You can buy reference cards made just for this purpose in many camera stores for under $20.)

Position the reference card so that it receives the same lighting you'll use for your photo. Then follow these steps:

1. **Set the camera to the P, Tv, Av, or M exposure mode.**

   You can't create a custom setting in any of the fully automatic modes.

2. **Set the White Balance setting to Auto (AWB).**

   The preceding section shows you how.

3. **Set the lens to manual focusing.**

   This step helps because the camera may have a hard time autofocusing on the card stock.

4. **Frame the shot so that your reference card fills the center area of the viewfinder.**

   Make sure that at least the center autofocus point and the six surrounding points fall over the reference card.

5. **Set focus and make sure that the exposure settings are correct.**

   Just press the shutter button halfway to check exposure. If necessary, adjust ISO, aperture, or shutter speed to get a proper exposure; Chapter 7 explains how.

6. **Take the picture of your reference card.**

   The camera will use this picture to establish your custom White Balance setting.

7. **Display Shooting Menu 2 and choose Custom White Balance, as shown on the left in Figure 8-20.**

After you tap the option (or highlight it and press Set), you see the screen shown on the right in Figure 8-20. The image you just captured should appear in the display, along with a message that tells you that the camera will only display that image and others that are compatible with the custom white-balancing option. If your picture doesn't appear on the screen, press the right or left cross key to scroll to it. (Note that you may see additional data on the screen depending on the current playback display mode; press the Info button to cycle through the various displays.)

8. **Tap the Set icon (or press the Set button) to select the displayed image as the basis for your custom white balance reference.**

   You see the message shown on the left in Figure 8-21, asking you to confirm that you want the camera to use the image to create the custom White Balance setting.

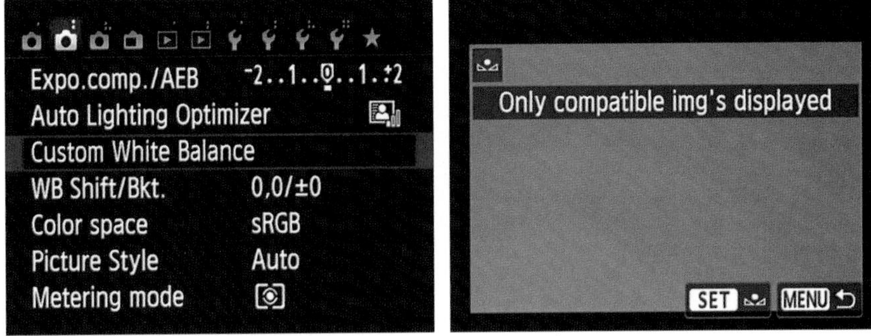

Figure 8-20: You can create a custom White Balance setting from Shooting Menu 2.

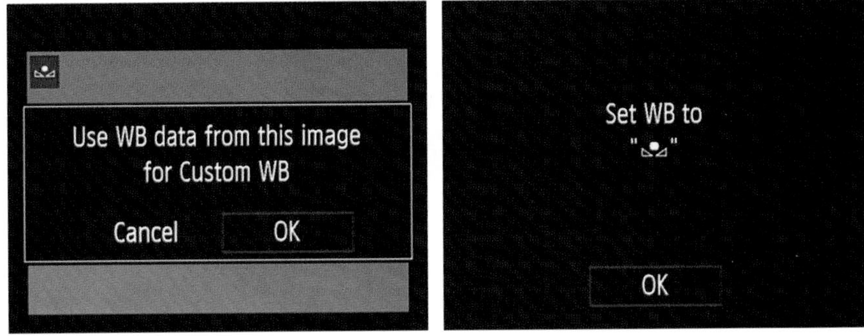

Figure 8-21: This message indicates that your White Balance setting is stored.

9. **Tap OK or highlight it and press the Set button.**

   Now you see the screen shown on the right in Figure 8-21. This message tells you that the White Balance setting is now stored. The little icon in the message area represents the custom setting.

10. **Tap OK (or highlight it and press Set).**

Your custom White Balance setting remains stored until the next time you work your way through these steps. Anytime you're shooting in the same lighting conditions and want to apply the same white balance correction, just select the Custom option as your White Balance setting. Remember, the icon for that setting looks like the one in the right screen in Figure 8-21.

Fine-tuning White Balance settings

In addition to creating a custom White Balance setting based on a gray card, you can tell the camera to shift all colors to make them a little more blue, amber, magenta, or green no matter what White Balance setting you use. To access this option, White Balance Correction, follow these steps:

1. **Set the Mode dial to P, Tv, Av, or M exposure mode.**

   You can take advantage of White Balance Correction only in these modes.

2. **Display Shooting Menu 2 and choose WB Shift/Bkt, as shown on the left in Figure 8-22.**

   The first two numbers next to the option name indicate the current amount of fine-tuning, or *shift*, and the second value represents the amount of white balance bracketing enabled. (See the next section for details on that topic). In the figure, all values are 0, indicating that no fine-tuning or bracketing is enabled.

   After you tap the menu item (or highlight it and press Set),you see the screen shown on the right in the figure. The screen contains a grid that's oriented around two main color pairs: green and magenta (represented by the G and M labels) and blue and amber (represented by B and A). The little white square indicates the amount of white balance shift.

3. **Use the cross keys to move the shift indicator marker in the direction of the shift you want to achieve.**

   You also can tap the scroll arrows located on each side of the grid to move the marker. Either way, the Shift area of the display tells the amount of color bias you've selected. For example, in Figure 8-22, the shift is two levels toward amber and two toward magenta.

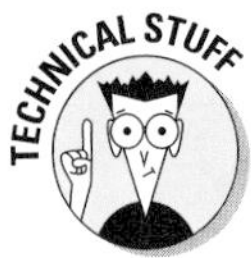

If you're familiar with traditional lens filters, you may know that the density of a filter, which determines the degree of color correction it provides, is measured in *mireds* (pronounced "my-reds"). The white balance grid is designed around this system: Moving the marker one level is the equivalent of adding a filter with a density of 5 mireds.

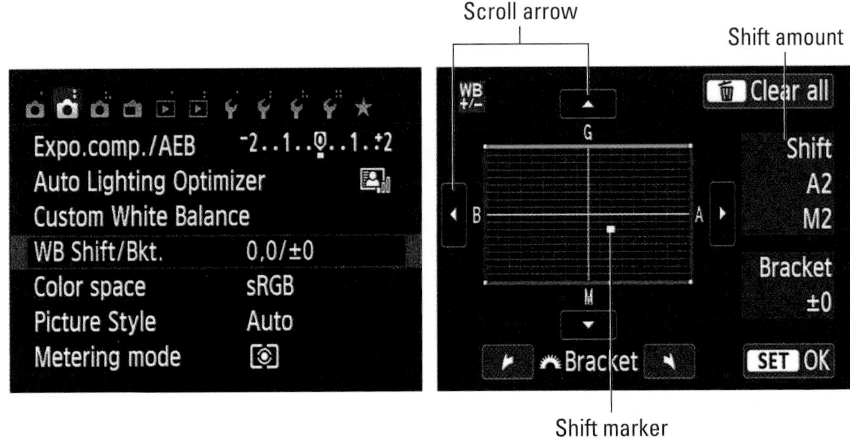

Figure 8-22: White Balance Correction offers one more way to control colors.

4. **Tap Set or press the Set button to apply the change and return to the menu.**

   After you apply White Balance Correction, a +/– sign appears next to the White Balance symbol in the Shooting Settings display, as shown on the left in Figure 8-23. It's your reminder that White Balance Shift is being applied. The same symbol appears in the viewfinder, right next to the ISO value.

   You can see the exact shift values in Shooting Menu 2, as shown on the right in Figure 8-23, and also in the Camera Settings display. (To go from the Shooting Settings display to the Camera Settings display, press the Info button twice.) For example, in Figure 8-23, the values indicate a shift two steps toward amber (A) and two toward magenta (M).

   Your adjustment remains in force for all advanced exposure modes until you change it. And the correction is applied no matter which White Balance setting you choose. Check the monitor or viewfinder before your next shoot; otherwise you may forget to adjust the white balance for the current light.

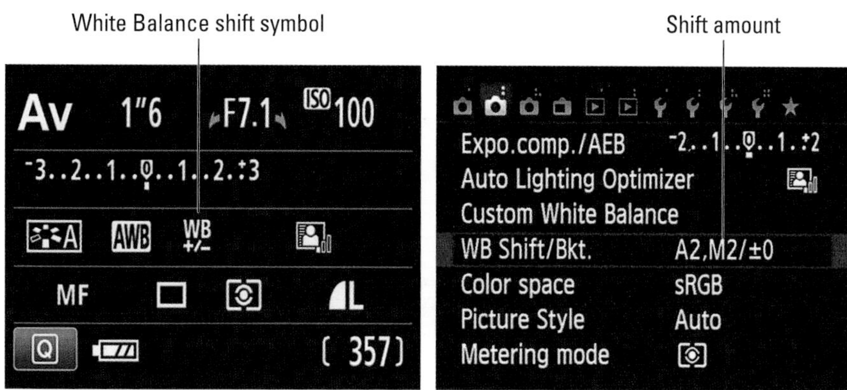

Figure 8-23: The +/– symbol lets you know that White Balance Shift is being applied.

5. **To cancel White Balance Correction, repeat the steps but move the marker back to the center of the grid in Step 3.**

   Be sure that both values in the Shift area of the display are set to 0.

   As an alternative, you can press the Erase button or tap its onscreen icon, found in the upper-right corner of the screen shown on the right in Figure 8-22. However, doing so also cancels White Balance Bracketing, which I explain in the next section.

Many film photography enthusiasts place colored filters on their lenses to either warm or cool their images. Portrait photographers, for example, often add a warming filter to give skin tones a healthy, golden glow. You can mimic the effects of these filters by simply fine-tuning your camera's White Balance settings as just described. Experiment with shifting the white balance a tad toward amber and magenta for a warming effect or toward blue and green for a cooling effect.

Bracketing shots with white balance

Chapter 7 introduces you to automatic exposure bracketing, which enables you to easily record the same image at three different exposure settings. Similarly, your camera offers automatic White Balance Bracketing. With this feature, the camera records the same image three times, using a slightly different white balance adjustment for each one. You might try this feature to experiment with different color takes on a scene, for example.

Eliminating color fringing (chromatic aberration)

When you view pictures taken with some lenses, close inspection may reveal *chromatic aberration,* which is geek-speak for a defect that creates weird color halos along the edges of objects. This phenomenon is also known as *color fringing.*

Your camera offers a Chromatic Aberration filter designed to address this problem. By default, the filter is turned off; you enable it via the Lens Aberration Correction option on Shooting Menu 1, as shown in the figures here.

As is the case with the companion filter, the Peripheral Illumination filter (covered in Chapter 7), you should turn this option on only if the second screen in the figure indicates that correction data is available for your lens. Otherwise, leave the option disabled, as it is by default. In fact, Canon recommends that you keep the option off when you use a non-Canon lens even if the screen indicates that correction data is available.

Note these other important aspects of the Chromatic Aberration filter:

- The correction is applied only to JPEG images. You can manually apply the correction to Raw images if you process them using Digital Photo Professional, a Canon photo program provided with your camera. See Chapter 6 for help with Raw processing. (Other Raw conversion programs typically have chromatic aberration correction tools as well.) Chapter 2 explains the difference between JPEG and Raw images.
- You can register additional lenses with the camera by using another of the free software tools, Canon EOS Utility. See that program's user manual, found on one of the CDs that ships with the camera, for instructions.
- Because the filter is applied after you take the shot, as the picture is being processed, enabling it slows down the camera's burst rate — the number of frames you can record per second when you use the Continuous Drive mode, covered in Chapter 2. For this reason, it's best to leave the filter off unless you notice strong chromatic aberration in your pictures and you don't want to deal with shooting in the Raw format and removing it yourself during the Raw processing stage.

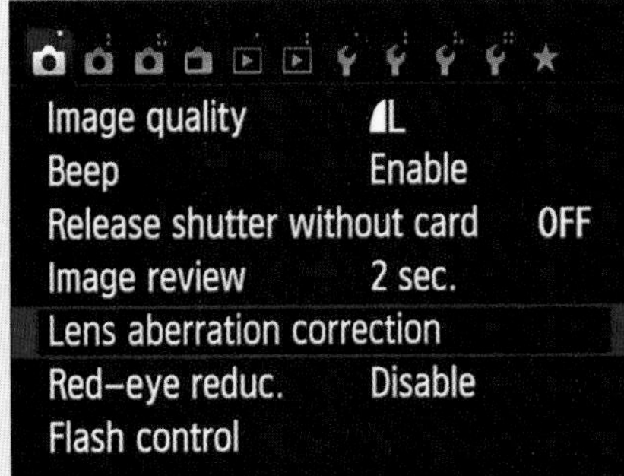

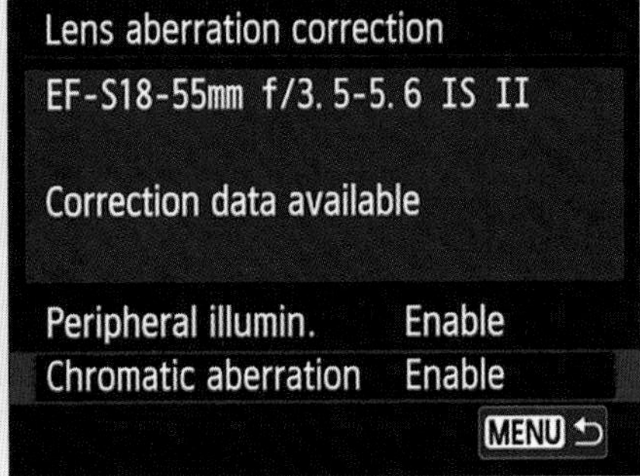

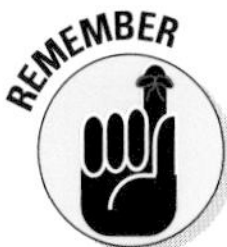

Note a couple of things about this feature:

- Because the camera records three images each time you press the shutter button, White Balance Bracketing reduces the maximum capture speed that's possible when you use the Continuous shooting mode. See Chapter 2 for more about Continuous mode. Of course, recording three images instead of one also eats up more space on your memory card.
- The White Balance Bracketing feature is designed around the same grid used for White Balance Correction, explained in the preceding section. As a reminder, the grid is based on two color pairs: green/magenta and blue/amber.
- When White Balance Bracketing is enabled, the camera always records the first of the three bracketed shots using a neutral white balance setting — or, at least, what it considers to be neutral, given its own measurement of the light. The second and third shots are then recorded using the specified shift along either the green/magenta or blue/amber axis of the color grid.

If all that is as clear as mud, just take a look at Figure 8-24 for an example. These images were shot using a single tungsten studio light and the candlelight. White Balance Bracketing was set to work along the blue/amber color axis. The camera recorded the first image at neutral, the second with a slightly blue color bias, and the third with an amber bias.

Neutral

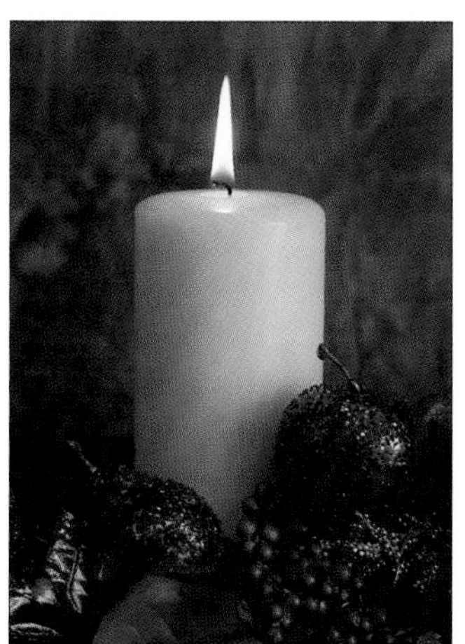

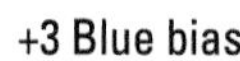

+3 Blue bias

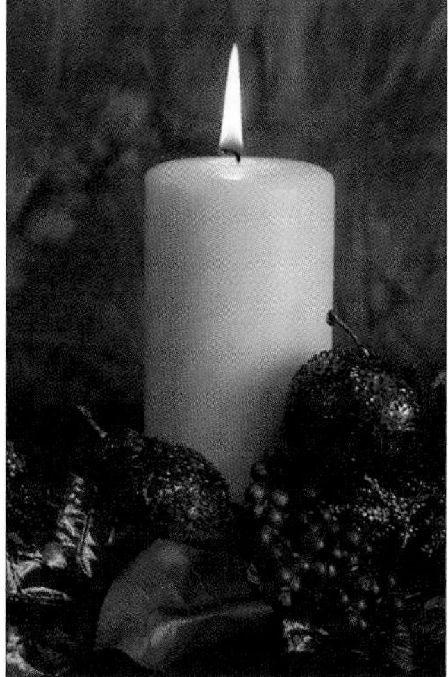

+3 Amber bias

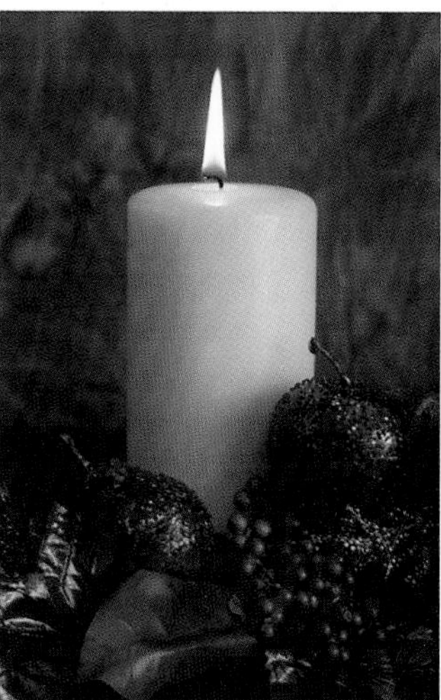

Figure 8-24: I captured one neutral image, one with a blue bias, and one with an amber bias.

To enable White Balance Bracketing, follow these steps:

1. **Set the Mode dial to P, Tv, Av, or M.**
2. **Display Shooting Menu 2 and choose WB/Shift Bkt, as shown on the left in Figure 8-25.**

   You see the screen shown on the right in the figure. It's the same screen that pops up for the White Balance Correction feature.

3. **Rotate the Main dial to set the amount and direction of the bracketing shift.**

   Rotate the dial as follows to specify whether you want the bracketing to be applied across the horizontal axis (blue to amber) or the vertical axis (green to magenta).

   - *Blue to amber bracketing:* Rotate the dial right.
   - *Green to magenta bracketing:* Rotate the dial left.

   As you rotate the dial, three markers appear on the grid, indicating the amount of shift that will be applied to your trio of bracketed images. You can apply a maximum shift of plus or minus three levels of adjustment.

   You also can tap the markers on either side of the word Bracket, at the bottom of the screen. Tap the right arrow to move markers along the blue to amber axis; tap the left one to move the markers along the green/blue axis. After you reach the maximum marker positions (+/-3), the arrow dims and then you can tap the opposite arrow to lower the bracketing amount until the marker returns to zero.

   The BKT area of the screen also indicates the shift; for example, in Figure 8-25, the display shows a bracketing amount of plus and minus three levels on the blue/amber axis. I used those settings to record the sample images in Figure 8-24. As you can see, even at the maximum shift (+/–3), the difference to the colors is subtle.

   If you want to get truly fancy, you can combine White Balance Bracketing with White Balance Shift. See the preceding section to learn about White Balance Shift.

4. **Tap the Set icon or press the Set button to apply your changes and return to the menu.**

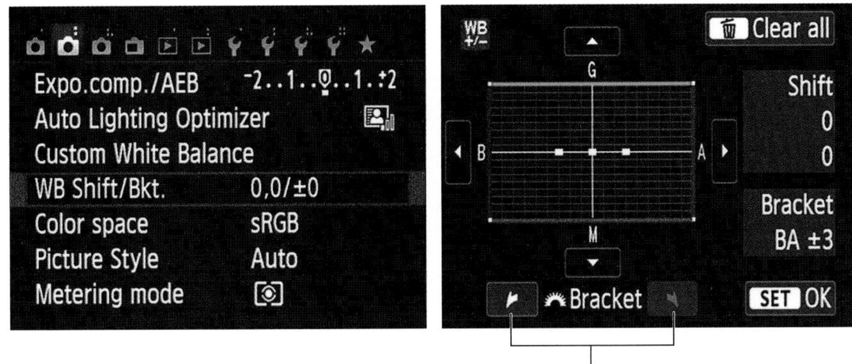

Figure 8-25: These settings were used to capture the bracketed candle images.

When White Balance bracketing is in effect, you see the symbol highlighted on the left in Figure 8-26 on the Shooting Settings screen. On Shooting Menu 2, the value after the slash shows you the bracketing setting, as shown on the right in the figure. (The two values to the left of the slash indicate the White Balance Shift amount.) The Camera Settings display, which you bring up by pressing Info twice when the Shooting Settings screen is displayed, also reports the bracketing setting.

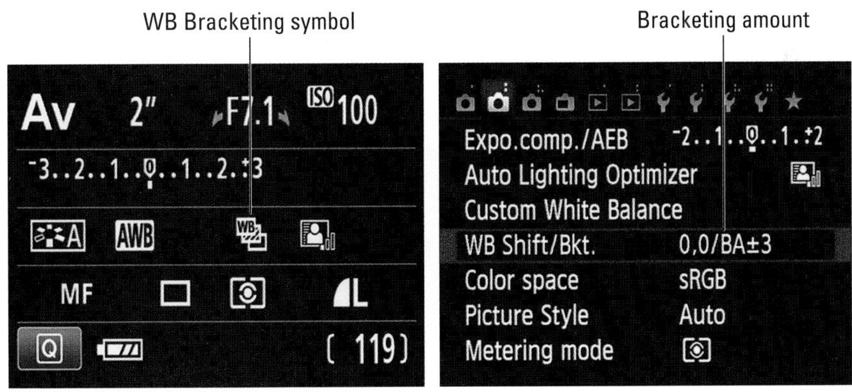

Figure 8-26: These symbols indicate that White Balance Bracketing is turned on.

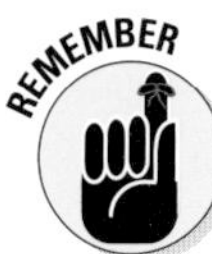

The bracketing setting remains in effect until you turn off the camera. You can also cancel bracketing by revisiting the grid screen shown earlier, in Figure 8-25, and either rotating the Main dial until you see only a single grid marker. You also can wipe out both your bracketing setting and any White Balance Shift amount by pressing the Erase button or tapping its icon (upper right corner of the screen). Either way, tap Set or press the Set button to officially turn off bracketing.

Although White Balance Bracketing is a fun feature, if you want to ensure color accuracy, creating a custom White Balance setting is a more reliable idea than bracketing white balance; after all, you can't be certain that shifting the white balance a couple steps is going to produce accurate colors.

If you're comfortable with shooting in the Raw format, that's the best color safety net, however: You can assign a White Balance setting when you process the Raw images, whether you're after a neutral color platform or want to lend a slight color tint to the scene.

See Chapter 2 for an introduction to Raw files; see Chapter 6 for help with the Raw conversion process.

Taking a Quick Look at Picture Styles

In addition to all the aforementioned focus and color features, your camera offers *Picture Styles.* Using Picture Styles, you can further tweak color as well as saturation, contrast, and image sharpening.

Sharpening is a software process that adjusts contrast in a way that creates the illusion of slightly sharper focus. The key word here is *slightly*: Sharpening cannot remedy poor focus, but instead produces a subtle tweak to this aspect of your pictures.

The camera offers the following Picture Styles:

- **Auto:** This is the default setting; the camera analyzes the scene and determines which Picture Style is the most appropriate.
- **Standard:** This option captures the image by using the characteristics that Canon offers as suitable for the majority of subjects.

- **Portrait:** This mode reduces sharpening slightly from the amount that's applied in Standard mode, with the goal of keeping skin texture soft. Color saturation, on the other hand, is slightly increased.
- **Landscape:** In a nod to traditions of landscape photography, this Picture Style emphasizes greens and blues and amps up color saturation and sharpness, resulting in bolder images.
- **Neutral:** This setting reduces saturation and contrast slightly compared to how the camera renders images when the Standard option is selected.
- **Faithful:** The Faithful style is designed to render colors as closely as possible to how your eye perceives them.
- **Monochrome:** This setting produces black-and-white photos, or, to be more precise, *grayscale images.* Technically speaking, a true black-and-white image contains only black and white, with no shades of gray.

If you set the Quality option to Raw (or Raw + Large/Fine), the camera displays your image on the monitor in black and white during playback. But during the Raw converter process, you can either choose to go with your grayscale version or view and save a full-color version. Or even better, you can process and save the image once as a grayscale photo and again as a color image.

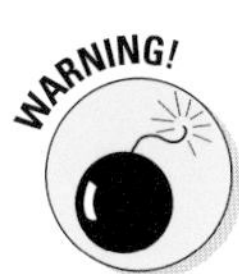

If you *don't* capture the image in the Raw format, you can't access the original image colors later. In other words, you're stuck with *only* a black-and-white image.

The extent to which Picture Styles affect your image depends on the subject as well as on exposure settings and lighting conditions. But Figure 8-27 offers a test subject shot at each setting (except Auto) to give you a general idea of what to expect. As you can see, the differences are subtle, with the exception of the Monochrome option, of course.

The level of control you have over Picture Styles, like most other settings in this chapter, depends on your camera's exposure mode:

- **In Scene Intelligent Auto, Creative Auto, Flash Off, and the scene modes:** The camera sets the Picture Style for you.
- **In the advanced exposure modes (P, Tv, Av, and M):** You can not only select any Picture Style but also tweak each style to your liking and create up to three custom styles.

- **Movie mode:** If you set the Mode dial to P, Tv, Av, or M, you can select any Picture Style, including any custom styles you create. (Want to shoot a black-and-white movie? Set the Picture Style to Monochrome before you start recording.)

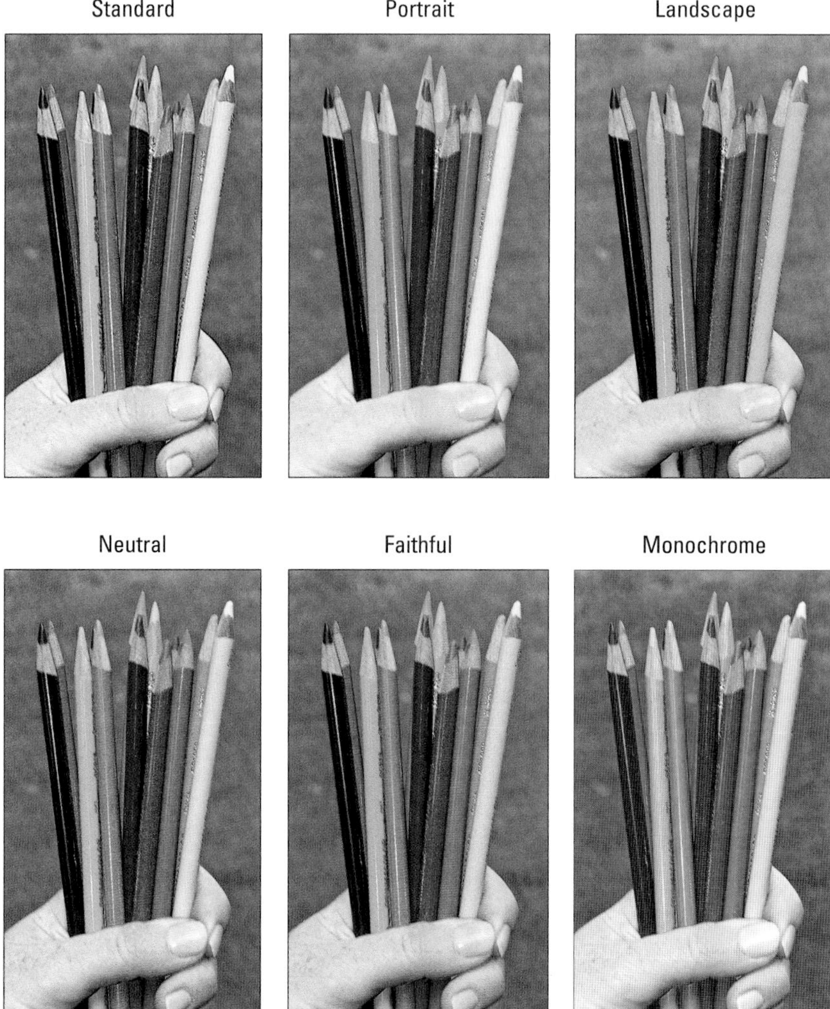

Figure 8-27: Each Picture Control produces a slightly different take on the scene.

Chapter 4 explains how to select movie-recording options. For still photography, you can select a Picture Style in three ways:

- **Quick Control screen:** Highlight the Picture Style icon, as shown on the left in Figure 8-28, and then rotate the Main dial to cycle through the available styles. (The figures show the normal Quick Control screen; in Live View mode, the settings appear on top of the image, as detailed in Chapter 4.) The User 1, 2, and 3 settings relate to custom Picture Styles that you can create; more on that topic momentarily. If you haven't created a custom style, the Auto style is used.

The numbers you see along with the style name at the bottom of the screen represent the four characteristics applied by the style: Sharpness, Contrast, Saturation, and Color Tone. Sharpness values range from 0 to 7; the higher the value, the more sharpening is applied. At 0, no sharpening is applied. The other values, however, are all set to 0, which represents the default setting for the selected Picture Style. (Using certain advanced options, you can adjust all four settings; more on that momentarily.)

If you want to see all available styles, tap the Picture Style icon or press Set to display the screen you see on the right in Figure 8-28. Highlight the style you want to use, and the four style values appear along with the style name, as shown in the figure. Tap Set or press the Set button to wrap up.

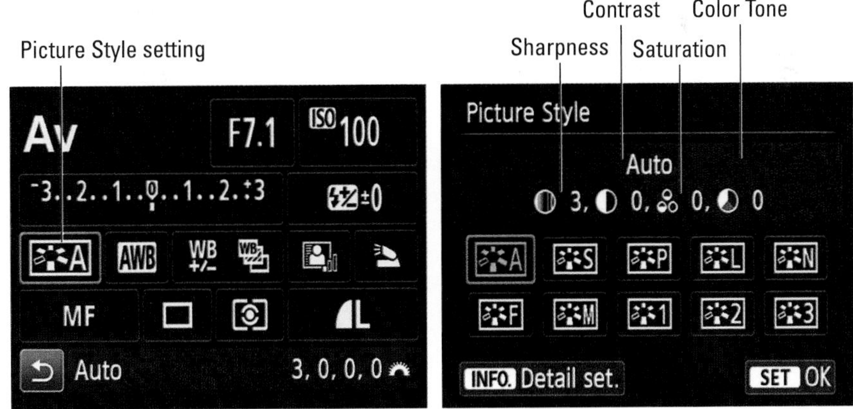

Figure 8-28: You can quickly select a Picture Style by using the Quick Control screen or pressing the bottom cross key.

- **Picture Style button (bottom cross key):** Press the key to display the same screen shown on the right in Figure 8-28. (Notice that the label on the key is the same as the icon that appears with the Picture Style setting on the Shooting Settings and Quick Control screens.) This technique works only for viewfinder shooting, however; the cross key serves a different purpose during Live View and Movie shooting.
- **Shooting Menu 2:** Choose Picture Style, as shown on the left in Figure 8-29 to display a list of all the styles, as shown on the right. You again can see the values for the four style characteristics on the screen shown on the right in the figure. To scroll the list of options, press the up or down cross keys or tap the scroll arrows, labeled in the figure. Choose an option and tap Set or press the Set button to exit the screen.

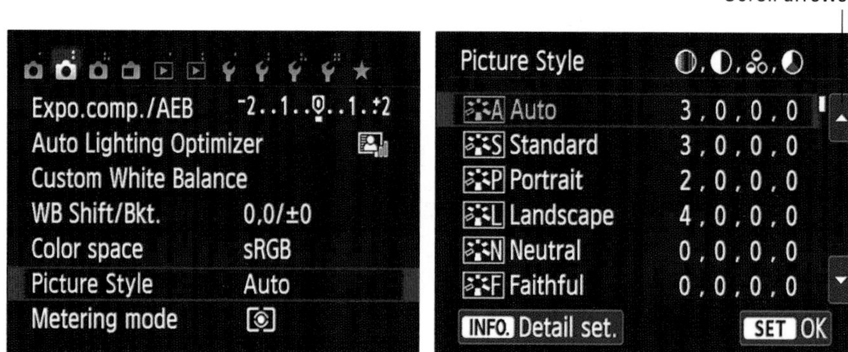

Figure 8-29: You also can access Picture Style options via Shooting Menu 2.

This discussion touches on just the basics of using Picture Styles. The camera also offers some advanced Picture Style features, including the following:

- **Modifying a Picture Style:** You can tweak each style, varying the amount of sharpness, contrast, saturation, and color tone adjustment that the style produces. After selecting a Picture Style — whether you're doing so from the Quick Setting screen shown on the right in Figure 8-28 or the menu screen shown on the right in Figure 8-29 — tap the Info icon or press the Info button to access a screen similar to the one you see on the left in Figure 8-30. Here, tap one of the adjustment options to display a screen that has a value scale. Drag along the scale, tap the arrows at either end, or use the right/left cross keys to change the setting. After you finish tweaking the style characteristics, tap Set or press the Set button. Then tap the Menu icon or press the Menu button.

- **Storing a custom style:** The process is the same as for modifying a style, except that instead of starting with an existing style, you choose one of the three User Defined options, as shown on the right in Figure 8-30.
- **Using your computer to create and download styles:** For übergeeks (you know who you are), the CD accompanying your camera includes a software package named — are you ready? — Picture Style Editor, where you can create and save Picture Style files to your heart's content. You then download the styles to your camera via the memory card. And I would be remiss if I didn't also mention that some Canon user groups swap Picture Styles with each other online. (I'd be equally remiss if I didn't warn you that you play at your own risk any time you download files from persons unknown to you.)

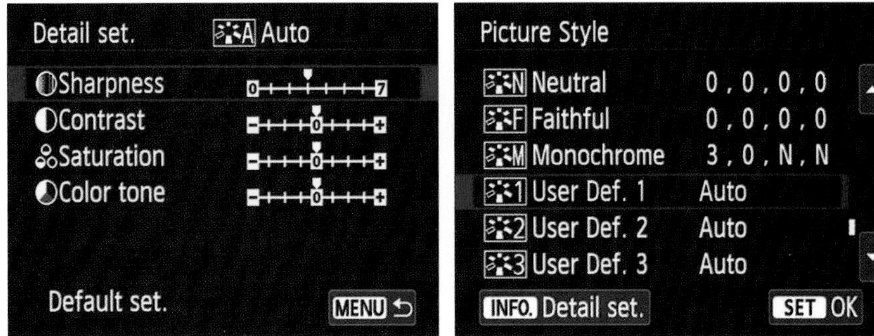

Figure 8-30: You can adjust the characteristics of one of the preset styles (left) or create your own custom style (right).

Unless you're just tickled pink by the prospect of experimenting with Picture Styles, I recommend that you just stick with the default settings. First, you have way more important camera settings to worry about — aperture, shutter speed, autofocus, and all the rest. Why add one more setting to your list, especially when the impact of changing it is minimal? Second, if you want to mess with the characteristics that the Picture Style options affect, you're much better off shooting in the Raw (CR2) format and then making those adjustments on a picture-by-picture basis in your Raw converter. In Canon Digital Photo Professional, which comes free with the camera, you can even assign any of the existing Picture Styles to your Raw files and then compare how each one affects the image. The camera tags your Raw file with whichever Picture Style is active at the time you take the shot, but the image adjustments are in no way set in stone or even in sand — you can tweak your photo at will. (The selected Picture Style does affect the JPEG preview that's used to display the Raw image thumbnails in Digital Photo Professional and other photo software.)

For these reasons, I opt in this book to present you with just this brief introduction to Picture Styles to make room for more details about functions that do make a big difference in your daily photography life, such as the white balance customization options presented earlier. But again, if you're really into Picture Styles and you can't figure out one of the advanced options from the descriptions here, the camera manual walks you step by step through all the various Picture Style features.

9

Putting It All Together

In This Chapter

- Reviewing the best all-around picture-taking settings
- Adjusting the camera for portrait photography
- Discovering the keys to super action shots
- Dialing in the right settings to capture landscapes and other scenic vistas
- Capturing close-up views of your subject
- Shooting through glass, capturing fireworks, and conquering other special challenges

Earlier chapters break down critical picture-taking features on your camera, detailing how the various controls affect exposure, picture quality, focus, color, and the like. This chapter pulls all that information together to help you set up your camera for specific types of photography.

Keep in mind, though, that there's no one "right way" to shoot a portrait, a landscape, or whatever. So feel free to wander off on your own, tweaking this exposure setting or adjusting that focus control, to discover your own creative vision. Experimentation is part of the fun of photography, after all, and thanks to your camera monitor and the Erase button, it's an easy, completely free proposition.

Recapping Basic Picture Settings

For some camera options, such as exposure mode, aperture, and shutter speed, the best settings depend on your subject, lighting conditions, and creative goals. But for certain basic options, you can rely on the same settings for almost every shooting scenario.

Table 9-1 offers recommendations for these basic settings and lists the chapter where you can find more information about each option. Figure 9-1 shows you where on the Shooting Settings screen you can find the symbols representing some settings along with a few not included in the table; don't forget that you can adjust these options via the Quick Control screen. Just tap the Quick Control icon or press the Quick Control button to shift from the Shooting Settings screen to the Quick Control display. (See Chapter 1 for the full story on using the Quick Control screen.)

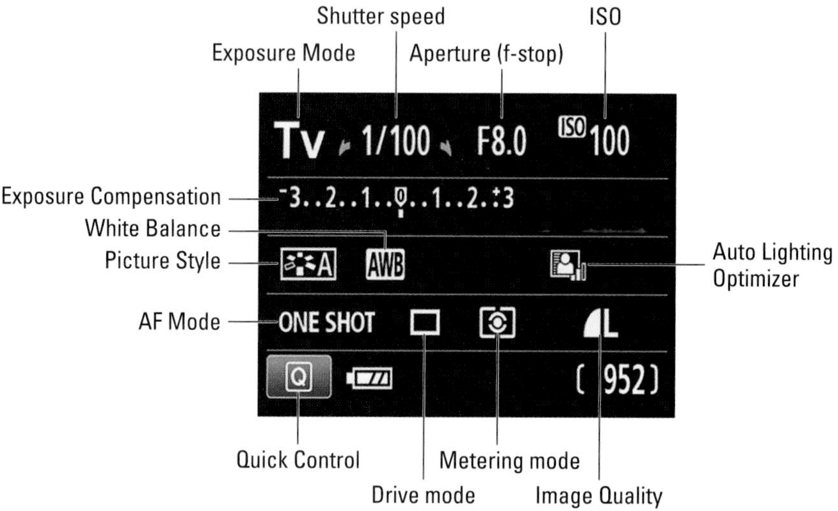

Figure 9-1: You can monitor these critical options on the Shooting Settings display.

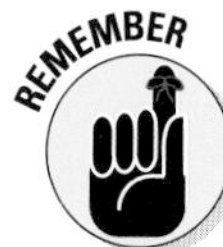

One key point: Instructions in this chapter assume that you set the exposure mode to P, Tv, Av, or M exposure mode, as indicated in the table. These modes, detailed in Chapter 7, are the only ones that give you access to the entire cadre of camera features. In most cases, I recommend using Tv (shutter-priority autoexposure) when controlling motion blur is important, and Av (aperture-priority autoexposure) when controlling depth of field is important. These two modes let you concentrate on one side of the exposure equation and let the camera handle the other. Of course, if you're comfortable making both the aperture and shutter speed decisions, you may prefer to work in M (manual) exposure mode instead. P (programmed autoexposure) is my last choice because it makes choosing a specific aperture or shutter speed more cumbersome.

What's my beef with the other exposure modes — Scene Intelligent Auto, Flash Off, Creative Auto, and the scene modes? The problem with these point-and-shoot modes is that they prevent you from accessing certain settings that can be critical to capturing great shots of certain subjects, especially in difficult lighting.

As you read through the rest of this chapter, also remember that it discusses choices for viewfinder photography; Chapter 4 guides you through the options available for Live View photography and movie recording. (For Live View photography, however, most settings work the same as discussed here, with the exception of the autofocus options.)

Table 9-1 All-Purpose Picture-Taking Settings

Option	*Recommended Setting*	*See This Chapter*
Exposure mode	P, Tv, Av, or M	2
Quality	Large/Fine (JPEG), Medium/Fine (JPEG), or Raw (CR2)	2
Drive mode	Action photos, Continuous; all others, Single	2
ISO	100 or 200 (available light permitting)	7
Metering mode	Evaluative	7
AF mode	Moving subjects, AI Servo; stationary subjects, One Shot	8
AF Point Selection	Moving subjects, Automatic; stationary subjects, Manual (single point)	8
White Balance	Auto	8
Auto Lighting Optimizer	Standard for P, Tv, and Av modes; Disable for M mode	7
Picture Style	Auto	8

Setting Up for Specific Scenes

For the most part, the settings detailed in the preceding section fall into the "set 'em and forget 'em" category. That leaves you free to concentrate on a handful of other camera settings that you can manipulate to achieve a specific photographic goal, such as adjusting aperture to affect depth of field. The next four sections explain which of these additional options typically produce the best results when you're shooting portraits, action shots, landscapes, and close-ups. You can discover a few compositional and creative tips along the way — but again, remember that beauty is in the eye of the beholder, and for every so-called rule, plenty of great images prove the exception. As Ansel Adams so wisely said, "There are no rules for good photographs; there are only good photographs."

Shooting still portraits

By *still portrait,* I mean that your subject isn't moving. For subjects who aren't keen on sitting still long enough to have their picture taken, skip to the next section and use the techniques given for action photography instead.

Assuming that you do have a subject willing to pose, the classic portraiture approach is to keep the subject sharply focused while throwing the background into soft focus, as shown in Figure 9-2. This artistic choice emphasizes the subject and helps diminish the impact of any distracting background objects in cases where you can't control the setting. The following steps show you how to achieve this look:

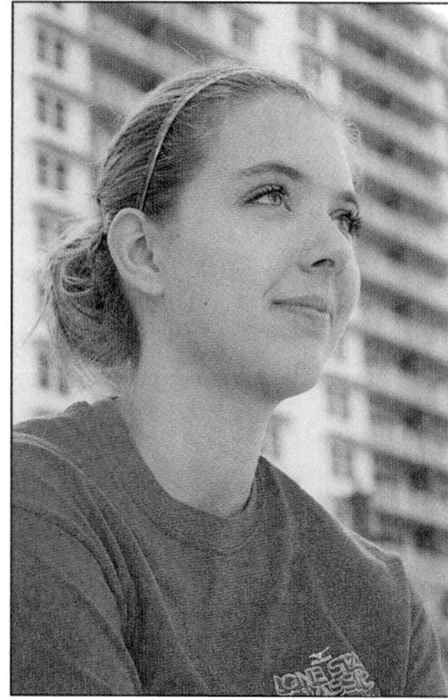

Figure 9-2: To diminish a distracting background and draw more attention on your subject, use camera settings that produce a short depth of field.

1. **Set the Mode dial to Av (aperture-priority autoexposure) and rotate the Main dial to select the lowest f-stop value possible.**

   As Chapter 7 explains, a low f-stop setting opens the aperture, which not only allows more light to enter the camera but also shortens depth of field, or the range of sharp focus. So dialing in a low f-stop value is the first step in softening your portrait background.

I recommend aperture-priority mode when depth of field is a primary concern because you can control the f-stop while relying on the camera to select the shutter speed that will properly expose the image. But you do need to pay attention to shutter speed also to make sure that it's not so slow that any movement of the subject or camera will blur the image.

You can monitor the current f-stop and shutter speed in the Shooting Settings display, as shown in Figure 9-1. The settings also appear in the viewfinder readout. (If you don't see the settings, give the shutter button a quick half-press and release to wake up the exposure meter.)

2. **To further soften the background, zoom in, get closer, and put more distance between subject and background.**

   As covered in Chapter 8, zooming in to a longer focal length also reduces depth of field, as does moving closer to your subject. And the greater the distance between the subject and background, the more the background blurs.

   A lens with a focal length of 85–120mm is ideal for a classic head-and-shoulders portrait. But don't fret if you have only the 18–55mm kit lens; just zoom all the way to the 55mm setting. You should avoid using a much shorter focal length (a wider-angle lens) for portraits. They can cause features to appear distorted — sort of like how people look when you view them through a security peephole in a door.

3. **For indoor portraits, shoot flash-free if possible.**

   Shooting by available light rather than flash produces softer illumination and avoids the problem of red-eye. To get enough light to go flash-free, turn on room lights or, during daylight, pose your subject next to a sunny window.

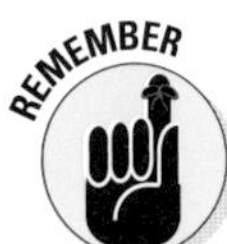

   In the Av exposure mode, simply keeping the built-in flash unit closed disables the flash. If flash is unavoidable, see the list of flash tips at the end of the steps to get better results.

4. **For outdoor portraits in daylight, use a flash if possible.**

   Even in daylight, a flash adds a beneficial pop of light to subjects' faces, as illustrated in Figure 9-3. A flash is especially important when the background is brighter than the subjects, as in this example; when the subject is wearing a hat; or when the sun is directly overhead, creating harsh shadows under the eyes, nose, and chin.

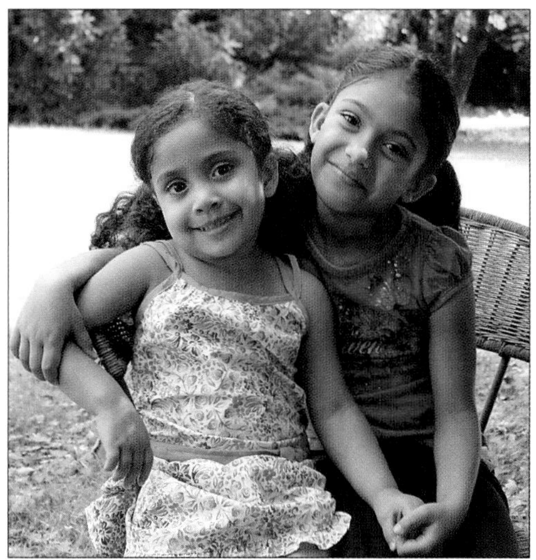

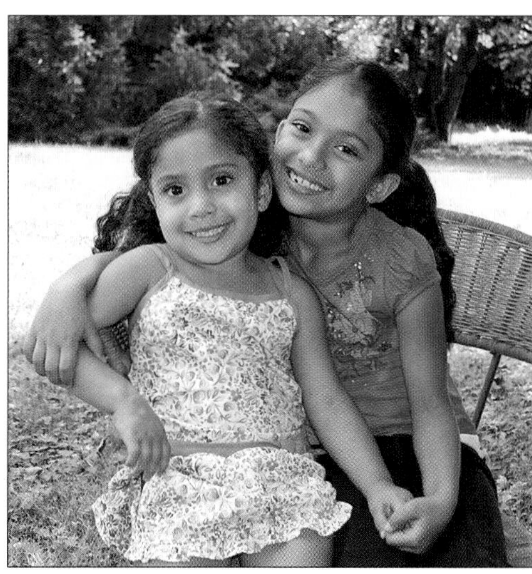

No flash / With flash

Figure 9-3: To better illuminate the face in outdoor portraits, use flash.

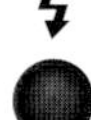

In the Av exposure mode, press the Flash button on the side of the camera to enable the built-in flash. For outdoor daytime portraits, disable the Red-Eye Reduction feature (Shooting Menu 1); you don't need it because the pupils are already constricted because of the bright ambient light.

One warning about using flash outdoors: The fastest shutter speed you can use with the built-in flash is 1/200 second, and in extremely bright conditions, that speed may be too slow to avoid overexposing the image even if you use the lowest ISO (light sensitivity) setting. If necessary, move your subject into the shade. (On some external Canon flashes, you can select a faster shutter speed than 1/200 second; see your flash manual for details.)

5. **Press and hold the shutter button halfway to engage exposure metering and, if using autofocusing, to establish focus.**

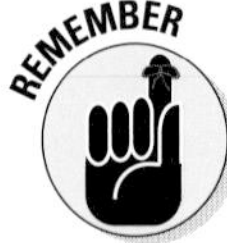

As spelled out in Table 9-1, the One Shot AF mode and Manual AF Point Selection options work best for portrait autofocusing. After selecting a focus point, position that point over one of your subject's eyes and then press and hold the shutter button halfway to lock focus.

Chapter 8 explains more about using autofocus, but if you have trouble, simply set your lens to manual focus mode and then turn the focusing ring to set focus.

6. **Press the shutter button the rest of the way to capture the image.**

Again, these steps give you only a starting point for taking better portraits. A few other tips can also improve your people pics:

- **Do a background check.** Scan the frame for intrusive objects that may distract the eye from the subject. If necessary (and possible), reposition the subject against a more flattering backdrop. Inside, a softly textured wall works well; outdoors, trees and shrubs can provide attractive backdrops as long as they aren't so ornate or colorful that they diminish the subject (for example, a magnolia tree laden with blooms).
- **Frame loosely to allow for later cropping to a variety of frame sizes.** Because your camera produces images that have an aspect ratio of 3:2, your portrait perfectly fits a 4-x-6-inch print size — but requires cropping to print at any other proportions, such as 5 x 7 or 8 x 10. The printing section of Chapter 6 talks more about this issue.
- **Pay attention to white balance if your subject is lit by both flash and ambient light.** If you use the automatic White Balance setting (AWB), as recommended in Table 9-1, photo colors may be slightly warmer or cooler than neutral because the camera can become confused by mixed light sources. A warming effect typically looks nice in portraits, giving the skin a subtle glow. Cooler tones, though, usually aren't as flattering. Either way, see Chapter 8 to find out how to fine-tune white balance.
- **For group portraits, be careful that depth of field doesn't get *too* shallow.** Otherwise, people in the front or back of the group may be beyond the zone of sharp focus. Depth of field may extend only a few inches from your focusing point, in fact, if you're using a long focal length (telephoto lens), select a very low f-stop value, and position yourself very close to your subjects. So it's easy to wind up with a wedding photo in which the bride's face is in sharp focus, for example, while that of her loving groom, standing just behind, is blurry. (Try explaining *that* to the mother of the groom. . . .)
- **When flash is unavoidable for indoor and nighttime portraits, try these tricks to produce better results:**

- *Indoors, turn on as many room lights as possible.* By using more ambient light, you reduce the flash power that's needed to expose the picture. This step also causes the pupils to constrict, further reducing the possibility of red-eye. (Pay heed to the preceding white-balance warning, however.) As an added benefit, the smaller pupil allows more of the subject's iris to be visible in the portrait, so you see more eye color.
- *Try setting the flash to Red-Eye Reduction mode.* Warn your subject to expect both a light coming from the Red-Eye Reduction lamp, which constricts pupils, and the actual flash. See Chapter 2 for details about using this flash mode, which you enable on Shooting Menu 1.
- *Pay extra attention to shutter speed.* In dim lighting, the camera may select a shutter speed as slow as 30 seconds when you enable the built-in flash in Av mode, so keep an eye on that value and use a tripod if necessary to avoid blurring from camera shake. Also warn your subject to remain as still as possible.
- *For nighttime pictures, try switching to Tv exposure mode and purposely selecting a slow shutter speed.* The longer exposure time enables the camera to soak up more ambient light, producing a brighter background and reducing the flash power needed to light the subject. Again, though, a slow shutter means that you need to take extra precautions to ensure that neither camera nor subject moves during the exposure.
- *For professional results, use an external flash with a rotating flash head.* Then aim the flash head upward so that the flash light bounces off the ceiling and falls softly down on the subject. (This is called *bounce lighting.*) An external flash isn't cheap, but the results make the purchase worthwhile if you shoot lots of portraits. Compare the portraits in Figure 9-4 for an illustration. In the first example, the built-in flash resulted in strong shadowing behind the subject and harsh, concentrated light. Bounced lighting produced the better result on the right.

  Make sure that the ceiling or other surface you use to bounce the light is white; otherwise the flash's light will pick up the color of the surface and influence the color of your subject.

- *Invest in a flash diffuser to further soften the light.* Whether you use the built-in flash or an external flash, attaching a diffuser is also a good idea. A *diffuser* is simply a piece of translucent plastic or fabric that you place over the flash to soften and spread the light — much like sheer curtains diffuse window light. Diffusers come in lots of different designs, including small, fold-flat models that fit over the built-in flash.

- *To reduce shadowing from the flash, move your subject farther from the background.* Moving the subject away from the wall helped eliminate the background shadow in the second example in Figure 9-4. The increased distance also softened the focus of the wall a bit (because of the short depth of field resulting from the f-stop and focal length).

  Positioning subjects far enough from the background that they can't touch it is a good general rule. If that isn't possible, though, try going in the other direction: If the person's head is smack against the background, any shadow will be smaller and less noticeable. For example, less shadowing is created when a subject's head is resting against a sofa cushion than if he sits upright with his head a foot or so away from the cushion.

- *Study the flash information in Chapter 7 and practice before you need to take important portraits.* How the camera calculates the aperture, shutter speed, and flash power needed to expose your subject and background varies depending on the exposure mode you use. To fully understand how to create the flash results you want, you have to experiment with every advanced exposure mode, all covered in Chapter 7.

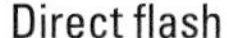

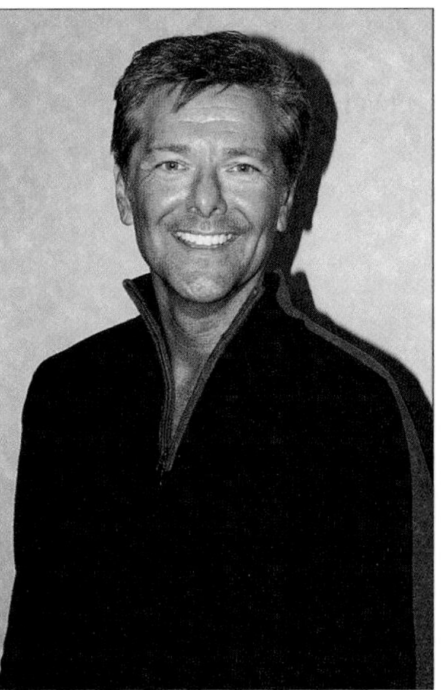

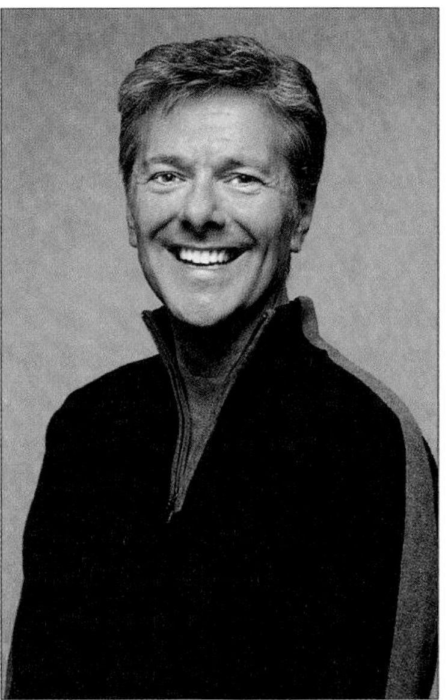

Figure 9-4: To eliminate harsh lighting and strong shadows (left), use bounce flash and move the subject farther from the background (right).

Capturing action

A fast shutter speed is the key to capturing a blur-free shot of any moving subject, whether it's a spinning Ferris wheel, a butterfly flitting from flower to flower, or, in the case of Figures 9-5 and 9-6, a hockey-playing teen. In the first image, a shutter speed of 1/125 second was too slow to catch the subject without blur. For this subject, who was moving at a fairly rapid speed, the shutter speed was all the way up to 1/1000 second to freeze the action cleanly, as shown in Figure 9-5. (The backgrounds are blurry in both shots because the camera settings I used produced a shallow depth of field; in the first image, the skater is a little farther from the background, blurring the background more than in the second image.)

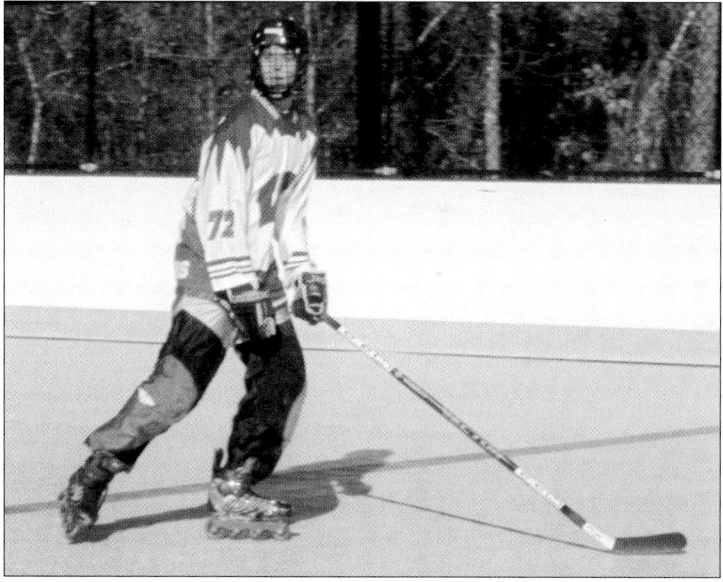

Figure 9-5: A too-slow shutter speed (1/125 second) causes the skater to appear blurry.

Along with the basic capture settings outlined earlier (refer to Table 9-1), try the techniques in the following steps to photograph a subject in motion:

1. **Set the Mode dial to Tv (shutter-priority autoexposure).**

   In this mode, you control the shutter speed, and the camera takes care of choosing an aperture setting that will produce a good exposure.

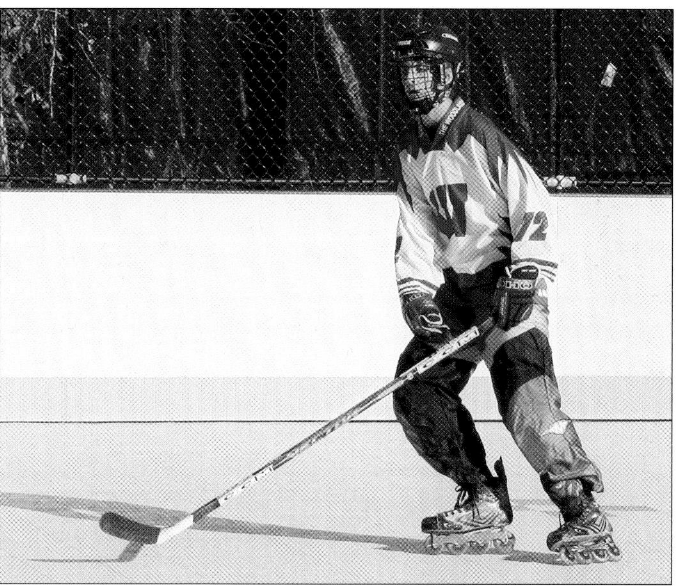

Figure 9-6: Raising the shutter speed to 1/1000 second freezes the action.

2. **Rotate the Main dial to select the shutter speed.**

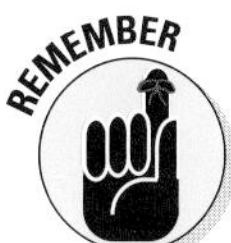

In the Shooting Settings display, the option that appears highlighted, with the little arrow pointers at each side, is the one that you can adjust with the Main dial. (Refer to Figure 9-1.) In Tv mode (and M mode), the shutter speed is the active option.

The shutter speed you need depends on how fast your subject is moving, so you have to experiment. Another factor that affects your ability to stop action is the *direction* of subject motion. A car moving toward you can be stopped with a lower shutter speed than one moving across your field of view, for example. Generally speaking, 1/500 second should be plenty for all but the fastest subjects — speeding hockey players, race cars, or boats, for example. For slower subjects, you can even go as low as 1/250 or 1/125 second.

Remember, though, that when you increase shutter speed, the camera opens the aperture to maintain the same exposure in Tv mode. At low f-stop numbers, depth of field becomes shorter, so you have to be more careful to keep your subject within the sharp-focus zone as you compose and focus the shot.

You also can take an entirely different approach to capturing action: Instead of choosing a fast shutter speed, select a speed slow enough to blur the moving objects, which can create a heightened sense of motion and, in scenes that feature very colorful subjects, cool abstract images. I took this approach when shooting the carnival ride featured in Figure 9-7, for example. For the left image, I set the shutter speed to 1/30 second; for the right version, I slowed things down to 1/5 second. In both cases, I used a tripod, but because nearly everything in the frame was moving, the entirety of both photos is blurry — the 1/5 second version is simply more blurry because of the slower shutter.

If the aperture value blinks after you set the shutter speed, the camera can't select an f-stop that will properly expose the photo at that shutter speed. See Chapter 7 for more details about how the camera notifies you of potential exposure problems.

3. **Raise the ISO setting to produce a brighter exposure, if needed.**

   In dim lighting, you may not be able to create a good exposure at your chosen shutter speed without taking this step. Raising the ISO increases the possibility of noise, but a noisy shot is better than a blurry shot. (The current ISO setting appears in the upper-right corner of the Shooting Settings display, as shown in Figure 9-1; press the ISO button or use the Quick Control screen to adjust the setting.)

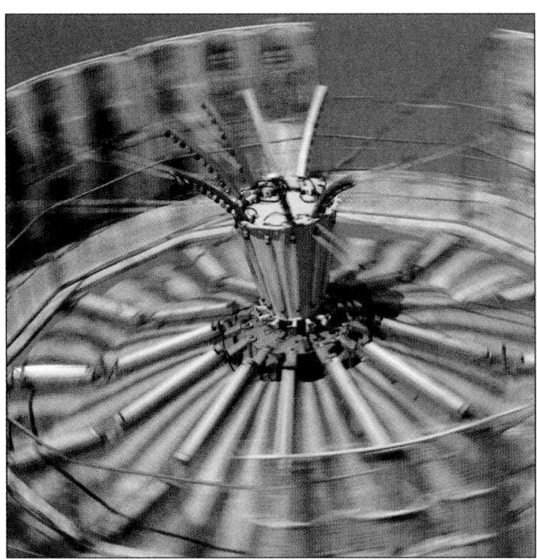

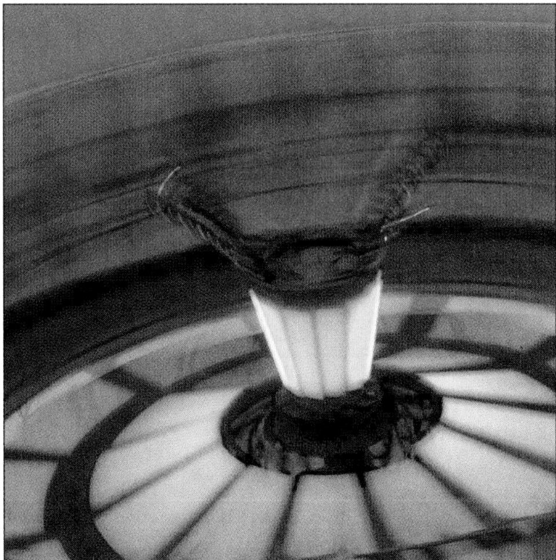

Figure 9-7: Using a shutter speed slow enough to blur moving objects can be a fun creative choice, too.

If auto ISO override is in force, ISO may go up automatically when you increase the shutter speed — Chapter 7 has details on that feature. Auto ISO can be a big help when you're shooting fast-paced action; just be sure to limit the camera to choosing an ISO setting that doesn't produce an objectionable level of noise. (Set that limit via the ISO Auto option on Shooting Menu 3.)

Why not just add flash to throw some extra light on the scene? That solution has a number of drawbacks. First, the flash needs time to recycle between shots, which slows down your shooting pace. Second, the fastest possible shutter speed when you enable the built-in flash is 1/200 second, which may not be fast enough to capture a quickly moving subject without blur. (You can use a faster shutter speed with certain Canon external flash units, however.) And finally, the built-in flash has a limited range, so unless your subject is pretty close to the camera, you're just wasting battery power with flash, anyway.

4. **For rapid-fire shooting, set the Drive mode to Continuous.**

   In this mode, you can take approximately five frames per second. The camera continues to record images as long as the shutter button is pressed. You can switch the Drive mode by pressing the left cross key or using the Quick Control screen. The icon representing the current mode appears in the Shooting Settings display. (Refer to the labeling in Figure 9-1.)

5. **If possible, use manual focusing; otherwise select AI Servo AF (autofocus) mode and Automatic AF Point Selection.**

   With manual focusing, you eliminate the time the camera needs to lock focus in Autofocus mode. Chapter 1 shows you how to focus manually, if you need help. Of course, focusing manually gets a little tricky if your subject is moving in a way that requires you to change the focusing distance quickly from shot to shot. In that case, try these two autofocus settings for best performance:

   - *Set the AF Point Selection mode to Automatic.* Press the button shown in the margin to adjust this setting. If Manual selection is in force, rotate the Main dial until all the focus points light up. Or tap the return to Auto Selection icon on the touchscreen (lower-left corner of the screen).
   - *Set the AF (autofocus) mode to AI Servo (continuous-servo autofocus).* Press the right cross key or use the Quick Control screen to access this setting. The name of the current setting appears in the Shooting Settings screen. (Refer to Figure 9-1.)

Frame your subject under the center focus point, press the shutter button halfway to set the initial focusing distance, and then just reframe as necessary to keep the subject within the 9-point autofocusing area. As long as you keep the shutter button pressed halfway, the camera continues to adjust focus up to the time you actually take the shot. Chapter 8 details these autofocus options.

6. **Compose the subject to allow for movement across the frame.**

   Don't zoom in so far that your subject might zip out of the frame before you take the shot — frame a little wider than usual. You can always crop the photo later to a tighter composition. (Many examples in this book were cropped to eliminate distracting elements.)

There action-shooting strategies also are helpful for shooting candid portraits of kids and pets. Even if they aren't running, leaping, or otherwise cavorting when you pick up your camera, snapping a shot before they move or change positions is often tough. So, if an interaction or scene catches your eye, set your camera into action mode and then just fire off a series of shots as fast as you can.

One other key to shooting sports, wildlife, or any moving subject: Before you even put your eye to the viewfinder, spend time studying your subject so that you get an idea of when it will move, where it will move, and how it will move. The more you can anticipate the action, the better your chances of capturing it.

Capturing scenic vistas

Providing specific camera settings for landscape photography is tricky because there's no single best approach to capturing a beautiful stretch of countryside, a city skyline, or another vast subject. Depth of field is an example: One person's idea of a super cityscape might be to keep all buildings in the scene sharply focused. Another photographer might prefer to shoot the same scene so that a foreground building is sharply focused while the others are less so, thus drawing the eye to that first building.

That said, here are a few tips to help you photograph a landscape the way *you* see it:

- **Shoot in aperture-priority autoexposure mode (Av) so that you can control depth of field.** If you want extreme depth of field so that both near and distant objects are sharply focused, as shown in Figure 9-8, select a high f-stop value. An aperture of f/22 worked for this shot.
- **If the exposure requires a slow shutter, use a tripod to avoid blurring.** The downside to a high f-stop is that you need a slower shutter speed to produce a good exposure. If the shutter speed is slower than you can comfortably handhold, use a tripod to avoid picture-blurring camera shake. No tripod handy? Look for any solid surface on which to steady

the camera. Using a remote-control to trigger the shutter release can also help avoid camera shake caused by the mere motion of pressing the shutter button.

You can always increase the ISO setting to increase light sensitivity, which in turn allows a faster shutter speed, too, but that option brings with it the chance of increased image noise. See Chapter 7 for details. Also see Chapter 1 for details about image stabilization, which can help you take sharper handheld shots at slow shutter speeds.

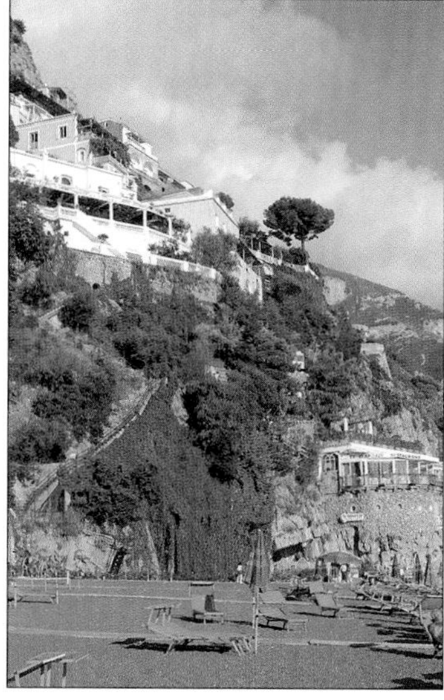

Figure 9-8: Use a high f-stop value to keep foreground and background sharply focused.

- **For dramatic waterfall and fountain shots, consider using a slow shutter to create that "misty" look.** The slow shutter blurs the water, giving it a soft, romantic appearance, as shown in Figure 9-9. Shutter speed for this shot was 1/15 second. Again, use a tripod to ensure that camera shake doesn't blur the rest of the scene.

In very bright light, using a slow shutter speed may overexpose the image even if you stop the aperture all the way down and select the camera's lowest ISO setting. As a solution, consider investing in a *neutral-density filter* for your lens. This type of filter works something like sunglasses for your camera: It simply reduces the amount of light that passes through the lens, without affecting image colors, so that you can use a slower shutter than would otherwise be possible.

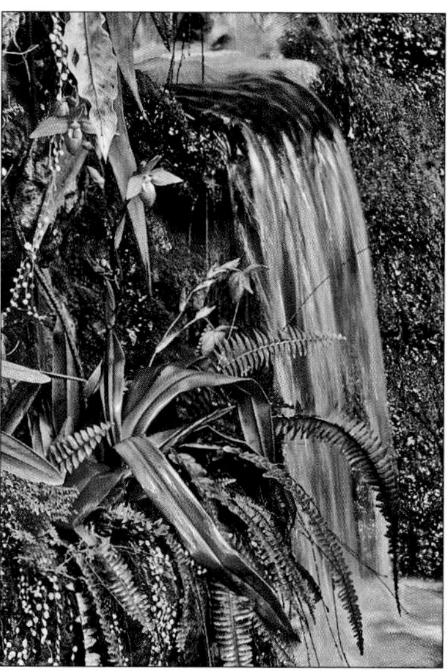

Figure 9-9: For misty water movement, use a slow shutter speed (and tripod).

- **At sunrise or sunset, base exposure on the sky.** The foreground will be dark, but you can usually brighten it in a photo editor, if needed. If you base exposure on the foreground, on the other hand, the sky will become so bright that all the color will be washed out — a problem you usually can't easily fix after the fact.

You can also invest in a graduated neutral-density filter, which is a filter that's clear on one side and dark on the other. You orient the filter so that the dark half falls over the sky and the clear side over the dimly lit portion of the scene. This setup enables you to better expose the foreground without blowing out the sky colors.

In the advanced exposure modes, experiment with enabling the Highlight Tone Priority option, too. Enabled via Custom Function 3 on Setup Menu 4, this feature can help you avoid blowing out highlights while still holding onto shadow detail. Chapter 7 offers more information.

- **For cool nighttime city pics, experiment with a slow shutter.** Assuming that cars or other vehicles are moving through the scene, the result is neon trails of light, like those you see in Figure 9-10. Shutter speed for this image was ten seconds. The longer your shutter speed, the blurrier the motion trails.

  Because long exposures can produce image noise, you also may want to enable the Long Exposure Noise Reduction feature. Chapter 7 discusses this option in more detail.

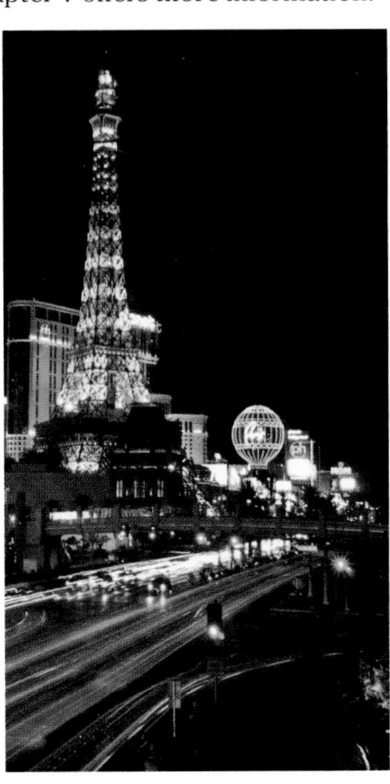

Figure 9-10: A slow shutter also creates neon light trails in city-street scenes.

- **For the best lighting, shoot during the "magic hours."** That's the term photographers use for early morning and late afternoon, when the light cast by the sun is soft and warm, giving everything that beautiful, gently warmed look.

  Can't wait for the perfect light? Tweak your camera's White Balance setting, using the instructions laid out in Chapter 8, to simulate magic-hour light.

- **In tricky light, bracket shots.** *Bracketing* simply means to take the same picture at several different exposures to increase the odds that at least one captures the scene the way you envision. Bracketing is especially a good idea in difficult lighting situations such as sunrise and sunset.

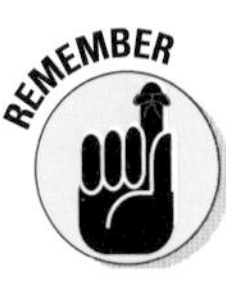

  Your camera offers automatic exposure bracketing (AEB) when you shoot in the advanced exposure modes. See Chapter 7 to find out how to take advantage of this feature.

Also experiment with the Auto Lighting Optimizer and Highlight Tone Priority options; capture some images with the features enabled and then take the same shots with the features turned off. See Chapter 7 for details. Remember, though, that you can't use both these tonality-enhancing features concurrently; turning on Highlight Tone Priority disables Auto Lighting Optimizer.

Capturing dynamic close-ups

For great close-up shots, start with the basic capture settings outlined earlier, in Table 9-1. Then try the following additional settings and techniques:

- **Check your owner's manual to find out the minimum close-focusing distance of your lens.** How "up close and personal" you can be to your subject depends on your lens, not on the camera body.
- **Take control over depth of field by setting the camera mode to Av (aperture-priority autoexposure) mode.** Whether you want a shallow or a medium or an extreme depth of field depends on the point of your photo. For the romantic scene shown in Figure 9-11, for example, setting the aperture to f/5.6 blurred the background, helping the subjects stand out more from the similarly colored background. But if you want the viewer to clearly see all details throughout the frame — for example, if you're shooting a product shot for your company's sales catalog — go in the other direction, stopping down the aperture as far as possible.

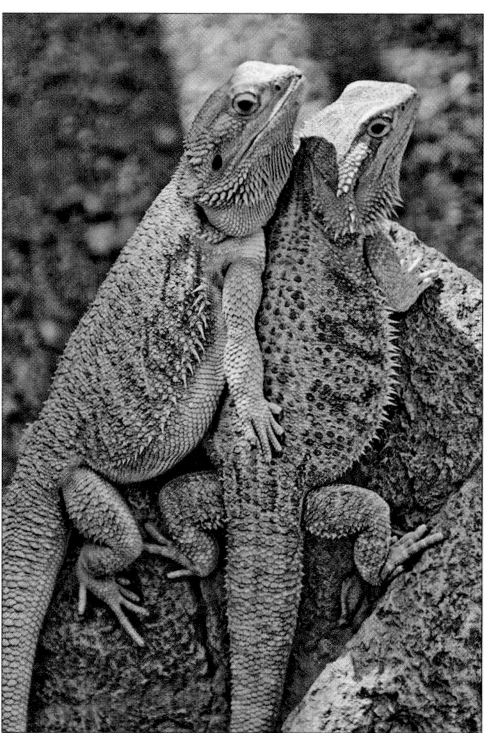

Figure 9-11: Shallow depth of field helps set the subject apart from the background.

- **Remember that both zooming in and getting close to your subject decrease depth of field.** Back to that product shot: If you need depth of field beyond what you can achieve with the aperture setting, you may need to back away or zoom out, or both. (You can always crop your image to show just the parts of the subject that you want to feature.)
- **When shooting flowers and other nature scenes outdoors, pay attention to shutter speed, too.** Even a slight breeze may cause your subject to move, causing blurring at slow shutter speeds.
- **Use fill flash for better outdoor lighting.** Just as with portraits, a tiny bit of flash typically improves close-ups when the sun is your primary light source. You may need to reduce the flash output slightly, via the camera's Flash Exposure Compensation control. Chapter 7 offers details.

  Keep in mind that the maximum shutter speed possible when you use the built-in flash is 1/200 second. So in extremely bright light, you may need to use a high f-stop setting to avoid overexposing the picture. You also can lower the ISO speed setting, if it's not already all the way down to ISO 100.
- **When shooting indoors, try not to use flash as your primary light source.** Because you're shooting at close range, the light from your flash may be too harsh even at a low Flash Exposure Compensation setting. If flash is inevitable, turn on as many room lights as possible to reduce the flash power that's needed — even a hardware store shop light can work in a pinch as a lighting source. Remember that if you have multiple light sources, though, you may need to tweak the White Balance setting.
- **To get *very* close to your subject, invest in a macro lens or a set of diopters.** A true macro lens is an expensive proposition; expect to pay around $200 or more. If you enjoy capturing the tiny details in life, it's worth the investment.

  For a less expensive way to go, you can spend about $40 for a set of *diopters,* which are sort of like reading glasses you screw onto your existing lens. Diopters come in several strengths: +1, +2, +4, and so on, with a higher number indicating a greater magnifying power. In fact, a diopter was used to capture the rose in Figure 9-12. The left image shows the closest shot possible with the regular lens; to produce the right image, a +6 diopter was attached. The downfall of diopters, sadly, is that they typically produce images that are very soft around the edges, as in Figure 9-12 — a problem that doesn't occur with a good macro lens.

No diopter

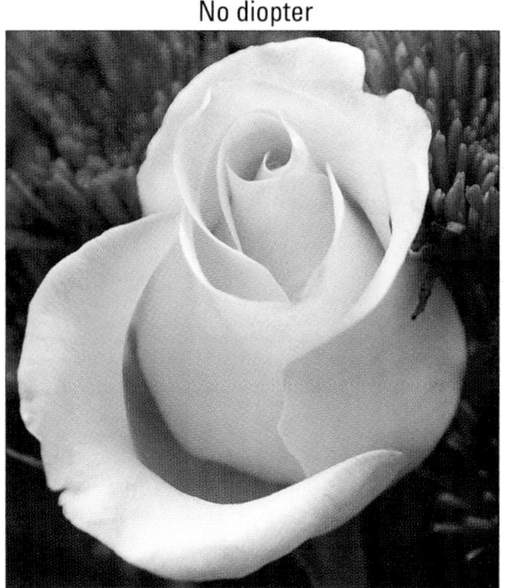

+6 diopter

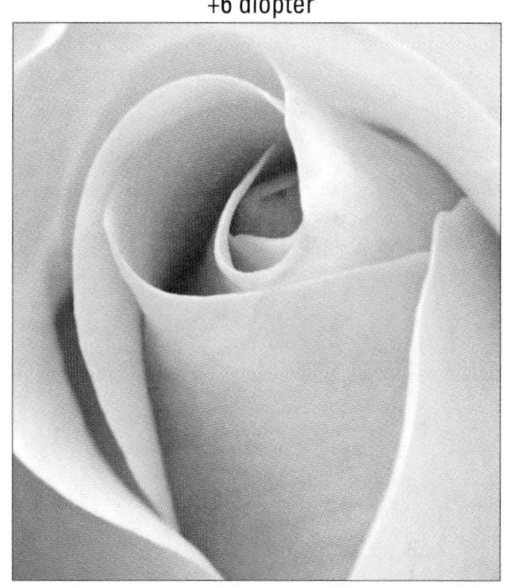

Figure 9-12: To extend the close-focus ability of a lens, add magnifying diopters.

Coping with Special Situations

A few subjects and shooting situations pose some additional challenges not already covered in earlier sections. So to close this chapter, here's a quick list of ideas for tackling a variety of common tough-shot photos:

- **Shooting through glass:** To capture subjects that are behind glass, such as animals at a zoo, you can try a couple tricks. First, set your camera to manual focusing — the glass barrier can give the autofocus mechanism fits. Disable your flash to avoid creating any unwanted reflections, too. Then, if you can get close enough, your best odds are to put the lens right up to the glass. (Be careful not to scratch your lens.) If you must stand farther away, try to position your lens at a 90-degree angle to the glass. I used this approach in Figure 9-13.

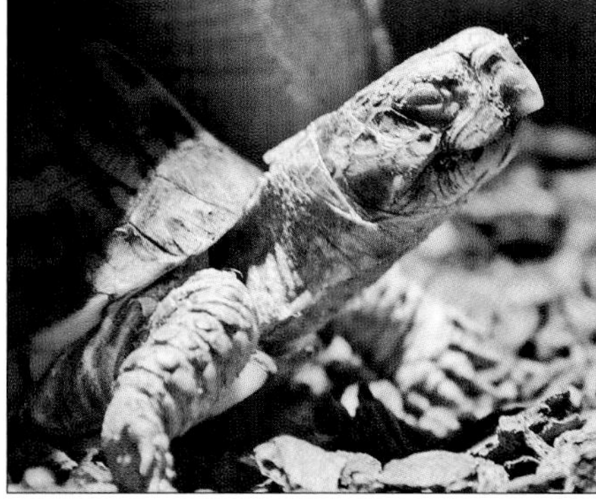

Figure 9-13: To photograph subjects that are behind glass, use manual focusing and disable flash.

- **Shooting out a car window:** Set the camera to shutter-priority autoexposure or manual mode and dial in a fast shutter speed to compensate for the movement of the car. Also turn on image stabilization, if your lens offers it. Oh, and keep a tight grip on your camera.
- **Shooting fireworks:** First off, use a tripod; fireworks require a long exposure, and trying to handhold your camera simply isn't going to work. If using a zoom lens, zoom out to the shortest focal length (widest angle). Switch to manual focusing and set focus at infinity (the farthest focus point possible on your lens). Set the exposure mode to manual, choose a relatively high f-stop setting — say, f/16 or so — and start at a shutter speed of 1 to 5 seconds. From there, it's simply a matter of experimenting with different shutter speeds. Also play with the timing of the shutter release, starting some exposures at the moment the fireworks are shot up, some at the moment they burst open, and so on. For the example featured in Figure 9-14, I used a shutter speed of about 5 seconds and began the exposure as the rocket was going up — that's what creates the "corkscrew" of light that rises up through the frame.

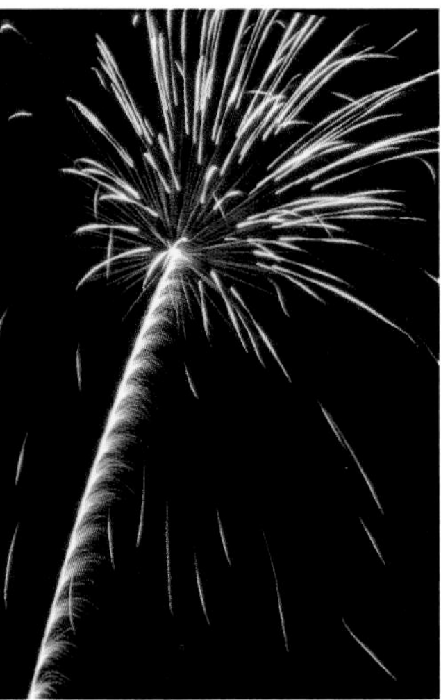

Figure 9-14: I used a shutter speed of 5 seconds to capture this fireworks shot.

Be especially gentle when you press the shutter button — with a very slow shutter, you can easily create enough camera movement to blur the image. If you purchased the accessory remote control for your camera, this is a good situation in which to use it. See the Drive mode discussion in Chapter 2 for more information about remote-control shooting.

- **Shooting in strong backlighting:** When the light behind your subject is very strong, the result is often an underexposed subject. You can try using flash to better expose the subject, assuming that you're shooting in an exposure mode that permits flash. The Highlight Tone Priority feature, which captures the image in a way that retains better detail in the shadows without blowing out highlights, may also help. (Chapter 7 offers an example.)

But for another creative choice, you can purposely underexpose the subject to create a silhouette effect, as shown in Figure 9-15. Base your exposure on the brightest areas of the background so that the darker areas of the frame remain dark.

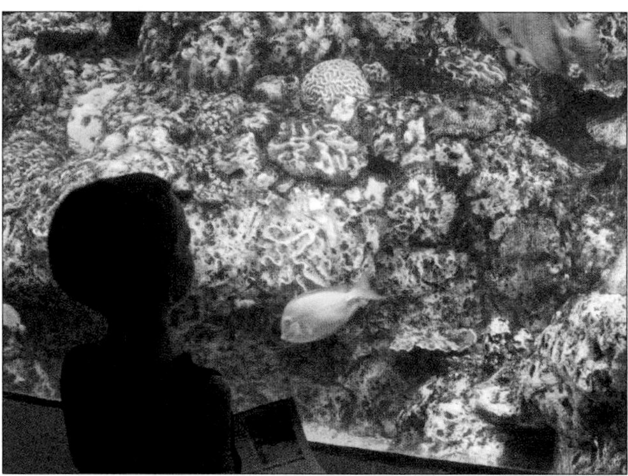

Figure 9-15: Experiment with shooting backlit subjects in silhouette.

Part IV
The Part of Tens

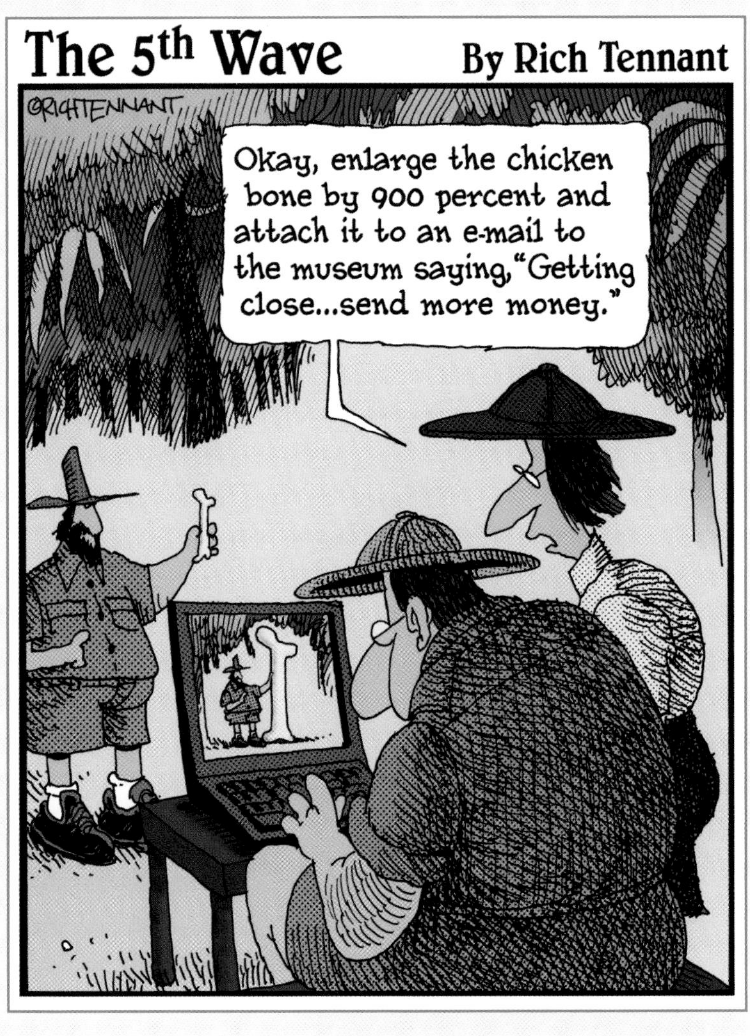

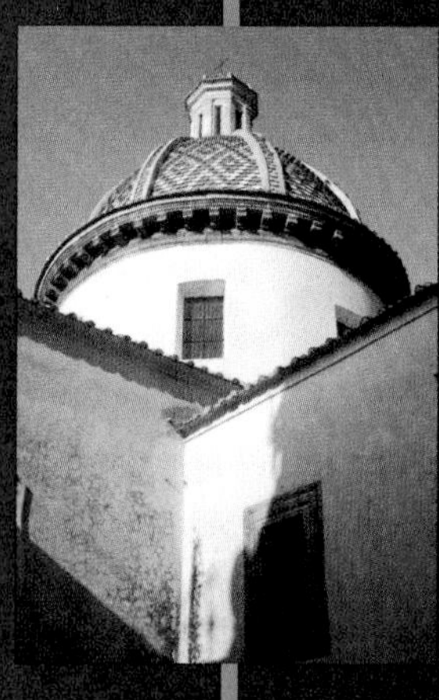

In this part . . .

In time-honored *For Dummies* tradition, this part of the book contains additional tidbits of information presented in the always popular Top Ten list format.

Chapter 10 shows you ten camera-customization options that have yet to make an appearance in the book, such as creating your own camera menu. Following that, Chapter 11 introduces you to ten camera functions that I consider specialty tools — bonus options that may not top the list of features I suggest you study, but are nonetheless interesting to explore when you have a free moment or two.

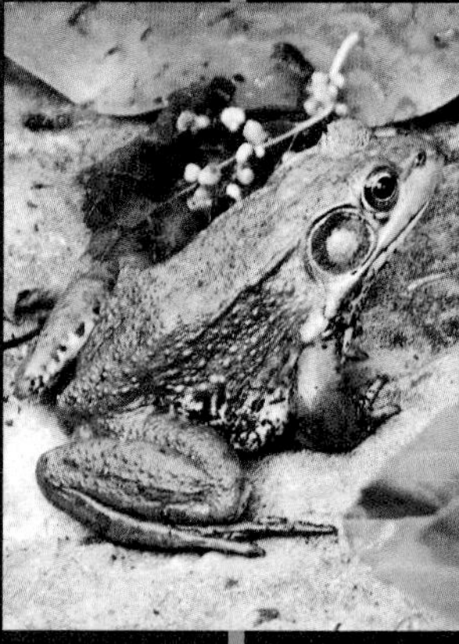

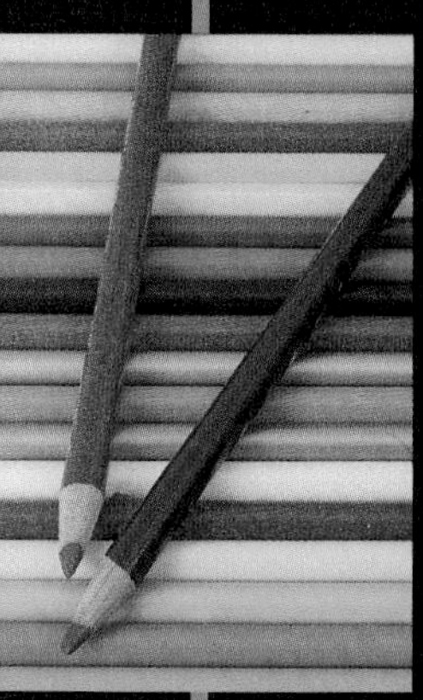

10

Ten More Ways to Customize Your Camera

In This Chapter

- Changing the function of the Set button
- Turning off the beep and AF-Assist beam
- Creating your own folders and camera menu
- Customizing a few other camera behaviors

Have you ever tried to cook dinner in someone else's house or work from another colleague's desk? Why is *nothing* stored in the right place? The coffee cups, for example, should be stowed in the cabinet above the coffee maker, and yet there they are, way across the kitchen, in the cupboard near the fridge. And everyone knows that the highlighter pens belong in the middle top drawer, not the second one on the left. Yeesh.

In the same way, you may find a particular aspect of your camera's design illogical or maybe a tad inconvenient. If so, check out this chapter, which introduces you to ten customization options not considered in earlier chapters. You can give the Set button a new job, for example, silence the camera's beeper, and even create your own camera menu.

Changing the Function of the Set Button

Normally, the main role of the Set button is to select items from the camera menus and Quick Settings screens. When you shoot in the P, Tv, Av, or M exposure modes, though, you can set the button to perform the following tasks when no menus are displayed:

- **Image Quality:** Displays the screen where you can change the Image Quality settings.
- **Flash Exposure Compensation:** Displays the meter that enables you to adjust flash power.
- **LCD Monitor On/Off.** Toggles the Shooting Settings screen on and off. Note that this function doesn't work in Live View mode.
- **Menu display:** Brings up the menus. After the menus are onscreen, you use the button to select menu options.
- **ISO Speed:** Displays the screen where you can adjust the ISO Speed setting, just as if you had pressed the ISO button.

You establish the button's purpose via Custom Function 7, as illustrated in Figure 10-1. To activate the options, just tap one or press the Set button. To scroll to the fourth and fifth options (not shown in the figure), press the up/down cross keys or tap the arrows on the right side of the screen (also not shown in the figure). Tap the Set icon or press the Set button to lock in your choice. Chapter 1 has a primer on navigating the Custom Function menus if you need additional help.

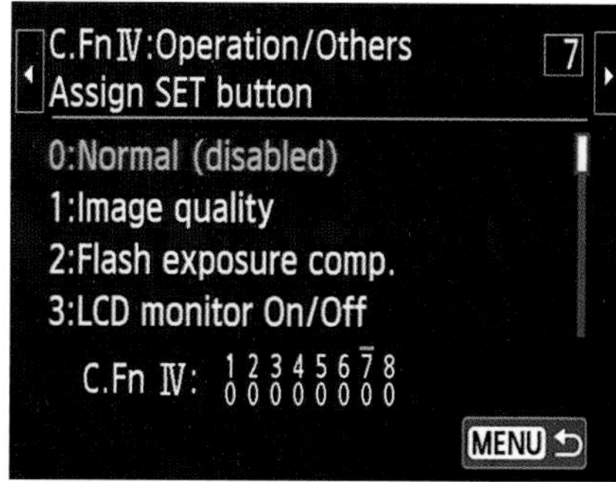

Figure 10-1: You can configure the Set button to perform an extra function during shooting.

To go back to the default setting, return to the Custom Function menu and select option 0 (Normal). The button then reverts to its original single-minded purpose, which is to lock in your menu and Quick Settings screen selections.

Customizing the AE Lock and Shutter Button

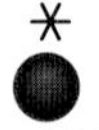

By default, you initiate autofocusing by pressing the shutter button halfway and lock autoexposure by pressing the AE (autoexposure) Lock button. I recommend that you stick with this setup while learning about your camera — otherwise, my instructions won't work. But after you feel more comfortable, you may want to customize the locking behaviors of the two buttons.

To configure the buttons, set the Mode dial to P, Tv, Av, or M. Then head for Custom Function 6. As shown in Figure 10-2, you can choose from the following configuration options. The part of the option name before the slash indicates the result of pressing the shutter button halfway; the name after the slash indicates the result of pressing the AE Lock button.

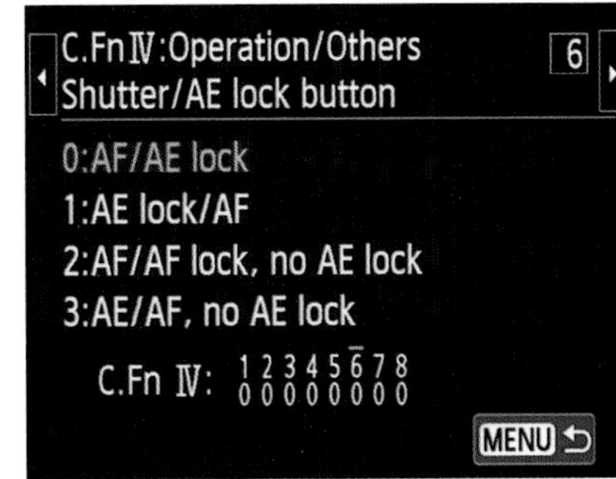

Figure 10-2: Adjust autoexposure and autofocus lock behavior via Custom Function 6.

- **AF/AE Lock:** This is the default setting. Pressing the shutter button halfway initiates autofocus; pressing the AE Lock button locks autoexposure.
- **AE Lock/AF:** With this option, pressing the shutter button halfway locks autoexposure. To initiate autofocusing, you instead press the AE Lock button. In other words, this mode is the exact opposite of the default setup.
- **AF/AF Lock, no AE Lock:** Pressing the shutter button halfway initiates autofocusing and exposure metering, and pressing the AE Lock button locks focus. Autoexposure lock isn't possible.

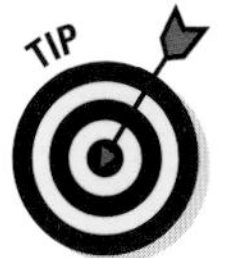

This option is designed to prevent focusing mishaps when you use AI Servo autofocusing, a viewfinder-shooting option explained in Chapter 8. In AI Servo mode, the autofocus motor continually adjusts focus from the time you press the shutter button halfway until the time you take the image. This feature helps keep moving objects focused. But if something moves in front of your subject, the camera may mistakenly focus on that object instead. To cope with that possibility, this locking option enables you to initiate autofocusing as usual, by pressing the shutter button halfway. But at any time before you take the picture, you can hold down the AE Lock button to stop the autofocusing motor from adjusting focus. Releasing the button restarts autofocusing. Exposure is set at the time you take the picture.

Additionally, when you enable continuous autofocusing in Live View or Movie modes, choosing this setting enables you to interrupt autofocusing by holding down the AE Lock button. Release the button to restart continous autofocusing. Chapter 4 has details on Live View and Movie mode autofocusing.

- **AE/AF, no AE Lock:** In this mode, press the shutter button halfway to initiate autoexposure and press the AE Lock button to autofocus. In AI Servo mode, continuous autofocusing occurs only while you hold down the AE Lock button, which is helpful if your subject repeatedly moves and then stops. Exposure is set at the moment you take the picture.

Disabling the AF-Assist Beam

In dim lighting, your camera may emit an AF (autofocus)-assist beam from the built-in flash when you press the shutter button halfway — assuming that the flash unit is open, of course. This pulse of light helps the camera "see" its target better, improving the performance of the autofocusing system.

If you're shooting in a situation where the AF-assist beam may be distracting, you can disable it in the P, TV, Av, or M exposure modes. Make the change via Custom Function 4, as shown in Figure 10-3. You get the following choices:

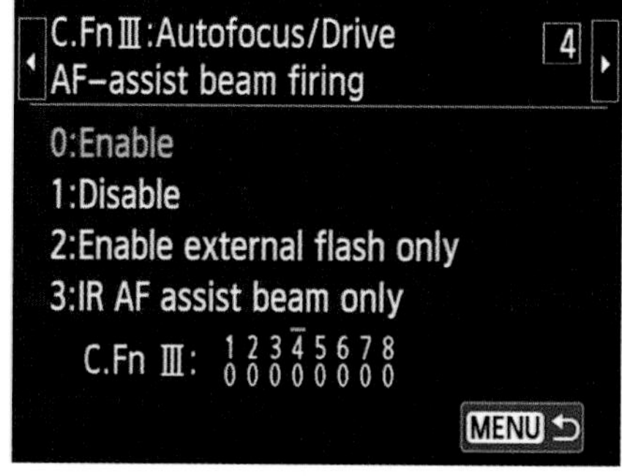

Figure 10-3: You can disable the autofocus-assist beam.

- **Enable:** This setting is the default and turns the AF-Assist Beam function on.
- **Disable:** I know you can figure this one out.
- **Enable External Flash Only:** Choose this setting to permit an external flash unit to emit the beam but prevent the built-in flash from doing so. (The idea is to save you the time and hassle of revisiting the Custom Function setting to enable or disable the beam every time you switch from the built-in flash to an external flash — two settings in one, if you will.) The external flash must be a compatible EX-series Speedlite unit.

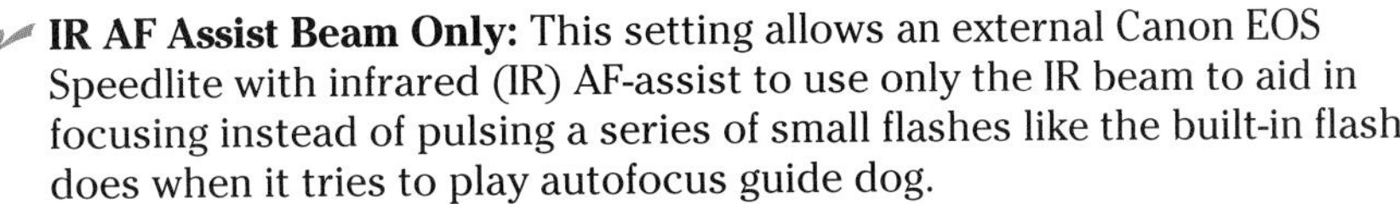

- **IR AF Assist Beam Only:** This setting allows an external Canon EOS Speedlite with infrared (IR) AF-assist to use only the IR beam to aid in focusing instead of pulsing a series of small flashes like the built-in flash does when it tries to play autofocus guide dog.

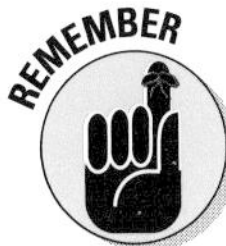

An external Canon Speedlite has its own provision to disable the AF-assist beam. If you turn off the beam on the flash unit, it won't light no matter which Custom Function setting you choose.

Keep in mind that without the aid of the assist beam, the camera may have trouble autofocusing in dim lighting. The easiest solution is to focus manually; Chapter 1 shows you how.

Silencing the Camera

By default, your camera beeps after certain operations, such as after it sets focus when you use autofocusing. If you need the camera to hush up, set the Beep option on Shooting Menu 1 to Disable, as shown in Figure 10-4.

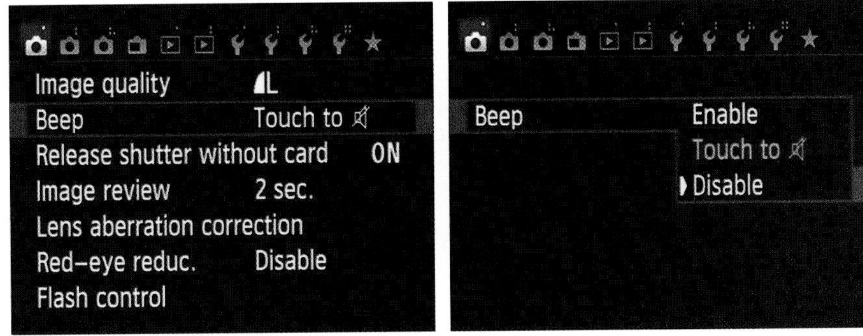

Figure 10-4: To quiet the camera's beeper, set this option to Off.

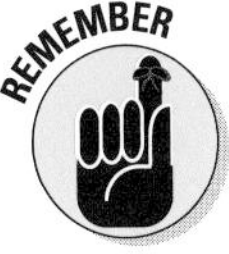

Note that if you set the option to Enable, you also hear a tone when you tap touchscreen-controlled options. If you don't want to hear that tone but still want the non-touchscreen beeps, set the option to Touch to Silence (instead of the word Silence, you see a speaker with a slash through it on the menu). That's the default setting, by the way; it's selected on the left in Figure 10-4. See "Using the Touchscreen" in Chapter 1 for details about this camera feature.

Preventing Shutter Release without a Memory Card

By default, you can take a picture without any memory card in the camera. Wait — let me rephrase that: When you press the shutter button, the camera will release the shutter to take a *temporary* photo that it stores in its internal memory. The picture appears on the monitor for a few seconds but then disappears and can't be retrieved. During the instant image-review period, your camera warns you that there's no card in the camera, as shown on the left in Figure 10-5. You also see a warning message on the monitor if no card is installed when you turn on the camera.

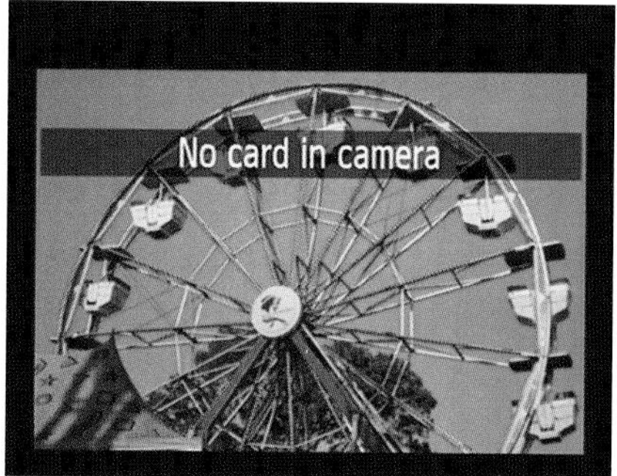

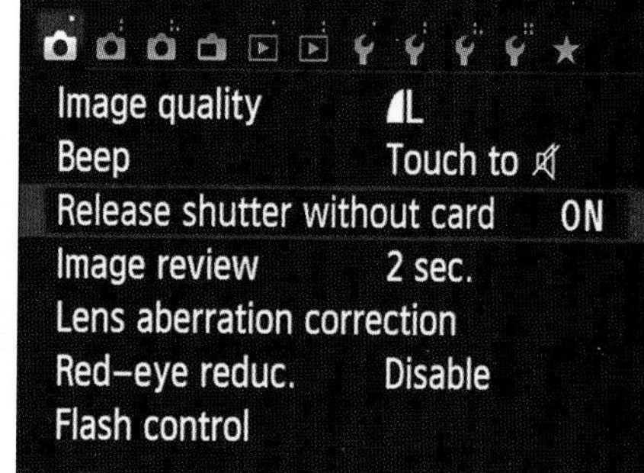

Figure 10-5: Pictures taken without a memory card live for only a few seconds.

If you're wondering about the point of this option, it's designed for use in camera stores, enabling salespeople to demonstrate cameras without having to keep a memory card in every model. For those of us not in that biz, I have mixed feelings: On one hand, if you turn the feature off, you can press the shutter button til the cows come home with no result — and you may not realize that the lack of the memory card is the issue. On the other hand, if you enable the feature but some distraction causes you to miss that instant-review warning, you may think you've recorded a picture when you haven't. I leave it up to you decide which route you want to go. You turn the feature on and off via the Release Shutter without Card option, found on Shooting Menu 1 and shown on the right in Figure 10-5.

Reducing the Number of Exposure Stops

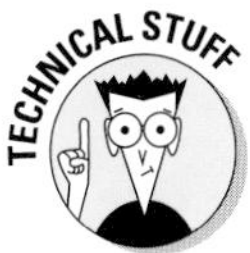

In photography, the term *stop* refers to an increment of exposure. To increase exposure by one stop means to adjust the aperture or shutter speed to allow twice as much light into the camera as the current settings permit. To reduce exposure a stop, you use settings that allow half as much light. Doubling or halving the ISO value also adjusts exposure by one stop.

By default, all the major exposure-related settings on your camera are based on one-third stop adjustments. For example, when you adjust the Exposure Compensation value, a feature that enables you to request a brighter or darker picture than the camera's autoexposure system thinks is correct, you can choose settings of EV 0.0 (no adjustment), +0.3, +0.7, and +1.0 (a full stop of adjustment).

If you prefer, you can tell the camera to present exposure adjustments in half-stop increments so that you don't have to cycle through as many settings each time you want to make a change. Make your preferences known via Custom Function 1, as illustrated in Figure 10-6.

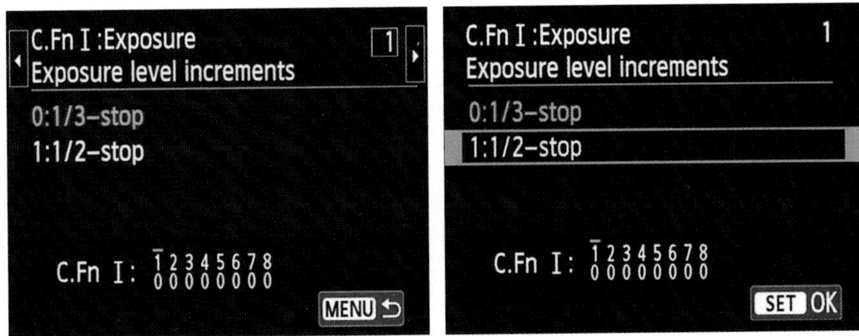

Figure 10-6: By default, exposure settings are based on 1/3-stop adjustments; you can change to 1/2-stop adjustments via this Custom Function.

Note that when you use the 1/2-stop setting, the exposure meter appears slightly different in the Shooting Settings display and Live View display than you see it in this book: Only one intermediate notch appears between each number on the meter instead of the usual two. The viewfinder meter doesn't change, but the exposure indicator bar appears as a double line if you set the Exposure Compensation value to a half-step value (+0.5, +1.5, and so on).

Check out Chapter 7 for the complete story on exposure.

Creating Your Very Own Camera Menu

Canon does a good job of making it easy to change the most commonly used camera settings. You can access many critical options by pressing the buttons on the camera body, and others require only a quick trip to the camera menus. To make the process even simpler, you can create your own, custom menu containing up to six items from the camera's other menus, as shown in Figure 10-7. Logically enough, the custom menu goes by the name My Menu and is represented by the green star icon.

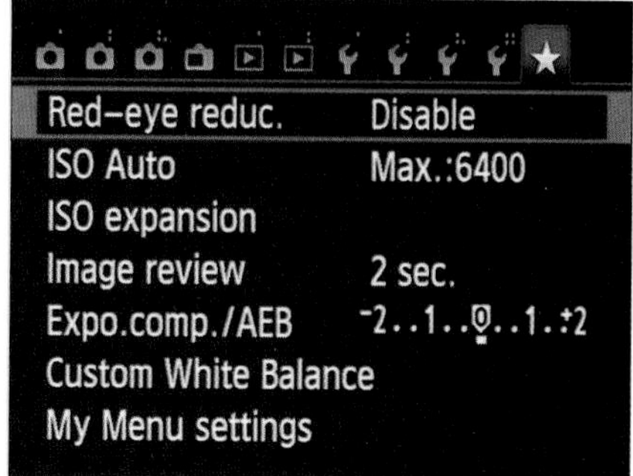

Figure 10-7: Group your top six menu items together by using the My Menu feature.

To create your menu, take these steps:

1. **Set the camera Mode dial to P, Tv, Av, or M.**

   You can create and order from the custom menu only in these exposure modes.

2. **Display the My Menu screen.**

   Initially, the screen shows only a single item, as shown on the left in Figure 10-8.

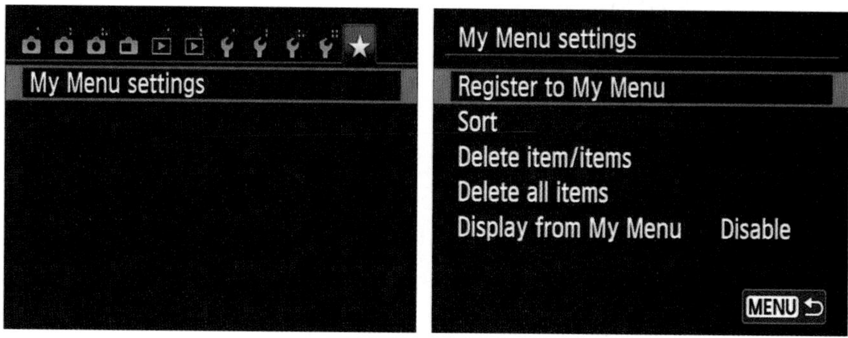

Figure 10-8: Choose Register to My Menu to add an item to your custom menu.

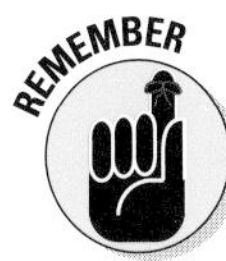

3. **Choose My Menu Settings.**

   To choose a menu item, either tap it or highlight it and press the Set button. Either way, you see the screen on the right in Figure 10-8.

4. **Choose Register to My Menu.**

   You see a scrolling list that contains every item found on the camera's other menus, as shown on the left in Figure 10-9.

5. **Choose the first item to include on your custom menu.**

   Again, you choose the item by tapping it and then tapping Set or by highlighting it and pressing the Set button. You can scroll the menu screen by using the up/down cross keys or tapping the scroll arrows, labeled in Figure 10-9.

   To add a specific Custom Function to your menu, scroll *past* the item named Custom Functions to find and highlight the individual function. (The item named Custom Functions simply puts the Custom Functions menu item on your menu, and you still have to wade through multiple levels of steps to reach your function.)

   After you choose the item, you see a confirmation screen, as shown on the right in Figure 10-9.

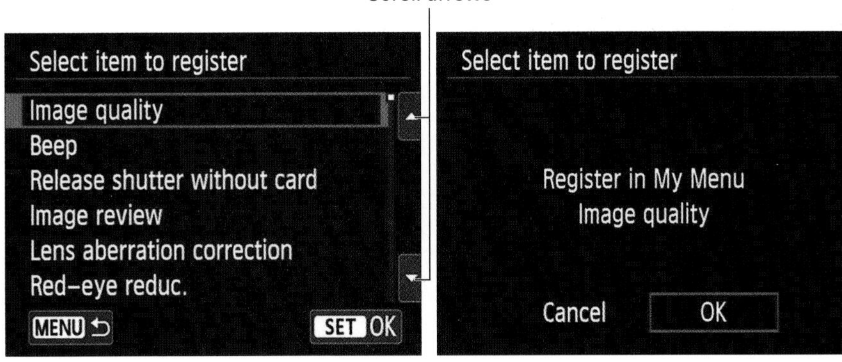

Figure 10-9: Highlight an item to put on your menu and press Set.

6. **Tap OK or highlight it and press Set.**

   You return to the list of menu options. The option you just added to your menu is dimmed in the list.

7. **Repeat Steps 5 and 6 to add up to five additional items to your menu.**

8. **Tap the Menu icon or press the Menu button.**

   You then see the My Menu settings screen.

9. **Tap the Menu icon or press the Menu button again.**

   The My Menu screen appears, with the items you added listed on the menu.

After creating your menu, you can further customize and manage it as follows:

- **Give your menu priority.** You can tell the camera that you want it to automatically display your menu anytime you press the Menu button. To do so, choose My Menu Settings on the main My Menu screen to display the screen shown on the right side of Figure 10-8. Then set the Display from My Menu option to Enable.
- **Change the order of the list of menu items.** Once again, navigate to the right screen in Figure 10-8. This time, choose the Sort option. Choose a menu item and then tap the up/down arrows at the bottom of the screen or press the up/down cross keys to move the menu item up or down in the list. Tap the Set icon or press the Set button to glue the menu item in its new position. Tap the Menu icon or press the menu button to return to the My Menu Settings screen; press or tap Menu again to return to your custom menu.
- **Delete menu items.** Display your menu, choose My Menu Settings, and then choose Delete Item/Items (refer to the right screen in Figure 10-8). Choose the menu item that you want to delete; on the resulting confirmation screen, tap OK or highlight it and press the Set button.

  To remove all items from your custom menu, choose Delete All Items (again, refer to the right side of Figure 10-8) and then tap OK on the confirmation screen or highlight it and press the Set button.

Creating Custom Folders

Normally, your camera automatically creates folders to store your images. The first folder has the name 100Canon; the second, 101Canon; the third, 102Canon; and so on. Each folder can hold 9999 photos. If you want to create a new folder before the existing one is full, choose Select Folder from Setup Menu 1 and then choose Create Folder, as illustrated in Figure 10-10. You might take this organizational step so that you can segregate work photos from personal photos, for example.

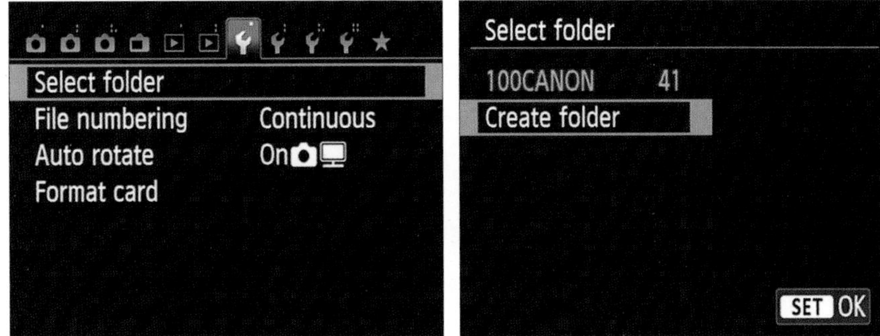

Figure 10-10: You can create a new image-storage folder at any time.

The camera asks for permission to create the folder; tap OK or highlight it and press Set. The folder is automatically assigned the next available folder number and is selected as the active folder — the one that will hold any new photos you shoot. Tap Set or press the Set button to return to Setup Menu 1.

To make a different folder as the active folder, choose Select Folder again, choose the folder you want to use, and tap Set or press the Set button.

Turning Off the Shooting Settings Screen

When you turn on your camera, the monitor automatically displays the Shooting Settings screen. At least, it does if you stick with the default setting selected for Custom Function 8, which bears the lengthy name LCD Display When Power On and appears in Figure 10-11.

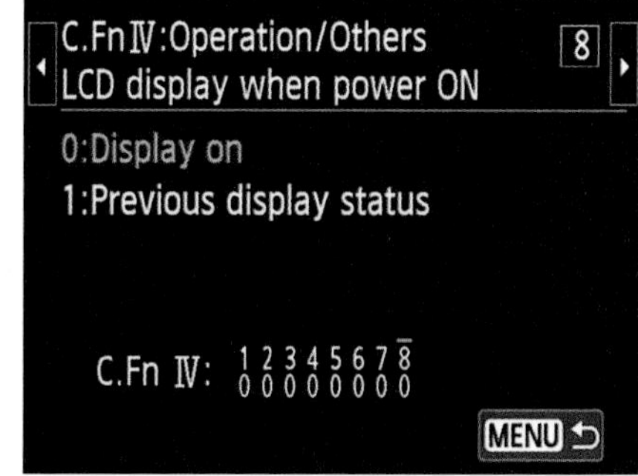

Figure 10-11: This option affects whether the Shooting Settings screen appears when you turn on the camera.

You can prevent the monitor from displaying the screen every time you power up the camera, if you choose. The monitor is one of the biggest drains on the camera battery, so limiting it to displaying information only when you need it can extend the time between battery charges.

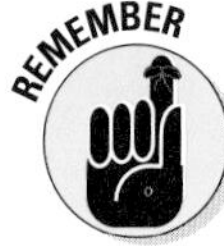

As with other Custom Functions, this option works only when the camera is set to one of the advanced exposure modes — in other modes, the screen still appears automatically. Still, any battery savings can be helpful when you're running low on juice.

To take advantage of this feature, set Custom Function 8 to Previous Display Status, exit the menus, and then press the shutter button halfway and release it. You get a temporary display of the Shooting Settings screen. Press the Info button to turn off the monitor and then turn off the camera.

When you turn on the camera again, the monitor doesn't automatically display the Shooting Settings screen — as long as the Mode dial is set to an advanced shooting mode, that is. To view the screen, press the Info button. Your first press displays the Camera Settings screen, press again to get to the Shooting Settings screen.

However, note that if the Shooting Settings screen is displayed when you turn off the camera, it *does* appear the next time you turn on the camera. Note the Custom Function setting name: Previous Display Status. It means what the name implies: The camera preserves the current monitor status even if you turn the camera off and then back on again. I don't know about you, but I'm already memory-challenged — I don't need to add one more thing to the list of items to remember. So I leave this option at the default and use the Info button to turn the monitor off when needed.

Changing the Color Space from sRGB to Adobe RGB

By default, your camera captures images using the *sRGB color mode,* which simply refers to an industry-standard spectrum of colors. (The *s* is for *standard,* and the *RGB* is for *red, green, blue,* which are the primary colors in the digital color world.) The sRGB color mode was created to help ensure color consistency as an image moves from camera (or scanner) to monitor and printer; the idea was to create a spectrum of colors that all these devices can reproduce.

However, the sRGB color spectrum leaves out some colors that *can* be reproduced in print and onscreen, at least by some devices. So, as an alternative, your camera also enables you to shoot in the Adobe RGB color mode — which includes a larger spectrum (or *gamut*) of colors. Figure 10-12 offers an illustration of the two spectrums.

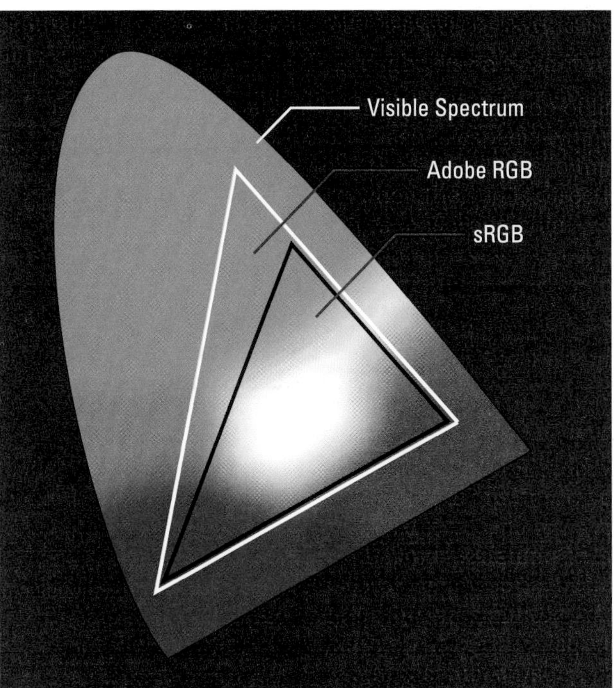

Figure 10-12: Adobe RGB includes some colors not found in the sRGB spectrum but requires some color-management savvy to use to its full advantage.

Some colors in the Adobe RGB spectrum can't be reproduced in print. (The printer just substitutes the closest printable color, if necessary.) Still, I usually shoot in Adobe RGB mode because I see no reason to limit myself to a smaller spectrum from the get-go.

However, just because I use Adobe RGB doesn't mean that it's right for you. First, if you plan to print and share your photos without making any adjustments in your photo editor, you're better off sticking with sRGB because most printers and web browsers are designed around that color space. Second, to retain all your original Adobe RGB colors when you work with your photos, your editing software must support that color space — not all programs do. You also must be willing to study the whole topic of digital color a little bit because you need to use some specific settings to avoid really mucking up the color works.

If you want to capture images in Adobe RGB instead of sRGB, you can make the adjustment via the Color Space option on Shooting Menu 2, shown in Figure 10-13.

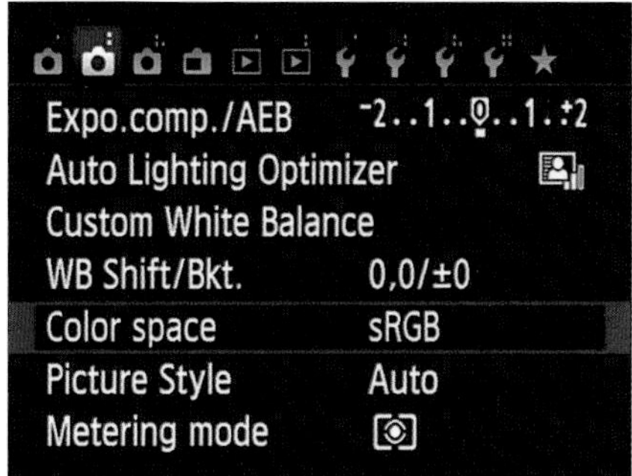

Figure 10-13: Choose sRGB unless you're savvy about image color management.

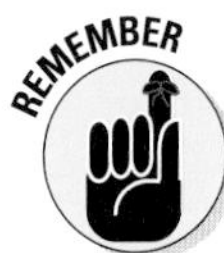

You can choose this color mode — in fact, all the options on Shooting Menus 2 and 3 — only when you shoot in the advanced exposure modes: P, Tv, Av, and M. In all other modes, the camera automatically selects sRGB as the color space. Additionally, your color space selection is applied to only your JPEG images; with Raw captures, you can select the color space as you process the Raw image. (See Chapter 6 for details about Raw-image processing.)

After you transfer pictures to your computer, you can tell whether you captured an image in the Adobe RGB color space by looking at its filename: Adobe RGB images start with an underscore, as in _MG_0627.jpg. Pictures captured in the sRGB color space start with the letter *I,* as in IMG_0627.jpg.

11

Ten Features to Explore on a Rainy Day

In This Chapter

- Taking advantage of Mirror Lockup shooting
- Tagging files with cleaning instructions and copyright data
- Investigating printing features and special-effects filters
- Creating slide shows and video snapshots
- Trimming frames from the beginning and end of a movie

Consider this chapter the literary equivalent of the end of one of those late-night infomercial offers — the part where the host exclaims, "But wait! There's more!" Options covered here aren't the sort of features that drive people to choose one camera over another, and they may come in handy only for certain users, on certain occasions. Still, they're included at no extra charge with your camera, so check 'em out when you have a spare moment. Who knows; you may discover just the solution you need for one of your photography problems.

Enabling Mirror Lockup

One component in the optical system of a dSLR camera is a mirror that moves when you press the shutter button. The vibration caused by the mirror movement can result in image blur when you use a very slow shutter speed, shoot with a long telephoto lens, or take extreme close-ups. To eliminate this possibility, your camera offers *mirror lockup.* When you enable this feature, the mirror movement is completed well before the shot is recorded, thus preventing mirror-related camera shake.

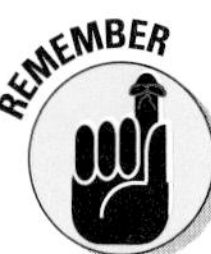

Mirror-lockup shooting requires a special picture-taking process:

1. **Set the Mode dial to P, Tv, Av, or M.**

   Mirror lockup isn't available in the other exposure modes.

2. **Set Custom Function 5, Mirror Lockup, to Enable, as shown in Figure 11-1.**

   For help navigating Custom Functions, see Chapter 1.

3. **Frame your shot.**
4. **If you're using manual focusing, set focus.**
5. **Press and hold the shutter button halfway.**

   This step engages autoexposure and autofocusing, if you're using that focusing method.

6. **Press the shutter button all the way down to lock up the mirror. Then release the button.**

   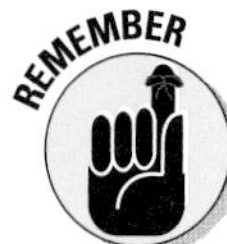

   You can no longer see anything through the viewfinder now. Don't panic — that's normal. The mirror's function is to display in the viewfinder the scene that the lens will capture, and mirror lockup prevents it from serving that purpose.

7. **Press the shutter button all the way again.**

   The camera takes the picture.

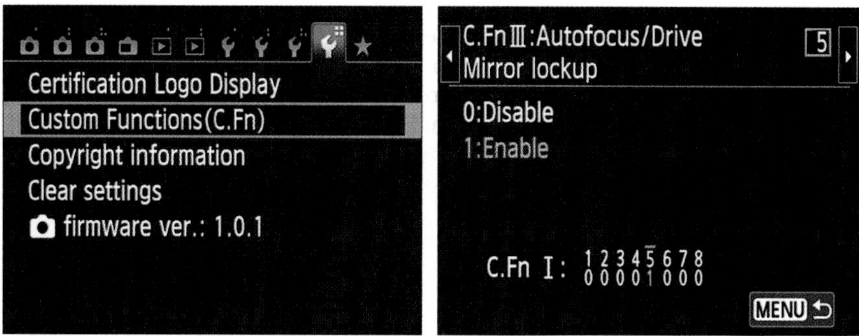

Figure 11-1: Mirror lockup prevents camera shake caused by the movement of the optical system's mirror.

Using a tripod or other support is critical to getting shake-free shots in situations that call for mirror lockup. For even more protection, set your camera to the Self-Timer: 2 second mode, introduced in Chapter 2, and take your hands off the camera after you press the shutter button in Step 6. The picture is taken two seconds after mirror lockup occurs. If you own a remote control unit, you can instead use it to trigger the shutter release.

A couple more fine points:

- **Drive mode:** Even if the Drive mode is set to Continuous or Self-Timer: Continuous, the camera behaves as it does in Single mode: You get one picture for each press of the shutter button.
- **Auto shutoff:** If you don't press any buttons for 30 seconds after you lock up the mirror, it automatically flips back down.

Adding Cleaning Instructions to Images

By default, your camera performs a sensor-cleaning routine every time you turn the camera on or off. (This feature is controlled via the Sensor Clean option on Setup Menu 3, covered in Chapter 1.) This automated sensor cleaning normally is enough to keep the sensor dust-free. But if small spots appear consistently on your images, your sensor may need deeper cleaning. The best solution is to take your camera to a repair shop for professional cleaning; I don't recommend that you clean the sensor yourself because you can easily ruin your camera if you don't know what you're doing.

Until you can have the camera cleaned, however, you can use a software-based dust-removal filter found in Digital Photo Professional, one of the programs that ships with your camera. You start by recording a data file that maps the location of the dust spots on the sensor. To do this, you need a white piece of paper or another white surface and a lens that can achieve a focal length of 55mm or greater. (Both of the kit lenses available for your camera qualify.) Then take these steps:

1. **Set the lens focal length at 55mm or longer.**
2. **Switch the lens to manual focusing.**
3. **Set focus at infinity.**

Some lenses have a mark that indicates the infinity position — the symbol looks like a number 8 lying on its side. If your lens doesn't have the marking, hold the camera so that the lens is facing you and then turn the lens focusing ring clockwise until it stops.

4. **Set the camera to the P, Tv, Av, or M exposure mode.**

   You can create the dust data file only in these modes.

5. **Display Shooting Menu 3 and choose Dust Delete Data, as shown on the left in Figure 11-2.**

   You see the message shown on the right side of Figure 11-2.

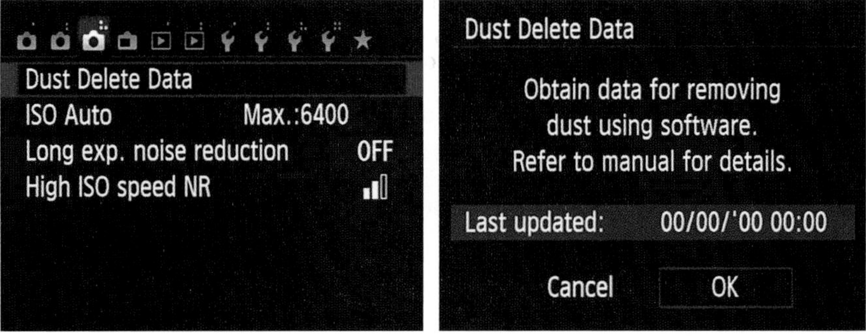

Figure 11-2: You can record dust-removal data that can be read by Digital Photo Professional.

6. **Choose OK.**

   The camera performs its normal internal sensor-cleaning ritual, which takes a second or two. Then you see the instruction screen shown in Figure 11-3.

7. **Position the camera 8 to 12 inches from your white paper.**

   The paper must be large enough to fill the viewfinder.

8. **Press the shutter button all the way to record the Dust Delete Data.**

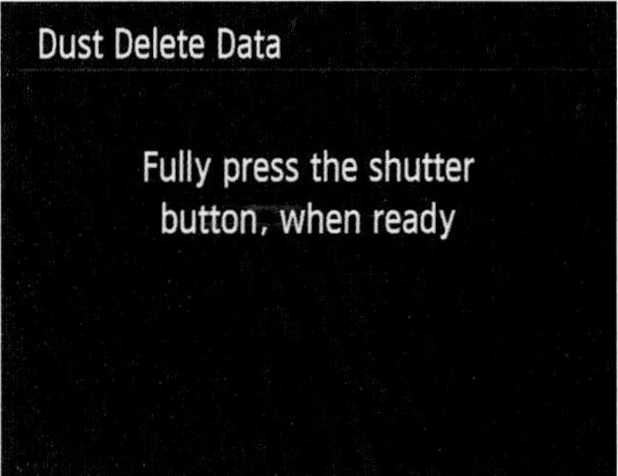

Figure 11-3: You take a picture of a piece of plain white paper to record the dust data.

No picture is taken; the camera just records the Dust Delete Data in its internal memory. If the process was successful, you see a screen with the message "Data obtained."

If the camera can't record the data, the lighting conditions are likely to blame. Make sure that the lighting is even across the entire surface of your paper and that the paper is sufficiently illuminated, and then try again.

9. **Choose OK.**

   The current date appears on the initial Dust Delete Data screen. (Refer to the right screen in Figure 11-2.)

After you create your Dust Delete Data file, the camera attaches the data to every subsequent image, regardless of whether you shoot in the fully automatic or advanced exposure modes.

To clean a photo, open it in Digital Photo Professional and choose Tools➪Start Stamp Tool. Your photo appears in an editing window; click the Apply Dust Delete Data button to start the dust-busting feature. The program's Help system (choose Help➪Digital Photo Professional Help) offers details.

Tagging Files with Your Copyright Claim

By using the Copyright Information feature on Setup Menu 4, you can add copyright information to the image *metadata* (extra data) recorded with the image file. You can view metadata in the Canon software; Chapter 6 shows you how.

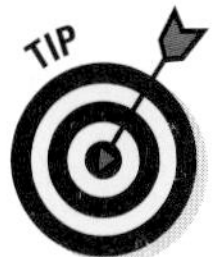

Including a copyright notice is a reasonable first step to prevent people from using your pictures without permission. Anyone who views your picture in a program that can display metadata can see your copyright notice. Obviously, that won't be enough to completely prevent unauthorized use of your images. And technically speaking, you hold the copyright to your photo whether you mark it with your name. But if you ever come to the point of pressing legal action, you can show that you did your due diligence in letting people know that you hold the copyright.

To turn on the copyright function, take these steps:

1. **Set the camera Mode dial to P, Tv, Av, or M.**

   You can create copyright data only in these modes. However, the data is stored with all images you shoot, whether you take them in the advanced or fully automatic exposure modes.

2. **Display Setup Menu 4 and chose Copyright Information, as shown on the left in Figure 11-4.**

   You see the screen shown on the right.

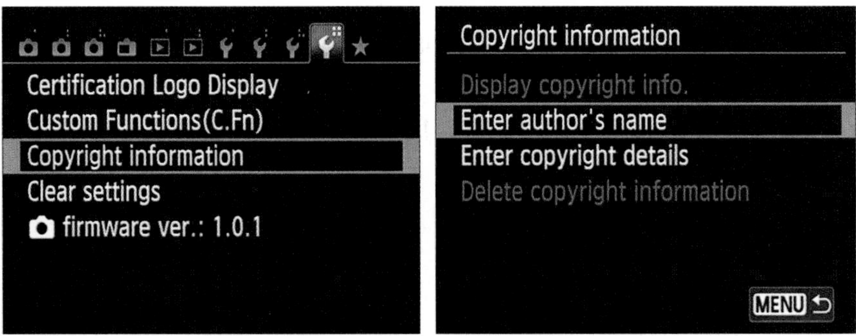

Figure 11-4: Tagging files with your copyright notice lets people know who owns the rights to the picture.

3. **Choose Enter Author's Name.**

   This step opens the data-entry screen, shown on the left side of Figure 11-5.

4. **Enter your name in the text box.**

   Your fastest and easiest option is to use the touchscreen-enabled keyboard: Just tap the letters you want to enter. Tap the symbol labeled Caps/lowercase/numbers in the figure to switch the keyboard from displaying all uppercase letters, all lowercase letters, or numbers and symbols. To move the cursor, tap inside the text or tap the arrows at the end of the text entry box; to erase the character to the left of the cursor, tap the Erase icon, also labeled in the figure.

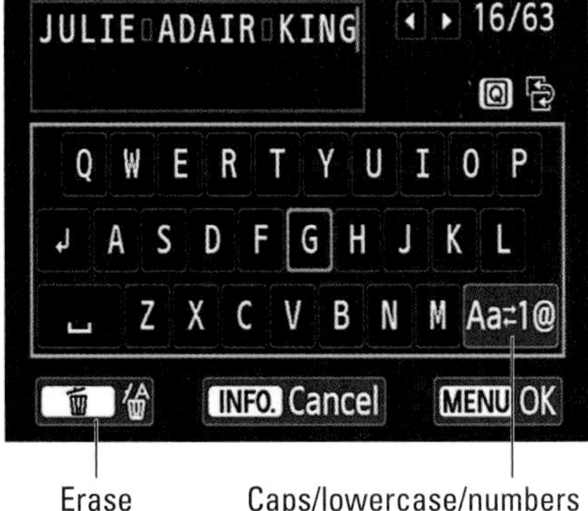

Figure 11-5: Enter your name by tapping on the keyboard.

If you don't want to use the touchscreen, use these button-based techniques instead:

- Press the Quick Control button to alternate between the text box and the keyboard.
- In the keyboard, use the cross keys to highlight the character you want to enter. Then press Set to enter the character in the text box.
- In the text box, use the cross keys to move the cursor.
- To delete a character, move the cursor just past the letter and press the Erase button.

5. **Tap the Menu icon or press the Menu button.**

   You see a screen saying that your text will be saved.

6. **Choose OK.**

   You see the Copyright Information screen shown on the left in Figure 11-6.

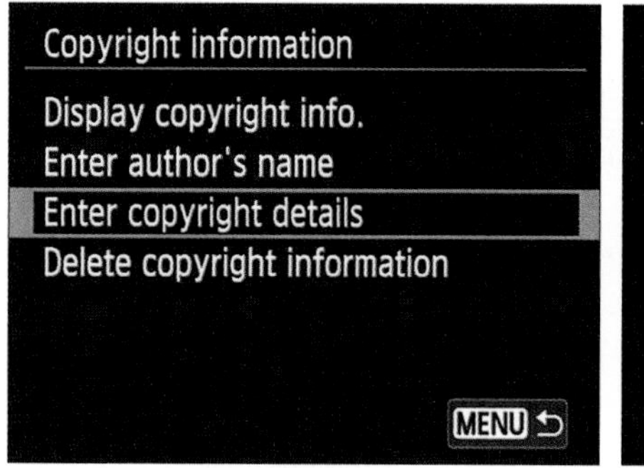

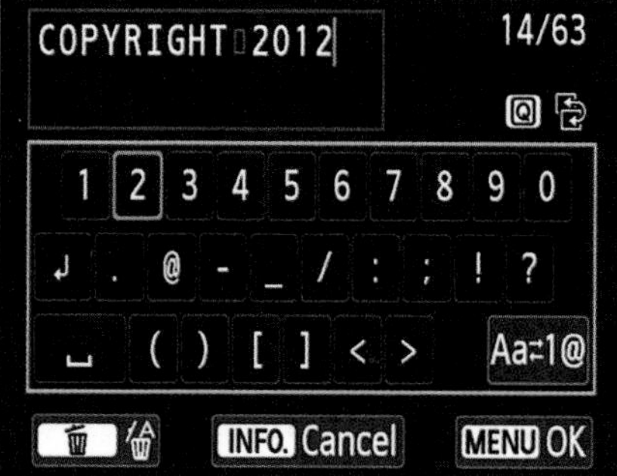

Figure 11-6: Enter the copyright data next.

7. **Choose Enter Copyright Details and enter additional copyright data.**

   You might want to add the word Copyright and the year, for example, or your company name. Use the same text entry process you used to enter your name.

8. **Tap the Menu icon or press the Menu button.**

   Wait for the camera to save the additional data.

9. **Choose OK.**

   Back you go to the main Copyright Information screen.

10. **To check the accuracy of your data, choose Display Copyright Info, as shown on the left in Figure 11-7.**

    You see a screen similar to the one on the right in the figure.

Figure 11-7: Double-check the copyright notice.

11. **Exit to Setup Menu 4 by tapping Menu twice or pressing the Menu button twice.**

You can later disable the copyright tagging by using the Delete Copyright Information option (shown on the left in Figure 11-7).

Exploring Two Special Printing Options

Through the Print Order option on Playback Menu 1, shown in Figure 11-8, you can access two features that enable you to print directly from your memory card or the camera:

- **DPOF (Digital Print Order Format):** With this option, you select pictures from your memory card and then specify how many prints you want of each image. Then, if your photo printer has a card reader compatible with your memory card and supports DPOF, you just pop the card into the reader. The printer checks your "print order" and outputs just the requested prints. You also can print by connecting the camera to the printer using the USB cable supplied in the camera box.

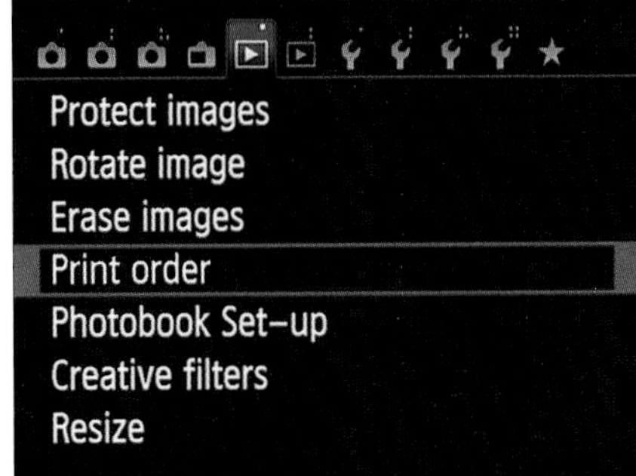

Figure 11-8: This option enables you to print directly from your memory card or camera.

- **PictBridge:** With a PictBridge-enabled photo printer, you can send pictures to the printer by connecting the two devices with the same USB cable you use for picture downloads.

If you're interested in exploring either printing feature, look for details in your camera manual.

Playing with the Creative Filters

Enough of the dry technical stuff — time for something a bit more entertaining. With the Creative Filters, you can add special effects to your pictures. For example, I used this feature to create the three versions of my city scene shown in Figure 11-9.

You can choose from the following filters:

- **Grainy B/W:** This filter turns your photos into old-fashioned, grainy, black-and-white photos.
- **Soft Focus:** This filter blurs the photo so details look all soft and fuzzy, as if you had rubbed petroleum jelly on the lens.
- **Fish-eye:** This option distorts your photo so that it appears to have been shot using a fish-eye lens, as shown in the top-right example in Figure 11-9.
- **Art Bold:** Like your colors bold — I mean, really, over-the-top vivid? Give this filter a try.
- **Water Painting:** Sort of the opposite of Art Bold, this filter sucks some color out of your image. The resulting image looks similar to a painting done in pastel colors.
- **Toy Camera:** This filter creates an image with dark corners — called a *vignette* effect. Vignetting is caused by poor-quality lenses not letting enough light in to expose the entire frame of film (like in toy cameras). When you choose this effect, you can also add a warm (yellowish) or cool (blue) tint. For example, I applied the effect with a warm tint to create the lower-left variation in Figure 11-9.

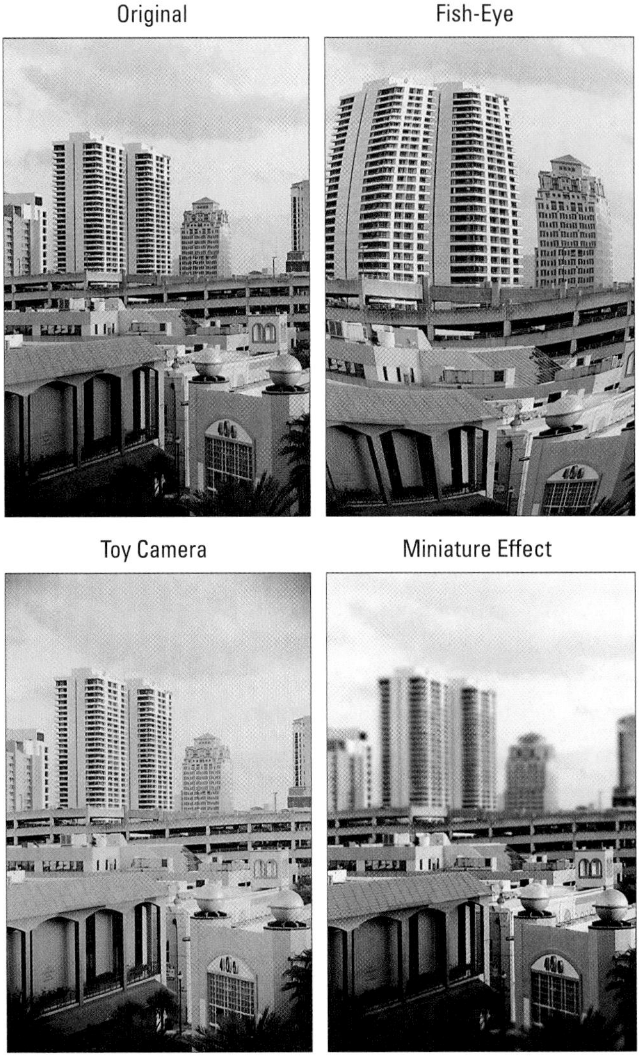

Original

Fish-Eye

Toy Camera

Miniature Effect

Figure 11-9: I used the Creative Filters feature to create these variations on a city scene.

- **Miniature:** This filter creates a trick of the eye by playing with depth of field. It blurs all but a very small area of the photo to create a result that looks something like one of those miniature dioramas you see in museums. I applied the filter to my city scene to produce the lower-right variation in Figure 11-9. This effect works best on pictures taken from a high angle, like the one featured in the figure.

You can apply the filters to still photos only. The fastest option is to use the Quick Control screen during Playback mode, as follows:

1. **Switch to Playback mode and display the photo in single-image view.**

2. **Press the Quick Control button to enter Quick Control mode.**

   The Quick Control icons appear on the screen, as shown in Figure 11-10.

3. **Choose the Creative Filters icon, labeled in the figure.**

   Either tap the icon or use the up/down cross keys to highlight it. You then see a row of icons along the bottom of the screen: seven representing the filters and one Off icon to remove a filter effect.

4. **Press the right/left cross keys or rotate the Main dial to select a filter. Or just tap the filter's icon.**

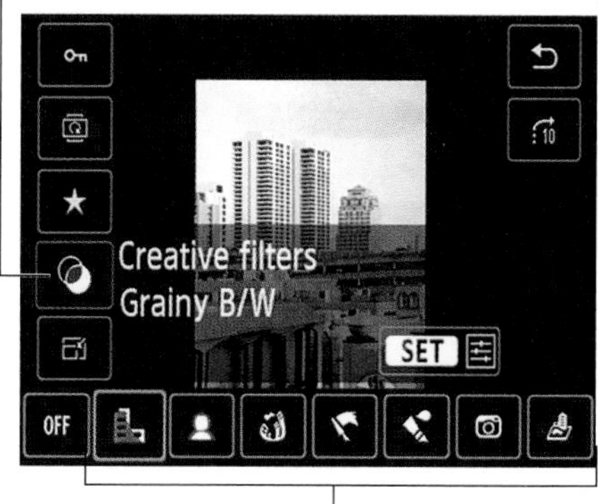

Figure 11-10: Rotate the Main dial to cycle through the available filters.

   As you do, the name of the filter appears on the screen, but the image itself doesn't change to reflect the filter's effects.

5. **Press the Set button or tap the Set icon.**

   Now you see a screen similar to the one in Figure 11-11, with options available for the selected filter.

6. **Adjust the effect as desired.**

   Which controls appear depend on the effect, as follows:

   - *Grainy B/W:* You see a scale that lets you set the level of contrast to Low, Standard, or High. Press the right or left cross keys to change the value or just tap the bars of the effect scale, labeled in Figure 11-11. The onscreen preview updates to show you the result.

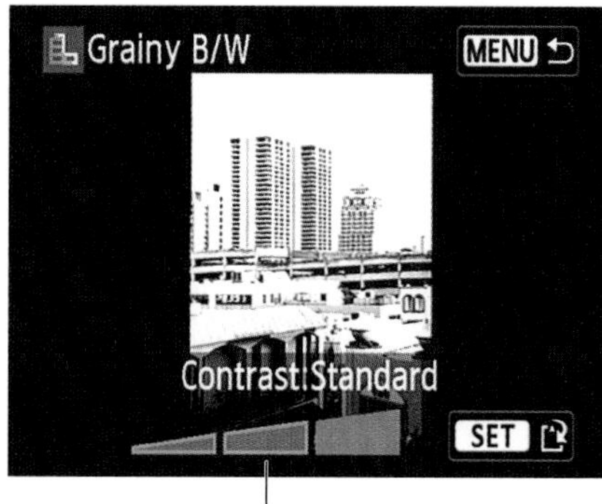

Figure 11-11: For the Grainy B/W filter, you can adjust the amount of contrast in the black-and-white image.

- *Soft Focus, Fish-eye, and Art Bold:* You also can adjust the intensity of the effect for these filters, setting the effect to Low, Standard, or Strong. Again, choose from three levels by using the cross keys or tapping the effect scale.
- *Water Painting:* This filter's three effect options — Light, Standard, and Deep — affect color density.
- *Toy Camera Effect:* Choose from three color tones: Cool, Standard, or Warm. Cool makes the photo look bluer, and Warm makes it look more golden. Standard leaves colors alone.
- *Miniature Effect:* This one's a little different: A box appears to indicate the area that will remain in sharp focus when the rest of the image is blurred. Use the cross keys to move the box up or down or tap the spot on the screen where you want to position the box. To change the box orientation from horizontal to vertical, press the Info button or tap the Info icon.

7. **Press Set or tap the Set icon.**

   You're asked to confirm that you want to save the adjusted image as a new file.

8. **Tap OK or highlight it and press the Set button.**

   The camera creates a copy of your image, applies the effect, and then displays a message telling you the folder number and last four digits of the file number of the altered photo. If the original was captured using the Raw Quality setting, the altered image is stored in the JPEG format.

9. **Tap OK or press the Set button one more time.**

   You're returned to the Quick Control screen. Tap the return arrow (upper-right corner of the screen) or press the Quick Control button to exit the screen and return to Playback mode.

As an alternative to using the Quick Control screen, you can access the filters via Playback Menu 1, as illustrated in Figure 11-12. After you choose Creative Filters from the menu, you see your most recent photo along with the data shown on the right in the figure. (You may see additional data depending on the Playback display mode; Chapter 5 details those display options.) Tap the Set icon or press the Set button to display the same filter icons and controls available via the Quick Control screen. From there, things progress as explained in the preceding steps. The only difference is that you can't use the Main dial to highlight the filter you want to use as in Step 4; you must use the right/left cross keys or just tap the filter icon.

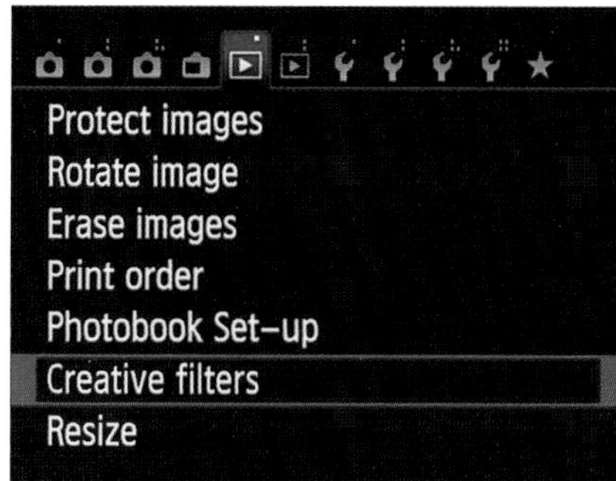

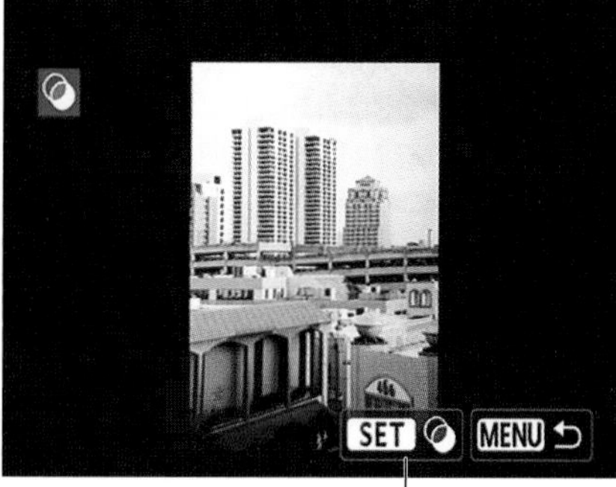

Figure 11-12: You also can access the Creative Filters from Playback Menu 1.

You can apply multiple filters to the same photo. For example, you can create a fish-eye effect and then apply the Grainy B/W filter to the altered image to create a monochrome fish-eye photo.

Tagging Pictures for a Photo Book

Many online and retail photo printing sites make it easy to print books featuring your favorite images. The Photobook Setup option on Playback Menu 1 is a nod to this popular trend. Using this feature, you can tag photos that you want to include in a photo book. Then, if you use the Canon EOS Utility software to transfer pictures to your computer, tagged photos are dumped into a separate folder so that they're easy to find. This feature only works when you download pictures by connecting the camera to the computer. In addition, it doesn't work with Raw (CR2) files.

Unfortunately, I don't have room in this book to provide steps for the process of creating your photo books this way, but if you're interested, the camera manual tells you how to tag pictures for inclusion in the book. You can find instructions about the software side of the photo-book function on the software instruction CD that shipped with your camera.

Presenting a Slide Show

Through the Slide Show function on Playback Menu 2, you can create a digital slide show featuring the best images and movies on your memory card. You can play the show on the camera monitor or, by connecting your camera to a TV as outlined in Chapter 5, present the show to a roomful of people. Follow these steps:

1. **Display Playback Menu 2 and choose Slide Show, as shown on the left in Figure 11-13.**

   You see the screen shown on the right in Figure 11-13. The thumbnail shows the first image to appear in the slide show.

   Also on this screen, you see the total number of images slated for inclusion in the show — 37, in the figure. On your first trip to this menu screen, all images on the card are selected for the show.

2. **Tap the Select Files option (labeled in Figure 11-14) or highlight it using the cross keys and press Set.**

   The option box becomes active, as shown in the figure, enabling you to specify which images or movies you want to include in the show. In the figure, the option is set to select photos by date.

3. **Press the up or down cross keys to scroll through the following settings:**

   - *All Images:* Choose this setting to include all files, regardless of whether they're still photos or movies.
   - *Date:* Select this option to play only pictures or movies taken on a single date. As soon as you select the option, the little Info label underneath the option box turns white, clueing you in to the fact that you can press the Info button or tap the icon to display a screen listing all the shooting dates on the memory card, as shown on the right in Figure 11-14. Again, press the up or down cross keys to select a date — or just tap it — and then tap Set or press the Set button to exit the date list.
   - *Folder:* This option includes still photos and movies in the selected folder. Again, press the Info button or tap the Info icon to display a list of folders and highlight the one you want to use, and then press the Set button or tap the Set icon to exit the folder list.
   - *Movies:* Select this option to include only movies and video snapshots in your show.
   - *Stills:* Select this option to include only still photos.

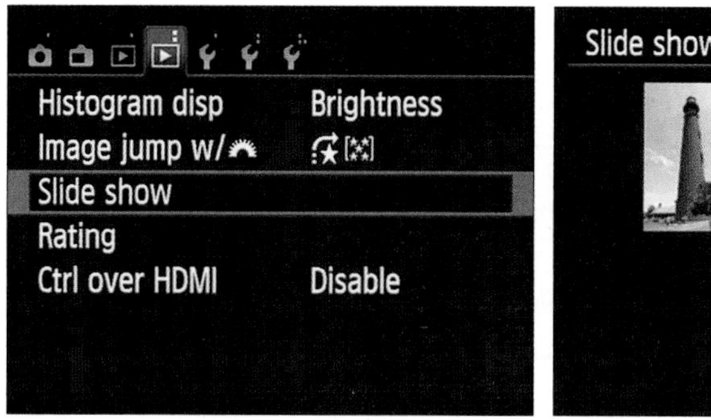

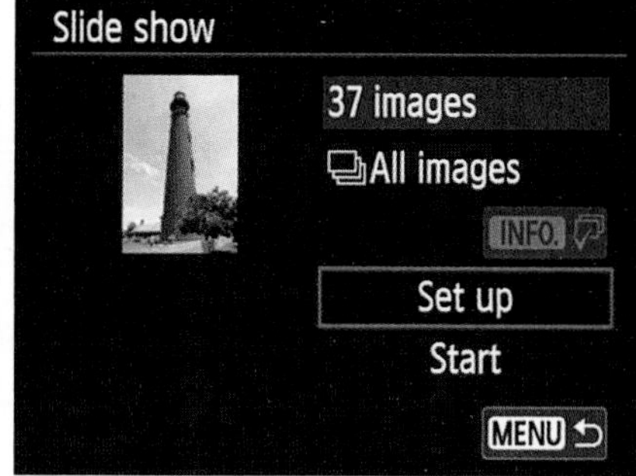

Figure 11-13: Choose Slide Show and then use the options to customize playback.

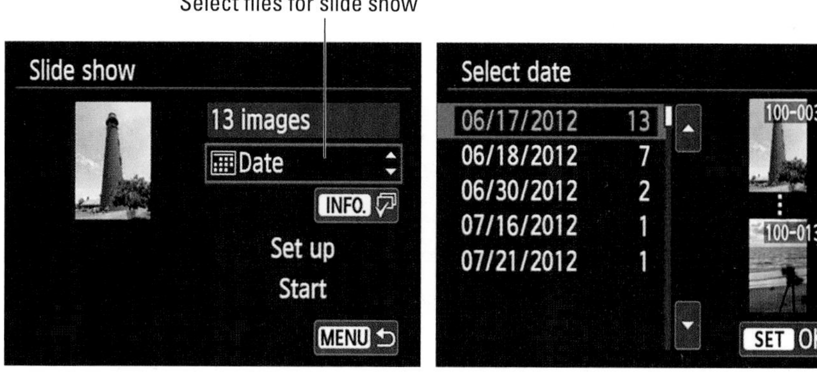

Figure 11-14: Use this option to specify which photos or movies you want to include in the show.

- *Rating:* This option enables you to select the photos and movies you want to see based on their ratings. Press Info or tap the Info icon to display a screen where you can specify the rating and see how many photos you assigned that rating. After selecting the rating, press Set or tap the Set icon to exit the rating screen.

You also can tap the Select Files box to display a screen containing all six options. After choosing an option, tap Set twice or press the Set button. You can then adjust settings by using the Info button or icon as described for those options that require it.

4. **Press the Set button to deactivate the Select Files box.**

5. **Choose the Set Up option, as shown on the left in Figure 11-15.**

   You cruise to the screen shown on the right in the figure, which offers the following options:

   - *Display Time:* This option determines how long each photo appears, with settings ranging from 1 to 20 seconds. Movies are always played in their entirety.
   - *Repeat:* Set this option to Enable if you want the show to play over and over until you decide you've had enough. Choose Disable to play the show only once.
   - *Transition Effect:* You can enable one of five different transition effects; experiment to see which one you like best. (They're a little difficult to describe in print.) Choose Off if you don't want any effects between slides.
   - *Background Music:* By using the EOS Utility software that ships with your camera, you can transfer music files to the camera memory card and then use the files as audio tracks for your slide show. In fact, Canon even supplies sample music files. If you're interested, the EOS Utility user manual (found on another disc that ships with the camera) provides instructions.

     If you do copy music to the card, set the Background Music option to on; then press the Set button or tap the Set icon to choose the music file you want to use.

6. **After selecting playback options, tap Menu or press the Menu button to return to the main Slide Show screen.**
7. **Tap Start or highlight it and press Set.**

   Your slide show begins playing.

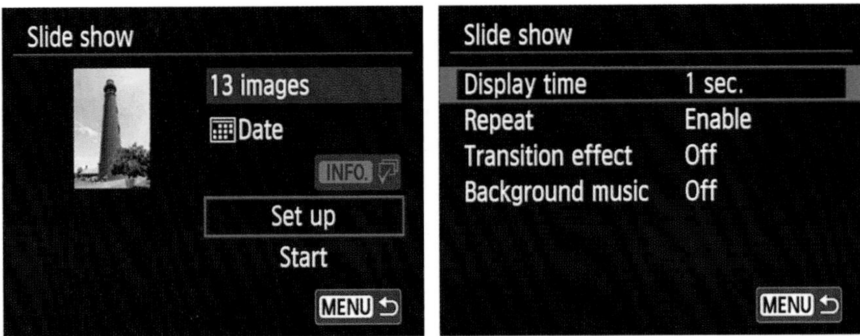

Figure 11-15: Use these options to specify playback preferences.

During the show, you can do the following to control the display:

- **Pause playback:** Press the Set button. While the show is paused, you can press the right or left cross key to view the next or previous photo. Press Set again or tap the onscreen Set icon to restart playback.
- **Change the information display style:** Press the Info button. (See the Chapter 5 section "Viewing Picture Data" for details about the available display styles.)
- **Adjust sound volume:** Rotate the Main dial.
- **Exit the show:** To exit to the Slide Show setup screen, press the Menu button or, if the show is paused, tap the Menu icon. To return to normal playback mode, press the Playback button.

Creating Video Snapshots

This feature enables you to capture short video clips that you stitch into a single recording, called a *video album*. A few pertinent facts before I show you the steps:

- Each clip can be no more than 8 seconds long. You also can record 2- and 4-second clips.
- All clips in an album must be the same length.

Because of the recording-time limitation, I suspect you'll find other features of your camera more engaging, so I'm opting to limit coverage to showing you how to create your first album. If you're interested, the camera manual explains how you can edit albums.

1. **Set the On/Off switch to Movie mode.**
2. **Display Movie Menu 2 and choose Video Snapshot, shown on the left in Figure 11-16.**

   The option is disabled by default.
3. **Set the Video Snapshot option to Enable, as shown on the right in the figure.**
4. **Choose Album Settings, as shown on the left in Figure 11-17.**

   You see the screen shown on the right in the figure.
5. **Choose Create a New Album.**

   You see the screen shown on the left in Figure 11-18.

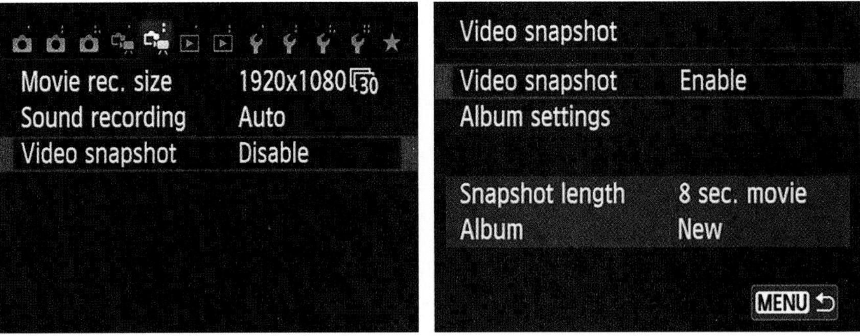

Figure 11-16: Set up your video snapshot initially via Movie Menu 2.

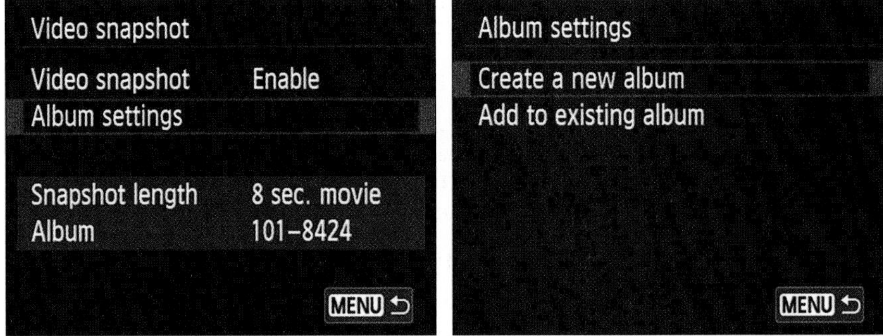

Figure 11-17: Choose Album Settings and then specify whether you want to create a new album or add the next clip you record to an existing album.

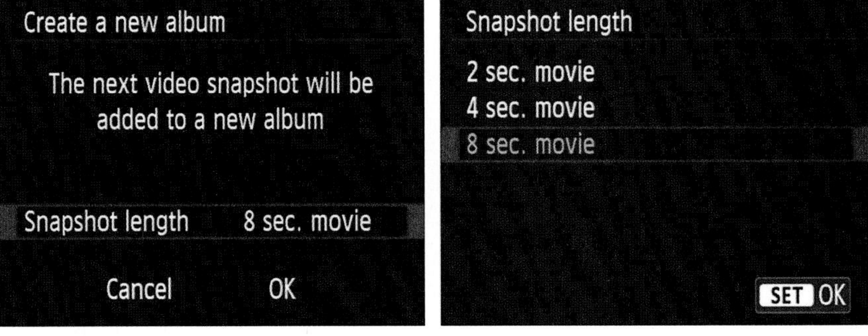

Figure 11-18: Choose the Snapshot Length option to set the clip length to 2, 4, or 8 seconds.

6. **Choose Snapshot Length to display the screen shown on the right in Figure 11-19.**
7. **Set the snapshot length to 2, 4, or 8 seconds and tap Set or press the Set button.**

   You see a confirmation screen.
8. **Tap OK or highlight the OK icon and press Set.**

   You're returned to the Video Snapshot setup screen.
9. **Tap the Menu icon or press the Menu button to return to Shooting Menu 2.**
10. **Return to shooting mode by pressing the shutter button halfway and releasing it.**

    You see a blue progress bar across the bottom of the screen, as shown on the left in Figure 11-19.
11. **Press the Live View button to start the recording.**

    The progress bar shrinks as the camera ticks off the seconds of your recording. When you reach the maximum clip length, recording stops automatically. The monitor temporarily shuts off, and then you see the last frame of the clip along with the options shown on the right in Figure 11-19.
12. **Tell the camera what to do with the clip.**

    Your choices, represented by the icons labeled in Figure 11-19:
    - Add the snapshot to your new album.
    - Play the clip.
    - Delete the clip.

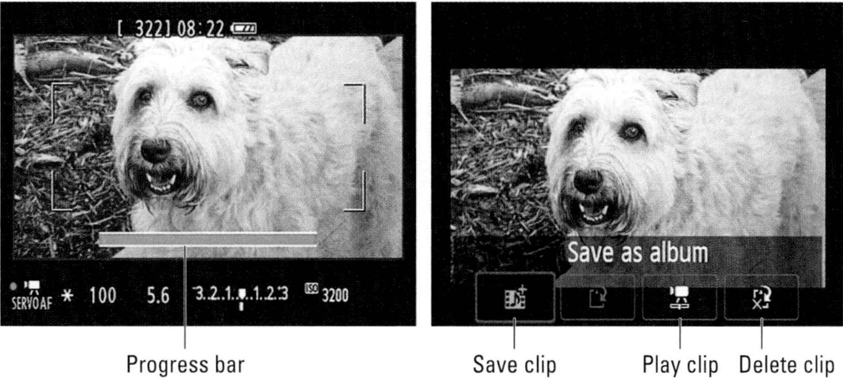

Figure 11-19: After recording a clip, you can save, play, or trash it.

To choose an option, tap its icon or use the cross keys to highlight the icon and press Set. If you play the clip, control playback by using the "buttons" labeled in Figure 11-20. Either tap a control icon or use the cross keys to highlight it and press Set. Rotate the Main dial to adjust playback volume. Press the Menu button or tap the Menu icon to return to the right screen in Figure 11-19.

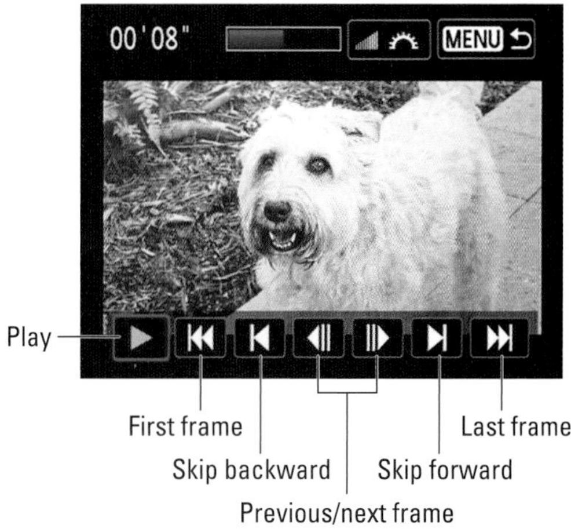

Figure 11-20: Highlight a playback control and press Set to "push" the selected "button."

13. **After saving your first clip, press the Live View button to record a second one.**

14. **When your second clip is recorded, choose one of the options shown in Figure 11-21.**

    This time, you get the same three options described in Step 11. But you also can create a new album for this clip.

15. **To stop capturing snapshots, return to Movie Menu 2 and set the Video Snapshot option to Disable.**

    You can then shoot regular movies again.

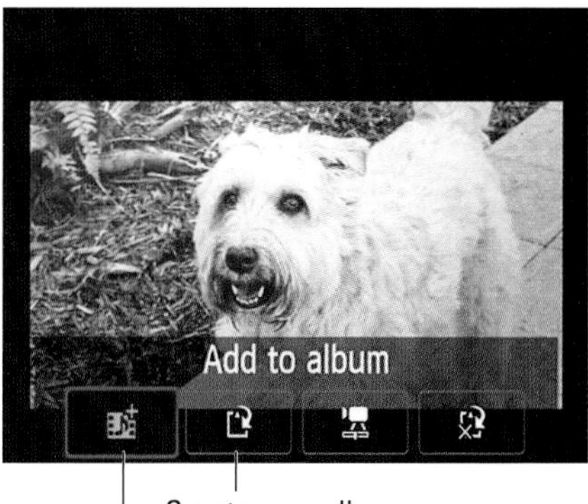

Figure 11-21: You can choose to add the second clip to the album you just created or start another new album.

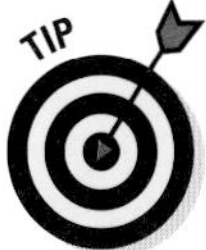

You also can use the Quick Control screen to enable and disable Video Snapshot recording, as shown in Figure 11-22. Tap or highlight the icon and then tap the Off icon at the bottom of the screen. Tap the neighboring icon to enable the feature using the snapshot length that's currently selected via Movie Menu 2. (You can't adjust the snapshot length using the Quick Control options.)

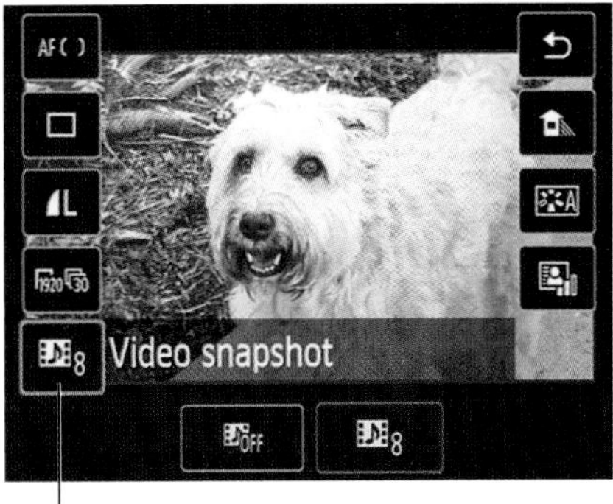

Figure 11-22: You also can enable and disable the Video Snapshot feature via the Quick Settings screen.

Just a few notes about recording video snapshots:

- **Sound recording:** By default, audio is recorded; you can control audio recording through the Sound Recording option on Movie Menu 2, just as for regular movies.
- **Movie Recording Size:** All clips in an album must use the same Movie Recording Size option (adjusted via Movie Menu 2). If you change the setting, the camera automatically creates a new album for your next snapshot.
- **Autofocusing:** Your options are the same as for normal movie recording; Chapter 4 has details.
- **Grid Display and Metering Timer options (Movie Menu 2):** Similarly, these options are available, as they are for normal movie recording, if the Mode dial is set to P, Tv, Av, or M. Again, Chapter 4 explains both options.
- **Normal playback:** To play a video snapshot after you exit the creation process, use the normal movie-playback steps, detailed at the end of Chapter 4.

Editing Movies

Although not a substitute for computer-based video-editing software, the T4i/650D movie-edit feature makes it easy to remove unwanted frames from the beginning or end of a movie. Here are the steps for trimming frames from the start of a movie:

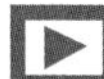

1. **Set the camera to Playback mode and display the movie file.**
2. **Press the Set button or tap the Set icon to display the playback controls shown on the left in Figure 11-23.**
3. **Tap the Edit icon (or highlight it and press Set) to enter the Editing screen.**

   You can see the screen on the right side of Figure 11-23.
4. **Tap the Cut Beginning icon, labeled in Figure 11-23. Or highlight it and press Set.**

   The bar at the top of the screen becomes active, as shown on the left in Figure 11-24, and little arrows appear under the bar. The bar indicates the current length of the movie.
5. **Press and hold the right cross key to advance frame by frame to the last frame you want to cut. Press the left key to rewind frame by frame.**

   Or tap those little arrows under the length bar to advance and rewind frame by frame.

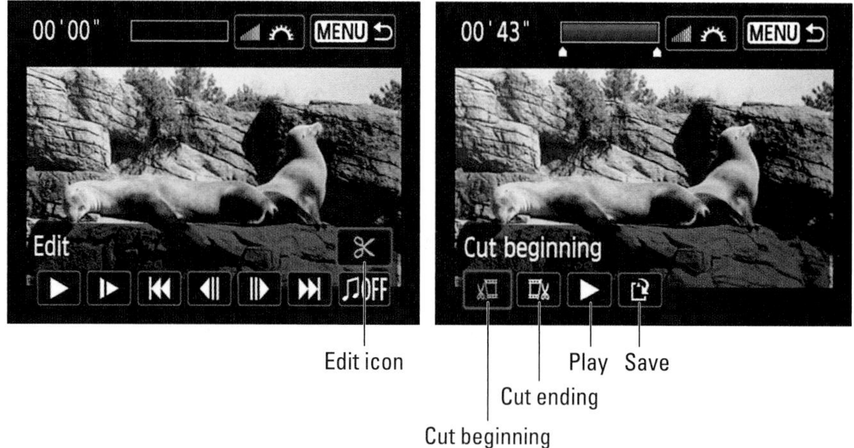

Figure 11-23: From the playback screen, tap the scissors icon to get to the editing functions.

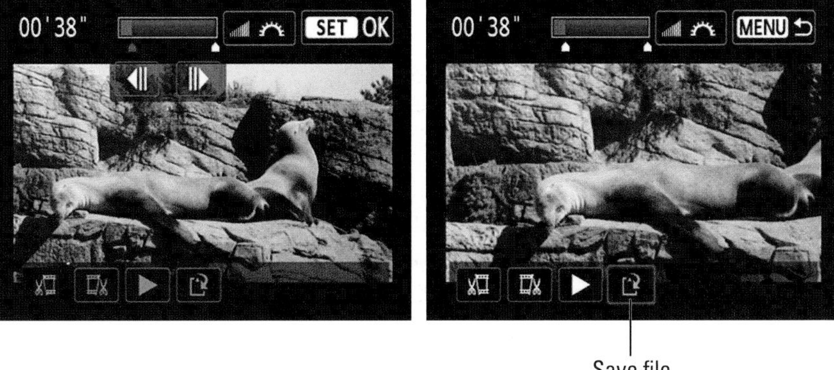

Figure 11-24: Press the right cross key to advance to the frame you want to use as the new first frame (left); then select the Save File icon to save the edited movie (right).

6. **Tap the Set icon or press the Set button to display the screen shown on the right in Figure 11-24.**
7. **Tap the Save File icon, labeled on the right in Figure 11-24.**

   Or use the cross keys to highlight it and then press the Set button. Either way, you see the screen shown in Figure 11-25.

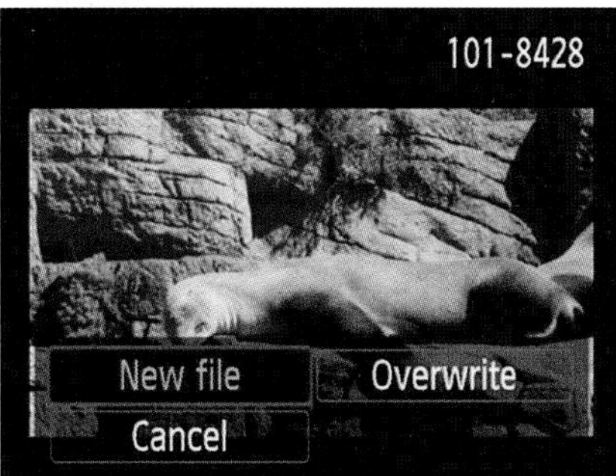

Figure 11-25: Choose New File to avoid overwriting your original movie.

8. **To save the trimmed movie as a separate file from your original, choose New File.**

   Just tap the New File icon or highlight it and press Set to get the job done.

   It's safer to save the edited version as a new file. That way, if you decide that you did a lousy editing job, you still have your original. But if you know you never want the original back, choose Overwrite instead.

To trim the end of a movie, follow the same process, but choose Cut Ending in Step 4.

Getting Free Help and Creative Ideas

Okay, so this last tip is a bit of a cheat: It isn't actually found on your camera, but it will help you better understand the features that are. I speak of Canon's website. For the American version of the site, go to `www.usa.canon.com`. (To access other versions, start at `www.canon.com` and then click the link for the version you want to see.)

If you haven't yet visited the site, I encourage you to do so. In the Support section of the site, you can get free technical support for camera problems and even download an electronic copy of your camera manual, should you happen to misplace the one that came with your camera. Most importantly, check periodically to make sure that your camera is running the latest *firmware,* which is the geekspeak term for the camera's internal software.

Be sure to also check out the Learning Center area of the site. At `www.usa.canon.com`, go to the Consumer and Home Office section. Then look for the Resources and Learning link, which leads to tutorials and other instructional offerings not only about your camera but also about the software that ships with it.

Appendix

Glossary of Digital Photography Terms

Can't remember the difference between a pixel and a bit? Resolution and resampling? Turn here for a quick refresher on that digital photography term that's stuck somewhere in the dark recesses of your brain and refuses to come out and play.

For more information about a topic, check the book's index.

24-bit image: An image containing approximately 16.7 million colors.

Adobe RGB: One of two color space options available on your camera; determines the spectrum of colors that can be contained in the image. Adobe RGB includes more colors than the default option, sRGB, but also involves some complications that make it a better choice for advanced photographers than beginners.

AEB: *Auto Exposure Bracketing,* a feature that automatically records three exposures: one at the selected exposure settings; one using settings that produce a darker image; and one using settings that produce a brighter image. A useful tool for ensuring that at least one exposure is good when you shoot in tricky lighting.

AE lock: A way to prevent the camera's autoexposure (AE) system from changing the current exposure settings if you reframe the picture or the lighting changes before the image is recorded.

AF mode: Short for *autofocus mode.* A setting that determines whether the camera locks focus when you press the shutter button halfway, continuously adjusts focusing up to the time you take the shot, or chooses which of the two strategies to employ. See also AI Servo, AI Focus, and One Shot AF mode.

AF Point Selection mode: The setting that tells the camera whether to base focus on any of its autofocus points (automatic point selection) or on a single point that you select (manual point selection). Available for viewfinder photography in the P, Tv, Av, and M exposure modes.

AI Focus: One of three AF mode settings available for viewfinder photography; the camera locks focus when you press the shutter button halfway unless it senses motion, in which case it adjusts focus to track the subject continuously, up to the time you press the shutter button all the way to take the shot.

AI Servo: A viewfinder-photography autofocus mode in which the camera continually adjusts focus up to the moment you take the picture; useful for focusing on moving subjects.

aperture: One of three critical exposure controls; an opening in an adjustable diaphragm in the camera lens. The size of the opening is measured in f-stops (f/2.8, f/8, and so on), with a smaller number resulting in a larger aperture opening. Aperture also affects depth of field (the distance over which focus remains acceptably sharp).

aspect ratio: The proportions of an image. Pictures from your camera have an aspect ratio of 3:2, the same as a 35mm-film photo. But in Live View mode, you can select from a few other aspect ratios. Movies have an aspect ratio of 16:9 or 4:3, depending on the Movie Recording Size setting (Movie Menu 2).

autoexposure: A feature that puts the camera in control of choosing the proper exposure settings.

Auto Lighting Optimizer: A feature designed to improve underexposed or low contrast shots automatically.

Av mode (aperture-priority autoexposure): A semiautomatic exposure mode: The photographer sets the aperture and the camera selects the appropriate shutter speed to produce a good exposure at the current ISO (light-sensitivity) setting. *Av* stands for *aperture value.*

Basic Zone modes: Canon's way of referring to all exposure modes except the advanced modes (P, Tv, Av, and M). Exposure modes in this category provide automated exposure control and limit access to advanced camera features.

backlight: Bright light coming from behind your subject, which can cause your subject to be underexposed in autoexposure shooting modes.

bit: Stands for *binary digit;* the basic unit of digital information. Eight bits equals one *byte.*

bit depth: Refers to the number of bits available to store color information. More bits means more data.

bulb mode: A shutter speed setting that keeps the shutter open as long as you hold down the shutter button. Available only in the M (manual) exposure mode.

burst mode: Another name for the Continuous Drive mode setting, which records several images in rapid succession with one press of the shutter button.

byte: Eight bits. ***See also*** bit.

Camera Raw: A file format that records the photo without applying any of the in-camera processing or file compression that is usually done automatically when saving photos in the other standard format, JPEG. Also known as *Raw.* Indicated by the file extension .CR2 on the T4i/650D.

camera shake: Any movement of the camera during the image exposure. Can lead to allover blurring of the photo and is common when photographers handhold their cameras and use a long exposure time. (Use a tripod to prevent it.)

card reader: A device used to transfer images from your camera memory card to your computer.

chromatic aberration: A defect produced by some lenses; looks like small halos of color along object edges. May be lessened by enabling the Chromatic Aberration feature (available through the Lens Aberration Correction function on Shooting Menu 1).

Close-up mode: An automated exposure mode designed for shooting subjects at close range; chooses settings designed to produce a blurry background, thereby emphasizing your subject.

color model: A way of defining colors. In the RGB color model, for example, all colors are created by blending red, green, and blue light.

color space: A specific spectrum of colors that can be rendered by a camera or other digital device. *See also* sRGB and Adobe RGB.

color temperature: Refers to the color cast emitted by a light source; measured on the Kelvin scale.

compression: A process that reduces the size of the image file by eliminating some image data.

continuous autofocus: An autofocus feature that continuously adjusts focus as needed to keep a moving subject in focus. Enabled by selecting the AI Servo AF mode; also occurs in AI Focus mode if the camera detects subject motion.

contrast: The amount of difference between the brightest and darkest values in an image. High-contrast images contain both very dark and very bright areas.

CR2: The Canon Camera Raw format.

Creative Auto exposure mode: An automatic-exposure mode that gives you a little more flexibility than the other fully automatic modes; for example, offers an option that enables you to specify whether you prefer the background to be blurry or sharp.

Creative Zone mode: Canon's term for the advanced exposure modes: P (programmed autoexposure), Tv (shutter-priority autoexposure), Av (aperture-priority autoexposure), and M (manual exposure).

crop: To trim away unwanted areas around the perimeter of a photo, typically done in a photo-editing program.

Custom Functions: A group of eight advanced camera options accessed via Shooting Menu 4 and available only in the P, Tv, Av, and M exposure modes.

depth of field: The distance from the subject over which focus appears acceptably sharp. With shallow depth of field, the subject is sharp but distant objects are not; with large depth of field, both the subject and distant objects are in focus. Manipulated by adjusting the aperture, lens focal length, or camera-to-subject distance.

diopter adjustment control: The wheel next to the viewfinder that enables you to adjust the viewfinder to your eyesight.

downloading: Transferring data from your camera to a computer.

dpi: Short for *dots per inch.* A measurement of how many dots of color a printer can create per linear inch. Higher dpi means better print quality on some types of printers; on other printers, dpi is not as crucial.

DPOF: Stands for *digital print order format.* A feature that enables you to add print instructions to the image file and then print directly from the memory card. Requires a DPOF-capable printer.

Drive mode: The camera setting that determines when and how the shutter is released when you press the shutter button. Options include Single, which produces one picture for each button press; Continuous, which records a continuous burst of images as long as you hold down the button; and three self-timer modes (one of which also works for remote-control operation).

dSLR: Stands for *digital single-lens reflex;* one type of digital camera that accepts interchangeable lenses.

dynamic range: The overall range of brightness values in a photo, from black to white. Also refers to the range of brightness values that a camera, scanner, or other digital device can record or reproduce.

edges: Areas where neighboring image pixels are significantly different in color; in other words, areas of high contrast.

EV compensation: A control that slightly increases or decreases the exposure chosen by the camera's autoexposure mechanism. EV stands for *exposure value;* EV settings appear as EV 1.0, EV 0.0, EV –1.0, and so on.

EXIF metadata: ***See*** metadata.

exposure: The overall brightness and contrast of a photograph, determined mainly by three settings: aperture, shutter speed, and ISO.

exposure compensation: Another name for EV compensation.

Face+Tracking AF: A Live View and movie-only autofocus method that searches for faces in the scene and, if it finds them, automatically focuses on them and tracks them through the frame if they move.

FE Lock: Stands for *flash exposure lock.* A feature that forces the camera to base flash exposure only on the subject at the center of the frame.

file format: A way of storing image data in a digital file; your camera offers two formats, JPEG and Camera Raw (CR2).

fill flash: Using a flash to fill in darker areas of an image, such as shadows cast on subjects' faces by bright overhead sunlight or backlighting.

firmware: The internal software that runs the camera's "brain." Canon occasionally releases firmware updates that you should download and install in your camera (follow the instructions at the download site).

flash exposure (EV) compensation: A feature that enables the photographer to adjust the strength of the camera flash.

Flash Off mode: The same as Scene Intelligent Auto exposure mode (fully automated shooting), but with flash disabled.

FlexiZone-Multi AF: A Live View and movie-only autofocus option; the camera automatically selects the focus point from all available points or from a specific zone of points that you select.

FlexiZone-Single AF: A Live View and movie-only autofocus option; you specify a single focus point for the camera to use when setting focus.

formatting: An in-camera process that wipes all data off the memory card and prepares the card for storing pictures.

frame rate: In a movie, the number of frames recorded per second (fps). A higher frame rate translates to crisper video quality.

f-number, f-stop: Refers to the size of the camera aperture opening. A higher number indicates a smaller aperture opening. Written as f/2, f/8, and so on. Affects both exposure and depth of field.

gamut: Say it *gamm-ut.* The range of colors that a monitor, printer, or other device can produce. Colors that a device can't create are said to be *out of gamut.*

gigabyte: Approximately 1,000 megabytes, or 1 billion bytes. In other words, a really big collection of bytes. Abbreviated as GB.

grayscale: An image consisting solely of shades of gray, from white to black. Often referred to generically as a *black-and-white image* (although, in the truest sense, an actual black-and-white image contains only black and white with no grays).

Handheld Night Scene mode: An automatic exposure mode designed to produce sharper images when you shoot in dim lighting and handhold the camera. Records a burst of four shots and then merges those shots for the final result.

HDR: Stands for *high dynamic range* and refers to a picture that's created by merging multiple exposures of the subject into one image using special computer software. The resulting picture contains a greater range of brightness values — a greater dynamic range — than can be captured in a single shot.

HDR Backlight Control mode: An automated exposure mode designed to produce a better exposure when you shoot high-contrast scenes. Records a burst of three shots at three different exposures and then merges them for the final image.

Highlight Tone Priority: A feature designed to produce better results when you shoot high-contrast scenes; brightens shadows without making highlights too bright. Available only in the P, Tv, Av, and M exposure modes.

histogram: A graph that maps out shadow, midtone, and highlight brightness values in a digital image; an exposure-monitoring tool that can be displayed during image playback. During Live View shooting, can also be displayed over the live image.

hot shoe: The connection on top of the camera where you attach an auxiliary flash.

image sensor: The array of light-sensitive computer chips in your camera that senses light and converts it into digital information.

Image Stabilization: A feature designed to compensate for small amounts of camera shake, which can blur a photo. Indicated on Canon lenses by the initials IS; enabled via the Stabilizer switch on the lens.

Image Zone modes: Canon nomenclature for the automated, scene specific exposure modes that are part of the Basic Zone modes. Includes Portrait, Landscape, Close-up, Sports, Night Portrait, Handheld Night Scene, and HDR Backlight Control modes.

Index mode: A playback feature that displays four or nine image thumbnails at a time.

ISO: Traditionally, a measure of film speed; the higher the number, the faster the film. On a digital camera, it means how sensitive the image sensor is to light. Raising the ISO allows faster shutter speed, smaller aperture, or both, but also can result in a noisy (grainy) image. Stands for *International Organization for Standardization,* the group that devised the ISO standards..

jaggies: Refers to the jagged, stairstepped appearance of curved and diagonal lines in low-resolution photos that are printed at large sizes.

JPEG: Pronounced *jay-peg.* The primary file format used by digital cameras; also the leading format for online and web pictures. Uses *lossy compression,* which eliminates some data in order to reduce file size. A small amount of compression does little discernible damage, but a high amount destroys picture quality. Stands for *Joint Photographic Experts Group,* the group that developed the format.

JPEG artifact: A defect created by too much JPEG compression.

Jump mode: A playback feature that enables you to jump through images 10 at a time, 100 at a time, or by date, by type of file (photo or movie), by folder, or by rating.

Kelvin: A scale for measuring the color temperature of light. Sometimes abbreviated as *K,* as in 5000K. (Note that in computer-speak, the initial *K* more often refers to kilobytes, as described next.)

kilobyte: One thousand bytes. Abbreviated as *K*, as in 64K.

Landscape mode: An automated exposure mode designed to render landscapes in the traditional fashion, with high contrast and bold, crisp colors, especially in the blue and green spectrums.

LCD: Stands for *liquid crystal display.* Often used to refer to the display screen included on digital cameras.

Live View: The feature that enables you to use the camera monitor instead of the viewfinder to compose your shots.

lossless compression: A file-compression scheme that doesn't sacrifice any vital image data in the compression process, used by file formats such as TIFF. Lossless compression tosses only redundant data, so image quality is unaffected.

lossy compression: A compression scheme that eliminates important image data in the name of achieving smaller file sizes, used by file formats such as JPEG. High amounts of lossy compression reduce image quality.

M (manual) exposure mode: An exposure mode that enables you to control both aperture and shutter speed.

manual focus: A setting that turns off autofocus and instead enables you to set focus by twisting the focusing ring on the lens.

megabyte: One million bytes. Abbreviated as MB. ***See also*** bit.

megapixel: One million pixels; used to describe the resolution offered by a digital camera.

metadata: Extra data that gets stored along with the primary image data in an image file. Metadata often includes information such as aperture, shutter speed, and EV compensation setting used to capture the picture, and can be viewed using special software. Often referred to as *EXIF metadata;* EXIF stands for *Exchangeable Image File Format.*

metering mode: Refers to the way a camera's autoexposure mechanism reads the light in a scene. Modes available on your camera include *spot,* which bases exposure on a small area at the center of the frame*; partial,* which uses a little larger metering area than spot; *center-weighted average,* which reads the entire scene but gives more emphasis to the subject in the center of the frame; and *evaluative,* which calculates exposure based on the entire frame.

mirror lockup: A feature that ensures that the movement of the camera's internal mirror is completed long before the shutter is released; used for long-exposure shots to ensure that the mirror movement doesn't blur the image.

monopod: A telescoping, single-legged pole on which you can mount a camera and lens in order to hold it more stably while shooting. It will not stand on its own, unlike a tripod.

Movie Servo AF: The continuous autofocusing option available during movie recording.

Night Portrait mode: Designed for photographing people at night or in dim lighting; combines a slow shutter speed with flash for brighter backgrounds and softer flash lighting. For good results, use a tripod and ask your subject to remain very still.

noise: Graininess in an image, caused by a very long exposure, a too-high ISO setting, or both.

NTSC: A video format used by televisions, DVD players, and VCRs in North America, Mexico, and some parts of Asia (such as Japan, Taiwan, South Korea, and the Philippines). Many digital cameras can send picture signals to a TV, DVD player, or VCR in this format.

One Shot AF: An autofocus mode for viewfinder photography (that is, not Live View or Movie mode) that locks focus when you press the shutter button halfway. Focus remains locked as long as you hold the button down halfway. Useful for photographing portraits and other non-moving subjects.

P mode: *Programmed autoexposure* shooting mode. The camera selects both f-stop and shutter speed, but you can select from different combinations of the two and access all other camera features.

PAL: The video format common in Europe, China, Australia, Brazil, and several other countries in Asia, South America, and Africa. ***See also*** NTSC.

Peripheral Illumination: A feature designed to correct *vignetting,* a lens defect that causes the corners of the image to appear darker than the rest of the scene. (Accessed via the Lens Aberration Correction option on Shooting Menu 1.)

PictBridge: A feature that enables you to connect your camera to a PictBridge-enabled printer for direct printing.

Picture Styles: Settings designed to render images using different color, sharpness, and contrast characteristics; options include Auto, Standard, Portrait, Landscape, Neutral, Faithful, and Monochrome. You can also create three custom styles.

pixel: Short for *picture element.* The basic building block of every image.

pixelation: A defect that occurs when an image has too few pixels for the size at which it is printed; pixels become so large that the image takes on a mosaic-like or stairstepped appearance.

platform: A fancy way of saying "type of computer operating system." Most folks work either on the Windows platform or the Macintosh platform.

ppi: Stands for *pixels per inch.* Used to state image output (print) resolution. Measured in terms of the number of pixels per linear inch. A higher ppi usually translates to better-looking printed images.

Portrait mode: An automated mode designed to render portraits in the traditional style, with softer skin texture, warmer skin tones, and a blurry background.

Quick Control screen: The monitor display that enables you to adjust critical camera settings quickly by using the touchscreen or the camera buttons rather than menus.

Quick Mode AF: A Live View-only autofocusing option; you tell the camera to automatically select from one of the same nine autofocus points used for viewfinder photography or to base focus on a specific point that you select.

Raw: ***See*** Camera Raw.

Raw converter: A software utility that translates Camera Raw files into a standard image format such as JPEG or TIFF. Canon Digital Photo Professional, provided free with your camera, offers this tool.

red-eye: Light from a flash being reflected from a subject's retina, causing the pupil to appear red in photographs. Can sometimes be prevented by using the Red-Eye Reduction flash setting; can also be removed later in most image-editing programs.

resampling: Adding or deleting image pixels. Adding a large amount of pixels degrades images.

resolution: A term used to describe the number of pixels in a digital image. Also a specification describing the rendering capabilities of scanners, printers, and monitors; means different things depending on the device.

RGB: The standard color model for digital images; all colors are created by mixing red, green, and blue light.

Scene Intelligent Auto: The most automatic of automatic exposure modes on your camera, represented by the A+ symbol on the Mode dial. The camera analyzes the subject and selects the settings it deems appropriate for capturing the photo.

SD card: The type of memory card used by your camera; stands for *Secure Digital.*

SDHC card: A high-capacity form of the SD card; stands for *Secure Digital High Capacity* and refers to cards with capacities ranging from 4MB to 32MB.

SDXC card: *Secure Digital Extended Capacity;* used to indicate an SD memory card with a capacity greater than 32MB.

sharpening: Applying an image-correction filter inside a photo editor to create the appearance of sharper focus.

shutter: A light-barrier inside the camera that opens when you press the shutter button, allowing light to strike the image sensor and expose the image.

shutter-priority autoexposure: A semiautomatic exposure mode in which the photographer sets the shutter speed and the camera selects the appropriate aperture. Selected via the Tv option on the Mode dial.

shutter speed: The length of time the shutter remains open; or, to put it another way, the duration of the image exposure. Measured in fractions of a second, as in 1/60 or 1/250 second.

slow-sync flash: A special flash setting that allows (or forces) a slower shutter speed than is typical for the normal flash setting. Results in a brighter background than normal flash.

Sports mode: An automated exposure mode designed for capturing action; selects a fast shutter speed to “freeze” the subject in mid-motion.

sRGB: Stands for *standard RGB,* the default color space setting on your camera (and the one recommended for most users). Developed to create a standard color spectrum that (theoretically) all devices could capture or reproduce.

Stop: An increment of exposure adjustment. Increasing the exposure by one stop means to select exposure settings that double the light; decreasing by one stop means to cut the light in half.

TIFF: Pronounced *tiff,* as in a little quarrel. Stands for *tagged image file format.* A popular image format supported by most Macintosh and Windows programs. It is *lossless,* meaning that it retains image data in a way that maintains maximum image quality. Often used to save Raw files after processing.

tripod: Used to mount and stabilize a camera, preventing camera shake that can blur an image; characterized by three telescoping legs.

Tv mode: Shutter-priority autoexposure; you set the shutter speed and the camera selects the f-stop to properly expose the image. Tv stands for *time value* (length of exposure).

UHS: A classification assigned to some SD memory cards; stands for *Ultra High Speed.*

UHS-1: At present, the fastest rated UHS type card.

USB: Stands for *Universal Serial Bus.* A type of port for connecting your camera to your computer. Your camera ships with the USB cable necessary for the connection.

Video Snapshot: A special movie mode that records a 2-, 4-, or 8-second movie clip. Multiple clips can be combined into a snapshot *album.*

white balance: Adjusting the camera to compensate for the color temperature of the lighting. Ensures accurate rendition of colors in digital photographs.

Index

• Numerics •

• A •

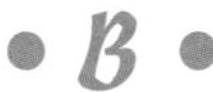

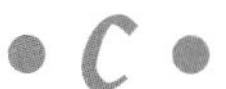

• D •

• E •

• J •

• K •

• L •

• N •

• O •

• P •

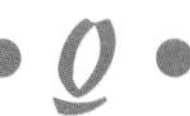

• R •

• S •

• T •

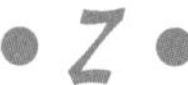